A TRAILS BOOKS GUIDE

PADDLING SOUTHERN MINNESOTA

85 GREAT TRIPS BY CANOE AND KAYAK

Lynne and Robert Diebel

trails books

AN IMPRINT OF BOWER HOUSE

DENVER

BowerHouseBooks.com

Editor: Mark Knickelbine
Design: Colin Harrington
Cover Photo: Robert Diebel

Printed in Canada

Library of Congress Control Number: 2007920220
ISBN 978-1-931599-78-8

10 9 8 7 6 5 4 3 2

Disclaimer: Many of the activities described in this book can be dangerous, especially when weather is adverse or unpredictable, and when unforeseen events or conditions create a hazardous situation. The author has done his best to provide the reader with accurate information about water travel, as well as to point out some of its potential hazards. It is the responsibility of the users of this guide to learn the necessary skills for safe water travel, and to exercise caution in potentially hazardous areas. The author and publisher disclaim any liability for injury or other damage caused by water travel or performing any other activity described in this book.

CONTENTS

4

ACKNOWLEDGMENTS

In memory of my mother, Mary Kingham Smith (1914-2006)

My husband, Bob, and I paddled almost 1,300 miles of rivers researching this guide, right on the heels of researching the northern book, which also involved about 1,300 miles of paddling. I'm deeply indebted to Bob for being my partner in both projects. Neither of us guessed how big they would be (or how rewarding!).

Of all my many southern Minnesota relatives, my mother took care of us most often, more times than I can count, and always with unconditional generosity, enthusiasm, and love. (She and my father, Lucian Smith, both of whom loved Minnesota's waters, taught me to paddle a canoe when I was a child.) In addition, Sue and Larry Leonard fed us, and Larry ran shuttles. Ginny Smith, Julie Quinn-Autrey and Bill Autrey (and Hannah and Colin Quinn), and Patty and Mike Marsh all fed and housed us, and Mike answered my Zumbro questions. Bob Smith fielded all my railroad bridge questions, and Mike Smith, all my geology questions. Our children helped as well. Matt calculated all the gradients and read the manuscript for river-science accuracy. Greg saved the project from disaster by retrieving all the files when my hard drive crashed and I hadn't backed up in two months. James did long-distance computer consultations when Greg wasn't available. Anne read the manuscript for clarity. Rebecca Gass offered her enthusiastic support for my projects. To my wonderful family, thank you.

Out on the rivers, thanks go first to Peggy Kreber and Warren Wagner of the Mankato Paddling & Outings Club (MPOC), with whom we paddled the Rush, the Sand, and the High Island. These two are an inspiration: they would paddle every day of the year if they could, and their knowledge of Minnesota rivers is awesome. I'm also grateful to MPOC members Brand Frentz and Mark Bosacker from North Mankato and Tom McDonald from the Twin Cities. I thank Hank Wells of Roseville, who, along with Ansel Krannich, joined us on the North Fork of the Crow. Hank's help on the manuscript is also appreciated. Thanks to Carol Brewton and Sue O'Brien of Winona who paddled with us on the Root and for Sue's guidance on Mississippi River information. Thanks to Richard Halterman, Patrick Moore, Gary Lentz, and Greg Wyum of CURE for great paddles on Hawk Creek and Yellow Medicine, and to the River Ramblers with whom we paddled the Lower Snake, the Cannon, and the Rice. I'm particularly grateful to Linda and Dave Hopper for joining us on a memorable trip down the Straight.

The following generous folks helped me with my seemingly endless research: Steve Mueller and Peter Hark of DNR Trails and Waterways; Thomas F. Waters, professor emeritus at the University of Minnesota; Joel Wagar, Brad Koonen, and Trygve Hanson of the DNR; Whitney Clark of Friends of the Mississippi River; Tim King and Kitty Tepley of Long Prairie; Diane Sander of Buffalo; Tom Bender of Friends of Rush River Park; Jeff McKay, Parks and Recreation Director in Owatonna; Scott Sparlin of the Coalition for a Clean Minnesota River; Joe Deden of the Eagle Bluff Environmental Center; and Robert Douglas, professor of geography at Gustavus Adolphus College in St. Peter.

A big thanks goes to Mike Cichanowski of Wenonah Canoe (the epicenter of Minnesota paddling!) for the great all-around river canoe, a royalex Spirit II, and for his advice and support of this project.

I'm very grateful to have worked with the supportive and professional staff at Trails Books, especially Mark Knickelbine, Eva Šolcová, and Stan Stoga.

—LSD

Also in memory of paddler John Austin (1945–2005), who loved "simply messing about in boats."

Like the state's northern half, southern Minnesota is blessed with an abundance of rivers. All the way from the South Dakota border to the Mississippi River, the restless song of the river sounds its call, and paddlers answer. There's whitewater (yes, southern Minnesota whitewater) and quiet water. There are intimate woodland streams, broad river highways, and wooded prairie rivers that carve deep into the flat land of southwestern Minnesota. There's exciting urban paddling in the Twin Cities area. Southern Minnesota waterways offer wonderful opportunities for paddlers of all abilities—beginner to expert. This guide is a collection of paddling trips that will take you to the best of these rivers.

HOW WERE THE RIVERS CHOSEN?

So many river miles lace the rolling land of southern Minnesota that including every paddleable stretch would be impossible. I narrowed the field by talking with other paddlers about their favorite runs and focusing on segments that seemed both fun and reasonably safe. Fun is in the mind of the paddler, so I considered a wide variety of river sizes and styles. The segments I chose to research are scenic, relatively undeveloped, and have accesses that range from acceptable to quite good. I included several series of trips where canoe camping is possible. Bob and I paddled every mile of every river in this guide, a total of just over 1,000 miles. In addition, we paddled about 260 miles that we decided not to include.

I avoided long stretches of treeless agricultural land, excessive motorboat traffic, and heavily polluted waters. (Pollution is the unfortunate reality of southern Minnesota rivers, but some are definitely cleaner than others. For information on organizations devoted to improving the health of Minnesota's rivers, see Appendix 5.) I stayed away from areas where riverbank development destroys the river's charm, river segments that require portages around dams and other hazards, and rivers that only run a few

days each season. For every rule I made about which rivers to exclude, however, at least one river breaks the rule and is included anyway. In each case, some wonderful attribute balances out that river's flaws.

Because so many of southern Minnesota's river miles are on the Minnesota and the Mississippi, those rivers would dominate the book if I included more than a sampler. For this reason, I describe only three trips on the Minnesota and three on the Mississippi.

WHERE ARE ALL THESE RIVERS LOCATED?

For the purposes of this guide, southern Minnesota lies south of a line running through Mille Lacs Lake, although the line is a rather indefinite divider. For example, the Kettle River is described in my earlier guidebook, *Paddling Northern Minnesota*, while its geographical cohort, the Snake, is included in this guidebook. The Long Prairie, one of the rivers in this southern Minnesota book, flows into the Crow Wing, a river that I cover in the northern Minnesota book.

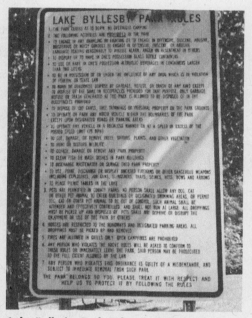

Lake Byllesby Park Rules: Don't even think about it.

South of that arbitrary dividing line, the rivers lie mostly in two watersheds: those of the Minnesota River and the Mississippi River. In fact, 31 of the 34 rivers described in this guide are in these two drainage basins. In addition, the St. Croix watershed contributes three rivers to the list. The waters of the three main rivers are generally free of rapids, with a few notable exceptions. The final reaches of their tributaries often have great stretches of rocky riffles and whitewater. What follows is a brief tour of the regions where these varying river networks are located.

In the **southwestern** counties, the Upper Minnesota River is fed by five main tributaries: the Pomme de Terre, the Chippewa, Hawk Creek, the Lac qui Parle, and the Yellow Medicine. The best runs on these prairie rivers are in their wooded final reaches, where they drop swiftly into the broad, deep valley of the Minnesota. A nice stretch of the Upper Minnesota River—good for canoe camping—rivals North Woods river corridors in isolation and wooded beauty. Another southwestern prairie river with a beautiful wooded reach is the West Fork of the Des Moines.

The Cottonwood joins the Middle Minnesota River at New Ulm. In the **Mankato** area, five fast-moving rivers traverse Blue Earth County on their way to the Middle Minnesota: the Le Sueur, the Maple, the Big Cobb, the Blue Earth, and the Watonwan. Between St. Peter and Jordan, three speedy streams that feed the Lower

Riverside DNR campsites, like this one on the Rum River, are nearly always marked with this sign.

Minnesota—High Island Creek, Rush River, and Sand Creek—offer high-water paddling adventures.

Moving east into the Mississippi watershed, the dramatic bluff country of the southeastern counties is home to a beautiful river quartet: the Root, the Whitewater, the Zumbro, and the Cannon (and its own tributary, the Straight). The former three flow into the Mississippi along the scenic stretch designated as the Upper Mississippi National Wildlife Refuge. In the Winona area, numerous quiet backwater channels offer good canoeing territory.

Swallow nest holes cover the soft rock of riverside cliffs in buckshot patterns.

In the Twin Cities, paddling opportunities include the Mississippi—especially through its dramatic Gorge—and two lively tributaries, Rice Creek and Minnehaha Creek. Within an hour's drive are four Mississippi tributaries: the Crow, the Vermillion, the lower Rum, and the Elk. Farther upstream, the Sauk joins the Mississippi at St. Cloud and the Platte, near Royalton. One of the northernmost rivers in this guide is the Long Prairie, flowing north into the Crow Wing near that river's confluence with the Mississippi. Farther east, the upper Rum runs south, draining Mille Lacs Lake.

In the St. Croix watershed east of Mille Lacs, the Snake races south and then east to meet the St. Croix. Farther south, the little Sunrise also feeds the St. Croix. The St. Croix itself defines Minnesota's eastern border for 145 miles. Several St. Croix trips are less than an hour from the Twin Cities. Designated a National Wild and Scenic River in 1968, the St. Croix is one of the state's premier paddling treasures.

A river needn't be classified as "wild" to offer rewarding experiences. For example, it may surprise readers to learn that wildlife is often as abundant along southern rivers as in the North Woods. Bald eagles have staged a remarkable comeback in Minnesota, as elsewhere. On almost every river we paddled in researching this guide, I saw at least one bald eagle, and often many more.

Sightings of their massive nests attest to their permanent residency. And forested riverbanks aren't confined to rural areas. "Great urban paddling" may sound like an oxymoron, yet Minnehaha and Rice creeks in the Twin Cities run through beautiful wooded corridors. The easily accessible respite from urban life that these city rivers afford makes them great substitutes for trips to remote North Woods rivers.

WHAT'S IN THE BOOK

Trips are organized alphabetically by river. Each trip is designed to be a one-day paddle, although information on shortening, lengthening, or combining the trips is also provided. For each daylong trip, there's a map, a summary of essential trip-planning information, and a detailed narrative describing the river segment. Reading a trip's introductory paragraph is a good way to decide whether you might or might not want to paddle it. This introduction includes an assessment of difficulty, a mention of rapids or other challenges, and a short description of the trip's attractions. I also mention if there's a good place at the end of the trip to grab a burger.

Maps

The maps have been kept simple for easy readability. Included are only the most essential details: roads that lead to the accesses, shuttle route roads, access points, the paddling route with mile markers, notable rapids, railroads, cities and towns, campsites and campgrounds, parkland, and bicycle trails. A key identifies the symbols used for these items.

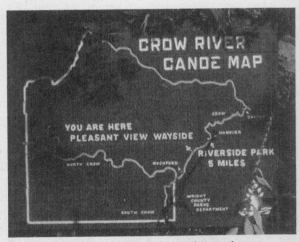

Pleasant View Wayside on the Crow has a pleasant wooded picnic spot.

Notable rapids are shown with hash marks and a rating. For an explanation of rapids ratings, see the "Paddling Safety" section later in this introduction.

Useful landmarks like tributaries, large islands, bridges, and power lines are shown to help you determine your location on the map. You may want to carry a compass to check the direction of the river's flow at a given point. Comparing the compass reading to the direction of the river on the map can help you find out where you are. Most of the mile markers for the river segments were determined using global positioning system (GPS) readings and all can be confidently used for trip planning. However, everyone takes a different route down a river, and mileages may vary slightly as a result.

A note about names and numbers of roads: in recent years, Minnesota has been renaming and renumbering roads to conform to the needs of the 911 system. While we have made every effort to ensure that the maps have the most up-to-date and accurate designations, the renaming and renumbering process continues in a few areas. The result is that occasional discrepancies may exist between our maps and new designations.

The maps in this guide provide all the information you need to take the trips. If you want more maps (and who doesn't?), the *Minnesota Atlas and Gazetteer*, published by DeLorme Mapping Company (www.delorme.com/atlasgaz), divides the state into 77 detailed maps, especially helpful in navigating back roads. This must-have book should live in your vehicle.

Topographical maps, especially the 7.5-minute quadrangle series, provide a detailed three-dimensional picture of the land and markings for roads and towns. Order these fascinating maps from USGS Information Services, Box 25286, Denver, CO 80225, (888) 275-8747, http://www.usgs.gov/.

DNR state canoe-route maps are available for 17 of the 38 rivers. These maps have shading that differentiates public and private land, useful information when you need to stop unexpectedly along a river. To order free copies, call the DNR, (888) 646-6367. A list of the routes and updated digital versions of the maps is online (http://www.dnr.state.mn.us/canoeing/index.html). DNR Public Recreation Information Maps (PRIM) divide the state into 51 separate area maps, identifying public and private land and showing all public water access points. Selected copies can usually be purchased at state parks. All PRIM maps may be purchased online from Minnesota's Bookstore (http://www.comm.media.state.mn.us/bookstore/bookstore.asp).

A historical map that may interest paddlers is Joseph N. Nicollet's *Map of the Hydrographical Basin of the Upper Mississippi River*, originally published in 1843 by the U.S. Government and reprinted from the original copperplates in 1965 by the Minnesota Historical Society. There's more about Nicollet's travels and about obtaining a copy of his map in Appendix 3.

Biking Trails

Minnesota has more miles of paved rail-to-trail bikeways than any other state. For paddlers who enjoy biking, the trip descriptions mention any nearby trails. *Minnesota Monthly*'s Web site (www.minnesotamonthly.com/sponsoredSection/biking/index.html) has links to maps and information for the most popular trails. A useful guidebook, *Bicycle Trails of Minnesota* (second edition), published by American Bike Trails, contains maps and descriptions for over 100 trails throughout Minnesota, including many in the Twin Cities area. In the section on Shuttle Logistics (below), I include tips on bicycle shuttles.

Camping

When camping facilities are available, either along the river or within 25 miles, these are listed in the narrative and shown on the map. On the rivers, you can spot **DNR riverside campsites** by looking for a brown-and-gold wooden sign with a canoe camp symbol. These sites almost always have a picnic table, a fire ring, a tent pad, and an open-air latrine.

Minnesota's wonderful system of **state parks** offers campgrounds with visitor centers, electrical hookups, and hot showers. When a state park is within 25 miles of the river, it's mentioned in the narrative, along with the phone number of the visitor center. Campsite reservations ([866] 857-2757, www.stayatmnparks.com) are arranged through a central booking agency. On weekends and holidays, reservations are recommended.

A historic truss bridge crosses the North Fork of the Crow.

Canoe Rental and Shuttle Service

Outfitters located within a reasonable distance of the river are listed. Some outfitters will provide shuttle service for a fee even if you don't rent a boat from them.

Shuttle Routes

Each trip includes a description of what I consider the best shuttle route from the put-in to the take-out. It's not always the shortest route. That's because I generally suggest paved rather than gravel roads, even when the latter are shorter. Nevertheless, in some cases, gravel roads are the only choice. Other possible shuttle roads are shown on the map.

Shuttle Logistics

If you've never shuttled people, boats, and equipment between the put-in and the take-out and wonder how it works, here are some tips.

For groups with more than one vehicle, the process is usually simple. One factor is whether you're more pressed for time at the beginning or end of the paddling. Other variables are changing weather and impending darkness. The most common routine is for the whole group to drive to the put-in at the designated time and drop off all canoes and gear, as well as people to watch the stuff. One person drives each vehicle to the take-out. The drivers leave all vehicles but one at the take-out and return to the put-in in that one vehicle. After everyone paddles downriver to the waiting vehicles, two people in one vehicle drive back to the put-in to fetch the vehicle. The others are free to load up and leave. For all but the two drivers, this arrangement saves time at the end of the trip.

Another option is to meet at the take-out and leave one vehicle there. Stuff everyone and all canoes and equipment into the remaining vehicles, drive to the put-in, and paddle down the river. Two (or more, depending on the number of vehicles) people then drive back to the put-in together and pick up the vehicles. This method saves time at the beginning of the trip but requires extra roof-rack space to carry the canoe that was on the vehicle left at the take-out.

Yet another method, when some paddlers want to take out early, is to leave their vehicle at an alternate access so they can take out there.

For those with only one vehicle and lots of energy, a **bicycle shuttle** works well, and pedaling makes for a nice change from paddling. Just chain the bike to a tree or some other permanent fixture at the take-out, drive to the put-in, leave the vehicle there, and paddle downriver. One person then stays with the canoe and the other rides the bicycle back to the put-in. Another strategy is to carry the bicycle in the canoe, eliminating the need to leave it at the take-out and offering the flexibility to choose an alternate take-out. Some bicycle shuttlers add a small motorized friction drive to make a long or hilly journey easier.

Rapidan Dam Park posts a useful park map.

Staton, Inc., (405) 605-3765 or www.staton-inc.com, and several other companies make an easily installed friction drive kit that will motorize your bike. This is a noisy contraption, but the gas mileage is great: about 130 mpg. One last tip: When there's a paved trail available, some folks like to do their shuttles on inline skates.

A shuttle bike nestles nicely into the canoe.

Gradient

Gradient refers to the steepness of the riverbed, expressed in feet per mile (fpm). The average gradient of a river segment is calculated by dividing the number of feet of elevation that the river drops in that segment by the length of the segment in miles. The importance of knowing the gradient of a river is that riffles and rapids are usually found on rivers with a gradient of higher than 3 fpm. On a river with a gradient of 10 fpm or more, you can generally expect challenging whitewater. Gradient is only one factor in predicting what the water will be like, but it can definitely alert you to the possibility of dangerous conditions.

Important: A river segment with a relatively low average gradient may have short, high-gradient drops that are balanced by long stretches of flat water. For example, the Upper Snake, mostly Class I to II, also drops through two very steep stretches. Always check both the average gradient and the gradient of any significant rapids on the river. Appendix 1 lists the average gradient, distance, and difficulty of each river trip.

Water Levels

The water level is one of the most important things to know about a river, primarily for you and your boat's safety. Moderate water levels generally yield the most enjoyable paddles. When you hear a river described as "bankfull," the water reaches the top of the banks. A river that's overflowing its banks is at flood stage. Never paddle a river that's at flood stage. Rivers are usually high in the spring and are often filled with debris racing downstream in icy cold water. Although you may be tempted by the excitement of spring's high water, never paddle a river that has this lethal combination of fast water, obstacles, and hypothermia-inducing cold. EVERY RIVER IN THIS BOOK IS DANGEROUS TO PADDLE AT HIGH WATER.

At the other extreme, a river that's too low is no fun to paddle. Scraping your way down a shallow, boulder-strewn river is frustrating for you and terrible for your equipment.

Each river trip lists available sources of water-level information, some online. For U.S. Geological Survey (USGS) automated gages ("gage" is the USGS standard variant of "gauge"), data is available on their Web site (http://nwis.waterdata.usgs.gov/mn/nwis/rt). USGS "Daily Streamflow Conditions" are presented in two formats: discharge in cubic feet per second (cfs) and gage height in feet. These readings are "real-time" data that are less than four hours old. In addition to listing streamflow for many of the rivers in this guide, the site chronicles recent rainfall, historical data, gage locations, and other information for the same gage areas. It's well worth getting acquainted with this useful Web site. Another Web source, the U.S. Army Corps of Engineers (USACE) Web site (www.mvp-wc. usace.army.mil/dcp/), gives "stage" (height in feet) readings

A bridge access often involves sliding down a grassy slope.

for some of the rivers that are not on the USGS site. The National Weather Service office at Chahassen, part of the National Oceanic and Atmos-pheric Administration (NOAA), has a Web site (www. crh.noaa.gov/ahps2/index. php?wfo=mpx) that lists readings from gauges owned by various agencies. However, none of these sites interprets the data for you.

On some rivers, there's a gauge painted onto a bridge pier. Volunteers read these gauges and the data are available from the DNR, (888) 646-6367, www.dnr.state.mn.us/ river_levels/index.html, along with DNR interpretations of the data for most, but not all, rivers. The interpretations indicate which levels the DNR feels are best for paddling. Please note that these DNR readings are updated at best weekly, not daily. Because volunteers do the readings, the data may only be reported occasionally. Many rivers change quickly, so be sure to note the date of the report. The DNR is converting the data sources for many river

The Maple is the victim of several dumpsites.

11

This is what happens when a canoe and a snag mix it up during a flood on the Cannon.

routes from volunteer readings to automated USGS gages and providing links to the USGS website. In these cases, the old data interpretation may not apply to the USGS data.

Some rivers have no gauges, and thus no readings are available. Paddlers often call nearby state parks, campgrounds, or outfitters to find out what conditions are like on a river that has no gauge. Information from these experienced sources is likely to be accurate. In addition, rainfall in the river's watershed or readings from a nearby gauged river in the same watershed can be somewhat useful in predicting levels.

On rivers where water-level readings are available, the trip description includes an **interpretation of water levels**. These interpretations are based on my own experience as well as on reports from other paddlers and from the DNR. The levels I list are suggestions only and not a guarantee of a safe or enjoyable paddle. Many other factors, including the equipment you use and the weight of the load in your boat, will determine whether you scrape or float.

Water level is also a partial predictor of how long your trip will take. The higher the water, the faster it flows. If a river flows at 1 to 2 miles per hour at moderate levels, which most do, then moderately high water may bump that speed up to 3 to 4 miles per hour, significantly shortening your paddling time. At low water, you may want to shorten your trip by using an alternate access. Water level is only one factor in your speed. The way you paddle—letting the river do the work, or racing downriver, calling "Hut!"—also helps determine your speed.

Finding accurate water-level information ahead of time can sometimes be confusing and frustrating. In addition, data reports can be inaccurate: the gauge may be calibrated improperly or the readings reported inaccurately. The result is that you may arrive at a river only to find that it's too high or too low to paddle. THE FINAL DECISION ON WHETHER TO PADDLE A RIVER IS YOURS ALONE. Use your judgment: if a river looks too high to paddle, then it almost always is. (See the "Paddling Safely" section for some indicators of dangerous water.) Pack up and go home, or find some other outdoor

A warning sign for a cable fence crossing a river escaped from its moorings, losing its effectiveness.

activity. Conversely, if the water looks too low, do your boat a favor and don't paddle.

Accesses

Accesses range from developed landings with ramps and parking areas to undeveloped access points by bridges on quiet country roads. Those at bridges may adjoin private land; be careful to use only the road right-of-way for your parking and access. Parking on the shoulder is common on quiet rural roads, but do lock your vehicle. Most accesses in this guide are easy to spot from the river; I've noted the less visible ones. If you're concerned that you might paddle right past a take-out, tie a bright ribbon or bandana on a branch at the take-out when you run the shuttle.

The hungry Zumbro has eaten another canoe.

Trip Descriptions

The remainder of each narrative provides a description of what paddlers can expect to see along their journey, including river conditions, obstacles, landmarks, flora and fauna, and other items worth noting. Reading the whole narrative before you paddle will help you decide if you would enjoy that particular trip.

Fishing

Whether or not you catch dinner, fishing on a canoe trip can be lots of fun. Whenever a river is known for great fishing, like the flathead catfish on the Minnesota or the smallmouth bass on the Snake, this is mentioned in the trip description. Also noted are fish populations known to exist at particular places on a river. If you plan to fish, you will of course need a Minnesota fishing license, available at many gas stations and most sporting-goods stores.

RIVER READING AND MANEUVERS

Many of the rivers described in this guide are primarily quiet water, offering safe and pleasant floats for paddlers of all skill levels, even beginners, provided that they have river-reading skills. If you've only paddled on lakes, you'll find that river paddling is quite different. All river paddlers should know how to read a river, maneuver the boat, and handle unexpected situations or difficulties.

Reading the river is a skill that improves with practice. A class with an accredited instructor is the best place to start. Learn to predict what lies in those waves ahead, the appearance of downstream and upstream V's (surface patterns on the water, which indicate either safe passage or an obstacle), what an eddy line does to a boat, the dangers of strainers and other obstacles, the difference between a pillow rock and a standing wave, the hazards of holes, and the intricacies of rock-garden navigation. Once you have instruction, practice on gentle rivers until you feel confident enough to attempt a more difficult trip. Paddling a river is far more fun when you have the skills to boldly meet the challenges.

PADDLING SAFELY

If you've ever been in a tight situation on a paddling trip, you already know the importance of knowledge, skills, good judgment, and proper equipment in dealing with the problem. In general, the more experienced you are, the more respect you have for the inherent risks a paddler faces and the keener your skills and judgment become.

Before you even plan a river trip, be sure you have the skills to paddle a river safely, the ability to read the water, and knowledge of the potential risks of paddling and how to deal with difficulties. Practice your skills, especially rescues, on safe and familiar waters. Develop the necessary respect for risk that will prevent you from overestimating your skills. Take the right equipment (see the checklist later in this section) including a snug-fitting,

The oft-flooding Zumbro stole a warning sign from the Silver Lake dam.

comfortable personal floatation device (PFD, or life jacket) for each paddler. ALWAYS WEAR YOUR PFD. Most canoe and kayak fatalities involve paddlers who aren't wearing a PFD. After years of constantly reminding our four children to be safe in the water sports they love, I never go out in a canoe or kayak without my PFD.

As you plan your river adventures, learn as much as you can about the river you want to paddle. Paddle with friends who are experienced or with a group or club that has experienced paddlers. Minnesota has many great paddling organizations and schools that hold regular outings on many of the rivers in this guide. (See the list of organizations, schools, and clubs in Appendix 4.)

When a Zumbro flood flushes out the storm drains of Rochester, the river suffers.

The following are some of the hazards you may face while on the river. This list is intended as an introduction to the subject, certainly not the last word. The best strategy before paddling rivers—especially whitewater rivers—is taking a class with an accredited instructor.

1. Broaching

When your canoe is pushed sideways, or broadside, to the current, the force of the current may pin it against an exposed rock, bridge pier, or other obstacle. This is known as broaching or pinning. If you're a beginning paddler, your instinct is to lean upstream away from the rock and into the onrushing water. If you do that, your boat quickly begins to fill with water. A strong enough current will then wrap the boat, with you in it, around the rock or bridge pier. However, if you remain calm and immediately do a hard downstream lean toward the rock, you can prevent this potential catastrophe. Maintain the downstream lean to keep the boat from filling with water and you may be able to wiggle it off the rock. You may also be able to climb onto the rock to lighten and free the boat. If other paddlers are with you, they may be able to help. A rescue

Although this lowhead dam on the Lower Snake looks innocuous, two recreational kayakers drowned trying to run it.

3. Holes

When fast water flows over a ledge or a rock, it curls back on itself on the downstream side, forming a turbulent depression in the water known as a hole, a souse hole, a reversal, or a hydraulic. Small to moderate holes form on Patterson's Rapids on the Minnesota River and also on other rivers in this guide. At moderate levels, most of these can be run or surfed by experienced paddlers. Some large holes become quite "sticky" and are called stoppers or keepers. These dangerous holes can trap and kill a swimmer and should be avoided, by portaging if necessary. Paddlers who cannot recognize the difference should avoid all but the smallest holes. At moderate to high water levels, large holes form on the Sauk Rapids of the Mississippi at St. Cloud and on the Upper Snake. Lowhead dams, like the one just upstream of the put-in on Snake River 6, always form stoppers. Never try to run a lowhead dam.

4. High Water

In early spring, and after heavy or sustained rainfall, rivers like the Zumbro, the Root, the Yellow Medicine, Hawk Creek, the Snake, and many others rise quickly and dangerously. The result can be very fast, unpredictable currents; huge waves; and big, sticky holes. In spring, tree branches and other debris may be racing downstream in ice-cold water as well. If the water rushes through the riverbank trees and shrubs, is turbulent and muddy with whirlpools visible, or contains floating branches or other debris, it is too high to paddle.

5. Strainers

When a tree extends into the current, it's called a strainer, a sweeper, or a snag. Water flows through the branches, but paddlers and canoes can be caught and trapped. Debris jams, bridge piers, jumbles of boulders, and undercut rocks also act like strainers. The current can trap and hold both paddlers and their boats underwater in the tangle of branches, logs, or rock, with potentially fatal results. Steer clear of strainers.

6. Ledges and Falls

You'll find ledges on the Upper Snake, in the Kettle Slough of the St. Croix, and at the Sauk Rapids on the Mississippi. Although the rapids of the Upper Snake are named "falls," they are really Class III to Class IV rapids with ledges. A ledge is signaled by a horizon line, a clear line across the river where the river drops over, often accompanied by mist or a roar. Falls are more dramatic, with a sudden

from shore using throw ropes may be necessary if the boat is pinned and filled with water.

To avoid a broach, keep your boat parallel to the current, pointed either upstream or downstream, so that it either hits obstacles head-on or slides alongside of them.

2. Cold

Springtime paddlers in Minnesota face the very real risk of dumping into the ice-cold water of rivers that have only recently thawed. Immersion in water this cold often leads to hypothermia, a potentially fatal chilling of the body's core that also quickly drains a paddler's strength, as well as his or her ability, and will, to survive. If you paddle when the water is below 55°F, or when the water temperature and the air temperature don't add up to over 100°F, it's essential to wear a wet suit or dry suit and carry extra clothes in a dry bag. If you're not an experienced paddler, wait until warmer weather and water before paddling.

Parking is sometimes a challenge.

Here's an example of "Worst Management Practices" along the Zumbro.

vertical drop of five feet or more. When approaching a ledge or falls, scout carefully before running it. If in doubt, always portage. The current often increases as you get nearer to a falls or rapids, so don't get too close if you're boat-scouting.

7. Dams

Several trips in this book take you near relatively high dams, like the Jordan Dam on Sand Creek, the Carp Dam on High Island Creek, and the Malt-O-Meal Dam on Cannon River 1. In addition, there are lowhead dams on several rivers, like the Cross Lake Dam on Snake River 6. Never underestimate the great danger of getting too close to the edge of a dam. Always take out as far from the dam as possible to avoid the strong current that builds near the edge. When you put in below a dam, stay away from the recirculating currents that form just below the dam.

A bicycle shuttler: note the motor, the helmet, and the reflective vest.

8. Capsizing

Anyone who paddles regularly will at some time capsize. Dumping is simply part of paddling. Don't panic. Hang on to your boat, keeping it downstream of you to avoid being crushed between the boat and a rock. Your PFD will help protect you from rocks, but only if you're wearing it! If you're headed into dangerous rapids or toward a hazard, let go of the boat and swim on your back, with your feet downstream and your toes out of the water. If you're near an eddy, swim that way. Don't attempt to stand in rapids; your feet may get trapped between rocks, and the fast water will push you under and keep you there. This is a common cause of drowning for paddlers.

Occasionally a cab is the best shuttle option for paddlers with only one vehicle.

If you're paddling in a group, the other people should help you first and your boat later. This brings up both the importance of paddling with at least one other person and learning river-rescue skills. As part of becoming a better paddler, you should learn and practice rescues. Using a throw bag effectively can help a fellow paddler out of a dangerous situation.

9. Rapids

Successfully negotiating riffles and rapids is exciting and fun—one of the great joys of river paddling. The Snake is the only river in this guide with significant whitewater. On the Upper Snake are two stretches of dangerous Class II-IV rapids and long stretches of Class I-II rapids. Below the Cross Lake Dam, Class I-II rapids characterize much of the lower river. Sand Creek has Class II rapids. Many other rivers—including the Sauk, the Big Cobb, High Island Creek, the Yellow Medicine, Hawk Creek, and many others—run through less challenging, but still quite exciting rapids. Most of the rivers in this guide have at least a few riffles and easy Class I

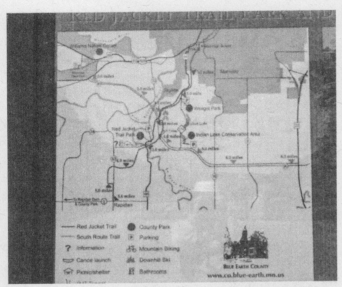

Bike trails, such as here on the Le Sueur, often make great shuttle routes.

what draws many paddlers to the rivers, and yet the excitement comes from the inherent danger of the fast water, danger that must be assessed thoroughly. Inexperienced paddlers often underestimate the risks, with sometimes catastrophic results. An expert paddler knows when a rapid is unrunnable and steadfastly respects all safety precautions. However, even experienced paddlers make mistakes that result from inadequate scouting, underestimating the difficulty of a drop, or paddling when the water is too high. Each paddler is responsible for understanding the difficulty of a river and its rapids before paddling.

To paraphrase Tolstoy in his pronouncement on families, all rapids resemble one another, but each difficult rapid is difficult in its own way. The International Scale of River Difficulty attempts to find the ways in which rapids are alike and rates them using these similarities. But because each rapid is different, these ratings always have degrees of subjectivity and imperfection. Here are the categories used to rate rapids. (Descriptions of Class V and VI are included for information only.) Remember that whenever the water is high or cold, a run becomes one class more difficult.

Class I: A step up from riffles, with fast water and waves, but not too big; and some obstructions, but not too many. These are run easily by beginning whitewater paddlers who have river-paddling experience and good maneuvering skills. The dangers are small if you have to swim. The Rum, the Chippewa, the Root, and many others in this guide have frequent stretches of Class I rapids.

Class II: Fast water with big waves, ledges, and more rocks, often close together and awkward to maneuver around. Excellent river-reading skills are needed to weave through the boulder gardens that characterize a Class II river. Broaching is a definite possibility, and rescue may be difficult. Some Class II rapids, like the Lower Snake at high water, can be quite long, with the poten-

rapids.

Riffles are fast, mostly unobstructed water with small waves—water that is easy and fun to paddle, great for beginning river paddlers to learn to maneuver on, and enjoyable for experienced paddlers as well.

Standing waves, also called haystacks, often form in rapids when the river races through a tight spot or over a drop and into slower water. These wave chains usually mark deep water and the best route for paddlers to follow. If the waves are too big, however, they can swamp an open canoe. At moderate to high water, High Island Creek, Sand Creek, and stretches of the Platte, the Elk, the Straight, the Des Moines, the Watonwan, and many others have chains of standing waves.

Rapids are classified to help paddlers predict which rivers they can run safely. The excitement of rapids is

Crossing the Le Sueur, a bicyclist runs the shuttle.

tial for problems becoming much greater than on a short rapid. Class II rapids are also found on Sand Creek, Bradbury Rapids on the Upper Rum, and the Lower Sauk at high water, among others. These Class II rapids are appropriate for experienced whitewater paddlers only; others should portage.

Class III: Very difficult rapids, with large, irregular waves that may be difficult to avoid and that can swamp an open canoe; drops of 3 feet or more; a strong, pushy current; and the presence of holes, strong eddies, and other powerful current effects, especially on large-volume rivers. Complex maneuvers are required. Long swims and injuries while swimming are more likely. Rescue can be quite difficult. Class III rapids are suitable for experienced advanced paddlers only. The Upper Snake River Falls has Class III rapids.

Class IV: Intense, powerful, but predictable rapids requiring precise boat handling in turbulent water. There may be big, unavoidable waves, holes, and constricted passages, all demanding fast moves under pressure. Capsize may be catastrophic and rescue is quite difficult. These rapids are appropriate only for highly skilled paddlers with extensive experience in difficult whitewater. The Lower Snake River Falls, with Class III and Class IV rapids, is the most difficult rapids in this guide.

Class V: Extremely long, obstructed, or very violent rapids that expose a paddler to added risk. Big drops may contain large, unavoidable waves and keeper holes; steep, congested chutes with complex, demanding routes; and broaching situations. Rapids are often long, demanding a high level of fitness. Class V rapids pose serious danger to life and little chance of rescue. These rapids are appropriate only for teams of experts under perfect water levels and weather conditions.

Class VI: Extreme and exploratory, these runs have almost never been attempted. The consequences of error are probably fatal and rescue is nearly impossible.

An Important Warning

If you are at all unsure of an approaching rapid, get out above the rapid and scout it carefully. Scouting is a chance to learn more about a river, and it's also an essential safety measure when you are unsure. **If in doubt, always portage.** Never let pride or pressure from others push you into attempting a rapid that is too difficult for your skills and experience. Sometimes the most "skilled" paddler is the one who portages when others paddle. A good test is to ask yourself, "Could I run this safely 9 out of 10 times?" If the answer is no, portage. Always wear your PFD and don't paddle alone.

A CANOE TRIP CHECKLIST

Beginning paddlers may want to use this basic checklist. A personally customized checklist is a good thing to develop if you do a lot of paddling. Even people who paddle frequently sometimes forget things they really need.

- A snug-fitting and comfortable PFD (lifejacket) for each paddler
- An extra paddle for each boat
- Sunscreen and bug spray
- Hat
- Shoes or sandals that protect your feet from rocks
- Rain gear
- First-aid kit
- Food and plenty of water in plastic containers
- Bailer and sponge
- Keys to shuttle vehicle or bike lock
- A dry bag to hold a change of clothes, wallet, camera, and cell phone
- Map and compass
- For whitewater: floatation bag, tie-downs, whitewater helmet, and wet suit (depending on conditions)
- For camping: camping equipment and food packed in dry bags

PRIVATE PROPERTY ISSUES

Minnesota's position on paddlers' rights is somewhat ambiguous and more restrictive of paddlers than that of its

Ready, set, go!

neighbor, Wisconsin. There are several issues to consider, the first being ownership of the waterways. Much of the land along Minnesota's rivers and lakes is privately owned, but all navigable waters in Minnesota are public waters, where the State of Minnesota owns the streambed *below the ordinary low-water level.* Navigability is defined by Minnesota as "when they are used, or are susceptible of being used, in their natural ordinary condition, as highways for commerce, over which trade or travel are or may be conducted." All the waterways described in this book are navigable and thus public waters.

The public may legally use any public waters, but getting to that water is another question. This leads to the second issue: riparian rights. Riparian rights are shoreland property rights. Where a public road with its right-of-way or a public access abuts a river or lake (navigable or not), the public has riparian rights and may access that water. In places along a public waterway where there is no public-access point, the landowner has the riparian rights and members of the public must get verbal or written permission from the landowner to cross that property. Crossing private property to get to a public waterway is trespassing and grounds for prosecution.

Once safely on the water, paddlers must still remember the shoreline issues. The legality of using private shoreline is a fuzzy area. Strictly speaking, paddlers may only use the surface of the water or anchor on that water. Landing on private shoreline or wading in the shallow water along private property may be interpreted as trespassing. It is particularly important to observe this rule where "No Trespassing" or "Keep Out" signs are posted. Paddlers who land on a shoreline and are asked by the landowner to leave should do so immediately, without argument. However, if a paddler is briefly on private shoreline in the natural course of paddling down the river for the purposes of taking a short rest, wading through a shallow area, or using a well-established-but-private portage trail around a rapid, the attorney general's office deems such activity legal.

Most of the rivers in this guide run through private woodlands, rather than state forests. Many run through agricultural areas. According to the DNR, state forested areas are open unless posted but agricultural land does not need to be posted for trespassing to be illegal. Paddlers have the final responsibility to determine whether the land is private or public and to obtain any necessary permission to camp on private property.

Property owners do have one responsibility. They may not build fences or dams that interfere with the normal passage of boats that are typical to the waterway. On the Rush River, a landowner has strung two barbed-wire fences across the river, endangering canoeists at some water levels. This fence is probably illegal because it is considered a danger to the public. It is, however, also illegal and definitely inadvisable for canoeists to cut fences. Fortunately, a fence like this is a rare occurrence. In over a thousand miles of paddling, we only encountered four, and one was later removed. Cooperation and mutual respect should be the goal of both paddlers and landowners in all these issues.

BOAT REGISTRATION

All canoes and kayaks owned by Minnesota residents and used on rivers and lakes in Minnesota must be registered with the State of Minnesota. The dealer from whom you buy the boat will tell you how to do this or you can contact the DNR for more information: (888) 646-6367; http://www.dnr.state.mn.us/licenses/water craft/index.html. If you are paddling a boat from another state, it must be registered in that state. If your stare does

Some landowners leave little doubt. (Snake)

not require registration, you must purchase a Minnesota registration sticker. One nice thing to remember about boat license fees is that they are used to build and maintain public-water accesses.

PADDLING ETIQUETTE

The same rules of courtesy that apply in most human endeavors apply in paddling: treat others as you would wish to be treated, respect private property, take responsibility for your own safety but help others when you can do so without endangering yourself, leave alcohol and drugs at home, don't bring the noise of the modern world into the quiet of the river environment, and share the work (and the fun) when you paddle in a group. Finally, LEAVE NO TRACE, so that others will find the same beautiful river that you found.

The loaded canoe will be slid, bicycle and all, down the steep, grassy slope to the riverbank.

GRASSROOTS ENVIRONMENTAL GROUPS

In the past few decades, Minnesotans have become increasingly aware of the environmental problems that challenge their rivers. The wonderful result of this awareness is that people have joined forces to restore their rivers. The Minnesota River is a good example. In the mid-1990s, the river was included on American Rivers' infamous list of our country's most threatened rivers. Action was clearly needed. The Minnesota Pollution Control Agency was charged with solving these water quality problems and putting extensive governmental resources to work on the challenge, an effort that is ongoing.

Folks in the Minnesota River valley decided to add their own grassroots approach as well. Groups fromed like Clean Up the River Environment (CURE) and Coalition for a Clean Minnesota River, springing from a sense of place, the love of one's own home landscape that Minnesota essayist Paul Gruchow wrote about in *Grass Roots: The Universe of Home* and *The Necessity of Empty Places*. These grassroots groups spring from the particular needs and goals of their citizens, and from a desire to make things better for their area in many ways. They seek economic and personal health as well as health for the land and waters that are so precious to them. They're organized and dedicated to making things happen. Each year, more groups form and more rivers gain advocates. Because paddlers are often in the forefront of those dedicated to river health, I weave information about the evolution of this great movement and how to get involved into the trip descriptions and sidebars. Appendix 5 provides a list of organizations and contact information—there's strength in numbers.

BIG COBB RIVER 1
County Road 10 to County Road 16 (12.2 miles)

Snags, Sweepers, and Strainers

A dead tree in the river by any other name is still a hazard. Beginning river paddlers often have trouble understanding this because a dead tree lying in the water just doesn't look very dangerous. The drama of boulder-filled rapids makes rocky challenges seem much more threatening. The truth is that strainers can be more dangerous than rapids, especially on a fast, high-volume river. A paddler who is swept by a strong current into the branches of a strainer is trapped and held underwater by the tangle of branches. A life jacket doesn't help and rescue is sometimes impossible. On a river with beautifully wooded banks, a strainer may lurk around any bend. To make things worse, dead trees often fall on the outside of bends. The current pushes the boat to the outside of the bend, making the tree harder to avoid. To ensure a safe trip down the river, learn the strokes and maneuvers that will help you evade the clutches of these deadfall demons. Draws, cross-draws, back paddles, back ferries, and side-slips are among your weapons.

Labeled simply the "Cobb River" on topographic maps, this tributary of the Le Sueur is actually called the "Big Cobb," to distinguish it from its tributary, the Little Cobb. This first route on the Big Cobb is plagued with strainers: tall, shallow-rooted cottonwoods that love to drop across the river. Chances are good that paddlers will have to portage several times. The Big Cobb's combination of fast water and frequent snags means that paddlers should have good maneuvering skills and be alert at every turn in the channel.

That said, a paddle on this part of the Big Cobb is well worth the trouble. Winding along the quiet wooded corridor of this appealing prairie river, it's easy to forget that vast expanses of farmland lie beyond the trees. The river runs swiftly down its quiet stretches and drops through some entertaining riffles and easy Class I rapids. The Big Cobb is also good bird-watching territory. The wooded banks are habitat for a number of birds: migrating warblers, orioles, cowbirds, catbirds, cardinals, flycatchers. Blue herons and kingfishers are common. Hawks perch in high trees. Raccoons look for mussels on shore, and turtles (including some big snappers) and otters play in the water. Although you only see two houses on the entire trip, there's other evidence of people: junk dumped on riverbanks. Fortunately, that bad habit is now out of style. Unfortunately, some of that old junk's still there.

Camping is available at Minneopa State Park, (507) 389-5464, or Mankato's Land of Memories Campground, (507) 387-8649. See the Blue Earth River for information on campsites at nearby Rapidan Dam Park.

The 5.2-mile **shuttle route** runs east on County Road 10, north on Highway 22 for 2 miles to Beauford, and west on County Road 16.

The gradient is 5.9 feet per mile.

A water level gauge painted on the County Road 16 bridge is visible from the landing. If the water level is in the middle of a numeral, that's the level; the dots are the .5 marks. Below 2 feet is too low. Over 4 feet, the combination of fast water and strainers can be dangerous.

From Mankato, take Highway 22 south to the little crossroads town of Beauford and then take County Road 10 west to the river. There's no official access at the beginning of the route. Park on the shoulder downstream right and slide your canoe down the long, grassy slope. Steep, slippery clay banks can make putting in a bit tricky.

The Big Cobb is winding and narrow, about 40 feet wide at the put-in. The flow is swift, over a streambed of sand and small gravel. Gravel bars are sprinkled with mussel shells. Many of the banks are sheer cliffs—layer cakes of glacial drift, clay, and topsoil, sliced open to display their history. Others are wooded down to the water.

Cliffs are common on the Big Cobb.

Ash, elm, willow, cottonwood, and silver maple shade the channel. Snags and deadfalls that block the channel either partly or completely are an integral part of this trip. Less than a half mile down from the put-in, a dead tree is often lodged in the hairpin curve, necessitating a portage.

The Big Cobb begins to run through short drops after mile 3, a pattern that continues to the take-out. Mostly gravel bar riffles at first, boulder riffles gradually become more common. At mile 5.9, the piers of an old bridge flank the river.

At mile 7, the river runs through a long, rocky drop. Downstream, occasional layer-cake banks are even higher and more spectacular. You pass some nice sandbars. Take out on river right at the County Road 16 bridge.

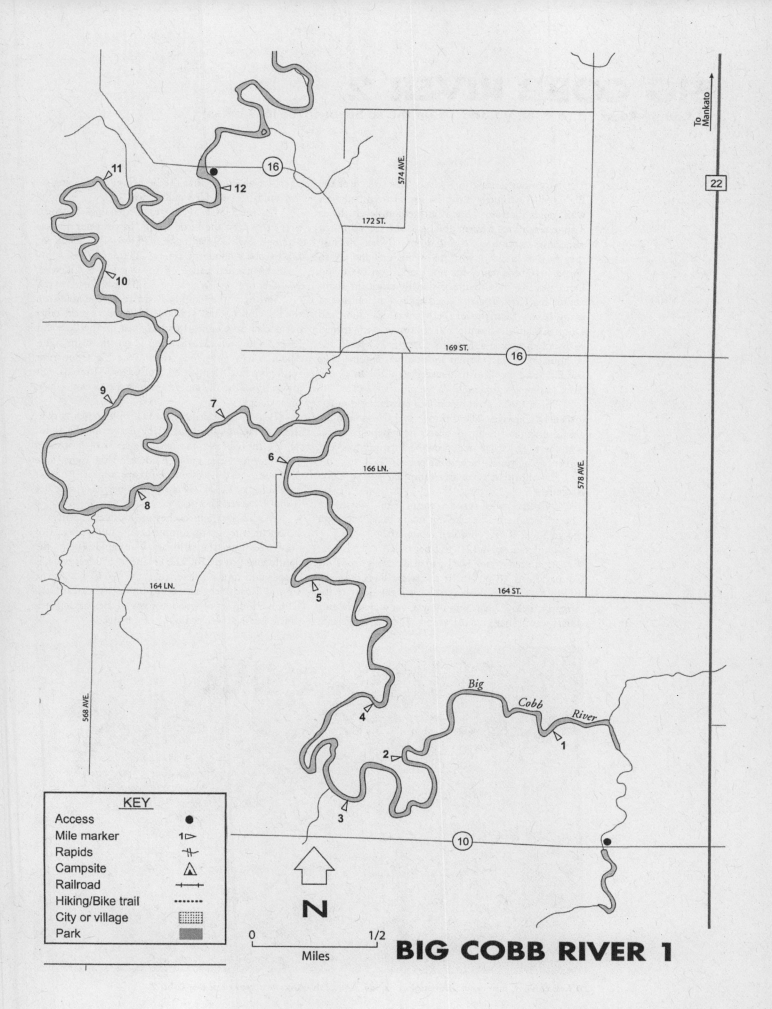

KEY

Access	●
Mile marker	1 ▷
Rapids	⫲
Campsite	△
Railroad	┼┼┼
Hiking/Bike trail	....
City or village	▦
Park	▬

0   1/2
Miles

N

BIG COBB RIVER 1

To Mankato

22

16

574 AVE.

172 ST.

169 ST.

16

166 LN.

578 AVE.

164 ST.

164 LN.

568 AVE.

Big Cobb River

10

BIG COBB RIVER 2
County Road 16 to County Road 16 on the Le Sueur River (6.4 miles)

Notorious among local rivers, this stretch of the Big Cobb is definitely a trip for experienced paddlers, with rapids that rate Class II at medium levels. In its rush to reach the Le Sueur, the Big Cobb races through sometimes-continuous rocky drops. (Note: Because they vary in intensity with the water level and are so numerous, these rapids are not marked on the map.) Deadfalls, like those that occasionally block the channel on Big Cobb I, are wedged against the outside of many bends. Members of the Mankato Paddling and Outings Club do cleanup and trimming every spring, so paddlers may not have to portage. However, the combination of fast current and strainers requires alert paddling and excellent maneuvering skills. On a swift river, strainers can be more dangerous than rapids.

This route's a great mix of fun rapids and dramatic scenery. The river valley burrows ever deeper into the glacial drift, and banks of sliced-away deposits tower over the river. Cedar trees grow on high sandy slopes and snapping turtles lurk in the pools.

For information on area **camping**, see Big Cobb River 1.

The 2.6-mile **shuttle route** runs north on County Road 16. The take-out is an official access on the Le Sueur River, on downstream left.

The **gradient** is 12.1 feet per mile.

A painted **water** level gauge is visible from the County Road 16 put-in. If the water level is in the middle of a numeral, that's the level; the dots are the .5 marks. Below 2 feet is too low. Over 4 feet, the mix of fast water, sharp curves, and strainers is dangerous.

Local kayakers say that the best level for playing on the rapids is between 3 and 4 feet.

On the USGS Web site, use readings from the river's tributary, the Little Cobb. To correlate the two readings: a USGS reading of 6.75 feet (170 cfs) on the Little Cobb is about the same as 2.5 feet on the County Road 16 painted gauge on the Big Cobb. Likewise, 9.31 feet (494 cfs) is about the same as 4 feet.

Put in at the County Road 16 bridge access on the Big Cobb, south of Mankato. (Note that the takeout is also on County Road 16, but on the Le Sueur River.) The well-used landing is on upstream right. About a half mile downstream, the Big Cobb runs through a fairly long stretch of Class I-II rapids, followed by a line of boulders across the river that you must dodge.

Beginning at mile 2.3, a half mile of nearly continuous rapids races past a log house on the right. After a short break, another long series of drops and pools begins. After another house on the right (mile 3.8) some nice limestone outcrops appear. Another long series of Class I-II rapids that begins at mile 4.4 rushes by several houses.

As the river approaches its confluence with the Le Sueur, the rapids diminish and huge pileups of dead trees litter the sandbars. The rapids end at the confluence (mile 5.8). The Le Sueur, 150 feet wide, is deeper and much quieter than the Big Cobb. At the County Road 16 bridge, **take out** on downstream left. Climb a long set of wooden steps to the parking area of the Le Sueur River Public Water Access.

A fast current, numerous challenging rapids, and high banks are typical of Big Cobb 2.

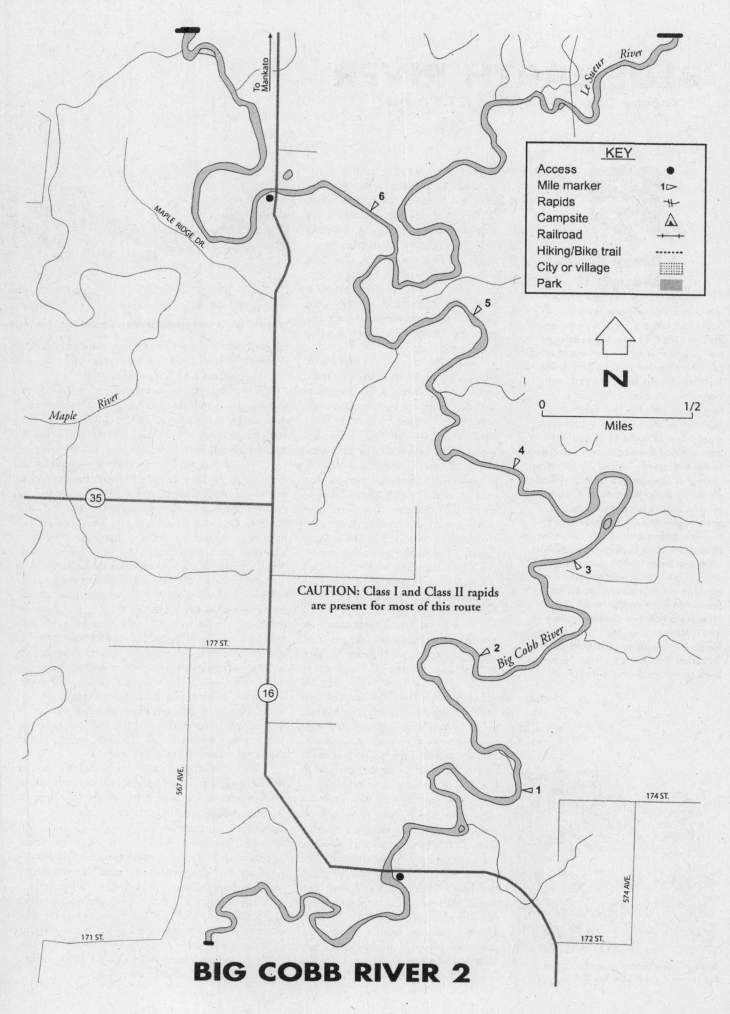

KEY

Access	●
Mile marker	1▷
Rapids	
Campsite	△
Railroad	
Hiking/Bike trail	....
City or village	
Park	

N

0   1/2
Miles

Le Sueur River

Maple River

MAPLE RIDGE DR.

To Mankato

6

5

4

3

2 *Big Cobb River*

1

CAUTION: Class I and Class II rapids
are present for most of this route

35

177 ST.

16

567 AVE.

574 AVE.

174 ST.

171 ST.

172 ST.

BIG COBB RIVER 2

BLUE EARTH RIVER
Rapidan Dam to Sibley Park (11.8 miles)

A River Runs Through It

Minnesota's environmental movement started on a river. In December 1962, a broken pipeline at the Richards Oil Company in Savage dumped over a million gallons of diesel oil, which poured into the Minnesota. Just two months later, at Mankato's Honeymead plant by the river's confluence with the Blue Earth, a soybean-oil storage tank ruptured. A giant surge of soybean oil gushed into the river and flooded nearby icy streets. In the end, nearly half of the 3.5 million gallons of Honeymead oil that spilled ended up in the Minnesota. Mixing with diesel oil slicks along the way, the gooey mess floated downstream. By the time it reached Lake Pepin on the Mississippi River in April, thick oil had coated at least 10,000 ducks—most died. Public outcry led the state government to pass environmental protection laws and to create the Minnesota Pollution Control Agency in 1967. Minnesotans drew national notice for their environmental activism. As Governor Karl Rolvaag said, "Spend a buck to save a duck."

Below the Rapidan Dam, the Blue Earth is a great combination of fun Class I rapids, dramatic rock outcrops, high wooded bluffs, and a pair of tributary waterfalls. Paddlers often spot owls, bald eagles, and great blue herons. Taking out at County Road 33 shortens the trip to 8.1 miles and avoids the final not-so-scenic stretch in Mankato, but also means missing the confluence with the Le Sueur. Members of the Mankato Paddling and Outings Club (MPOC), which has adopted this segment of the Blue Earth, do a thorough spring cleaning every year.

Rapidan Dam Park (http://www.co. blue-earth.mn.us/dept/parks/rapidan. php3) has primitive riverside campsites (drinking water and outhouses) past the canoe access. Register for camping at the Dam Store, (507) 546-9997. The Dam Store also sells food, and it's far from primitive. In addition to burgers and fries, this tiny store serves homemade pies that were featured in the August 2003 edition of *Food & Wine* magazine. They also sell firewood if you'd rather cook over a campfire. (*Food & Wine* feels you'd be making a big mistake.) Less primitive camping is available at Mankato's Land of Memories Park (a.k.a. Dakota Wokiksuye Makoce City Park), (507) 387-8649; or at Minneopa State Park, (507) 389-5464.

The 10.4-mile car shuttle route runs east on County Road 9 from the put-in. At Rapidan, go north on Highway 33. Turn right on U.S. Highway 169, and exit at South Riverfront Drive. Turn right on South Riverfront Drive, left on Hubbell Street, and then left on Mound Avenue. Sibley Park is at the end of Mound. Turn right at the "Division of Water" sign and go around the park. The carry-in access area is along the Blue Earth, just before the confluence. Find a spot where the bank is low and sloping (this changes from flood to flood). There's parking across the road.

A bike shuttle works well. From the take-out at Sibley Park, turn right on Mound Avenue and right on Hubbell Street. Turn left on South Riverfront Drive and go under the highway underpass. The trailhead is on the right just after the underpass, between the YMCA and West High School. Ride the trail 6 miles south to its end. Ride a half mile south on County Road 33 into Rapidan and west for 2 miles on the designated bike-lane shoulder of County Road 9. Note: If you take out at County Road 33, catch the South Route Trail by rid-

Wooded bluffs and glacial boulders grace the Blue Earth.

ing northeast on County Road 33 for a mile. The South Route intersects the Red Jacket a mile southeast.

The gradient is 5.0 feet per mile.

Water level readings are available for the USGS gage near Rapidan (http://waterdata.usgs.gov/usa/nwis/uv?site_ no=05320000). A reading of 880 cfs (2.9 feet) is low but adequate. Readings of 2,000 to 4,500 cfs (4 to 6 feet) is medium. Over 6 feet is high and 15 feet is flood stage.

Put in at Rapidan Dam Park, on downstream left at the Rapidan Hydtoelectric Dam. There's parking and a toilet at the access. Carry down 150 yards of gravel trail to the river. The Blue Earth is about 250 feet wide and fast. Avoid the Rapidan Dam just upstream. The current can be unpredictable: upstream eddies, whirlpools, a strong flow. The Blue Earth runs through frequent boulder-strewn drops, riffles to Class I, before it meets the Le Sueur.

Just past the power lines with the airplane warning balls (mile 2.5), a rock outcrop on river right marks a small ravine known locally as Devil's Gulch. (The name is etched into the sandstone.) At most water levels, you can walk back into the ravine, where the rock walls converge and the temperature drops. After about 100 yards, the ravine opens up to a waterfall. Farther downstream on the river, watch carefully on the left for a small grotto (mile 3.3) known as Triple Falls. Back in the woods, a tributary stream drops three times over limestone ledges, delicate little waterfalls splashing down to join the Blue Earth. At mile 6, a huge boulder (named "Big Moe" by members of the MPOC) stands guard in midstream.

While the County Road 33 bridge (mile 8.1) isn't an official access, a gravel road and a well-used path lead to the river on downstream left. If you take out here, you miss the confluence with the Le Sueur, but the rest of the trip is considerably less attractive. The Blue Earth is almost 400 feet wide. After County Road 90 (mile 9.3) the river is not a pretty sight: long stretches of riprap on the banks, drainpipes, and the Honeymead plant (Cenex Harvest States) of soybean oil–spill infamy (see "A River Runs Through It," left). The Highway 169 Bridge is followed quickly by the DM&E Railroad bridge. A half mile downstream, take out on river right at any point where the ever-changing bank seems most accommodating. (A birdhouse on a pole makes a good landmark.) Sibley Park has picnic shelters, drinking water, and toilets by the parking area.

You can see the Rapidan Dam from the put-in on the Blue Earth.

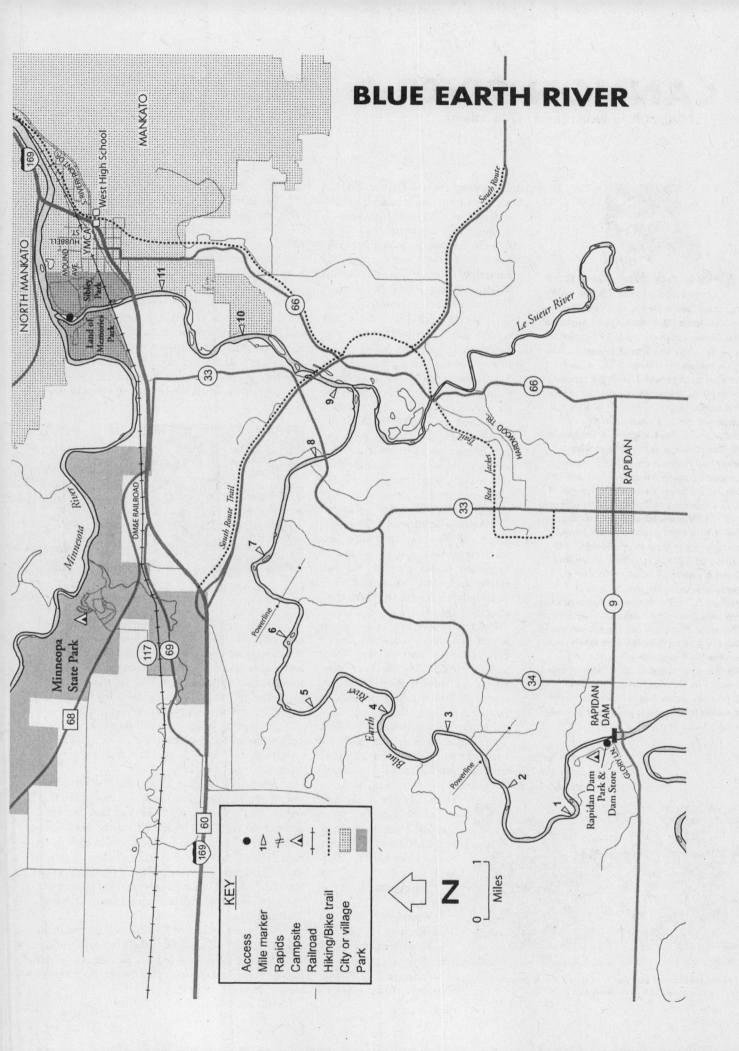

BLUE EARTH RIVER

CANNON RIVER 1
Faribault to Northfield (17.8 miles)

Shiva on the Cannon

Carved into a tall sandstone bluff, the improbable image of Shiva (the Hindu God of Destruction) has watched the Cannon rush by since 1986. Not exactly what one would expect to see on a midwestern river. It's at a spot known as Scott's Mill, and the remains of dry-laid limestone abutments along the banks are all that's left of that old structure. Shiva's creator (in this case only...) was Jim Langford, a student at St. Olaf College in Northfield who designed a decidedly off-beat senior project merging Asian religion and art. For his sculpture's execution, Langford chose this remote Cannon River cliff and reportedly worked on it for months (with help from assistant Paul Monson), completing in time to graduate in the spring of 1986. Ever since, Shiva has been a source of amusement for paddlers, irritation for some area residents, and defacement opportunities for kids (and a few adults). Members of the River Ramblers use it as a landmark for the trail to their favorite lunch spot on the bluff top. Gary Mogren of Faribault, a member of a citizens' group known as the Cannon and Straight River Explorers, is writing a book about the Cannon River, which includes this and many other stories.

The beautiful Cannon, a state-designated Wild and Scenic River, has a fast current and numerous riffles—entertaining at moderate levels. When it's high, however, beginners may have trouble avoiding the frequent strainers. At moderate to high water levels, the Cannon riffles over submerged boulder beds in Cannon Wilderness County Park. At low water, this stretch is nearly impassable.

From Shields Lake in the lake country west of Faribault, the Cannon flows across glacial plains before its steep descent into the Mississippi River valley. Six dams impound the river above Cannon Falls. This first trip on the Cannon begins below the fourth dam, once used to power the Faribault Woolen Mills. The mill is going strong, but the dam no longer produces water power. Just downstream from the dam, the Straight River enters, looking less like a tributary than a main stem. High cliffs often flank the winding Cannon; wildflowers—hepatica, bloodroot, wild ginger, and rare dwarf trout lilies—carpet the forest floor in the spring; and the hardwood forests glow in the fall. Hawks, eagles, blue herons, turkey vultures, and numerous songbirds are common sightings.

Primitive riverside **campsites** are located in Cannon Wilderness County Park. Nearby Nerstrand Big Woods State Park, (507) 333-4840, has a campground. See Straight River 2 for information on Sakatah Lake State Park.

The 13.5-mile **shuttle route** runs north on Highway 3 into Northfield. Turn right and cross the river on the 5th Street bridge. Turn right on Water Street and right again on 7th Street. Riverside Lions Park has parking, drinking water, and toilets. If you arrive on a Tuesday or Friday between 11:45 a.m. and 1:00 p.m. or on a Saturday between 9:00 a.m. and 12:00 a.m., a farmers' market often features home-baked treats.

The **gradient** is 3.1 feet per mile.

Water-level information from the gauge at Northfield is available from the DNR: http://www.dnr.mn.us/river_levels/index.html; (888) 646-6367. Below 13 feet is low, 13 to 16 feet is moderate, and above 16 feet is high.

Two Rivers Park is next to the parking lot of the Faribault Woolen Mill Store on 2nd Avenue NW. The official canoe access is just downstream of the confluence with the Straight River. You can also put in near the fishing platform upstream of the confluence, where the current is quieter.

Low limestone outcrops underlie the wooded banks at first. Less than a mile downstream, mossy cliffs rise above the river and the Cannon runs under a railroad bridge. Snags are common at bends. You pass wooded islands, beautiful high cliffs—some streaked with mineral stains—and a pair of old, dry-laid limestone abutments crumbling into the river. On the right, a trail up the bluff above the sandstone cliff carving leads to a popular picnic spot with a great view.

High rock cliffs flank this reach of the Cannon.

Soon after the Cannon flows under County Road 29, it enters Cannon Wilderness County Park, a lovely blend of woods and bluffs and another good picnic area. On the left, you see a sign for the park (mile 7.2) and a short access path. A second access point on the left, harder to spot, has timber steps and a trail to the parking area, picnic shelter, toilets, and drinking water. If you reach the footbridge, you already passed it. It's also possible to take out on upstream left at the footbridge. On the right bank across the bridge is a campsite. About a mile downriver from the bridge, another campsite is on the left bank under the power line.

As you leave the park, wooded islands often split the channel. At one island, Wolf Creek joins the Cannon from the left and a smaller stream flows in from the right. Between the Highway 3 bridge and a footbridge, Dundas City Park has a small, hard-to-spot access (mile 14) on the right. (Many paddlers prefer to take out here as the current slows considerably between Dundas and Northfield, where the Malt-O-Meal Dam impounds the river.) Downstream of the footbridge are the interesting remains of historic Archibald Mill.

On your way out of Dundas, you go under the County Road 1 bridge. After the Highway 3 bridge (mile 17.6) in Northfield and just past a group of willows on the right, **take out** at a small inlet. Up the grassy slope is Riverside Lions Park.

The footbridge at Dundas is a good vantage point for viewing the old Archibald Mill.

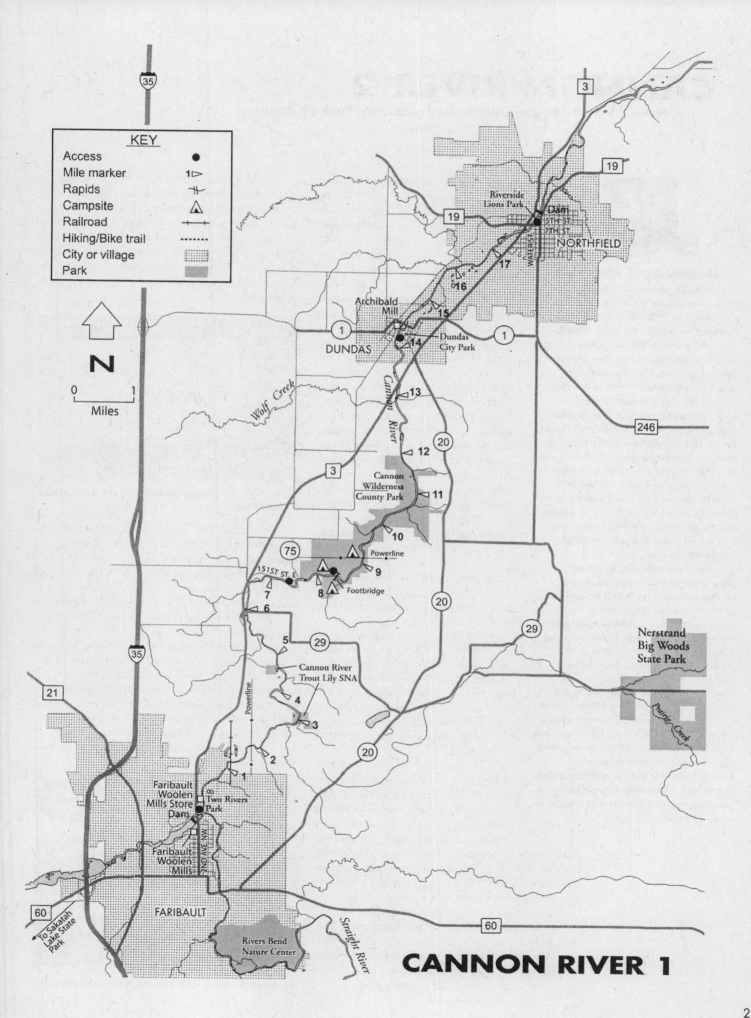

KEY

Access   ●
Mile marker   1▷
Rapids
Campsite   △
Railroad
Hiking/Bike trail
City or village
Park

N

0   1
Miles

Riverside Lions Park

Dam
5TH ST.
7TH ST.
NORTHFIELD

17

16

Archibald Mill

15

DUNDAS

14   Dundas City Park

Wolf Creek

Cannon River

13

12

Cannon Wilderness County Park

11

10

Powerline

9

151ST ST. E

7

8   Footbridge

6

5

29

Cannon River Trout Lily SNA

4

Powerline

3

Nerstrand Big Woods State Park

Prairie Creek

2

1

Faribault Woolen Mills Store Dam

Two Rivers Park

2ND AVE. NW

Faribault Woolen Mills

FARIBAULT

To Sakatah Lake State Park

Rivers Bend Nature Center

Straight River

CANNON RIVER 1

CANNON RIVER 2
Waterford Iron Bridge to Lake Byllesby County Park (9.2 miles)

Dams and Mussels

In 1855, a dam was built across the Cannon to power the Ames Flour Mill in Northfield. In 1927, the Malt-O-Meal Corporation bought the dam. Malt-O-Meal still owns it, but the deteriorating structure no longer generates power, the impoundment is filled with silt, and the corporation wants to sell the dam to the city. The downstream impoundment known as Lake Byllesby is also silt-filled. All this sediment is terrible for mussel populations. River scientists who study these humble organisms say that they quickly die when their river's substrate is coated with silt. When mussels die, so do the creatures that eat them. As Aldo Leopold wrote in *A Sand County Almanac*, "To keep every cog and wheel is the first precaution of intelligent tinkering."

The issue isn't simple. Although dam removal seems like an easy fix, all that sediment must first be removed or it will head downstream to cause more trouble. In the 1980s, releasing the sediment behind the Byllesby Dam did extensive damage to wildlife in the Cannon River Bottoms. Dam-removal methods can be ecologically sound, however, and removal is usually the best option for everyone. Citizens often oppose dam removal because it means change, but it also costs a lot to maintain a dam. Some dams still generate power, but more expensively than newer technologies. Back when building a dam just meant cheap power, these complex questions weren't even considered. Now we're all paying the price.

It's possible—but quite challenging—to portage around the Malt-O-Meal Dam that impounds the Cannon in downtown Northfield. High retaining walls and riprap flank the river all through the downtown. For this reason, this guide omits the 3.3-mile stretch between the dam and the Waterford Bridge.

This is a short trip, and you're lulled at first by long, straight stretches of quiet water riffled only occasionally by gravel bars. Then the river wakes up, dropping briefly but notably through an exciting series of wave chains as it heads east toward Lake Byllesby and the silt-filled upper end of the impoundment. Although the river channel is still traversing flat glacial-drift terrain, the scenery is pleasant and the river corridor is peaceful and mostly undeveloped. Those who prefer not to paddle Lake Byllesby—where wind and shallows can be issues—can take out at the Highway 56 Bridge, shortening the journey to 7.2 miles.

Across the impoundment, Lake Byllesby Regional Park has a **campground**: (507) 263-4447; www.co.dakota.mn.us/parks/byllesby.htm. See Cannon River 1 for information on Nerstrand Big Woods State Park.

The 11.4-mile **shuttle route** runs south on Canada Avenue (gravel), east on Highway 19 (paved), and north on Highway 56 (paved). Turn right on Sciota Trail (gravel) and left on 23rd Avenue Way (gravel). At the "Public Access to Lake" sign, turn left. There's a parking lot, a picnic area, and a toilet by the boat ramp.

The **gradient** is 2.5 feet per mile.

See Cannon River 1 for **water level** information.

To reach the historic Waterford Bridge from Northfield, go northeast on Highway 19 and turn left on Canada Avenue, a narrow gravel road. The bridge, built in 1909, is only one lane wide, and there's room for one car to park at a little gravel turnoff. (A new traffic bridge will probably be built upstream after 2007. If so, the county currently plans to keep the old one as a trail bridge.) **Put in** on upstream right: the path down to the river is steep and rocky.

Low banks, wooded with silver maples, willows, and walnuts, and underlain by limestone layers, flank the Cannon. Sand and gravel bars, often dotted with mussels, are common, and the river runs wide, swift, and straight. After the County Road 59 bridge, an unofficial access on downstream right has a good landing.

About 2 miles downstream of the bridge, the Cannon winds through a series of fast riffles and standing waves. Piles of dead trees lie at the bends. As you pass the old abutments of a railroad bridge and a road bridge (no longer crossing the river), the river quiets and the narrow river valley opens up. From there, it's about a half mile to the confluence with Chub Creek and the Highway 56 bridge. The access, which has parking, is on upstream left.

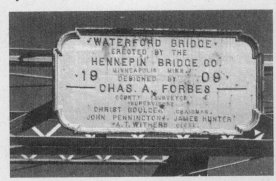

You find a taste of Cannon River history downstream of Northfield.

To continue into Lake Byllesby, paddle under the bridge, through the marshy shallows, and to the right of a large island. Stay right to avoid the worst of the shallows, then head past shoreline houses and around a wooded point. Take out at the concrete boat ramp at Lake Byllesby County Park. Two more miles of paddling will take you to Lake Byllesby Regional Park at the northeast end of the lake.

Other trips: Below the 60-foot dam that impounds Lake Byllesby, two rocky miles of the Cannon have a gradient of 15 feet per mile. Rated Class II, this stretch is **not** suitable for beginners. Expert whitewater kayakers who want to try it should look for a flow of 1,125 to 3,800 cfs on the USGS gage at Welch. Access is difficult: a steep, treacherous trail leads to the base of the dam on river left. The take-out is on river right at Highway 20 in Cannon Falls.

The Cannon runs quietly under the Waterford Bridge.

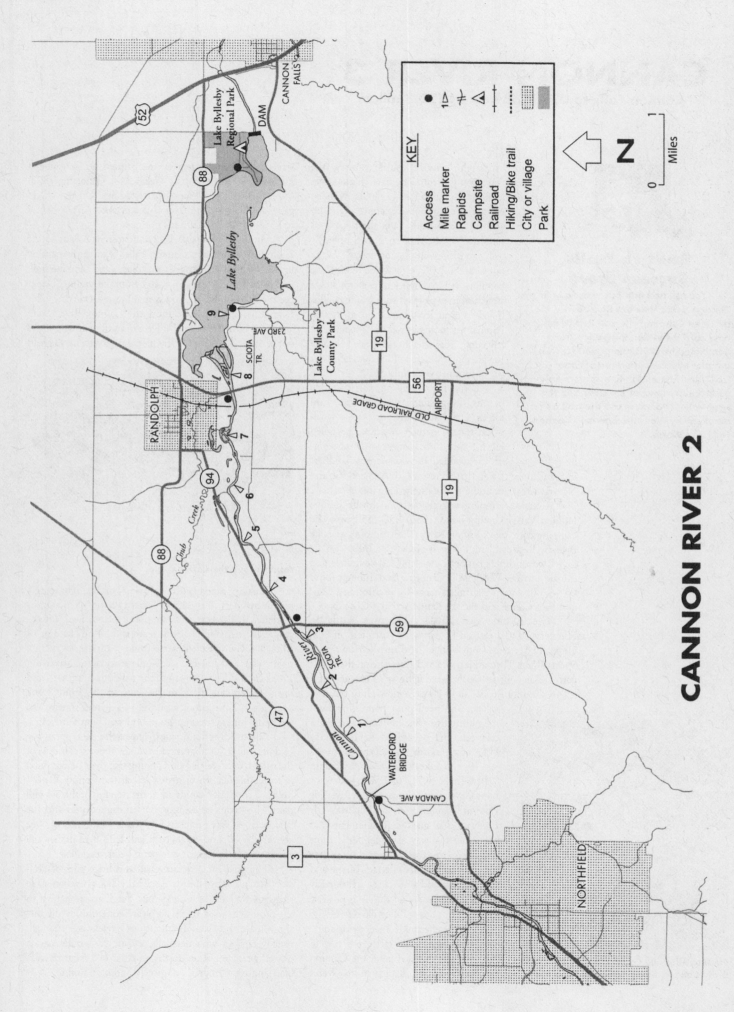

CANNON RIVER 2

KEY

- Access
- Mile marker
- Rapids
- Campsite
- Railroad
- Hiking/Bike trail
- City or village
- Park

N

Miles

0   1

Lake Byllesby Regional Park

Lake Byllesby

Lake Byllesby County Park

DAM

CANNON FALLS

RANDOLPH

23RD AVE.

SCIOTA TR.

OLD RAILROAD GRADE

AIRPORT

Chub Creek

Cannon River

SCIOTA TR.

WATERFORD BRIDGE

CANADA AVE.

NORTHFIELD

52

88

94

88

47

3

19

56

59

19

CANNON RIVER 3
Cannon Falls to U.S. Highway 61 (20.3 miles)

Rails to Trails Success Story

The rail bed that once carried the Chicago Great Western Railroad between Cannon Falls and Red Wing now carries the Cannon Valley Trail. Completed in 1992, the paved route is a nationally acclaimed recreational trail. Bicyclists and in-line skaters enjoy spectacular views of the river and the river valley. Paddlers use the trail as an excellent shuttle route between Cannon Falls and Welch.

Rambling through beautiful bluff country, the Cannon is at its finest on this run. The river chatters over gravel bars and races through two Class I rapids. Wooded bluffs rise up to 360 feet above the valley and sheer rock cliffs flank the river. This long trip can be shortened to 8 miles by using the Miesville Ravine access. Taking out at the tiny village of Welch reduces the paddling to 13.3 miles and eliminates a stretch of river plagued with strainers. Plus there's a great ice-cream shop in Welch. Popular for tubing as well as canoeing and kayaking, the stretch between Miesville Ravine and Welch will be crowded on warm summer weekends.

Look for snapping turtles, blue herons, kingfishers, wood ducks, and eagles. Denizens of the area's dense hardwood forests include owls and red-tailed hawks, and a lovely assortment of songbirds lives in both the wooded and open areas. Sandbars in the Cannon River Turtle Preserve SNA (Scientific and Natural Area) are home to the rare wood turtle.

Riverside **camping** is available at a private facility, Hidden Valley Campground: (651) 258-4550; www.hvcamping.com. See Cannon River 2 for **camping** at Lake Byllesby Regional Park just west of Cannon Falls.

Two outfitters supply **canoe** and **kayak rentals** and **shuttle service**: Welch Mill Canoeing and Tubing: (800) 657-6760; www.welchmillcanoeandtube.com; and Cannon Falls Canoe and Bicycle Rental, (877) 882-2663.

The 20-mile **car shuttle route** runs south on Highway 20 and east on Highway 19. Turn left on U.S. Highway 61, cross both bridges, and turn left on Green Spring Road. The parking area and access are on the left. If you're taking out at Welch, take Highway 19 east and turn left on County Road 7 (a lovely drive down into the river valley). You need prior permission from the outfitter to park and land here. For a take-out at Miesville Ravine, take Highway 20 north and 280th Street east.

For a **bike shuttle**, the Cannon Valley Trail: (507) 263-0508; www.cannonvalleytrail.org, runs from Riverside Park in Cannon Falls to Highway 61. Ride up the grassy embankment and along the highway shoulder for a short distance to the access. There's a small fee for a Wheel Pass, required for biking and rollerblading and available at Trailside Pay Stations. (Note: A trail shuttle is possible to Welch but not to Miesville Ravine.)

The **gradient** is 4.8 feet per mile.

This segment is rarely too low to run, but after a heavy rain, the Cannon can rise several feet in a few hours. Water levels from 1 to 3.5 feet on the painted bridge gauge at Highway 20 are optimal. Welch Mill Canoeing, (800) 657-6760, will give you current readings. On the USGS gage at Welch (http://waterdata.usgs.gov/mn/nwis/uv?05355200) 2.5 to 5.5 feet is optimal.

Put in at Riverside Park, on upstream right at the Highway 20 bridge in Cannon Falls. Next to the parking lot are shelters, drinking water, toilets, and the bike trail; the painted-bridge gauge is visible from the landing. Under the Highway 20 bridge, you swing through a curving Class I rapids at the mouth of the Little Cannon River. Soon after the North 3rd Street bridge and a utility bridge, you're out of town. The riffles are frequent and the scenery's great.

Anglers love the Cannon, too.

A pair of sandy landings (mile 7) on the right mark a picnic area next to the River Terrace Prairie SNA, a grassland area that's home to a rare prairie plant called "kittentail." Less than a mile downstream is the sandy landing of Miesville Ravine Park Reserve (mile 8) on the left, with a picnic area and toilets. A 0.1-mile carry across the Trout Brook footbridge takes you to the parking lot; please avoid using the eroded access downstream of the Trout Brook confluence. Trout Brook is a lovely, clear trout stream, and the park's hiking trails are good bird-watching territory.

About 3.5 miles downstream of the park, sprawling Hidden Valley Campground occupies about a half mile of the right bank. Welch Mill Landing (for their rentals only) is a mile further, on upstream left at the County Road 7 bridge. The Class I rapids are at the remains of the old mill dam. The second access is on the left immediately after the bridge. It's private property, but Welch Mill Canoeing (see above) allows paddlers to park and land here if they call ahead or stop in to ask permission before paddling.

The gradient now decreases and huge piles of dead trees accumulate at bends. Especially at high water, these snags are frequent and dangerous. Sandbars are habitat to the protected wood turtle, so please don't disturb any turtles you see. You pass the mouth of a backwater channel, usually choked with deadfalls. About 0.75 miles past a powerline, **take out** on upstream left at U.S. Highway 61. The landing is eroded, overgrown, and hard to find.

Passing Miesville County Ravine Park, the lively Cannon flows smoothly for a bit.

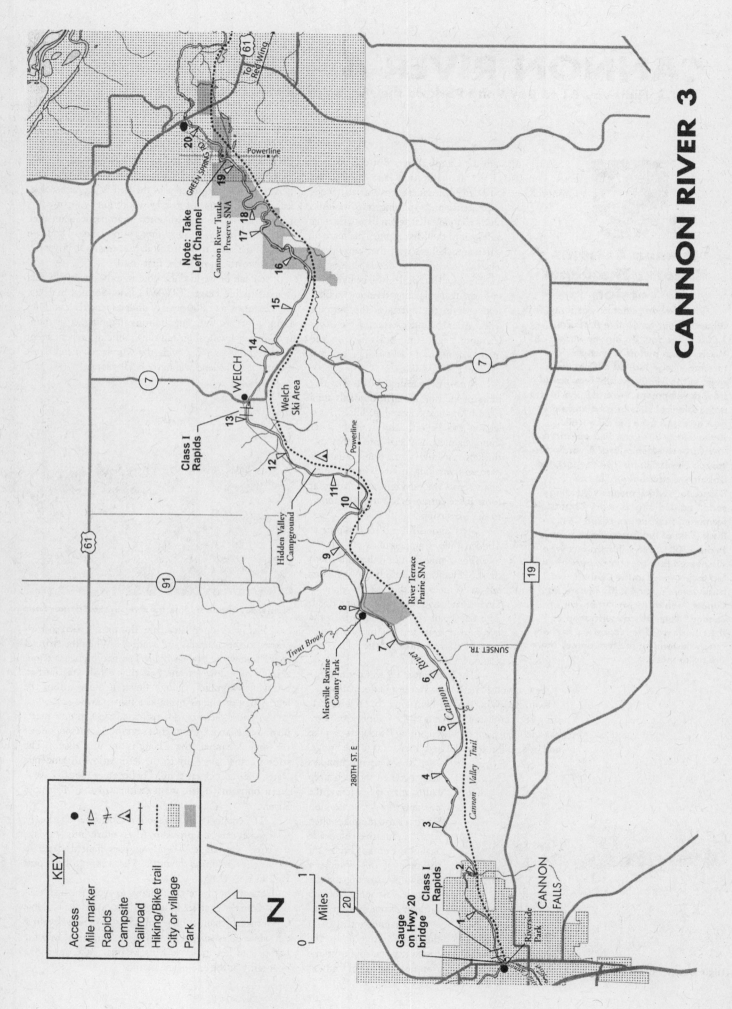

KEY

Access
Mile marker
Rapids
Campsite
Railroad
Hiking/Bike trail
City or village
Park

N

Miles

0   1

Gauge on Hwy 20 bridge

Class I Rapids

CANNON FALLS

Riverside Park

280TH ST. E

Miesville Ravine County Park

Trout Brook

River Terrace Prairie SNA

SUNSET TR.

Cannon Valley Trail

Cannon River

Hidden Valley Campground

Powerline

Welch Ski Area

WELCH

Class I Rapids

Note: Take Left Channel

Cannon River Turtle Preserve SNA

GREEN SPRING RD.

Powerline

To Red Wing

CANNON RIVER 4
U.S. Highway 61 to Bay Point Park on the Mississippi River (11.6 miles)

Cannon Bottoms History: The Short Version

The Cannon Bottoms was a major cultural center for Native Americans 1,000 years ago. During the Middle Mississippian period, a prehistoric farming village thrived next to the river. In the 1980s the site was saved from development. Several important archaeological sites located there are best accessed from the bike trail. Archaeology buffs can find out more at www.fromsitetostory.org. According to Joseph Nicollet in his 1843 report, the Dakota called the river "Inyan Bosndata," which means "standing rock," named after a nearby sandstone formation that settlers called Castle Rock (little of the formation remains). In the 1700s, French fur traders who discovered that tribal members often hid their canoes in the Cannon backwaters named it "la Rivière aux Canots," which means "the river of canoes." Later mispronunciation of the French word for canoe led to the river's misleading modern name. There are no cannons.

A trip through the Cannon River Bottoms offers a lovely contrast to the dramatic bluff land traveled on Cannon River 3. The river meanders across a vast, wide-open marshland, splitting into multiple sandy channels that rejoin before flowing quietly into the Mississippi. This maze of waterways changes with the water levels. The river corridor is undeveloped and the wildlife abundant. Birders will be interested to know that migrating cerulean warblers stop over in the forests of the bottomlands. After the quiet waters of the lower Cannon, negotiating 3.5 miles on the main channel of the Mississippi may feel a bit on the wild side.

A note of warning: In the first few miles of the run, frequent deadfalls are a hazard for inexperienced paddlers. Navigation can be difficult: At high water some channels may lead into impassable thickets. At low water some channels dead-end, making it necessary to drag boats across the sand and mud bars that form at the entrances to various channels to the Mississippi.

See Cannon River 3 for camping at Hidden Valley Campground.

The 7-mile shuttle route runs south on U.S. Highway 61 into Red Wing. Turn left at Withers Harbor Drive, right at Levee Road, and left at Bay Point Road. The Bay Point Park boat ramp is to the left, next to restrooms and picnic tables.

The 7-mile bike shuttle follows the Cannon Valley Trail.

The gradient is 1.2 feet per mile.

See Cannon River 3 for water-level information.

From Red Wing, go northwest on U.S. Highway 61, crossing both bridges (the first over the Cannon's backwater channel). Turn left on Green Spring Road, just past the second bridge. Put in at the steep bank next to the bridge.

The Cannon wanders lazily between the high steep bluffs that characterize the previous trip. At the Cannon Bottom Road, deadfalls often form a massive blockade against the unused bridge. At the time of this writing, a narrow passage on the far right leaves room to slip through. If not, portage left.

A channel (mile 1.5) on the right connects to the backwater that split from the river near the end of Cannon

River 3. At mile 2, the backwater joins the main channel for good. Just downstream, you see the bike trail that runs next to the river at the edge of the Red Wing Archaeological Preserve. A mile of marshy woods follows, crossed by remnants of an abandoned railroad spur trestle. Soon after, you paddle into vast, sprawling bottomlands. The main route of the same railway, still in use, crosses the river 0.8 mile downstream from the first trestle.

A flock of wood-duck houses and signs marks Red Wing Wildlife League (RWWL) land. Formed in 1935, the League owns 2,800 acres of undeveloped river bottom, using it for bird watching, hunting, trapping, cross-country skiing, snowshoeing, and snowmobiling. A permanent conservation easement with the Minnesota Land Trust ensures that the land will never be developed.

Numerous sandbars line the river in the Cannon Bottoms

Flat, wide-open Rice Lake Bottoms is covered with grasses, rushes, cattails, and sandbars. When the channel splits, follow the branch right. The two branches rejoin about a mile downstream. Less than a half mile farther, the wide Vermillion Slough flows in quietly from the left. A sign on the right marks a fish-spawning area.

A short distance downstream, the Cannon meets Diamond Island. (Although it's on the Minnesota side of the main channel, the island is in Wisconsin.) The stronger flow is usually to the left. At low to moderate water, the right channel quickly becomes too shallow. A green buoy marks the main channel of the Mississippi River.

The channel isn't huge, but if motor traffic is heavy, boat wakes can be a problem. Always turn into the wake to avoid capsizing. When you pass lighted daymark #794.9, it's 3.5 miles down the Mississippi to Bay Point Park in Red Wing.

Stay right of the green buoys to avoid the boat traffic. Where the channel splits, go right. (A bridge is visible down the left channel.) Bay Point Park is signaled by three tall white poles shaped like a teepee. Turn right into the harbor and left into Ole Miss Marina. Take out at the boat ramp at the end of the marina.

High wooded bluffs border the Cannon bottomland.

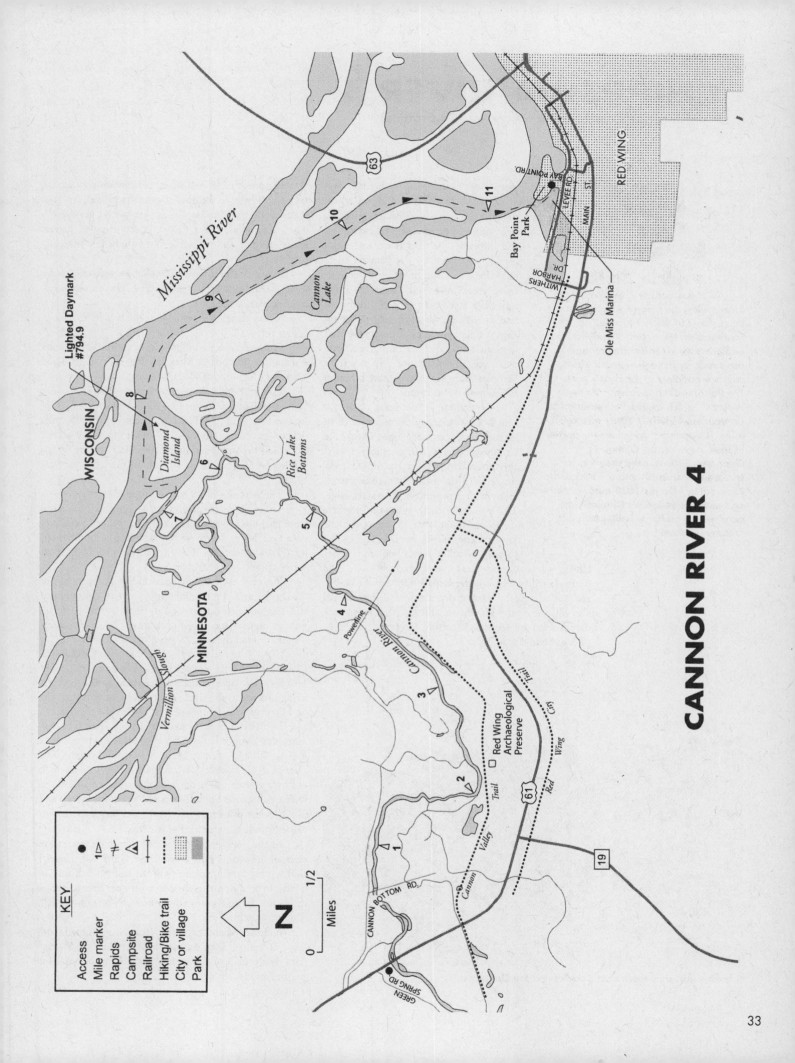

CANNON RIVER 4

CHIPPEWA RIVER 1
Shakopee Creek to Highway 40 (20.6 miles)

Prairie Bluffs

As it descends into the Minnesota River valley, the Chippewa carves a deep gorge in the flat prairies of southeastern Minnesota. Paddlers exploring the river for the first time are struck by its high wooded bluffs, as were paddlers in the river's past. The Dakota called the river "Manya Wakan," which means "of remarkable or wonderful bluffs." (They also called it the "Chippewa," because war parties of their enemies, the Ojibwa or Chippewa Indians, used the river to travel south on raids into the Minnesota River valley.) On his 1838 map, explorer and mapmaker Joseph Nicollet, who admired the bluffs as well, labeled it "Manya Wakan."

The Chippewa races through many boulder and gravel bar riffles (Class I at medium to high water) on this long, but fast and fun, trip. Five bridges cross the river, although access at all of them is steep and difficult. The river twists through a corridor canopied by overhanging silver maples and willows. Towering old cottonwood groves and banks that rise sometimes 100 feet lend a vertical dimension, and wooded islands often split the channel. At times, glimpses of the prairie land through which the river runs give a sense of space and distance. The terrain becomes more varied and more beautiful as you head downstream.

Originating in the lakes of northeast Douglas County, 90 miles north of its confluence with Shakopee Creek, the Chippewa cuts a narrow slice in level agricultural land. Above Shakopee Creek, the river runs past numerous farms, many with cows grazing at water's edge. This practice is partly responsible for the silt-laden water that characterizes the lower reaches of this river. In the 1830s, Joseph Nicollet described the lower Chippewa as running clear over a sandy bottom. The bottom's still sandy, but the water's now turbid. Floods are exacerbated by excessive wetland drainage, which also fills the river with silt. In addition, deadfalls swept downstream by frequent flooding lodge in hazardous piles at bends in the river.

Because the largest white pelican rookery in the Upper Midwest is nearby, paddlers are likely to spot these handsome birds, as well as blue herons, geese, swallows, sandpipers, cedar waxwings, bald eagles, hawks, white-tailed deer, and some imposingly big snapping turtles.

Riverside **camping** with hot showers is available for a fee at Ambush Park: (320) 843-4775; www.benson-mn.org/park, in Benson.

Kayak rentals are available at the Java River Cafe in Montevideo, (320) 269-7106.

Canoe rentals and rental canoe pickup at the takeout can be arranged at Mitlyng's Bait on County Road 13 west of Watson, (320) 269-5593.

The 13.8-mile **shuttle route** runs 0.5 miles south on gravel County Road 19 (45th Avenue SW). After intersecting County Road 6, continue south 7.5 miles on now-paved County Road 19, which jogs west several times and becomes County Road 8. At Highway 40, go 4 miles west to the Lentz Access, on the left before the bridge.

The **gradient** is 1.9 feet per mile.

The Chippewa usually can be paddled from April through July. A **water level** of 2 to 4 feet on the USGS gage near Milan (http://waterdata.usgs.gov/mn/nwis/uv?05304500) is optimal. The river runs up to 2,000 cfs at spring runoff.

Put in at the concrete boat landing at the mouth of Shakopee Creek. From Highway 29 between Montevideo and Benson, go west on County Road 6 and north on gravel County Road 19 (45th Avenue SW). The access is on the left after the road crosses Shakopee Creek.

With the addition of Shakopee Creek, the Chippewa widens considerably. Right after a rain, Shakopee also adds noticeable sediment to the flow. All along this reach, the river runs through intermittent riffles, increasing in frequency near the end of the trip.

In just a mile you reach the County Road 6 bridge. After the County Road 62 bridge (mile 5.4) the banks are higher and steeper. After the third bridge (70th Avenue NW) at mile 8.6, you pass some 100-foot-high cliffs, perforated with bank swallow holes and layered with stratification lines. Groves of huge cottonwoods and old oaks line this beautiful stretch, and there's lots of fast water from here to the end of the trip.

At the fourth bridge (mile 14.3), which crosses the river on the county line, a "Welcome North Side Hagen" sign is posted on upstream right. In another half mile, a handsome old iron truss bridge is number five. At about mile 18.1, an immense old cottonwood tree on the left is worth watching for.

A cluster of houses on the left announces the Highway 40 bridge. **Take out** on downstream left. A steep path leads to a parking area planted with beautiful prairie flowers.

A bovine audience checks out paddlers on the Chippewa.

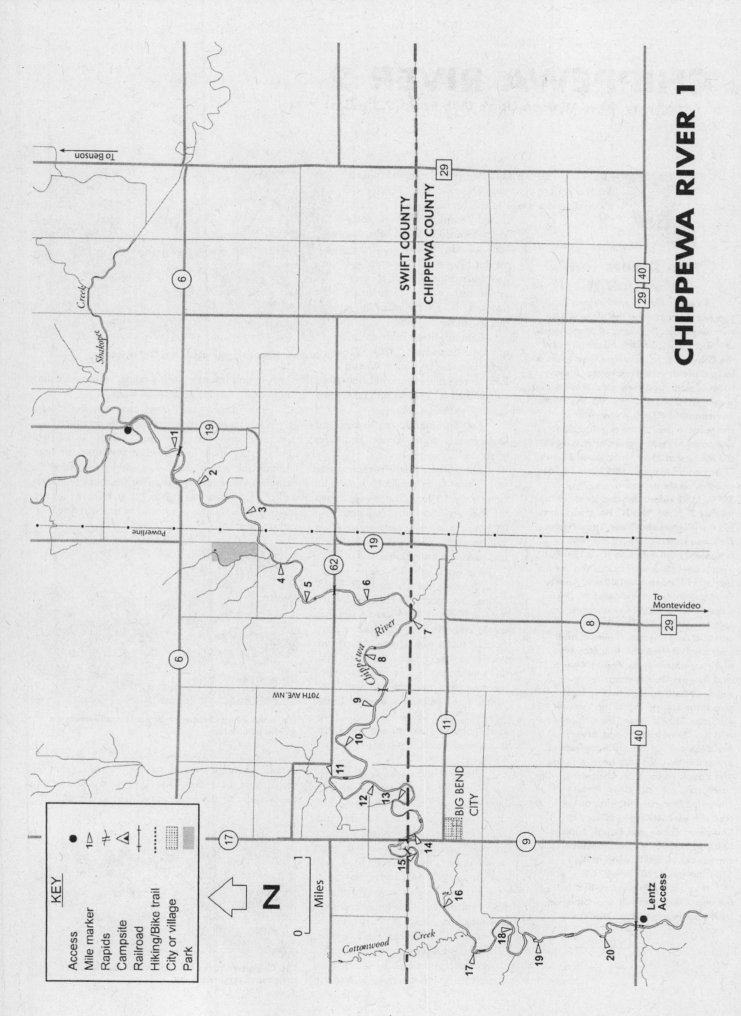

KEY

Access
Mile marker
Rapids
Campsite
Railroad
Hiking/Bike trail
City or village
Park

N

Miles

0   1

To Benson

Shakopee Creek

Powerline

SWIFT COUNTY
CHIPPEWA COUNTY

70TH AVE. NW

Chippewa River

To Montevideo

BIG BEND CITY

Cottonwood Creek

Lentz Access

CHIPPEWA RIVER 2
Highway 40 to Watson Lion's Club Park (9.5 miles)

Two Rivers Run Through It

An old Indian legend says a tornado will never hit the place where two rivers join. Residents of Montevideo, at the confluence of the Minnesota and the Chippewa, tell you that their town is indeed protected by the rivers. A lively town of dedicated river rats, Montevideo is the birthplace of **Clean Up the River Environment** (CURE, www.curemn river.org), a grassroots organization dedicated to restoring water quality in the Minnesota River watershed. As one of its annual events, CURE hosts spring paddles on three local rivers. Since 1999, CURE cofounder and local science teacher Richard "Butch" Halterman has led the **Minnesota River Expedition.** On these canoe-camping journeys (sometimes the entire river—335 miles!), high school students explore the natural beauty of the Minnesota River. Another CURE cofounder, Patrick Moore, started **Java River Café** (www.javariver cafe.com), where coffee fiends can also rent kayaks. Moore is now executive director of CURE. Members of Montevideo's **Twin Rivers Canoe and Kayak Club** organize regular paddling trips on five local rivers: the Lac qui Parle, the Yellow Medicine, Hawk Creek, the Chippewa, and the Minnesota. During **Riverfest Rendezvous**, an annual June festival in Montevideo, the club hosts a canoe and kayak race on the Chippewa, with cash prizes for each class. Paddlers interested in joining the club or the race can contact Ralph Heidorn at Chippewa Canoe and Kayak Supply: (320) 269-6081; www.chippewa canoe.com, or Bill Pauling at Bill's Supermarket, (320) 269-8274.

If you want to explore the rivers of the upper Minnesota River watershed, start your journey in Montevideo.

This trip is lots shorter (and more agricultural, at least at first) than Chippewa River 1, and there are more snags at the bends. It's just as pretty though, running through some lovely forested areas of oaks, big cottonwoods, willows, and silver maples. Fast-moving water and gravel-bar riffles (Class I at medium to high water) will entertain paddlers, as will the many birds that live in these woods.

Camping is available at Lac qui Parle State Park, (320) 752-4736. From the take-out at Watson Park, drive 5 miles west on County Road 13 and then 0.25 miles north on County Road 33 to the entrance.

For information on canoe and kayak rentals, shuttle services, and water levels, see Chippewa 1.

The 8.9-mile shuttle route runs east on Highway 40 for a mile, then south on County Road 9, which turns west, crosses the river, and then runs south again. Go 0.25 mile east on County Road 13 to Watson Lion's Club Park, where you'll find parking, a water pump, and toilets.

The **gradient** is 2.5 feet per mile.

To reach the put-in from Montevideo, drive north on Highway 29 and west on Highway 40. A short gravel road on the left before the bridge leads to Lentz Access. From a parking area planted with prairie flowers, a steep dirt path leads down to the **put-in**. For the first 2 miles, the Chippewa runs through open land with few trees growing on its grassy banks. You see grazing fields, fences, and cropland. The river flows through some shallows, where gravel bars create riffles, and past grassy islands.

The farmland is followed by a long, lovely wooded stretch, interrupted only by the County Road 9 bridge (mile 2.8), the sole bridge crossing on this trip. Thick groves of oaks edge the river, the fringe of their exposed roots like bangs on the brow of the high river bank.

At mile 3.3, you pass two tiny buildings that are also on the very brink of a high eroded bank, their future appearing somewhat uncertain. Between here and the mouth of Dry Weather Creek, another 2.8 miles downstream, the Chippewa swings through a series of big S-curves; its channel split by several large islands, its flow punctuated by riffles. This wooded stretch

A historic truss bridge crosses the Chippewa.

is narrow and intimate, with a border of trees shielding you from the outside agricultural world.

Dry Weather Creek flows clear and thin over a gravel bed as it meets the Chippewa. The river then flows through an area where level meadowland on the right tops a vertical bank and stretches away from the river, breaking the woods motif. On the left, between the channels of the Chippewa and Dry Weather Creek, a big wedge of land looms as high as 110 feet above the river. A mile past the mouth of a stream on the right, you meet a large island.

The often lively Chippewa flows smoothly around glacial boulders.

The current now slows because of the dam downstream. Where the river splits at the Watson Sag channel, go left toward the dam. Don't go near the dam or into the Watson Sag. Take out on the right at Watson Park.

The Chippewa races through numerous boulder riffles and light rapids.

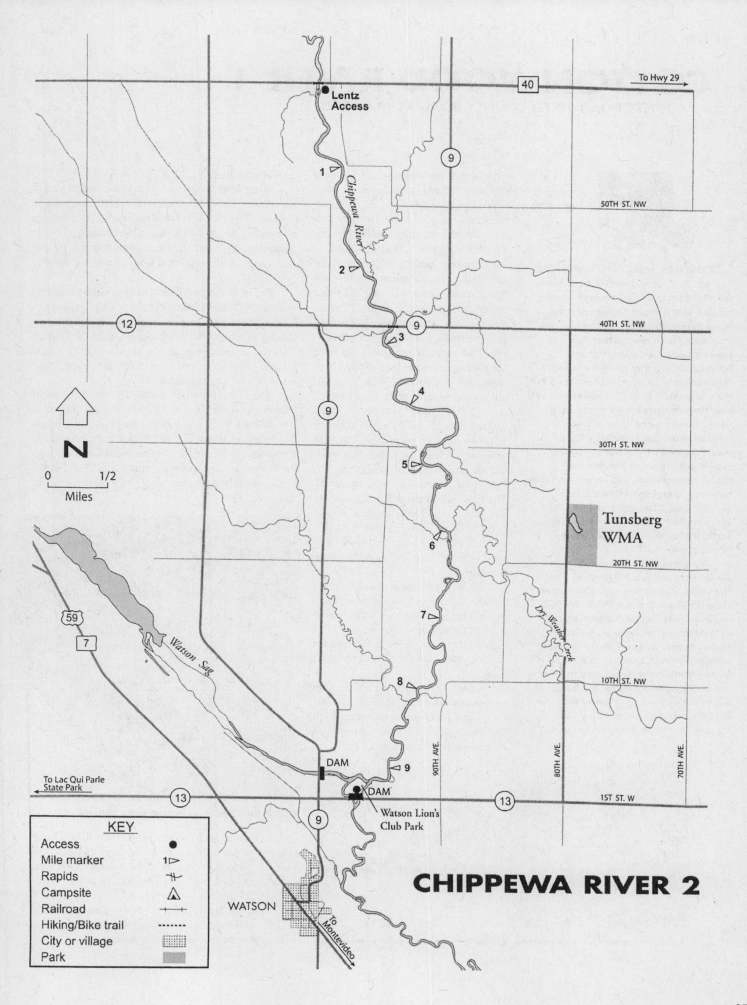

To Hwy 29

40

Lentz
Access

1

Chippewa River

9

50TH ST. NW

2

12

9

40TH ST. NW

3

9

4

30TH ST. NW

N

0   1/2
Miles

5

Tunsberg
WMA

6

20TH ST. NW

Watson Sag

59

7

7

Dry Weather Creek

10TH ST. NW

8

90TH AVE.

80TH AVE.

70TH AVE.

DAM

9

To Lac Qui Parle
State Park

13

DAM

1ST ST. W

13

9

Watson Lion's
Club Park

CHIPPEWA RIVER 2

WATSON

To
Montevideo

KEY

Access	●
Mile marker	1▷
Rapids	≠
Campsite	△
Railroad	+++
Hiking/Bike trail	-----
City or village	
Park	

COTTONWOOD RIVER 1
COUNTY ROAD 10 TO COUNTY ROAD 11 (6.8 MILES)

Eroded but Beautiful

In 1838, as he headed west across the Minnesota prairie, explorer Joseph Nicollet wrote about "a skirt of woods lining the Cottonwood." He noted that the "water is so transparent that one can see many little objects at the bottom." Today, that pretty wooded skirt probably looks much the same, but the water often doesn't. The Cottonwood now runs opaque brown when it's rising. Flooding and erosion from artificial drainage patterns, wetland reduction, and loss of deep-rooted prairie grasses wash the farmers' topsoil downstream and leave riverbank tree roots dangling in thin air. One paddler said, "You can smell the soil in the water." Filled with rich prairie earth, it's too thick to drink and too thin to plow.

The good news is that erosion on the Cottonwood is on a gradual decline. The Cottonwood often runs clear when there isn't runoff. Since 1983, the RCRCA has been notching up the improvement with education and grants. But an agency is only as good as the public it serves. What really needs to happen is for everyone in the watershed to take personal responsibility for the health of this beautiful river. That's why the RCRCA offers an annual canoe trip. Those who paddle the river, value it.

On this short, fast trip, the Cottonwood River races through frequent riffles and Class I rapids. Especially when the water's high, it's an exciting ride. Paddlers encounter one wavy drop after another; at high water, some drops form three-foot-high waves. This isn't a trip for beginning paddlers.

The river carves a deep gorge in the surrounding prairie and is often banked by high escarpments; one notable example is long, tall, and heavily eroded. There are a few islands (actually large gravel bars) and a few snags. Scarlet tanagers, wild turkeys, bald eagles, blue herons, little green herons, kingfishers, and lots of other birds make their homes here. Wild roses and phlox grow on some of the steep banks.

The Redwood-Cottonwood Rivers Control Area (RCRCA, www.rcrca.com) works to improve water quality in both watersheds. Check the Web site for information (and photos) about their annual June canoe trip down the Cottonwood. The trip includes a shuttle and is open to the public. Another celebration of area rivers is "River Blast," a river festival—with lots of music and a flotilla—held in New Ulm on Labor Day weekend (www.riverblast.org).

Note: The Minnesota State Pollution Control Agency periodically posts warnings at Flandrau State Park against swimming in the Cottonwood River because of high coliform bacteria levels. Paddling the river is safe, however. Definitely don't drink it.

Camping is available along the river at Flandrau State Park, (507) 233-9800.

The 8.3-mile **shuttle route** runs north on County Road 10, east on County Road 27, and south on County Road 11.

The **gradient** is 6.2 feet per mile.

Water level information is available online (http://waterdata.usgs.gov/mn/nwis/uv?05317000) for the USGS gage near New Ulm. The DNR says levels from 3 to 6 feet are optimal. Above 6 feet, expect big standing waves. In spring and early summer, the Cottonwood rises quickly after a rain. In late summer, it takes a heavy rain to bring the river up.

Put in at the Marti Landing, the public access on downstream left at County Road 10. To get there from New Ulm, go west on U.S. Highway 14 and south on County Road 10. There's a parking area by the landing. The river corridor is wooded, with mostly silver maples at water's edge and a mix of oaks and (not surprisingly) cottonwoods in the upland areas.

The Cottonwood is about 100 feet wide at the bridge, quickly growing to 125 feet after the first tributary flows in. If the river's rising, the many little streams that feed the Cottonwood will be out of their banks and the water will be turbid. About a half mile down from the bridge, intermittent wavy riffles and Class I rapids begin—some steep, some easy—and continue to the take-out.

Gravel bars are frequent along the Cottonwood.

At mile 1, you pass a gravel pit on the right. The riffles and rapids continue to be frequent, but short. At mile 4.74, a long, high, curving escarpment on the right is heavily eroded, with topsoil mounded at the bottom and cantilevered oak trees at the top.

Take out on upstream left at the County Road 11 bridge public access, with timber steps up the steep bank, a paved access road, and a parking area.

Although surrounded by farmland, the Cottonwood's corridor is wooded.

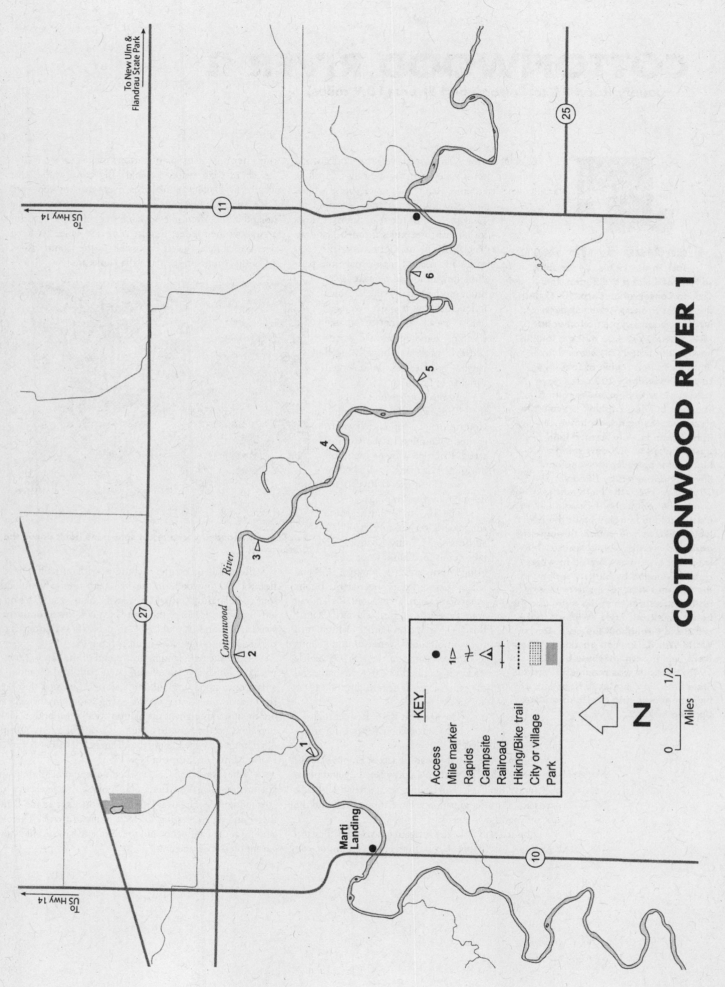

COTTONWOOD RIVER 1

KEY

- ● Access
- 1△ Mile marker
- ⊭ Rapids
- △ Campsite
- ┼ Railroad
- ⋯ Hiking/Bike trail
- ▦ City or village
- ▨ Park

N

0 — 1/2
Miles

Marti Landing

To US Hwy 14

To New Ulm &
Flandrau State Park

Cottonwood River

COTTONWOOD RIVER 2
County Road 11 to Cottonwood Street (13.9 miles)

Flandrau State Park

Back in the 1930s, when dams still seemed like a great idea, the Civilian Conservation Corps (CCC) and the Works Projects Administration (WPA) impounded the Cottonwood River. The idea was to make a lake in newly designated Cottonwood River State Park. In a region of few lakes, Lake Cottonwood's 200 acres gave folks a place to boat, swim, and fish. The dam builders couldn't prevent the river's increasing floods, however. Runoff from heavily farmed land upstream led to one devastating high-water episode after another. Severely damaged by floods in 1947, 1965, and 1969, the last vestiges of the dam were completely removed in 1995. It's possible to imagine what the lake looked like as you paddle through the park and see the wide expanse of low land that once was covered in water, clearly bounded by bluffs. Workers in the CCC and WPA camps left more lasting structures than the dam, like the handsome Rustic Style buildings that still stand throughout the park. During World War II, German prisoners of war were held in some of these buildings. In 1945, the park was renamed Flandrau State Park, for Charles E. Flandrau, an Indian agent during the Dakota Sioux Uprising in 1862.

As it nears the Minnesota River, the Cottonwood carves an ever-deeper valley, with dramatically high cliffs, heavily wooded banks, sand and gravel bars, willow thickets, and almost no development. Near the end of the trip, the river flows for almost three miles through Flandrau State Park. As on Cottonwood River 1, riffles and Class I rapids make the paddling fun, although there are fewer drops on this run. For the last three miles, the flow is quiet. Wooded banks mean a chance to see wildlife, including pileated woodpeckers, swallows, broad-winged hawks, bald eagles, and several varieties of herons.

As on Cottonwood River 1, the Minnesota State Pollution Control Agency periodically warns against swimming in the Cottonwood River because of high coliform bacteria levels.

See Cottonwood River 1 for information on camping.

The 10.7-mile shuttle route runs south on County Road 11 and east on County Road 25. To take out at the Cottonwood Street bridge, turn left on Highway 15/68 and left on Cottonwood Street at the public water access sign. To take out at Flandrau State Park instead, turn left onto County Road 13. At Martin Luther College, turn right on Summit Avenue and go 1 mile to the park entry on the right. A vehicle sticker is required to enter the park, and the canoe access is next to the main parking area.

The gradient is 4.7 feet per mile.

See Cottonwood River 1 for information on water levels.

Put in at the County Road 11 access. From the south side of New Ulm, go west on County Road 25 and north on County Road 11. The landing on upstream left has a paved access road and parking. The banks are low and the Cottonwood flows quietly.

About a half mile downstream, gravel bar riffles and bouldery Class I rapids begin. In the next four miles, you

run intermittent drops of various intensities along this stretch of high wooded banks. Big cottonwoods, for which the Dakota named this river, grow by the river. Oaks, with a few cedars sprinkled in, dominate the upland areas. After mile 9, watch the sandstone cliffs for a swallow metropolis: hundreds of nest holes scattered over a rock face. Access is possible at the County Road 13 bridge (mile 10.4), where the banks are low.

Swallow-nest condos pockmark a sandstone bank above the Cottonwood.

Relatively quiet after the bridge, with only a few little riffles, the Cottonwood's in the state park now. The unmarked state park landing (mile 11.3) may be hard to spot. It's on the left just downstream of the white lifeguard tower for the park's swimming pond. A trail leads through willow thickets and up timber steps to the park's main parking lot.

From the park landing to the end of the trip is 2.6 miles, much of which is remote-feeling state park land. At mile 12.9, a dam once stood, impounding Lake Cottonwood. Just before the bridge, you pass the USGS gaging station on the left. Take out on upstream right at the Cottonwood Street bridge. Timber steps lead up the bank to a parking area. For a tasty post-paddling burger, try the Lamplighter Family Sports Bar & Grill, on North Minnesota Street in New Ulm.

Other trips: The Cottonwood flows another 3 miles to its confluence with the Minnesota. Along this stretch, the river goes under the Highway 15 bridge (there's a canoe landing there) and an interesting DM&E Railroad trestle. There's no landing at the confluence and the next access is 6.7 miles downstream on the Minnesota.

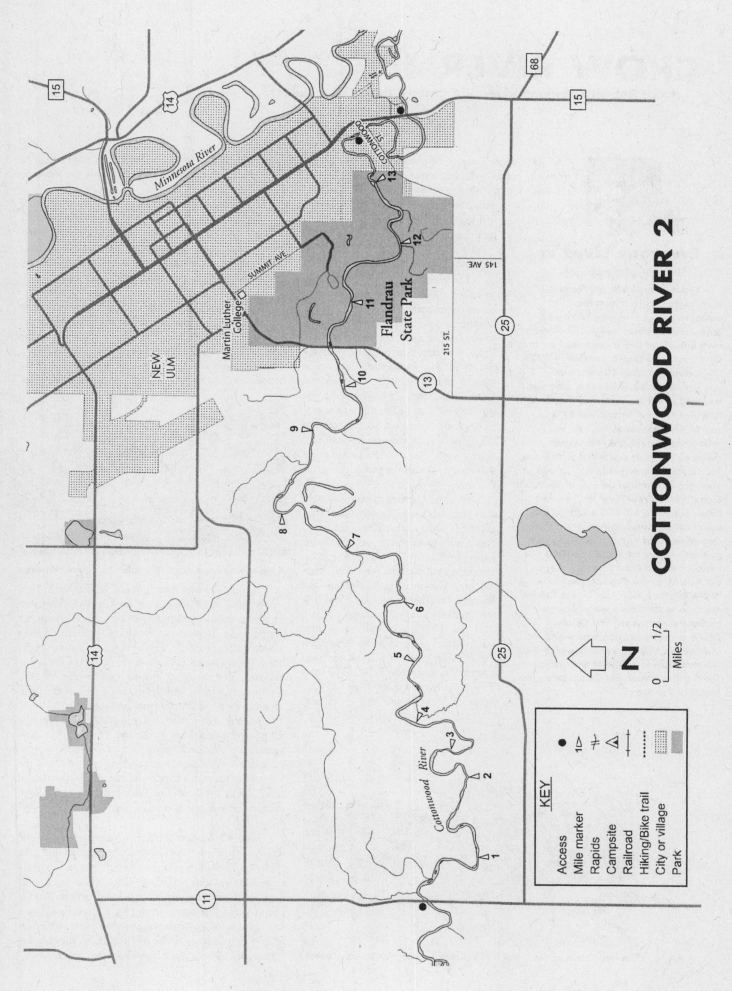

COTTONWOOD RIVER 2

N

0 1/2
Miles

KEY

Access
Mile marker
Rapids
Campsite
Railroad
Hiking/Bike trail
City or village
Park

CROW RIVER 1
Lake Rebecca Park to Riverside County Park (12.4 miles)

Everyone Lives in a Watershed

Picking up plastic pop bottles, aluminum cans, and fast-food containers, and dragging old tires, bikes, and furniture out of the water, may not sound like a great day on the Crow. But on a September day in 2005, 280 volunteers from 10 communities did just that. By noon, their trash collection weighed over nine tons, and they had had a great time. In addition to the satisfaction that came with cleaning up their favorite river, the enthusiastic cleanup crew was rewarded with lunch, T-shirts, and some good press. If you or your group wants to be part of the next Clean Up the Crow River Day, contact Diane Sander, (763) 682-1933, ext. 3, diane.sander@mn.nacdnet.net, at Crow Organization of Water (CROW), a joint powers watershed board. To learn more about the Crow's health, check out their Web site (www.crowriver.org). CROW is also looking for Citizen Stream Monitors to do simple weekly stream-testing between April and October. CROW provides the equipment and the instructions. Volunteers choose their own site and provide a little of their time. The result is a valuable database on the health of the river.

Just 30 miles west of Minneapolis, this journey on the Crow is suitable for beginning river paddlers—unless the water's high. Mostly quiet, the route is sprinkled with a few easy stretches of riffles. After a few miles on the South Fork, paddlers head down the main stem of the Crow. Putting in at Riverside Park in Rockford shortens the trip to 7.5 miles.

The Crow is feeling pressure of sprawling suburban growth: many new houses have been built along the river. Despite the development, the river offers a pleasant day of paddling close to the Twin Cities. Two large park preserves along the river help this fast-growing area retain some of its natural beauty. Unfortunately, Crow-Hassan Park Preserve, where this trip ends and Crow River 4 begins, is only on one bank of the river. Long stretches of the opposite bank are crowded with new development. Plenty of herons and eagles share the river with the people. There are few crows.

Primitive riverside **camping** is available free at Rockford's Riverside Park: (763) 477-6565, and at Riverside County Park (www.co.wright.mn.us/department/parks/parks.asp). There is also group camping, available for a fee and by reservation only, away from the river in Lake Rebecca Park Reserve: (763) 559-6700; www.threeriversparkdistrict.org/.

The 10.5-mile **shuttle route** runs northeast on County Road 50. After crossing Highway 55 in Rockford, the road becomes County Road 10 (Woodland Trail). Turn left on County Road 123 (Pioneer Trail) and angle left on County

Road 19. After crossing the river, turn right on River Road and right on Riverview Road, which you follow to its end.

The **gradient** is 1.4 feet per mile.

This reach of the Crow is almost always passable, making it a good late-summer paddle. Water level information from the USGS gage at Rockford is available online (http://waterdata.usgs.gov/mn/nwis/uv?05280000) or from the DNR, (888) 646-6367. Medium is 3 to 7.5 feet.

Put in at the Lake Rebecca Park Preserve's canoe landing. From Highway 55 in Rockford, go southwest on County Road 50. The primitive canoe landing on the right, less than a mile past the park entrance, has a short dirt path to the river. This is the South Fork of the Crow. Deadfalls at bends can be a hazard in the first few miles.

A mother and son peep through a bridge at Hanover.

At mile 2.3, the river is joined by the North Fork and becomes the main stem of the Crow. It flows into Rockford under a railroad trestle, the Highway 55 bridge, and a street bridge. At mile 4.9, there's a fishing platform and a recently improved canoe landing on the left at the north end of Riverside Park. There's also a picnic area, but camping isn't allowed at the landing. Campers may pitch tents in the main part of the park, between the flood-control berm and the river.

For the next 2 miles, noisy highways hide behind a fringe of silver maples on both sides. At mile 7.8, a small sign on the left marks a picnic area across the river from a big meadow. At an east–west powerline (mile 8.1), the Crow races through a curving half-mile of fast water and riffles. With the houses of Rockford gone and willow thickets covering the floodplain, this is the prettiest part of the trip.

Mile 9.9 features a return to development, as the Crow nears Hanover. On upstream right at the Hanover Bridge (mile 10.8) there's an access trail. Just past an interesting old iron truss bridge, the Crow riffles over a boulder bed. About a mile out of town, the river flows past the county park. The access on the left is unmarked, but a sand and gravel landing where you take out makes it easy to spot. A road leads up the hill to parking, the camping area, picnic tables, a drinking-water pump, and toilets.

The main stem of the Crow flows through some nice wooded areas.

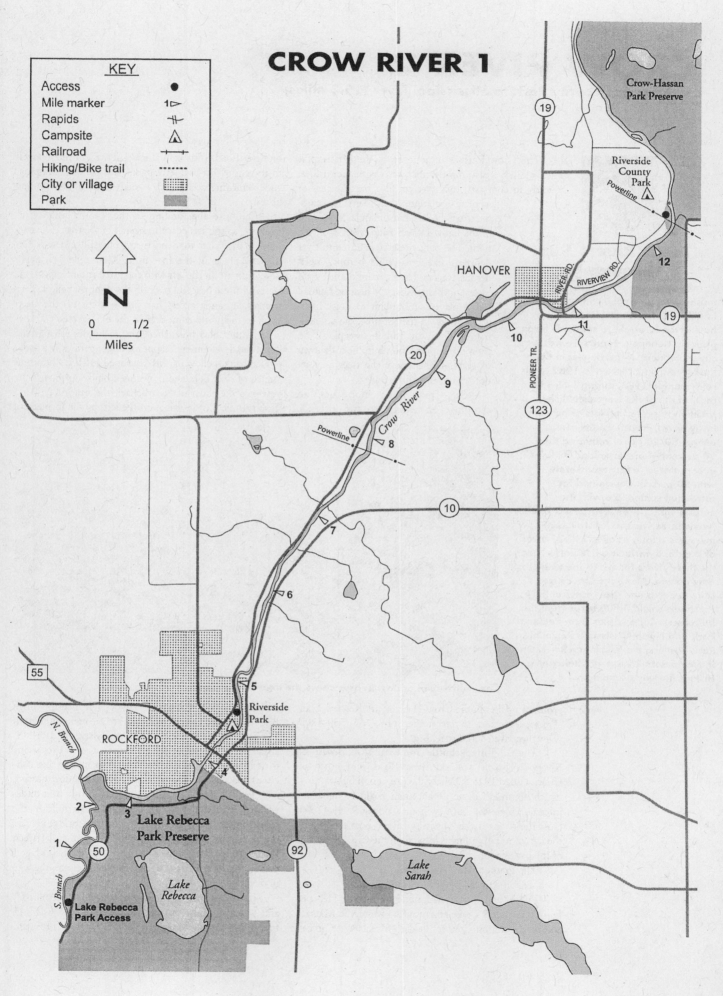

CROW RIVER 1

KEY

Access	●
Mile marker	1▷
Rapids	
Campsite	△
Railroad	
Hiking/Bike trail	----
City or village	
Park	

N

0   1/2
Miles

Crow-Hassan
Park Preserve

Riverside
County
Park

Powerline

HANOVER

12

11

20

9

10

Crow River

Powerline

8

10

7

6

55

N. Branch

5

Riverside
Park

ROCKFORD

4

2

3

Lake Rebecca
Park Preserve

1

50

92

Lake
Sarah

S. Branch

Lake Rebecca
Park Access

Lake
Rebecca

CROW RIVER 2

Riverside County Park to Mississippi River (15.3 miles)

Three Rivers Run Through It

As suburban development mushrooms, everyone can be grateful to Clifton E. French (1919–2006) for having the foresight to set aside large parks in Hennepin County. French was superintendent of the Hennepin County Parks from its inception in 1962 to his retirement in 1984, during which time most of the parks were established. In addition to protecting lots of acres in large parks, French established a unique 80/20 policy requiring that 80 percent of preserve land be kept in or restored to its natural state, with 20 percent designated for recreation compatible with that natural state. Three Rivers Park District (www.threeriversparkdistrict.org) now manages a total of over 27,000 acres of parkland, including five parks along the three rivers for which the district is now named. Along the Crow River, Lake Rebecca and Crow-Hassan Park Preserves shield 4,800 acres from the bulldozers. Coon Rapids Dam Regional Park and North Mississippi Regional Park lie along the Mississippi River. On the Minnesota River near Shakopee is Historic Murphy's Landing.

The Crow finishes its journey to the Mississippi. The paddling is easy, mostly quiet water with a few riffles. A study in contrasts, this river corridor has stretches of wooded isolation, then dense development on the left and the quiet woodland of the Crow-Hassan Park Preserve on the right. The park preserve is home to river denizens like great blue herons, green herons, marsh hawks, cormorants, bald eagles, and kingfishers. A historic railroad trestle plays counterpoint to noisy highway bridges. In the last mile, the development fades away and the steeple of St. John the Baptist Church in the little town of Dayton rises above the trees, a quiet note at the end of the trip.

See Crow 3 for information on camping. There are also two riverside on River Road. Turn right at Riverview Road and follow it to the end. It's a two-level park, with parking, camping, and picnicking above and a road down to the landing below.

Opposite the landing is the Crow-Hassan Park Preserve, so this is a peaceful stretch of the river. The current's a bit faster than upstream but still quiet. A few islands appear in the first mile. After mile 1.5, a big development on the left with the usual runoff pipes contrasts with the peaceful park on the right. At mile 1.8, an unmarked canoe access has timber steps up the steep bank to the group campsites in the park preserve.

In the third mile, there are no houses for a while. Then the development reappears, accompanied by a badly eroded bank. Following this developed patch is a beautiful stretch of river bordered by wooded bluffs on the left. As you pass the town of St. Michael, the historic Millside Tavern (mile 5.6) is visible on the left, by the former site

The church spire at Dayton rises above the trees on the Crow.

group campsites in the Crow-Hassan Park Reserve, available for a fee and by reservation only: (763) 559-6700; www.threeriversparkdistrict.org/.

The 12.5-mile **shuttle route** runs southwest on Riverview Road, west on River Road, and north on County Road 19 to St. Michael. Go east on Highway 241, which becomes County Road 36 after you go under the interstate highway. Turn right on County Road 42 and cross the river. At the Mississippi River boat landing on the left, a canoe landing is located on the Crow River side of the parking lot.

The **gradient** is 2.7 feet per mile.

See Crow 3 for **water level** information.

Put in at Riverside County Park outside Hanover. From Interstate 94, take Highway 241 west to St. Michael, and turn south on County Road 19. At Hanover, go east

of Berning's Mill (closed in 1996). The first Berning's Bridge was built here in 1885 to serve the main route from Minneapolis to St. Cloud and was replaced in 1931. Its attractive steel-span bridge replacement, a Warren pony truss bridge, was removed in 2006. Its uninspiring concrete replacement (County Road 116) is just downstream.

For the next 2.5 miles, the Crow flows past undeveloped wooded banks on both sides. At mile 8, the houses return, and a handsome railroad bridge crosses the river, just before the Interstate 94 bridge. Between the interstate and Highway 101 (mile 11.1) there's a golf course and its attendant houses, but little else in the way of development.

The final mile of the trip is wooded, undeveloped, and peaceful. **Take out** between the County Road 42 bridge and the confluence, at the dirt access on the right.

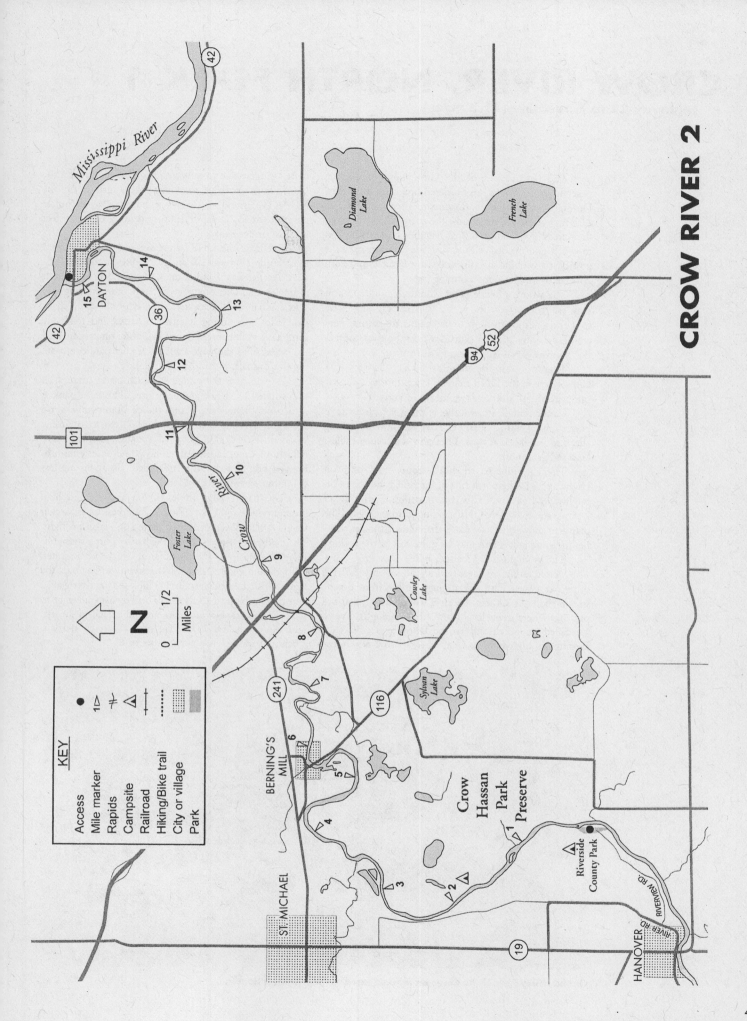

KEY

Access
Mile marker
Rapids
Campsite
Railroad
Hiking/Bike trail
City or village
Park

N
0   1/2
Miles

Mississippi River

DAYTON

Diamond Lake

French Lake

Foster Lake

Crow River

Cowley Lake

Sylvan Lake

BERNING'S MILL

ST. MICHAEL

Crow Hassan Park Preserve

HANOVER

Riverside County Park

RIVERVIEW RD.
RIVER RD.

CROW RIVER, NORTH FORK 1

Highway 22 to Forest City (11.2 miles)

The North Fork of the Crow flows through a peaceful wooded wetland bordered by farms and fields. Deadfalls are common and sometimes require portages. Although there are no rapids, the current is swift when the water's high, and good boat-handling skills are needed to get around the obstacles. A riverside campsite makes it possible to combine this trip with Crow River, North Fork 2 for an overnight canoe-camping trip.

The woods provide good wildlife habitat and you may see beavers, ducks, geese, bald eagles, and many songbirds. Although most of the banks are natural, several farms allow grazing right down to the river, a practice that the DNR is working to discourage.

There's no **camping** on this stretch of the Crow. On Crow River 2, the DNR maintains a primitive riverside campsite about 2 miles downstream of Forest City.

Canoe rentals are available at the Riverside Store in Forest City, (320) 693-6711. They recommend calling ahead for weekend rentals. They also rent canoe trailers (and sell groceries).

The 15.2-mile paved **shuttle route** runs south on Highway 22 to the north side of Litchfield, northeast on Highway 24 to Forest City, and north on County Road 2 across the river. The DNR landing is on the right. The map also shows alternate roads that allow a shorter shuttle; these are gravel and may be quite soft in the spring.

The **gradient** is 2.3 feet per mile.

Water levels are measured at the County Road 2 bridge at Forest City, on a gauge visible from downstream right. At 2.4 feet, the river will be bankfull at the put-in. General river level (low, medium, high) reports are called in sporadically to the DNR by a volunteer; medium to high water is best. There's also a new auto-mated gauge at the County Road 22 Bridge. Data for the North Fork of the Crow near Manannah is on the NOAA Web site (http://www.crh.noaa.gov/ahps2/index.php?wfo=mpx). In April 2006, a reading of 84.23 feet was just under bankfull.

Put in at the DNR canoe landing on downstream right at the Highway 22 bridge, 9 miles north of Litchfield. For the first 4 miles, the Crow wanders in and out of the lowland trees of a large wetland, often straying into side channels and backwaters. To stay on the main channel, follow the strongest current. Farms and roads are sometimes visible through the trees, other times hidden by the woods and the wide marsh. Deadfalls are common, but don't usually block the channel.

As you near the bridge at 328th Street (mile 4.1), the wooded left bank gradually rises. The right bank is sometimes higher as well, and there's a farm (mile 5) on the right. Meeker County 34 (mile 7) crosses on a low wooden trestle bridge. Between wetland areas, the channel is sometimes more defined now, and occasional submerged boulders dot the streambed. Deadfalls are less common. There's another farm.

You pass a farm (mile 10) on the left and high ground on the right as you approach Forest City. Meeker County's Shaw Memorial Park (mile 10.7) is on the right. The landing isn't marked and the bank's a little steep, but there's a trail up to the picnic area, which has a shelter, grills, drinking water, and toilets. As you paddle under the County Road 2 bridge (mile 11) look for the river gauge. You have to be next to the bank on downstream right to see the numbers. Downstream, around a bend to the left, **take out** at the DNR landing (mile 11.2) on the left. There's a parking circle next to the road.

On the North Fork of the Crow, an intrepid kayaker negotiates a deadfall.

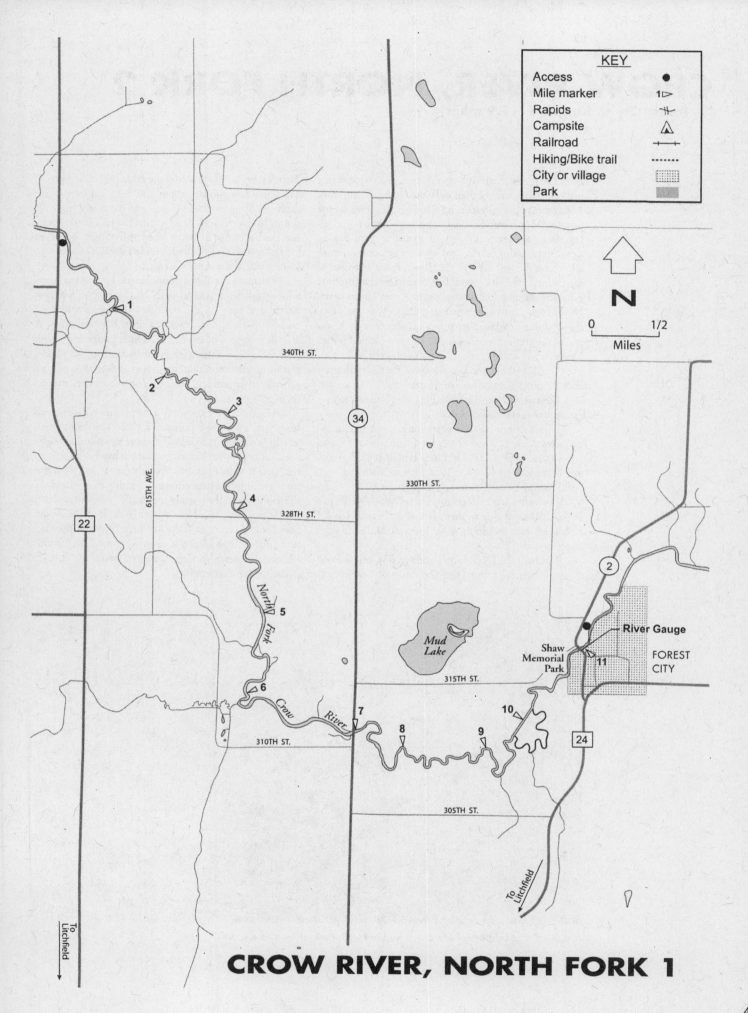

KEY

Access •
Mile marker 1▷
Rapids
Campsite ▲
Railroad ┼┼┼
Hiking/Bike trail ┄┄┄
City or village
Park

N

0 __ 1/2
Miles

340TH ST.

34

330TH ST.

328TH ST.

615TH AVE.

22

North Fork

5

6

Crow River

7

310TH ST.

8

9

10

305TH ST.

315TH ST.

Mud Lake

2

River Gauge

Shaw Memorial Park

11

FOREST CITY

24

To Litchfield

To Litchfield

CROW RIVER, NORTH FORK 1

CROW RIVER, NORTH FORK 2

Forest City to Kingston (11.9 miles)

The Crow flies faster on this trip, in a channel that is often more defined than on Crow River, North Fork 1. A few easy but entertaining Class I rapids spice up the paddling. High wooded banks and an often remote-feeling river corridor make this an appealing trip. Eagles, wood ducks, kingfishers, and white-tailed deer seem to appreciate the woodsy habitat as well. A few stretches of agricultural land and several riverside farms interrupt the generally natural feel of the route. As on Crow River, North Fork 1, this is deer-hunting territory, so you probably shouldn't paddle during the hunting season. At the end of the trip is Meeker County Kingston Park, Finnish Memorial, one of Meeker County's well-kept parks.

The DNR maintains a primitive riverside campsite about 2 miles downstream of the put-in.

See Crow River, North Fork 1, for information on canoe and canoe trailer rentals.

The 8.0-mile shuttle route runs south across the bridge on County Road 2, east on County Road 24, and east on County Road 27. The canoe landing is on the right, in Meeker County Kingston Park, Finnish Memorial.

The gradient is 3.4 feet per mile.

For water level information, see Crow River, North Fork 1. Because this segment has several rocky Class I rapids, it's best to paddle it between medium and high water.

Put in at the DNR canoe landing, on County Road 2, across the river from the tiny burg of Forest City.

There's room for parking and the ramp is grass and gravel. The Crow flows quietly, about 100 feet wide, over a generally sandy streambed. Occasional boulders begin to appear in the channel. After a mile, the farmland retreats and the banks rise higher. The campsite (mile 2.4) is on the right, across from a high wooded bank. There's a sign to alert you and a sign at the site.

Downstream of the campsite, the Crow races intermittently through boulder-bed Class I rapids on the most attractive stretch on the trip. You see deer stands (and numerous deer) in this wooded area, but no houses. A mile downstream of the 675th Avenue bridge (mile 4.8), look for a nice 1930s vintage car parked in the woods, rusting quietly. After that, the sylvan spell is broken by an agricultural processing plant, looming over the river on the high right bank.

Highway 24 crosses on a handsome old-fashioned bridge (mile 6.6), with potential for access on downstream left. In less than a mile, 690th Avenue also has an interesting old bridge, with a creosoted timber roadbed and intricate iron trusses. After mile 8.4, the banks by two farmyards are unfortunately eroded by grazing that extends all the way down to the river. In the last 1.5 miles of the route, the Crow flows through a big wetland, bordered by old oaks and cottonwoods. Take out (mile 11.9) on river left at the dirt ramp at Meeker County Kingston Park, Finnish Memorial. There's parking, a shelter, water, and a brick outhouse, but no camping.

A solo-canoe paddler spends a day on the North Fork of the Crow.

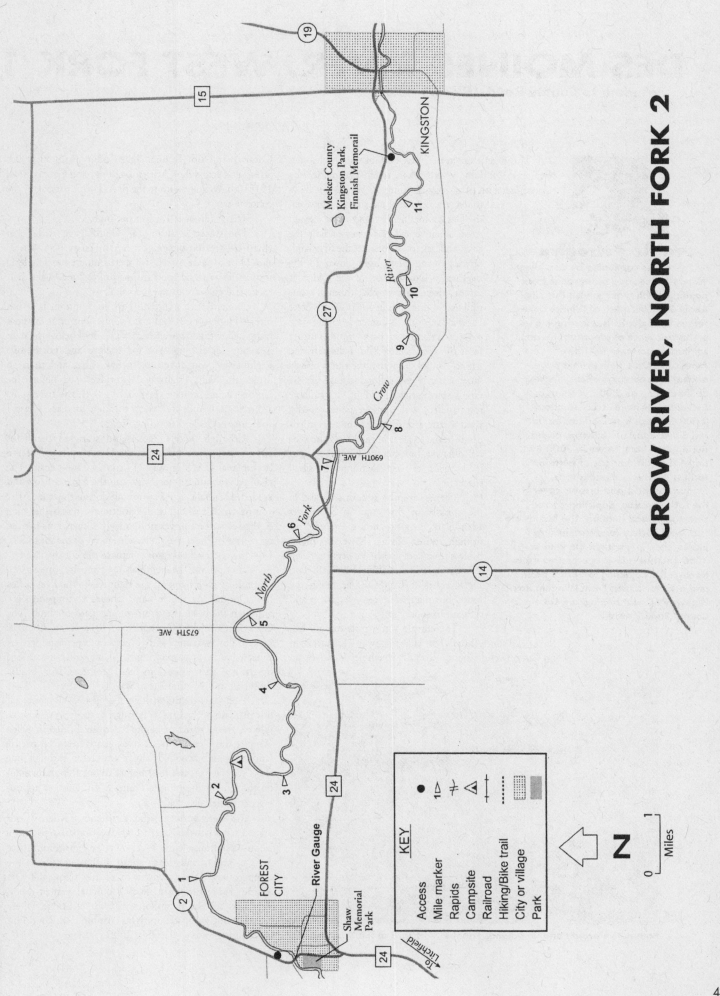

CROW RIVER, NORTH FORK 2

DES MOINES RIVER, WEST FORK 1
Windom to County Road 19 (16.1 miles)

Prairie Petroglyphs

Paddlers captivated by Boundary Waters Canoe Area pictographs (rock paintings) will want to visit this site. About 20 miles north of Windom, the Jeffers Petroglyphs is a fascinating prehistoric place of great cultural and spiritual importance to Native Americans. On a high prairie ridge, ancient rock carvings offer glimpses of life as long as 5,000 years ago. Archeologists have recorded about 2,000 carvings inscribed on the flat red Sioux quartzite outcrop, probably during the years between 3000 B.C. and 1700 A.D. Images of buffalo, turtles, deer, elk, thunderbirds, humans, atlatls, and arrows cover the rock surfaces, depicting sacred ceremonies and hunting. The Minnesota Historical Society (www.mnhs.org/places/sites/jp/) bought the land in 1966 and has added interpretive trails through the adjoining tall-grass prairie and a visitor center. From Windom, take Highway 60 east to Bingham Lake and County Road 2 north.

This paddle down the West Fork of the Des Moines begins at Windom, where urban riverbanks render the prairie river a bit of an ugly duckling. By the time it flows under the Christianna Bridge, however, the Des Moines has become a lovely swan. Areas of native, tall-grass prairie adjoin the river, and oak forests blanket the hilly land, often growing thick right down to the riverbanks. Downstream of the bridge, it carves a deep, narrow valley through beautiful glacial drift hills in Kilen Woods State Park. Because the cruise ends in the state park, it's a natural for park visitors. Putting in at the Christianna Bridge shortens the trip to 7 miles. Although the run is mostly quiet water, a few riffles and easy Class I rapids spice up the paddling. It's suitable for paddlers with some experience who want a taste of fast water. The river corridor is home to great horned owls and red-tailed hawks, blue herons, kingfishers, and bald eagles, as well as numerous small shore birds.

There's camping at both ends and in the middle of this trip. In Windom's Island Park, campsites near the access have drinking water, but no showers. A much more scenic spot (with showers) is Kilen Woods State Park, (507) 662-6258. Two DNR riverside campsites lie along the route, but these are often overgrown and difficult to spot.

The shuttle route runs east on 6th Street and south (briefly) on U.S. Highway 71. Turn right on Cottonwood County Road 25, which becomes Jackson County 17 (490th Avenue). Take County Road 30 (900th Street) east across the Christianna Bridge and County Road 19 (510th Avenue) south to the river. There's parking by the concrete ramp.

The gradient is 1.4 feet per mile.

The water level on the USGS gage at Jackson (http://waterdata.usgs.gov/mn/nwis/uv?05476000) should be at least 4 feet; 4.7 feet is moderate. The level is most likely to be good from April to June. After that, rocky stretches are usually too shallow.

The entrance to Island Park in Windom is at 6th Street (Highway 62) and 4th Avenue. Put in at the boat ramp below the lowhead dam. (The pool below the dam is a popular fishing spot for walleye and northerns.) Right away, you encounter a few riffles and then go under the U.S. Highway 71 bridge. Just before the Union Pacific railroad trestle (mile 0.4), the river splits around an island and runs through an easy Class I stretch of rocks and standing waves.

Although wooded areas and scattered cornfields appear in the first few miles, the Des Moines still feels a bit urban as U.S. Highway 71 (mile 2) crosses again. The channel is about 100 feet wide and the banks are low and eroded. Deadfalls are common all during this trip. After you pass a pair of old bridge abutments just before mile 3, the scenery improves quite nicely. Gravel bars backed by willow thickets line the inside curves of the meanders. Cottonwood and oak groves replace the cornfields.

To find the Mabel Nelson campsite (mile 6.2), watch for a high bank on the right where the river bends left. On the lower left bank, there's a campsite sign, although the bank is overgrown and hard to climb. The Christianna Bridge (County Road 30) is about 2.8 miles farther downstream, with access on upstream left. A short path leads to parking, a picnic area, and a sign describing the adjoining Des Moines River Prairie Scientific and Natural Area (SNA).

The Christianna Bridge Campsite, on river left downstream of the bridge, is tough to spot; no sign is visible on the overgrown bank. From the bridge to Kilen Woods, the Des Moines curves gently between prairie land and high wooded bluffs and races through one short stretch of riffles. Just before mile 14, look for signs on the left for the Holthe Prairie SNA, another appealing native prairie area.

You know you're on the north end of Kilen Woods State Park when you see a flight of timber steps and a wood-duck house (mile 15.1) on river right. From these steps, a hiking trail leads about a quarter mile to the campground. Just downstream of the steps, the Des Moines runs through a Class I boulder garden. Soon after, you see the new County Road 19 bridge, where you take out on upstream right. (An interesting old iron trestle bridge was replaced in 2005.)

Both native prairie and woodlands line the West Fork of the Des Moines.

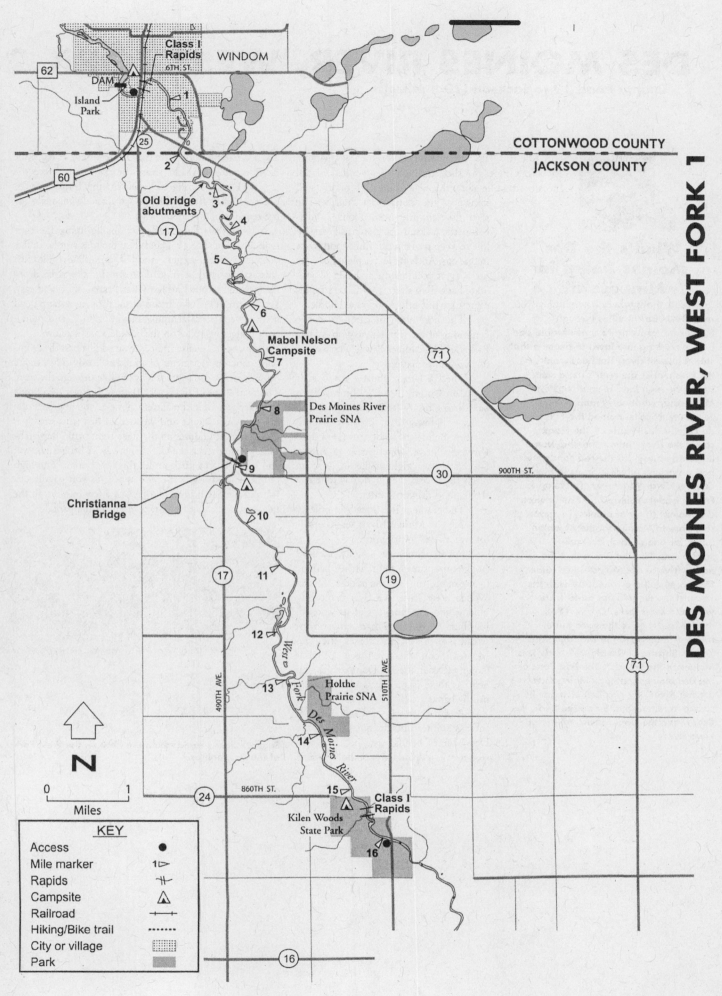

Class I Rapids

6TH ST.

WINDOM

62

DAM

Island Park

25

60

2

Old bridge abutments

17

3

4

5

6

Mabel Nelson Campsite

7

8 Des Moines River Prairie SNA

9

Christianna Bridge

10

17   11

12

13

Holthe Prairie SNA

14

15

Class I Rapids

Kilen Woods State Park

16

24   860TH ST.

490TH AVE.

510TH AVE.

West Fork Des Moines River

30   900TH ST.

19

71

71

COTTONWOOD COUNTY
JACKSON COUNTY

16

KEY

Access   ●
Mile marker   1▷
Rapids
Campsite   △
Railroad   ┼┼
Hiking/Bike trail   ·······
City or village
Park

N

0   1
Miles

DES MOINES RIVER, WEST FORK 2
County Road 19 to Jackson (10.8 miles)

What's the Des Moines Doing in Minnesota?

Well, that's where it originates. The river flows for 94 miles through Minnesota, growing to considerable size before crossing into Iowa to become that state's largest river. The headwaters of the West Fork—the river's main stem—are in the high land in southwestern Minnesota, what early mapmaker Joseph N. Nicollet named the "Plateau du Coteau des Prairies." The Sioux called the river "Inyan-sha-sha-watpa" (Redstone River) for the red sandstone gorge through which it flows in Marion County, Iowa. Various explorers and French traders referred to it as "rivière des Moins" (river of monks) in apparent reference to Moingona, the Algonkin name for one of their riverside settlements. Nicollet wrote that the name "rivière des Moins" later came to be associated erroneously with the Trappist monks (Moines de la Trappe) who also lived there. On his 1838 map, Nicollet gave the river three names: "Moingonan of the Algonkins," "Inyan Shasha of the Sioux," and "Des Moines of the French". The East Fork of the Des Moines (named "Moingonan Brother River" by Nicollet) also has its source in Minnesota. So do the Rock, the Cedar, and the Upper Iowa, all major Iowa rivers.

On this trip, the West Fork of the Des Moines River continues to slice through the wooded glacial moraines that lie along the edge of the high prairie land known as the Coteau des Prairies. The river flows swiftly until about 2 miles before the Jackson Dam, so paddlers who like to keep moving can finish both trips in one day. And that leaves plenty of time for a great picnic stop at Kilen Woods State Park. Two short, easy Class I rapids punctuate this otherwise quiet paddle.

The best place to **camp** is at the beginning of the trip, Kilen Woods State Park. See Des Moines River, West Fork 1 for more information.

The 10.1-mile **shuttle** route runs south on County Road 19 (gravel, then paved) to County Road 16, then east to U. S. Highway 71, then south into Jackson. Before the bridge, turn left onto Riverside Drive, which leads to Ashley City Park. Turn right at the log cabin to reach the access. The park has toilets, a shelter, and drinking water.

The **gradient** is 1.2 feet per mile.

See Des Moines River, West Fork 1, for water level information.

Put in at the new County Road 19 Bridge on upstream right. There's parking by the ramp. You're in the middle of Kilen Woods State Park, the river is flowing quietly, and the terrain is at its wooded, hilly best. A little more than a mile downstream, a powerline crosses the Des Moines. Soon after, you pass Belmont County Park on the left. Don't plan to stop here, as there is no access on the steep, brushy banks.

A short stretch of Class I rapids (mile 2.8) interrupts the quiet flow as the Des Moines bends east, narrows, and rushes over a drop. Large standing waves and scattered boulders are easy to negotiate. A half mile downstream, an island splits the river just before the County Road 16 bridge. The left channel is full of rocks, but the right offers clear passage. Just downstream are the remains of an older bridge.

Floodplain forests of silver maple lining the river replace the hills for a bit, and then the hills return. In this densely wooded section, another powerline (mile 5.8) crosses. Just over a mile downstream, the river drops through the second and last Class I rapid, short and easy. Less than a mile downstream of the drop, at a sharp bend in the river, snags accumulate in impressive (and potentially dangerous) piles on the boulders and shallows.

In about a quarter mile, as you paddle past the crumbling concrete abutments of an old railroad bridge, traffic noise from the interstate is now audible through the trees. The twin spans of Interstate 90 cross the river a half mile farther. Soon after, the current slows as you approach the Jackson Dam. Quiet and wooded at first, this stretch is later lined with houses on the steep right bank. Be watchful as you approach the U. S. Highway 71 bridge in town; you may need to duck under this low bridge. The high bluffs of Jackson's north side appear as you paddle out from under the bridge, and it's just a few minutes to the take-out, a dirt landing on river left in the park.

Several Class I rapids liven the flow on the West Fork of the Des Moines.

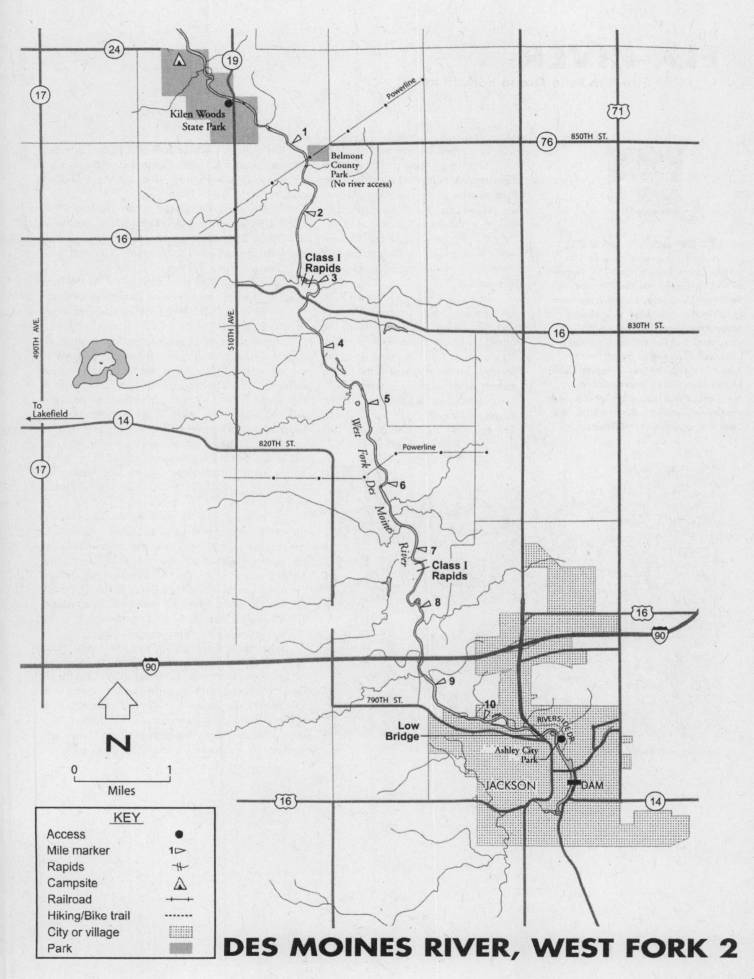

DES MOINES RIVER, WEST FORK 2

ELK RIVER

166th Street to Lake Orono Park (9 miles)

Tour Lake Orono

A dam has impounded the Elk River in some form since 1851. Instead of flowing freely into the Mississippi, the lively Elk is impounded in shallow Lake Orono. If the idea of paddling around the impoundment appeals to you, check out the online map and historical information (http://www.lakeorono.org/Pontoontourscript1.pdf) on the Lake Orono Improvement Association Web site. Highlights include the Orono Cemetery, Scout Island, the Dam Site, and the Storm Drains.

This lively ride down the Elk River ends quietly in Lake Orono, where the river is impounded by a dam a mile upstream of its confluence with the Mississippi River. Paddlers who are comfortable maneuvering in Class I rapids and dodging deadfalls will enjoy this river. Campers at Wapiti Park Private Campground can take out at the campground landing, shortening the trip to 6.3 miles and eliminating the lake paddle.

This area is feeling a lot of development pressure, evidenced by new houses along the river. For several miles of the trip, the din of traffic on U.S. Highway 10 is audible from the river. Even so, once you hit the stretch with the rapids, it's easy to forget all about traffic noise. For 2 miles, there are few houses. Eagles, herons, and kingfishers fly past. The fast-moving, rocky river with its high red-sand banks is all you think about.

Camping is available at Wapiti Park, (763) 441-1396, a private campground located along the river and accessed from U.S. Highway 10 on the west side of the causeway across Lake Orono.

The 6.3-mile **shuttle route** runs south on 166th Street NW and east on U.S. Highway 10. Just before the Orono Lake causeway, turn right on Gary Street into Lake Orono Park. The boat ramp is on the left.

The **gradient** is 3.7 feet per mile.

USGS **water level** measurements for the Elk River near Big Lake are available online (http://waterdata.usgs.gov/mn/nwis/uv?05275000). Look for a minimum flow of 200 cfs; 480 cfs is better.

Put in at the public water access 2 miles east of the City of Big Lake, a half mile north of U.S. Highway 10 on 166th Street NW. Where the road turns west just before the river, a public water access is tucked between two houses. There's room to park a few cars. Be careful as you launch: large riprap at the landing makes the riverbank rather treacherous.

The Elk, shallow and about 80 feet wide, runs quietly at first. Before and after County Road 15 (mile 1.6), houses are scattered along the wooded banks. The USGS gage is on the bridge. A stream (mile 2.2) races in from the left.

At mile 3.3, the Elk picks up the pace, running through a long series of riffles and Class I rapids alternating with quiet pools. There may be deadfalls along this stretch. High red-sand riverbanks topped with trees often flank the river. After the railroad trestle (mile 4) the rapids are a bit more intense but still Class I. At mile 6.1, the Elk quiets again and flows past the remains of an old bridge. The sandy landing (mile 6.3) at the Wapiti Park Campground appears on the right.

The Elk wanders slowly past the campground, which fills a horseshoe curve of land on the right bank. An interesting assortment of vintage cabins lines the left bank. At mile 7.5, the river widens and slows even more as it enters Lake Orono. It's about 1.3 miles across this shallow impoundment and under U.S. Highway 10 to the boat ramp where you **take out** at Lake Orono Park. There's a picnic area and toilets by the parking lot.

Morning mist floats over the Elk.

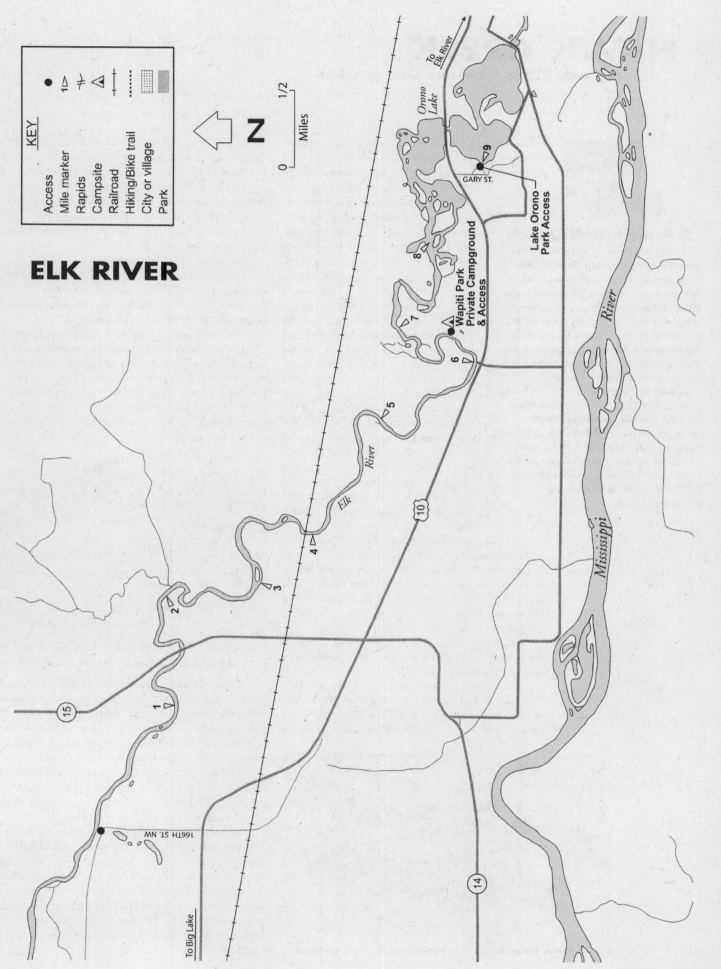

ELK RIVER

KEY

- Access ●
- Mile marker 1▷
- Rapids ≠
- Campsite △
- Railroad ┼
- Hiking/Bike trail ┈
- City or village ▦
- Park ▨

N

½ Miles

0

To Elk River

Orono Lake

9

GARY ST.

Lake Orono Park Access

Wapiti Park Private Campground & Access

8

7

6

5

4

Elk River

10

3

2

15

1

166TH ST. NW

14

Mississippi River

To Big Lake

HAWK CREEK
U.S. Highway 212 to Minnesota River (9 miles)

A Prairie Half-Dozen

Avid prairie river paddlers, take note. The citizens group Clean Up the River Environment (CURE, www.cure mnriver.org) awards a handsome Prairie River Paddler patch to any paddler who completes trips on each of the six CURE rivers: the Minnesota, the Lac qui Parle, the Pomme de Terre, the Chippewa, the Yellow Medicine, and Hawk Creek. Journeys on all these rivers are described in this guide, they're all fun to paddle, and CURE will take your word for your paddling accomplishments. Once you've paddled them all, call Dixie Tilden at CURE, (877) 269-2873, to find out about getting your well-earned patch. And definitely consider joining CURE; it's an effective, growing grassroots group.

Paddling Hawk Creek on a sunny spring day means a fun, fast trip down a beautiful stretch of river. When it's running, that is. This rocky tributary of the Minnesota definitely flashes up and down and in summer's low water, it's rarely passable. Although it's not a well-known canoe route, those who have paddled Hawk Creek will tell you that it's well worth the effort required to check the water levels. Carving a deep gorge down the north side of the Minnesota River valley, this reach drops 100 feet in 9 scenic miles. The Hawk races between high wooded banks and sheer cliffs and down steep, short, rocky Class I drops (Class II in high water) the whole route.

A major tributary of the Upper Minnesota, 65-mile Hawk Creek is one of six prairie rivers on which Clean Up the River Environment (CURE) focuses. The river is also the object of the Minnesota Pollution Control Agency (MPCA) Hawk Creek Watershed Project (see Appendix 5). Hawk Creek runs through private land until it reaches Skalbekken County Park at its mouth, thus paddlers should choose sandbars to stop for picnics.

Camping opportunities include Renville County's Skalbekken Park, (320) 523-3768, an attractive riverside campground on the Minnesota with a shelter and toilets, but no drinking water; and Upper Sioux Agency State Park, (320) 564-4777, which has all three, and camping tipis to boot. Both charge a fee and the tipis require reservations.

Kayak rentals are available from Java River in Montevideo, (320) 269-7106, and **canoe rentals** from Gary Lentz in Echo, (507) 925-4482.

The 7.7-mile **shuttle route** goes east on U.S. Highway 212 and south on County Road 10. A short distance before the bridge across the Minnesota River, turn right onto a dirt road. On the gate, a sign tells when

the park is open. Follow the dirt road all the way to a turnaround. A trail leads through the bushes to the mouth of Hawk Creek. Another part of the park, this one with an official canoe access, is through the gate on the east side of County Road 10. This access, in a camping area with a shelter and outhouses, is 0.8 mile down the Minnesota River from the mouth of Hawk Creek. The reward is an easier take-out.

The **gradient** is 10.2 feet per mile.

Water level readings are not available, although you can call experienced local paddler Gary Lentz, (507) 925-4482. Gary's not usually by his phone, but if he is, he can tell you if Hawk Creek is runnable.

Put in on upstream river left at the U.S. Highway 212 bridge. There's room to park on the wide shoulder, and the grassy slope makes it easy to slide a canoe down to the river. A drop is visible upstream, and soon after the bridge, more drops appear. The frequent Class I rapids that characterize the rest of the trip are intricate mazes of boulders. Watch out for strainers on the outside curves of the rapids.

Cliffs of glacial drift tower over Hawk Creek.

Oaks, cottonwoods, and cedars cover the banks and perch atop high walls in the wide gorge. Willow thickets soften the banks. Sheer cliffs of layered glacial drift add a dramatic note. Almost no houses are visible. A new bridge (822nd Avenue) crosses at mile 1.76, followed by a few, somewhat hazardous remnants of the old bridge.

Just past mile 4, the Hawk sprawls briefly into an intricate braid of small channels and grassy islands. At mile 5 is the 810th Avenue bridge, with an automated MPCA water monitor on downstream center.

In the last 2.5 miles, the drops are longer and steeper. A quarter mile before the confluence, a powerline is followed by a long sandbar on the left and an especially rocky drop. **Take out** at Skalbekken Park, on river left just before the confluence. The unofficial access, unmarked and usually overgrown, is at the end of a dirt park road that leads to County Road 10. Or continue 0.8 mile down the Minnesota to the official canoe access just upstream of the shelter on the left.

Speedy Hawk Creek demands constant attention from paddlers.

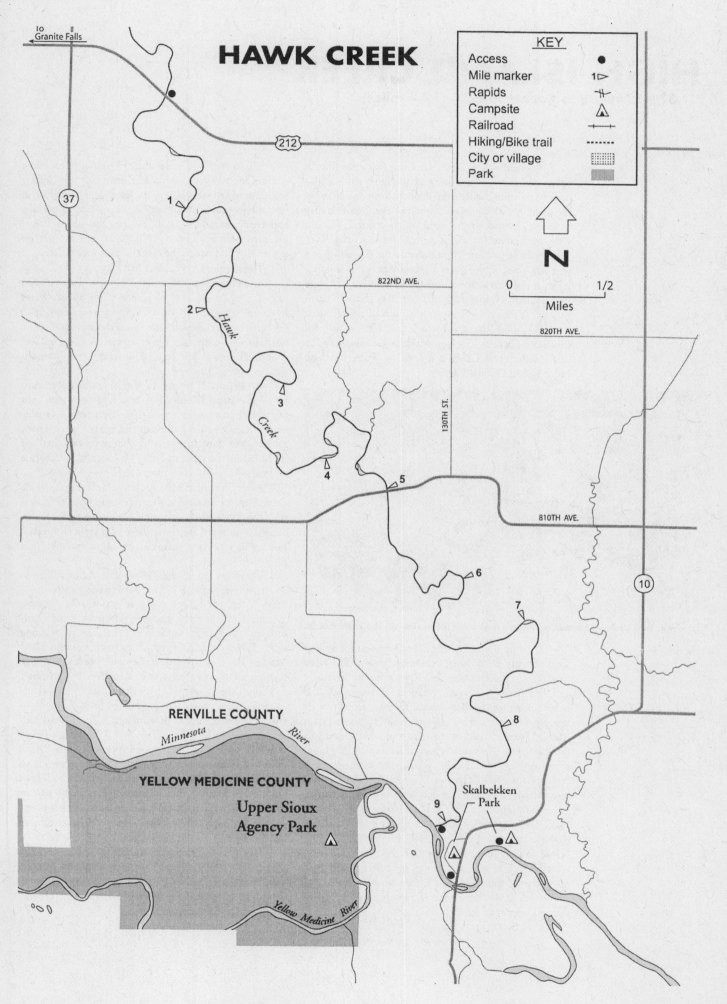

HAWK CREEK

HIGH ISLAND CREEK
371st Avenue to County Road 6 (12.4 miles)

When the High Island's running, it's great fun for expert paddlers. Long chains of standing waves and a narrow, twisting channel make for challenging and exciting paddling. In this heavily wooded area, deadfalls may cross the channel. If the water's high enough, you can slide over some; others require portaging. The Carp Dam *must* be portaged. Strainers and the possibility of a wire fence add to the list of hazards. The valley is popular with horseback riders, and the campground at High Island Creek County Park is one of their favorite destinations. Although you may see groups of riders, when the creek's high enough for paddling, it's too high for their horses to ford. They just watch as you paddle swiftly past. High Island Creek is a favorite of the Mankato Paddling and Outings Club.

Fast water and chains of standing waves make for a fun ride on the High Island.

The fun offered by this fast stream and the valley's scenic beauty far outweigh these challenges. The creek drops into the deep Minnesota River valley in this reach, and the banks are steep, wooded, undeveloped, and beautiful. In this unspoiled area, the only dwellings are deer stands, not houses. (Avoid paddling during deer season.) Near the end of the trip, numerous gravel bars flank the river. The creek is named for a small (but high) island in High Island Lake, which contributes to creek flow upstream of this trip. At flood stage, the creek flows into the lake instead of the lake flowing into the creek.

Camping is available at High Island Creek County Park, south of County Road 12 at the end of 341st Lane. Call the county, (507) 237-4092 or (507) 237-4330, before you arrive for a free permit. Although there's no vehicle access to the river, a long, steep hiking trail leads up to the campground. In Henderson, Allanson's Park, (507) 248-3234, with electrical hookups, toilets, and hot showers, charges a fee.

The 6.5-mile **shuttle route** runs north on 371st Avenue and east on 240th Street. Turn right on County Road 12, which takes you to the Jessenland Town Hall at the intersection with County Road 6. There's parking and a toilet at the town hall. You can also ask to park at the car-repair business right next to the take-out on upstream left. Just tell the owner about your Volare.

The **gradient** is 15.7 feet per mile.

The High Island runs in the spring and after a good rain. It drops quickly, so be sure to check ahead. **Water levels** are measured on the USGS gage near Henderson (http://waterdata.usgs.gov/usa/nwis/uv?site_no=05327000). The minimum is 3.9 feet, between 4.5 and 6.0 feet is optimal, and at 8.86 feet/1,290 cfs the High Island is spilling over its banks.

Put in from 371st Avenue, a quiet gravel road reached by County Road 12 and 240th Street. Downstream right offers the best access. It's a steep bank but not too brushy. There's a house on downstream left, the last you'll see for a while. Just downstream, a wire fence crossed the river in 2005 but was gone in 2006; be watchful. Serpentine and narrow, High Island moves fast.

High clay cliffs frequently flank the channel. Where the road first runs next to the river (mile 3.5) the bank is relatively low and access is possible on the right. Watch out for poison ivy. A narrow footbridge (mile 4) follows. Further downstream, there's a new house (mile 4.7) on the right.

Upstream left of the old wooden trestle bridge at 361st Avenue (mile 5.7) is a good place to stop for a break. After the bridge and just past an old concrete abutment on the right, the creek drops over the eight-foot-high Carp Dam (mile 5.9). There are no warning signs. Take out on river right for a short portage. Local paddlers often put in below the dam, but warn against parking there as one car was broken into. If you start a trip here, they suggest you park at the road by the bridge.

Watch out for a low footbridge (mile 7.3) draped with grapevines. Farther downstream, where a small tributary comes in on the left (mile 8.7), is High Island Creek County Park land, a good spot for a break. After this stop, High Island narrows and speeds up, with large standing waves. Until several years ago, the creek split here. Now the flow is all directed through one narrow channel. This fast stretch leads into an especially pretty part of the valley, wider now, with some great views of bluffs covered with cedars and oaks.

By mile 10.5, the gradient decreases and High Island Creek slows. The confluence with the creek's major tributary, Buffalo Creek (mile 11.6), is on the right. Take out on upstream left at County Road 6. The USGS gage station is on downstream left.

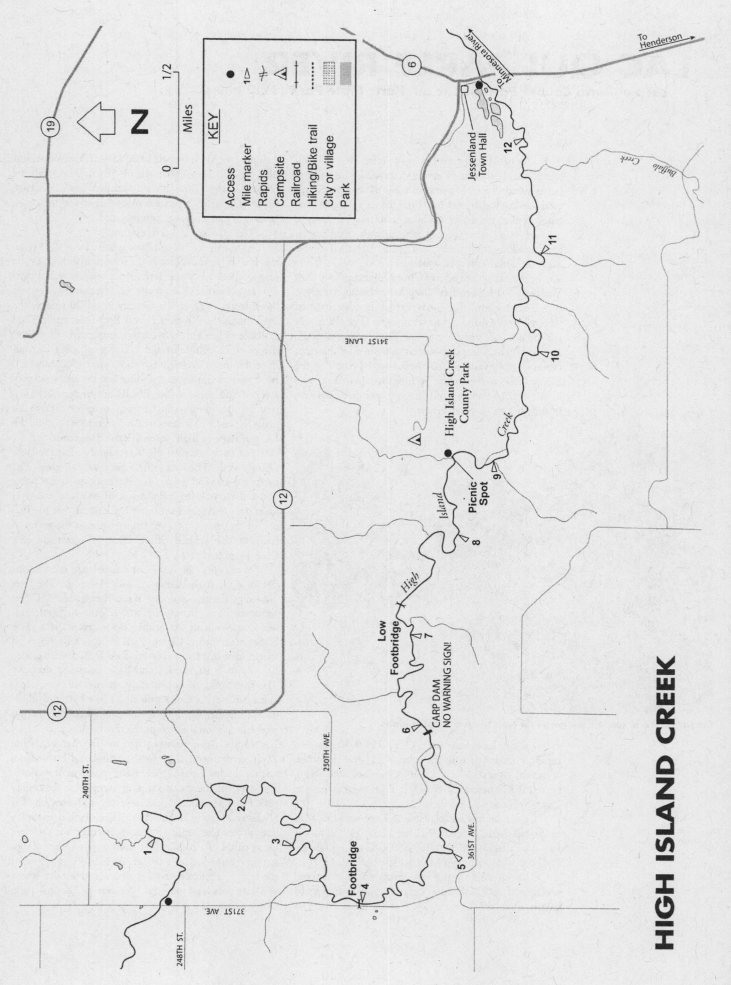

HIGH ISLAND CREEK

LAC QUI PARLE RIVER
Lac qui Parle County Park to Lac qui Parle State Park (12.9 miles)

This prairie river trip has lots to offer: long stretches of riffles and easy Class I rapids, dramatically high glacial banks sliced like layer cakes, and lots of wildlife. Sharp-eyed paddlers sometimes find bison bones on gravel bars, leftovers from the days when huge herds roamed this area. Pileated woodpeckers, green herons, owls, bald eagles, bank swallows, river otters, and foxes make their homes along its banks. This area, a premier birding region, is one site for the Audubon Society's Great Minnesota River Bird Watching Day, held each fall (http://www.birdingtrail.org/).

The Lac qui Parle has carved a deep channel through glacial drift, and towering cliffs of glacial rubble tell the geologic story of the area. Some of the cliffs are 150 feet high. A line of boulders deposited by the most recent glacial invasion (10,000 years ago) is visible on the exposed faces of these cliffs. Swallows like to nest in holes in the cliffs, swooping out in great clouds to feed on insects that hatch on the river.

The Lac qui Parle cuts a deep gorge through the surrounding plain.

Lac qui Parle State Park, (320) 734-4450, has two **campgrounds**; one is in the bottomland and the other, across the river on a windy hilltop, overlooks the broad, beautiful Minnesota River valley. Primitive camping is also possible at Lac qui Parle County Park.

Canoe rentals are available at Dawson Mini-Mall in Dawson, (320) 769-2036, or at Mitlyng's Bait by the Lac qui Parle Dam, (320) 269-5593. **Kayak rentals** are available at Java River in Montevideo, (320) 269-7106.

The 9.9-mile **shuttle route** runs on an unmarked gravel road to 226th Street (gravel), and then west to County Road 27 (paved). Take County Road 27 (331st

Avenue) north, County Road 20 (240th Street) east, and then County Road 48 north (365th Avenue) and east (246th Street). Turn left on County Road 33 (Lake Road). The park entrance is on the right and the canoe landing is past the lower campground.

The **gradient** is 3.6 feet per mile.

Although the Lac qui Parle is best run in the spring, rain may bring it up later in the season. In either case, be sure to check the **water level**. If it's too low, you'll definitely walk rather than paddle. On the painted gauge on downstream right at the County Road 20 bridge, the level should be 1.8 to 2.2 feet. Real-time readings are available online (http://waterdata.usgs.gov/usa/nwis/uv?site_no=05300000) for the USGS gage near Lac qui Parle. Optimal levels are 6.5 to 8.0 feet (360–600 cfs). By 7.5 feet, sediment-laden water laps the terrestrial vegetation, and some gravel islands are underwater. The river's quick to rise and frequent snags at river bends make the run hazardous above 8.5 feet. **Don't paddle the Lac qui Parle in high water: It's too dangerous.**

Put in by the riverside turnaround in Lac qui Parle County Park. There's room to park on the grass. The banks are low and grassy, the river's about 70 feet wide, and a thick wooded margin shields much of the river from the agricultural land that lies beyond. For the first half of the route, the river rushes through the waves of frequent boulder-bed riffles, some of which are easy Class I rapids.

At mile 6.9, the USGS automated gage is on downstream right at the County Road 31 bridge. The river now digs deeper, and one bank rises about 150 feet above the river. At mile 8.8, a river gauge is painted on the County Road 20 bridge, downstream right. The bridge near historic Lac qui Parle Village (mile 9.3) is no longer used by cars, and its roadbed is thick with grass.

By mile 10, the Lac qui Parle slows and deepens. The riverbanks are consistently lower, and more deadfalls appear. After County Road 33 (the Hagen Bridge), paddle another 0.2 mile to the unmarked **take-out** on river left. It's just a notch in the dirt bank.

Other trips: Another trip on the Lac qui Parle River, recommended by local paddler and high-school science teacher Greg Wyum, starts upstream of this one. You can combine the two trips by camping at the county park. From MacGuire Bridge, just east of Dawson on U.S. Highway 212, to Lac qui Parle County Park is about 14 river miles. The banks are less spectacular, but there are more riffles. To paddle this stretch, put in on downstream left at MacGuire Bridge. About 100 yards west of the bridge, a narrow gravel road leads to an area where you can park and put in. Take out at Lac qui Parle County Park.

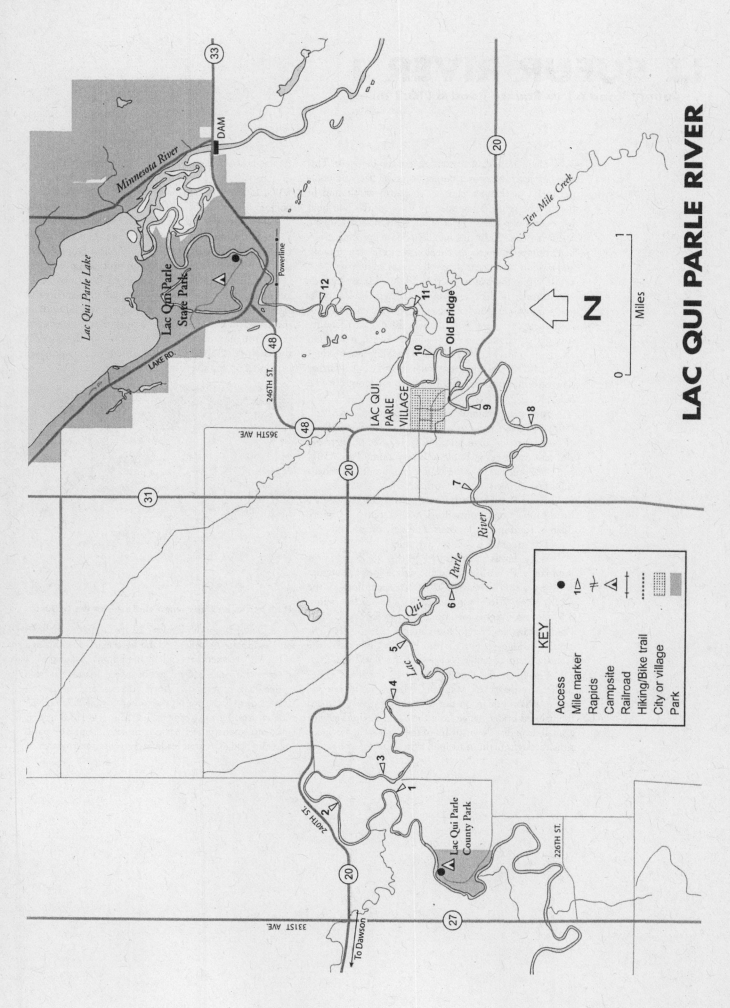

LAC QUI PARLE RIVER

LE SUEUR RIVER 1
County Road 41 to County Road 8 (10.8 miles)

There are lots of reasons to like the Le Sueur. This winding reach races over numerous gravel bars and boulder beds. Its channel varies in shape, in width, and in depth. The valley is bounded by wooded hills and high banks exposing layers of glacial till. Sadly, however, the Le Sueur has been badly manhandled. For many years, riverbank dumping, riverbank alterations, storm-water runoff, and erosion have taken their toll on this lovely river.

Despite the bad news, the riffles and Class I rapids on this reach are definitely fun for paddlers. Hawks, owls, and songbirds are fond of this wooded river valley as well. And the good news is that, with Blue Earth County strongly committed to improving its rivers, restoration efforts are underway. The Mankato Paddling and Outings Club (MPOC) has adopted a reach of the Le Sueur farther downstream, from County Road 16 to the mouth (see Le Sueur River 2).

Area **campgrounds** include Minneopa State Park, (507) 389-5464, west of Mankato, and Mankato's Land of Memories Campground, (507) 387-8649. There are also tent campsites at Rapidan Dam County Park, (507) 546-9997, managed by the Dam Store (home of the delicious pies extolled in Blue Earth River).

The 5.7-mile **shuttle route** runs south on County Road 41, west on County Road 90, and south on County Road 8. Parking for the access is on downstream left.

The **gradient** is 7.7 feet per mile.

Water levels are measured on the USGS gage near Rapidan, with readings available online (http://waterdata.usgs.gov/mn/nwis/uv?05320500). According to the DNR, below 2 feet is uncanoeable, 2 to 3.5 feet is low, 3.5 feet to 5.5 feet is medium, and over 5.5 feet is high. Paddlers are advised to use caution over 6 feet. The painted bridge gauges all read a little differently; the County Road 22 gauge is closest to the USGS readings.

Put in at the County Road 41 (589th Avenue) bridge, southeast of Mankato. There's no developed access; if you put in on downstream right, you can see the painted bridge gauge from the bank. Beginning with a small drop just downstream of the bridge, the Le Sueur runs through medium to long riffles and Class I rapids for the next 9 miles.

As you pass one of the high banks at about mile 2, watch for rows of bank-swallow nest holes that form a graphic design on the cliff face. At mile 3.7, the former site of the historic Hungry Hollow truss bridge (removed as this book went to press) is followed quickly by the County Road 90 bridge. Hungry Hollow Stop, a roadside area with a canoe access, is on upstream river left.

Beginning at mile 5, the river suffers: riprap, concrete wing dams, and riverbank dumping. Balancing this ugliness are ferns, wild iris, wild phlox, and wild roses on the banks and the dramatic beauty of the deep river gorge. You may meet pileups of cottonwood deadfalls. At the Highway 22 bridge (mile 6.7), MPOC's river gauge is painted on the river right bridge pier.

High banks and fast water characterize the Le Sueur.

Downstream of Highway 22 are numerous shallows and sandbars. At mile 8.3, the Le Sueur races through what MPOC members call "Stan's Rapids" (named for a fellow who once lodged a borrowed, brand-new solo canoe in a root wad). Short, curving, and steep, this Class I drop is the last on the route. At mile 8.7, a power line crosses. Downstream of the County Road 8 bridge, **take out** at the gravel bar on the left, about 100 yards past the bridge. A trail leads back to the parking area.

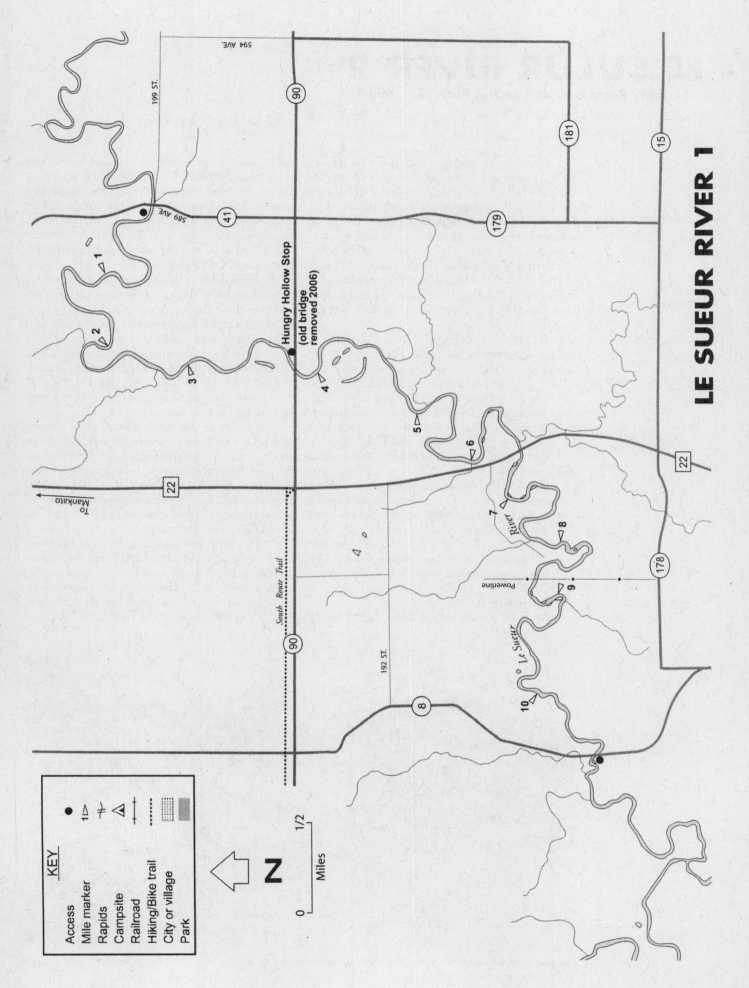

LE SUEUR RIVER 1

594 AVE.

199 ST.

90

181

15

589 AVE.

41

179

1

2

Hungry Hollow Stop
(old bridge
removed 2006)

3

4

5

6

22

To Mankato

22

7

River

8

178

Powerline

9

Le Sueur

South Route Trail

90

192 ST.

8

10

N

Miles

0   1/2

KEY

- Access
- 1 Mile marker
- Rapids
- Campsite
- Railroad
- Hiking/Bike trail
- City or village
- Park

LE SUEUR RIVER 2
County Road 8 to Red Jacket Park (8.7 miles)

On this mostly quiet float down the Le Sueur River, a lively current and occasional riffles spice up the paddling. As on Le Sueur River 1, the river corridor varies considerably in this segment. As the trip begins, the Le Sueur flows past many high cliffs of glacial drift. Sand and gravel bars, softened by willow thickets, are common along this reach. The narrow river occasionally sprawls into wide shallows. In the last 5 miles, high wooded bluffs flank a channel that has grown considerably in width and depth. In between, two major tributaries of the Le Sueur, the Maple and the Big Cobb, add their flow.

The Mankato Paddling and Outings Club (MPOC), which has adopted the last 7 miles of the river, does an annual cleanup on this reach. On a historic note, two interesting bridges cross this segment of the Le Sueur. The first is the Kerns-Yaeger Bridge, a bowstring arch-through iron truss bridge, built in 1873 and no longer used by traffic. A mile later is the stone Red Jacket train trestle, built in 1874 and now part of the Red Jacket Trail.

See Le Sueur River 1 for information on **camping** and **water levels**.

The 6.6-mile **car shuttle route** runs north on County Road 8, west on County Road 90, and south on County Road 66. A **bike shuttle** is possible on this route. Ride north on County Road 8 (generally quiet) to County Road 90. Hook up with the South Route Bike Trail that parallels County Road 90 (a busy road). This trail connects with the Red Jacket Trail, which takes you to the landing.

The **gradient** is 6.0 feet per mile.

Put in on downstream left at the County Road 8 public access. To get there from Mankato, take County Road 16 south, County Road 90 east, and County Road 8 south. A painted river gauge is visible from the parking area (if it's not obscured by logs). Between the parking area and the river, a detention pond filters parking lot runoff, evidence of Blue Earth County's commitment to its rivers. It's a 100-yard carry down a path to a gravel bar downstream of the bridge.

A big gravel bar marks the confluence with the Big Cobb River (mile 1.8) on the left and the Le Sueur widens to about 150 feet. At mile 2.4, the County Road 16 public access is on downstream left. Wooden steps climb the steep bank to a parking area.

An even bigger gravel bar lies at the confluence with the Maple (mile 3.7), and the Le Sueur widens to about 200 feet. The bluffs are impressively high now. A few riffles disturb the generally smooth flow of the river between here and the take-out.

As you reach mile 6, the wooded valley narrows. Watch for rock outcrops among the trees. Along this scenic stretch, the historic Kerns-Yaeger Bridge crosses the river. **Take out** on river right, just past the tall stone Red Jacket trestle. There's no sign, just a sandy landing. Red Jacket Park has a drinking water pump, toilets, and lots of parking. Steps lead up to the Red Jacket Trail that crosses the river on the trestle.

Other trips: This route ends 1.5 miles before the river's confluence with the Blue Earth River. From the confluence, the Blue Earth flows another 3.5 miles down to its confluence with the Minnesota River. There's an access on river right at Sibley Park, just before the confluence. Members of MPOC call this the Three Rivers Trip.

The power of a river to rearrange the earth is evident on the Le Sueur.

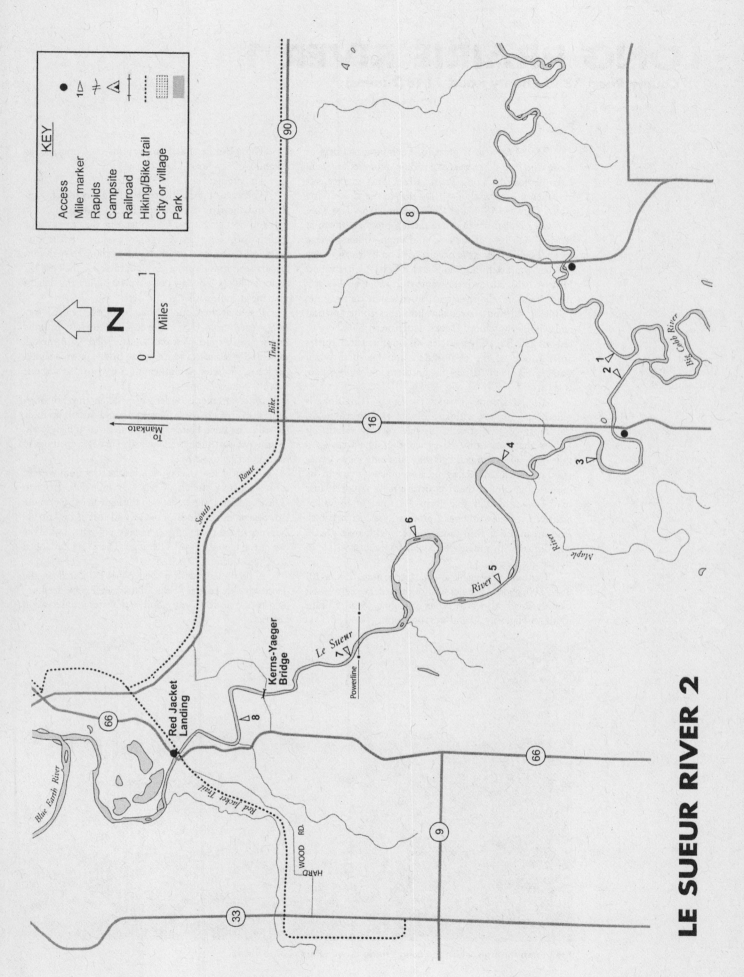

LE SUEUR RIVER 2

KEY

- ● Access
- 1△ Mile marker
- ≠ Rapids
- △ Campsite
- ┼ Railroad
- ⋯⋯ Hiking/Bike trail
- ▦ City or village
- ▨ Park

N

Miles
0 1

To Mankato

Big Cobb River

Maple River

Le Sueur River

Powerline

Kerns-Yaeger Bridge

Red Jacket Landing

Red Jacket Trail

Blue Earth River

South Route Bike Trail

HARDWOOD RD.

90
8
16
66
66
9
33

1
2
3
4
5
6
8

LONG PRAIRIE RIVER 1
County Road 38 to County Road 11 (8.2 miles)

This short trip is great for beginning paddlers or those who love a lazy, peaceful paddle. From its source in Lake Carlos, the Long Prairie River flows quietly east and then north for almost 100 miles to the Crow Wing River. Between 1995 and 1997, area residents Tim King and Greg Nolan began a stewardship program aimed at sharing their love of the river and urging others to care for it. Their efforts have been carried on by Kitty Tepley of the Todd County Soil and Water Conservation District, with steady improvement in water quality as a result. In 2001, the river was named a state canoe route. Paddlers will find a river that nourishes contemplation and wildlife watching. Ducks, kingfishers, blue herons, red-winged blackbirds, eagles, dragonflies, and turtles are denizens of the clear waters and marshes. When water levels are up, fishing for northern and walleye pike is good.

The land through which the Long Prairie flows is quietly agricultural, with small farms and diverse fields. For most of this stretch, a wide marshy floodplain buffers the river from the agriculture. The wide-open valley will appeal to paddlers who like long views better than the enclosed feeling of a woodland river. In its meandering course, the river occasionally wanders close to the wooded hills that form the sides of its valley. Scattered trees, mostly oaks, grow on the higher banks. The streambed is firm sand, streaked with river grasses and dotted with mussel shells and fragments, visible in the clear water.

Camping is available at Lake Carlos State Park, (320) 852-7200, about 16 miles west of the put-in. Go west on County Road 38, which becomes County Road 5. Turn south on Highway 29 and west on County Road 38.

The 4.7-mile **shuttle route** runs on County Road 38 and County Road 11.

The **gradient** is 1.8 feet per mile.

The Long Prairie's **water levels** fluctuate considerably, but the river is rarely too low to paddle. Between 150 and 350 cfs on the USGS gage at the city of Long Prairie (http://waterdata.usgs.gov/usa/nwis/uv?site_no=05245100) seems to qualify as the medium to high flow usually seen in the spring and fall; these are the best levels for paddlers. The low flows typical of July and August may mean some walking.

Put in at the County Road 38 bridge near Clotho. To get there from U.S. Highway 71 in the city of Long Prairie, go 10 miles west on County Road 38. Although there's no established access at the bridge, a wide shoulder leaves room for parking, and it's easy to drag a canoe down the grassy slopes.

Once summer is underway, paddlers travel through a marshy tunnel of reed canary grass and cattails up to six feet tall. The Long Prairie flows gently, even at high levels, twisting its way through the marsh. There are openings to several marshy oxbows.

At mile 3.3, a small creek joins the river from the left, through a long stretch of oaks. At mile 5.8, Freeman Creek, wide and weedy, flows in through an oxbow on the left. Several duck blinds in the second half of the trip are evidence of the river's large population of waterfowl. **Take out** at the County Road 11 bridge. There's no developed access; upstream right is best.

A flow meter with a solar panel is located on the upstream side of the bridge. This meter provides river data to the Todd County Soil and Water Conservation District.

The marsh through which the Long Prairie flows offers distant views.

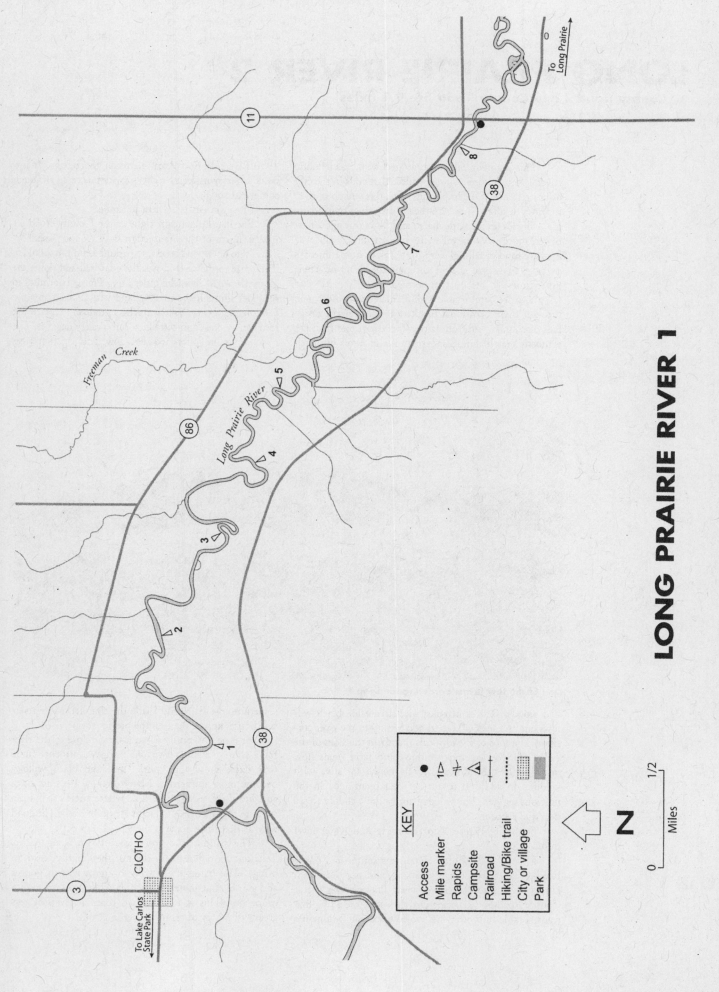

LONG PRAIRIE RIVER 1

To Long Prairie

0

11

38

8

7

6

5

4

3

2

1

38

Freeman Creek

Long Prairie River

86

3

CLOTHO

To Lake Carlos State Park

KEY

● Access
1▷ Mile marker
⇵ Rapids
△ Campsite
🕂 Railroad
⋯ Hiking/Bike trail
▦ City or village
▨ Park

N

0   1/2
Miles

LONG PRAIRIE RIVER 2
County Road 11 to County Road 56 (9.1 miles)

This segment can be combined with Long Prairie River 1 for a leisurely all-day paddle that ends in the city of Long Prairie. One important note: this stretch of river includes deadfall jams. As it heads east, the Long Prairie gradually leaves the wide marsh and flows through a narrower, more wooded valley. In the last mile, black willows are fond of falling over into the river. Sometimes it's possible to wiggle a boat through the resulting jams; other times it's necessary to portage.

If you're comfortable with maneuvering your canoe through these occasional blockades, don't let the deadfalls discourage you from taking this trip. Long Prairie 1 is mostly marshland; this segment is a nice mix of marsh

1990/Riverside Rest Area" to reach the bridge. A low bank on downstream right provides access, although somewhat rough.

The **gradient** is 1.4 feet per mile.

Put in on upstream right at the County Road 11 bridge, north of the intersection with County Road 38. There's no developed access, so parking is on the shoulder. The route to the river is over the guardrail and down the grassy slope. At first, the quiet Long Prairie continues to meander through the marshy land that characterizes the previous segment. Willow thickets gradually replace the reed canary grass and cattails, and the valley narrows. The river banks are often wooded now, and riparian trees

One of the few farms bordering the Long Prairie.

and woods. Groves of oaks; big, streamside black willows; and some small cedars add beauty to the river corridor. The tops of the low hills that form the sides of the valley are wooded and meadows and farm fields flow downhill to the floodplain. The banks are alive with wildlife. In addition to all the birds mentioned in the previous segment, the wooded areas offer a chance to see deer and raccoons.

See Long Prairie 1 for **camping** and **water level** information.

The 5.9-mile **shuttle route** runs south on County Road 11, east on County Road 38, and north on U.S. Highway 71 into the city of Long Prairie. Turn left at County Road 56 (Riverside Drive), just before a sign that reads "Prairie Improvements Project/Celebrate Minnesota

sometimes overhang and shade the channel. More riverside houses appear than on the previous trip.

At mile 2, County Road 38 runs close to the river for a short distance. Two old bridge abutments (mile 6.5) flank the Long Prairie, and the black willows become more numerous. Many of these trees are huge and beautiful. After mile 8.2, where there's a hairpin curve in the river, deadfall jams are quite likely. The good news is that this stretch is short.

The last mile takes you into the city of Long Prairie. **Take out** on downstream right at the County Road 56 bridge. The banks are usually overgrown with grasses and shrubs, but there's a low area where you can pull a canoe out. This is a designated roadside/riverside rest area with plenty of room for parking.

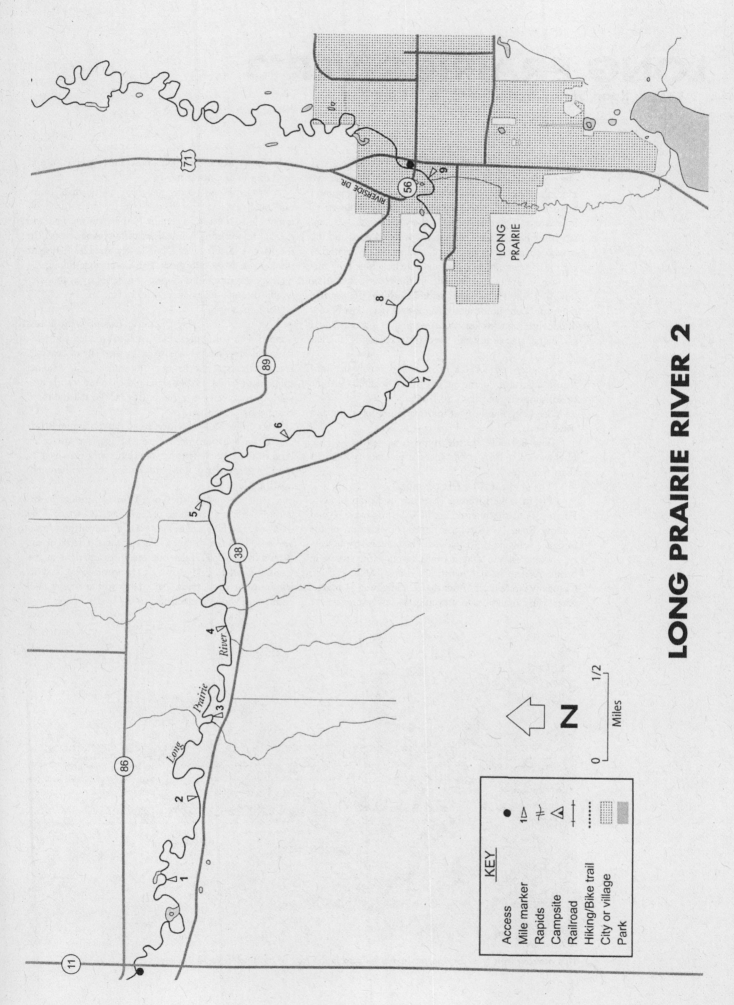

LONG PRAIRIE RIVER 2

KEY

Access
Mile marker
Rapids
Campsite
Railroad
Hiking/Bike trail
City or village
Park

N

Miles

0   1/2

LONG PRAIRIE

RIVERSIDE DR.

Long Prairie River

LONG PRAIRIE RIVER 3
County Road 56 to County Road 14 (14.6 miles)

Another quiet segment of the Long Prairie River, this one has wonderful bird-watching potential. Blue herons, sandhill cranes, kingfishers, blue-winged teals, common mergansers, grebes, and mergansers are some of the marsh inhabitants. Wood ducks, flickers, owls, marsh hawks, and red-tailed hawks frequent both the wooded areas and the marsh. In addition, clouds of multicolored dragonflies patrol for mosquitoes, and some truly huge snapping turtles can be spotted swimming in the clear water. After leaving Long Prairie and before reaching Browerville, there's only one house along 12 miles of river. The beauty of this river segment lies in the interplay of low marshland and higher glacial-outwash levees (ridges of sandy land left by the last glacier).

Be prepared for the occasional deadfall that may require a portage. Taking out at County Road 90 (Jasmine Road) shortens the trip to 10.1 miles.

See Long Prairie 1 for information on **camping and water levels**.

The 8.4-mile **shuttle route** runs north on U.S. Highway 71 to Browerville and east on County Road 14 (East 6th Street).

The **gradient** is 1.7 feet per mile.

Put in at the Riverside Rest Area in the city of Long Prairie. It's at the intersection of U.S. Highway 71 and County Road 56 (Riverside Drive), downstream of the bridge. There's no official access. The bank is low, however, and it's easy to drag a canoe through the riverbank brush. As you head downstream, Long Prairie Packing Company is on the left. After the U.S. Highway 71 bridge, where jams sometimes form, you pass a few houses on the right. Then, in less than half a mile, the town is gone and the Long Prairie heads north.

Black willows border the river just north of town, but the channel is now 80 to 90 feet wide, so deadfalls rarely block the way. By mile 1, the trees are few and sparse, and the Long Prairie flows through open marsh. To the west, U.S. Highway 71 is barely audible. A distant smokestack at the Northern Star Co-op that's along the highway appears and disappears mysteriously as the river winds through its wide prairie marsh. At mile 4.6, a power-line crosses.

At times, the Long Prairie follows outwash levees. Topped with oak groves, they are also wooded with willows and elms next to the river. In these areas, deadfalls create occasional blockages. After mile 7, the channel splits many times. Oxbows and old channels form a network of waterways to explore. (It's easy to tell the main channel by the current.)

At mile 10.1, County Road 90 (Jasmine Road) crosses on a handsome old iron bridge, the last of its kind in the area. When the water's up, you may have to duck to get under. If you want to end the trip here, use upstream left.

After the bridge, the Long Prairie continues meandering, passing a few more oxbows and backwaters. The highway is audible again; farms and a transmission tower are visible in the distance. There's a good view of the Browerville steeple. **Take out** on upstream right at the County Road 14 bridge (not a developed access). A short climb up the steep, grassy bank takes you to a quiet road with a nice wide shoulder next to the bridge.

This narrow iron truss bridge on Jasmine Road is the last of its kind in Todd County.

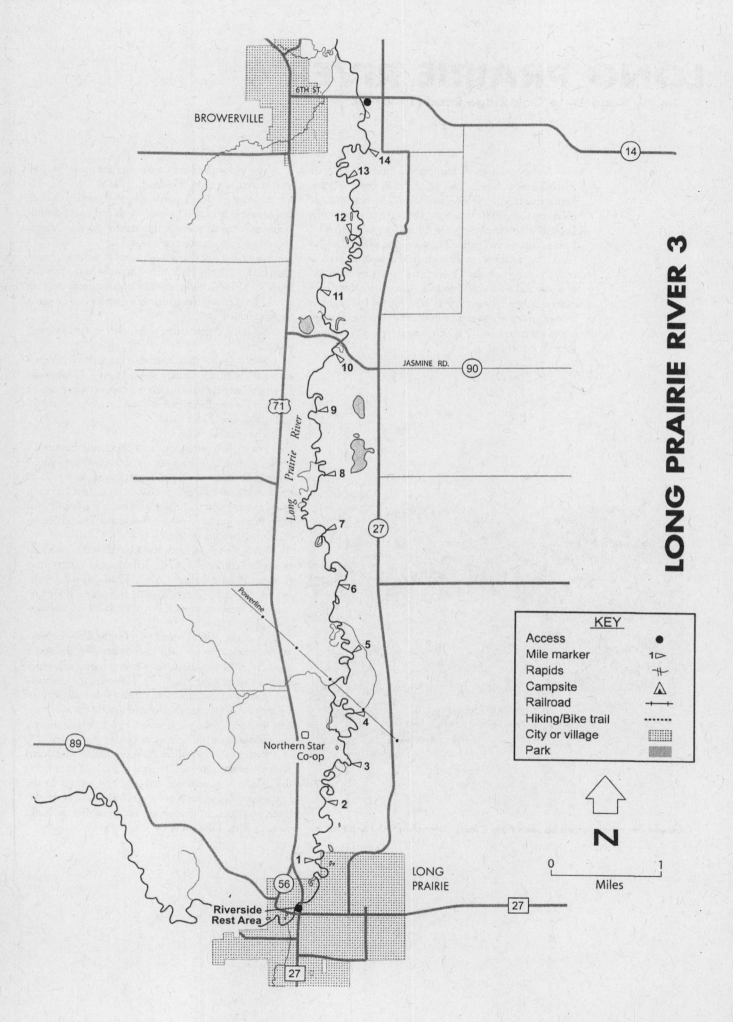

LONG PRAIRIE RIVER 3

BROWERVILLE

6TH ST.

14

13

12

11

JASMINE RD. 90

Long Prairie River

71

10

9

8

7

27

6

5

Powerline

4

Northern Star
Co-op

3

2

1

56

89

LONG
PRAIRIE

**Riverside
Rest Area**

27

27

KEY

Access	●
Mile marker	1▷
Rapids	⊬
Campsite	△
Railroad	+—
Hiking/Bike trail	····
City or village	▒
Park	▓

N

0   Miles   1

LONG PRAIRIE RIVER 4
County Road 14 to Oak Ridge Road (11.2 miles)

For several miles of this trip, the quiet Long Prairie River wanders through the Long Prairie State Wildlife Management Area (WMA), making this segment another good one for wildlife watchers (and what canoeist isn't?). Look for river otters, snapping turtles, kingfishers, hawks, herons, osprey, and eagles. During spring and fall migrations, the waterfowl population in the wetland areas is truly impressive. Around every bend, there's an explosion of wings and duck calls. Potential sightings include ducks of seemingly every variety, from blue-winged teal to grebes to mergansers. If you paddle in the fall, it's a good idea to know when the hunting season is open (generally October through November).

Browerville's steeple can be seen from a long distance on the Long Prairie.

The wide-open landscape makes the name "prairie" fit this river just right. The land in the WMA is a lovely mix of grass and shrub marsh, ridges of wooded upland, and prairie grassland. The river winds and twists considerably as it travels through the marshy prairie. Oxbows and divided channels are common. The Long Prairie is a gentle river, but one characteristic should be noted: floodplain trees, especially black willow, sometimes fall into and block the channel, either partially or completely. Paddlers should be comfortable maneuvering around or dragging over deadfalls.

See Long Prairie 1 for information on **camping** and **water levels.**

The 8.5-mile **shuttle route** runs east on County Route 14, north on County Route 16, and straight onto County Road 62. After crossing the river, County Road 62 becomes County Road 79. Go north on County Road 79 and east on Oak Ridge Road.

The **gradient** is 1.3 feet per mile.

Put in on upstream right at the County Route 14 bridge, east of U.S. Highway 71 on the edge of Browerville. This isn't a developed access, so you must park on the shoulder and slide your boat down a short but steep grassy slope. From the higher ground at Browerville, the Long Prairie quickly flows into low marshland broken by occasional stretches of wooded uplands.

In the first mile, Little Eagle Creek and a few smaller streams come in from the left. A quiet county road (County Road 16, then County Road 79) follows the river on the right. There's a house and a farm along that stretch. Upstream left at County Road 79 (mile 4) is a good place to land.

At about mile 5, the Long Prairie flows into the WMA, where there are no houses or farms for the next 4 miles. Wooded on both banks at first, this is an area where deadfalls often block the river. However, the channel's wide enough that a canoe can often get through without a portage. After leaving the wooded stretch, the river wanders through a vast marsh where cattails, marsh grasses, and willow thickets form a quiet canyon.

Before mile 8.7, where the wide channel that drains Sheets Lake flows in from the right, the Long Prairie leaves the WMA. You see occasional irrigation pumps on the banks now, and a group of corncribs is visible in the distance. More upland areas appear and trees cover the banks on both sides. **Take out** at the Oak Ridge Road bridge.

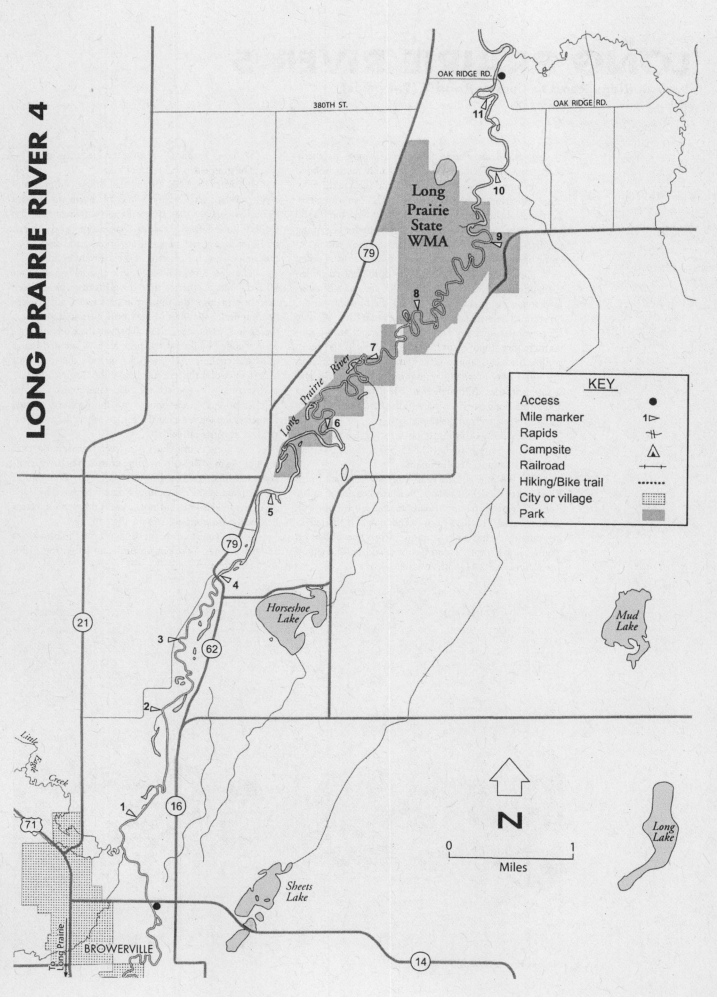

LONG PRAIRIE RIVER 4

OAK RIDGE RD.
OAK RIDGE RD.

11

380TH ST.

10

Long
Prairie
State
WMA

9

79

8

7

Long Prairie River

6

KEY

Access	●
Mile marker	1 ▷
Rapids	╫
Campsite	△
Railroad	┼─┼
Hiking/Bike trail	········
City or village	▨
Park	▨

5

79

4

Horseshoe
Lake

Mud
Lake

21

3

62

2

Little Eagle Creek

1

71

16

Long
Lake

N

0 ——————— 1
Miles

Sheets
Lake

14

BROWERVILLE

To Long Prairie

LONG PRAIRIE RIVER 5
Oak Ridge Road to County Road 7 (9.4 miles)

As the Long Prairie heads into a more northerly ecoregion, the riverbanks are higher and more wooded than on previous segments, with some birch and white pines appearing in the mix of hardwoods. Two tributaries, Turtle Creek and Moran Creek, add to its flow, but it's still a quiet river, making this another good one for beginning paddlers. For those who want a longer journey, taking out at the bridge near Philbrook extends the trip to 12.4 miles.

The best time to take this trip is during the fall, when the hardwoods are in full blazing color and the fall waterfowl migration is underway. (Avoid the hunting season, however!) The wetlands of the Long Prairie River Wildlife Management Area (see Long Prairie River 4) are a popular migratory stopover for huge flocks of ducks and geese, and the birds lay claim to most of the river while they're in the area. Other possible sightings include river otters and snapping turtles. Although there are a few more houses and farms along the river than on the first four segments, the area is relatively undeveloped.

The closest **camping** opportunity is fairly distant: Crow Wing State Park, (218) 825-3075, about 35 miles from the take-out, near Brainerd.

The 9.8-mile **shuttle route** runs west on Oak Ridge Road, north on County Road 79, which becomes County Road 21, east on County Road 66, and south (right) on County Road 7 for 100 yards to the bridge. If you're taking out near Philbrook, continue across the bridge on County Road 7, turn left on County Road 28, and left on Township Road 29 (313th Avenue).

See Long Prairie 1 for **water level** information.
The **gradient** is 1.5 feet per mile.

Put in at the Oak Ridge Road bridge. From Browerville, go east on County Route 14, north on County Route 16, straight on County Road 62 (which becomes County Road 79), and east on Oak Ridge Road. There's no established access: park on the shoulder and drag down the bank on either upstream or downstream right.

The slow-moving Long Prairie is shallow and about 80 feet wide. A quarter mile downstream, Turtle Creek meanders in from the right. You pass two houses before floating under the 400th Street bridge (mile 2.9), where there's another house. After the bridge, there are undeveloped wooded banks for the next mile. A wooded island splits the channel. At mile 5.3, you pass the mouth of Moran Creek on the left. Just before the County Road 26 bridge (mile 5.9) you see the fieldstone abutments of a defunct bridge. A few houses and the Moran Riverside Cemetery are located near the bridge, where access is possible on downstream left.

The Long Prairie flows past several farms in the next 3 miles. At mile 8.2, a powerline crosses. The river, shallow and quiet, is about 150 feet wide now. **Take out** on downstream left at the County Route 7 bridge. The slope up to the road is long but not steep. A drive-in for a farm field and a wide shoulder make the parking easy.

If you continue to the bridge near Philbrook, it's another 3 miles. Take out on upstream left at the 313th Avenue Bridge.

Birders love the Long Prairie.

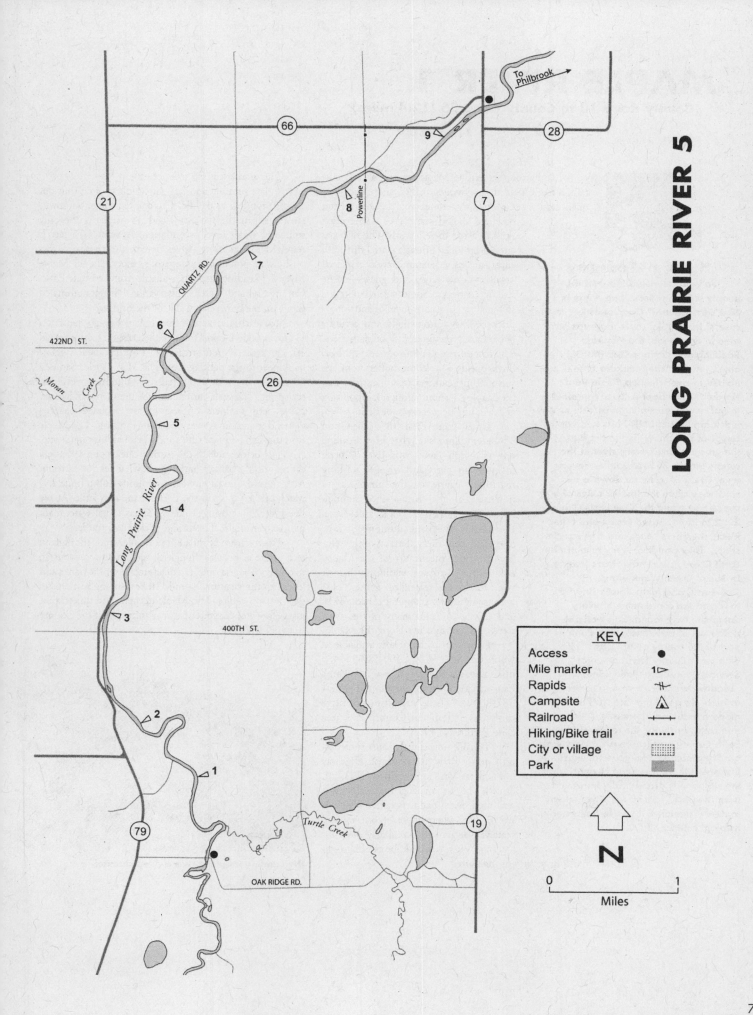

66

21

28

7

9

8 Powerline

QUARTZ RD.

7

6

422ND ST.

Moran Creek

26

5

Long Prairie River

4

3

400TH ST.

2

1

79

Turtle Creek

19

OAK RIDGE RD.

To Philbrook

KEY

Access	●
Mile marker	1▷
Rapids	≠
Campsite	△
Railroad	┼┼
Hiking/Bike trail	·····
City or village	
Park	

N

0   1
Miles

75

MAPLE RIVER 1
County Road 10 to County Road 35 (12.4 miles)

Spring Cleaning

So who cleans up the stuff that people once dumped along rivers in Blue Earth County? Good question. In the case of the Maple, several groups have tried to do the job, the Mankato Paddling and Outings Club (MPOC) among them. "The Mankato area is a hotbed of river cleanup," said Paul Nordell, DNR Adopt-A-River coordinator (http://www.dnr.state.mn.us/adoptriver/index.html). And MPOC has been at the center of the effort. Ten years ago, the group cleaned every river in the county—that's 300 river miles—every year. That's been toned down a bit. Now they clean the last 12 miles of both the Le Sueur and the Blue Earth. From 2002 to 2004, Brand Frentz and other MPOC members conducted a dump-site study. They paddled every mile of Blue Earth County's six main rivers (Maple, Le Sueur, Cobb, Watonwan, Blue Earth, and Minnesota) using GPS to record the coordinates of every dump site they found, an invaluable database. In one sense, "the dump is part of the county's rural past," said Blue Earth County Environmental Services coordinator Julie Conrad. "Landowners were trying to control erosion. It's good that the stuff is old: no modern industrial chemicals. Although dumpsites are ugly, the rivers of Blue Earth County have more pressing water quality problems and government funds just aren't there for dump cleanup. And the situation is dramatically improved from the past." So it's up to volunteers to do the cleaning. If you're interested in helping, contact MPOC.

The narrow, serpentine Maple features a swift current, a few Class I drops, frequent riffles, and equally frequent strainers. Deadfalls sometimes cross the channel and paddlers should have the maneuvering skills to avoid these hazards. The river has cut a deep valley through glacial drift. On cliffs bare of vegetation, layers of glacial deposits—clay, sand, and gravel—create striking patterns. Some steep banks are softened by baby cottonwoods and willow thickets. Big cottonwoods and scrubby red cedars grow among floodplain trees. The combination of lots of trees and high banks yields a welcome buffer from the surrounding countryside. On a sunny day, the Maple is a shimmering ribbon, riffling and winding between wooded banks.

Until you reach the old Good Thunder dump site, that is. Cascading down a high bank, this pile of trash includes car parts and wringer washing machines. Some of the junk washes downstream and litters the channel, becoming a hazard as well as an eyesore. Fortunately, riverbank dumping is now rare, and this mess detracts only temporarily from the beauty of the Maple. And there's plenty of wildlife to distract you. Raccoons, red-tailed hawks, blue herons, swallows, snapping turtles, owls, and turkey vultures: many of the usual riverbank denizens live along the Maple.

Camping in the area is available at Minneopa State Park, (507) 389-5464, 5 miles west of Mankato, and at Mankato's Land of Memories Campground, (507) 387-8649). There are also primitive campsites at Rapidan County Park (see Blue Earth River).

The 6.2-mile shuttle route runs west on County Road 10, north on Highway 66, and east on County Road 35 (179th Street). This isn't an official access, but it is well used. Most paddlers take out downstream left, where there's room to pull your vehicle into the flat grassy ditch for loading. When you park, be careful not to block driveways or mailboxes.

The gradient is 6.9 feet per mile.

In late summer and fall, the Maple is often (but not always!) too low to paddle. The painted gauge on downstream left at the County Road 35 bridge is the only source of water level information. At least 1.75 feet is required for paddling. Over 5 feet, the river becomes pushy and potentially dangerous, especially on Maple River 2. (Readings are not available from the Blue Earth County Soil and Water Conservation District automated gauge on the downstream side of the bridge.)

To reach the access from Mankato, go south on Highway 66 to Good Thunder, then east on County Road 10. The access is on upstream left. Put in at the low grassy bank next to the parking area. The Maple varies between 50 and 80 feet wide and often runs muddy, especially in the spring. The swift current and the prevalence of hairpin curves and strainers on the narrow wooded channel demand attention at every bend in the river. The Maple runs through frequent riffles and Class I rapids on this trip.

Just before mile 2, the rusting carcass of a 1940s-era car rests on the bank, a harbinger of what lies downstream. After the old Good Thunder community dump (mile 4.9) watch out for trash in the river for the next mile. At Ivy Road, the Stone Bridge (mile 5.33) has a high-water mark on upstream right. This bridge is closed to traffic.

Downstream of mile 8, the Maple winds through an area where it looks as though all the old cottonwoods go to die. For about a mile, big dead trees litter the banks and lean into the channel. At mile 10.8, a sliding seat crosses the river on cables. The Maple deepens and quiets a bit just before you take out on downstream left at the County Road 35 Bridge.

The winding Maple carves a deep channel.

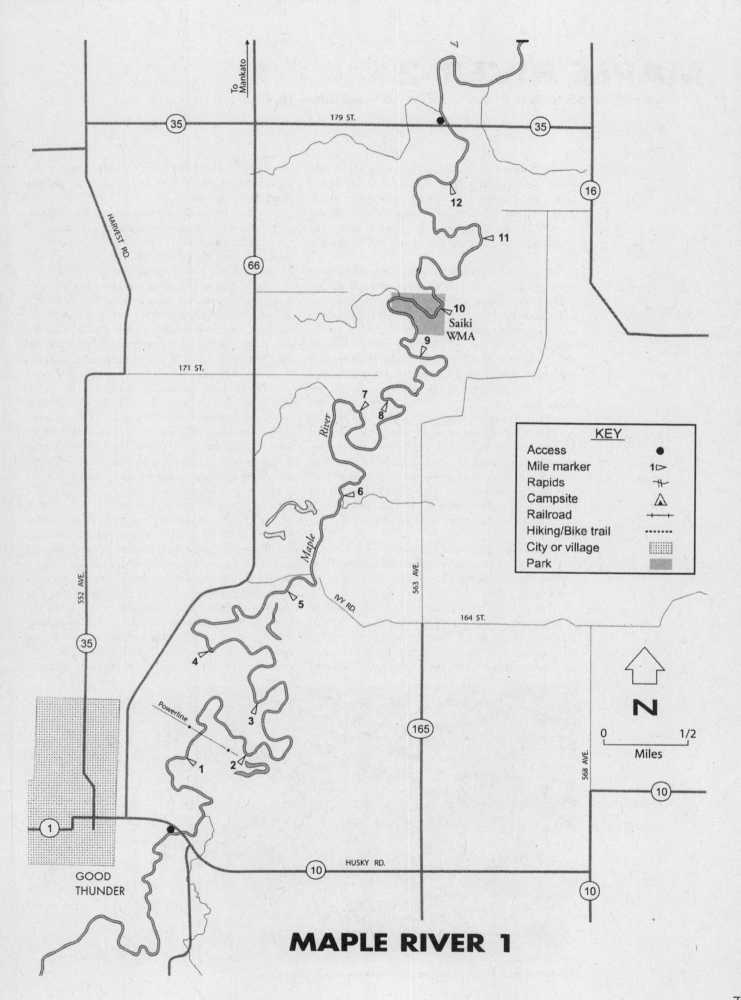

179 ST.

35

35

16

12

11

66

10
Saiki
WMA

9

171 ST.

7

8

River

6

KEY

Access

Mile marker 1

Rapids

Campsite

Railroad

Hiking/Bike trail

City or village

Park

563 AVE.

164 ST.

Maple

IVY RD.

5

4

568 AVE.

165

10

Powerline

3

N

0   1/2

Miles

2

1

552 AVE.

HARVEST RD.

35

1

GOOD
THUNDER

10   HUSKY RD.

10

MAPLE RIVER 1

MAPLE RIVER 2
County Road 35 to Red Jacket Park on Le Sueur River (8.4 miles)

The final reach of the Maple is even livelier than Maple River 1, dropping through numerous riffles and long Class I rapids before racing into the Le Sueur. Beginning river paddlers should not attempt this segment. Although there are fewer strainers along this stretch than upstream, paddlers should still be watchful for these hazards.

In the last 2 miles of the Maple, outcrops of the sandstone and limestone that underlie the glacial drift emerge, adding to the beauty of the wooded gorge. The confluence with the Le Sueur is a grand sight. After a fast run down its intimate wooded channel, the Maple bursts out into the expansive valley of the Le Sueur River, flanked by distant high bluffs. A 4.7-mile paddle down the Le Sueur takes you to Red Jacket Park. Local paddlers use two alternate access points along this stretch to shorten the trip (see shuttle route).

For area **camping** opportunities, see Maple River 1.

The 5-mile **shuttle route** goes west on County Road 35 and north on Highway 66. Paddlers who plan to take out early should turn right onto 193rd Street. This steep gravel road becomes 561st Avenue as it turns south and follows the river. River access is possible under the power line and by the gas pipeline crossing. If you plan to take out at one of these spots, tie a bright marker on the bushes so you don't miss it.

The **gradient** is 9.0 feet per mile.

See Maple River 1 for **water level** information. Local kayakers like levels between 3 and 4 feet for playing on the waves in this section.

Put in on downstream left at the County Road 35 (179th Street) bridge. When you park, please don't block driveways or mailboxes. You can check the painted bridge gauge from the landing. Just downstream, the Maple runs through a long, rocky Class I rapid, followed

quickly by another Class I that swings around a curve. Frequent boulder-strewn drops continue all the way down to the Le Sueur.

On the right bank near the end of the first mile, look for glimpses of the orange-striped sandstone bedrock that underlies the glacial drift. In the second mile, both sandstone and limestone outcrops show up on the left. The Maple's channel is now clearly defined by rocky banks.

As the river passes a house that appears to have been built from local stone, it races, notably, through about a half mile of curving boulder-bed Class I rapids. After several more stretches of rocky fast water, the Maple reaches the Le Sueur. A huge gravel bar marks the middle of the confluence, and cliffs to the northeast rise almost 200 feet above the Le Sueur.

The Le Sueur is about 200 feet wide at the confluence; its width varies downstream. This big river moves as fast as the Maple but with less fanfare. There are fewer, shorter stretches of riffles and the wide channel means far fewer deadfalls than on the Maple. High mounded bluffs, densely wooded and beautiful, flank the river much of the way. Along the left bank, a gravel road swings close to the river at the gas pipeline crossing (mile 4.9) and again right after the powerlines (mile 6.75) cross.

At mile 7.5, an old iron truss bridge with a wooden roadbed, no longer used for traffic, crosses the Le Sueur. The Red Jacket Trail bridge is next, an imposing stone and wood trestle. (In its former life, it was a railroad bridge—built in 1874 to link southwestern Minnesota's vast grain fields with mills in Mankato.) After the trail bridge, **take out** at an unmarked sandy landing on the right before you reach the highway bridge. Red Jacket Park has a picnic shelter, drinking water, and a toilet next to the parking area. If you climb the steps up to the bike trail, you get a great view of the river from the towering trestle bridge.

Handsome rock outcrops bound the Maple near its mouth.

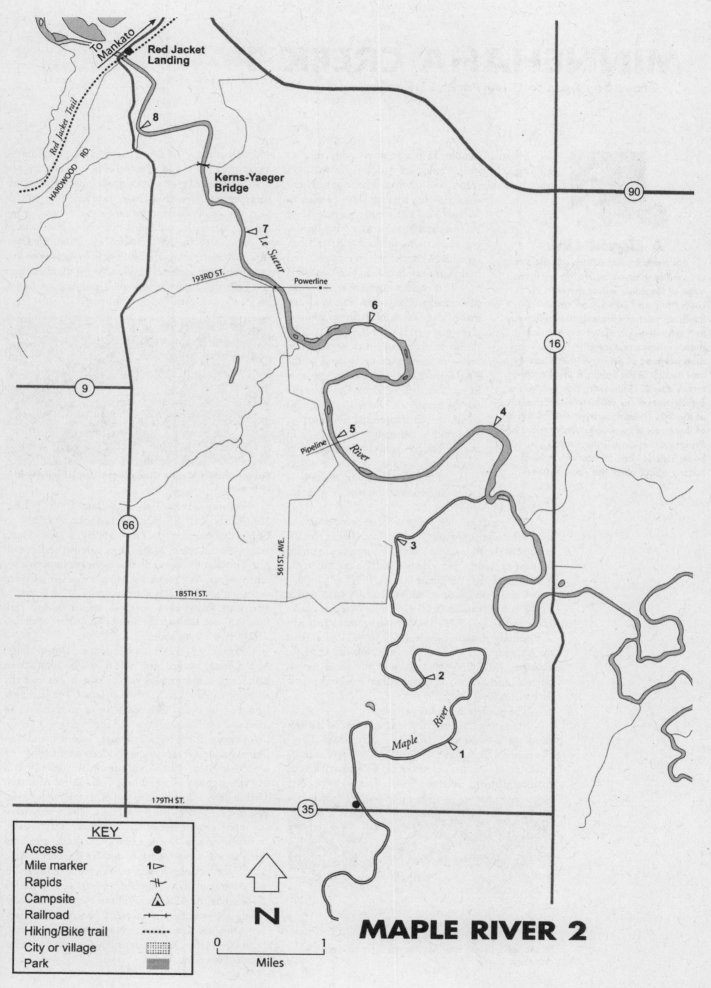

To Mankato

Red Jacket
Landing

Red Jacket Trail

HARDWOOD RD.

8

Kerns-Yaeger
Bridge

7

Le Sueur

193RD ST.

Powerline

6

9

66

561ST. AVE.

Pipeline

River

5

4

3

185TH ST.

2

Maple   River

1

179TH ST.

35

90

16

KEY

Access ●
Mile marker 1▷
Rapids
Campsite △
Railroad ┼
Hiking/Bike trail ┈┈
City or village
Park

N

0   1
Miles

MAPLE RIVER 2

MINNEHAHA CREEK 1

Grays Bay Dam to Utley Park (11.2 miles)

A Liquid Link

Minnehaha flows through the suburb of Minnetonka, skirts the northern edge of Hopkins, winds through St. Louis Park and Edina, and crosses the southern part of Minneapolis on its way to the Mississippi. Its watershed ties these communities together in the common purpose of preserving the beauty and health of the creek. A local architect, Victor C. Gilbertson, has published a collection of his watercolor renderings of the 101 (!) bridges over the full length of the creek in his book, *Watercolors of Bridges over Minnehaha Creek*. The book includes bits of interesting local history about all of the communities.

Suburban paddling at its most diverse, this cruise on winding Minnehaha Creek takes paddlers past wetlands, wooded natural areas, and manicured backyards. Numerous alternate landings allow paddlers to fashion a custom creek trip. Because of various hazards, this isn't a good trip for beginners to do alone. The River Ramblers lead Minnehaha trips each year, and beginners are welcome to join them.

The stream originates at Lake Minnetonka. After a slow start in a quiet marsh, the flow is often lively, running through several boulder bed Class I rapids. Plenty of nice suburban parks, a historic house to visit, a shopping stop at the Knollwood Target, and a lunchtime landing at Taco Bell or Dairy Queen round out the attractions. There's also the bridge count for entertainment. You'd expect some bridges over an intown waterway. In fact, 37 bridges—a fascinating array ranging from small wooden pedestrian bridges to massive interstate highway structures—cross Minnehaha on this trip. (They're not all shown on the map.)

On a practical note, many of the bridges are low and some are dangerous when they trap flood debris. The low culverts of the Highway 169 bridge are common spots for strainers to lodge. Obstructions should be reported to the Minnehaha Creek Watershed District, (952) 471-0590.

Canoe and kayak rentals are available from Aarcee Rental in Minneapolis, (612) 827-5746; Hoigaard's in St. Louis Park, (952) 929-1351 (www.hoigaards.com); REI in Bloomington and Roseville, (952) 884-4215; and from the Minneapolis Parks Board at Lake Nokomis and Lake Calhoun, (612) 230-6400. None of the rental sources offers shuttle service, and so many **shuttle routes** are possible that none is listed.

The **gradient** is 3.6 feet per mile.

Obtaining accurate **water level** information is tricky. Readings are available from the Minnehaha Creek Watershed District: (952) 471-0590; www.minnehaha creek.org, for the discharge from the Gray's Bay Dam on Lake Minnetonka. Medium flow is reported to be 75 to

Minnehaha Creek travels through several beautiful marshes.

150 cfs, but many paddlers report that these levels are too low, that it's safe to paddle at higher levels. There is a new USGS automated gage at Hiawatha Avenue (http:// water-data.usgs.gov/mn/nwis/uv/?site_no=05289800) but in July 2006, readings from this gage and the district gauge did not agree. The watershed district has also installed gauges at Interstate 494 and below the Browndale Dam. When correlated, real-time readings from these three sites will give a more accurate overall picture of the creek's flow and help the district update their paddling guidelines. Watch the watershed Web site for updates.

Suburban Minnehaha Creek looks surprisingly wild at times.

Put in just below Gray's Bay Dam. From Highway 101 (Chanhassen Road) in Minnetonka, turn east on Gray's Bay Boulevard. The canoe landing, at 16501 Gray's Bay Boulevard, has a parking area, a toilet, and a small pier. The clear shallow creek first meanders through a big cattail marsh. As it passes the Minnetonka Civic Center, watch out for the low pedestrian bridge. After Interstate 494, Minnehaha begins to speed up. At Burwell Park (mile 2.3), you can tour the historic house if it's open (call [952] 939-8219 for hours).

At mile 3.6, there's another low pedestrian bridge. After a bridge marked with mile 6.7 (West 36th Street), look for the canoe landing on the right if you have any shopping to do at the Knollwood Target. The landing is followed—in quick succession—by a combination of street and pedestrian bridges and the Highway 7 bridge. Downstream of the highway bridge, Taco Bell and then Dairy Queen have easy to spot landings on the left.

Minnehaha widens into a small lake (mile 9) as it flows through the Meadowbrook Golf Course. After paddling under a railroad bridge and St. Louis Park's Brookside Avenue bridge, you're in Edina. The speedy creek slows and widens as it flows under Highway 100 and enters an impoundment. This is a heavily residential area until after the Browndale Avenue bridge. It's also on the flight path for the Minneapolis airport, with the attendant noise.

At the end of the impoundment, **take out** to the left of the Edina Mills Dam at Williams Park. If you're continuing downstream, you can put in between the bridges, right below the dam. It's a turbulent, but relatively safe, launch spot. Utley Park (with parking, toilets, and water) is across Browndale Avenue.

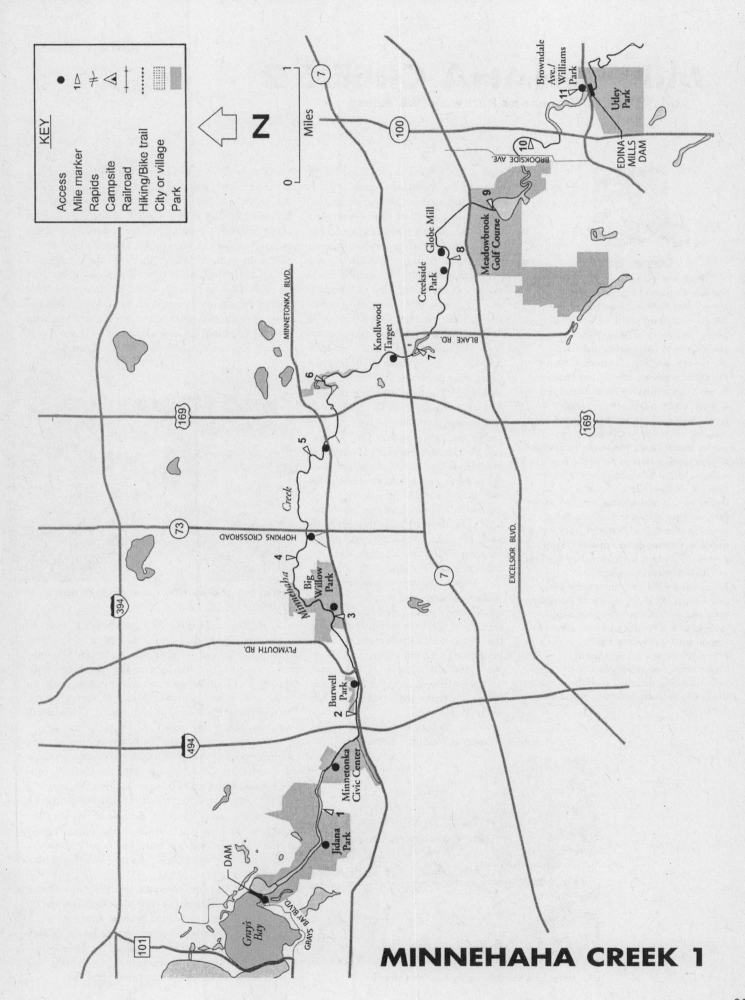

KEY

- Access
1△ Mile marker
≠ Rapids
△ Campsite
|—|— Railroad
····· Hiking/Bike trail
City or village
Park

N

Miles

0

MINNEHAHA CREEK 1

Brokdale Ave./ Williams Park
11
Utley Park
EDINA MILLS DAM

10

9

BROOKSIDE AVE.
Meadowbrook Golf Course

8
Globe Mill
Creekside Park

BLAKE RD.

7
Knollwood Target

6

5

MINNETONKA BLVD.

Creek

HOPKINS CROSSROAD

4
Big Willow Park

Minnehaha

3

PLYMOUTH RD.

2
Burwell Park

EXCELSIOR BLVD.

Minnetonka Civic Center

1
Jidana Park

DAM

Gray's Bay

GRAYS BAY BLVD.

MINNEHAHA CREEK 2
Utley Park to Minnehaha Parkway (9.8 miles)

Love Story

It all started with a photo. A friend's daguerreotype image of Minnehaha Falls inspired Henry Wadsworth Longfellow to write his epic poem, *The Song of Hiawatha.* Longfellow himself never visited Minnesota, and his information about the Ojibwa people came from Henry Rowe Schoolcraft's writings about the Ojibwa and the Dakota. Hiawatha was a real historical leader, but eastern Iroquois rather than Ojibwa. In one sense, Longfellow's Hiawatha resembled his namesake: he sought peace for his people. Longfellow's romantic tale of Ojibwa warrior Hiawatha and his lovely Dakota bride Minnehaha is really about forging a peace between these two warring tribes. Our romantic poet wove together threads from various Native American cultures and published his epic in 1855. Almost immediately, Minnehaha Falls became a must-see destination. As many as 39 trains a day, crowded with visitors to see the falls, arrived at the Princess Depot, a train station built in the late 1800s. Minnehaha Park is still a great destination. And after you finish your paddling adventure on the creek, the lovely waterfall awaits, just over the bridge.

This is the urban (as opposed to suburban) half of Minnehaha Creek. And like Minnehaha Creek 1, this is not a trip for beginners to take alone, as there are assorted hazards. Join the River Ramblers on their annual trip instead, and watch out for the deadfalls and numerous very low bridges.

After a short jaunt in Edina, the stream crosses south Minneapolis. Interestingly, there's more parkland bordering the city stream than along its suburban alter ego. Back in the 1800s, Minneapolis had the vision to create a park system, now nationally famous, that includes a parkway enclosing most of Minnehaha Creek. Bike paths now follow the creek as well, making a bicycle shuttle possible. The trip features a Class II drop (with an easy portage), stretches of Class I rapids, a paddle through Hiawatha Golf Course, and 54 bridges. (They're not all shown on the map.) This urban adventure ends about a half mile before the creek drops over the spectacular, 53-foot-high Minnehaha Falls. Below the falls at Minnehaha Park, the creek races through a half mile of rocky, wooded gorge to the Mississippi. Ten more bridges cross the creek after the take-out.

There's plenty of rather tame wildlife to keep you company. Habituated ducks, geese, green herons, white egrets, and northern harriers are among the inhabitants. Black-crowned night herons have been spotted hanging around West 54th Street.

See Minnehaha Creek 1 for information on **canoe and kayak rentals** and **water levels.**

The **gradient** is 7.6 feet per mile. (This includes the drop at West 54th Street.)

Put in on river left, downstream of the Browndale Avenue Bridge in Edina. The canoe access in Utley Park has parking, a picnic shelter, and bathrooms nearby. Minnehaha, shaded and narrow, winds tightly. Even when the creek's running low, you must duck at the arched Wooddale Avenue bridge to avoid the pipe that bisects the arch. At West 54th Street, the portage trail (mile 1.1) for the Class II rapids begins on the left. It's a short, boulder-filled drop served up in two separate pitches. For those who run it, it's most dangerous at low water. If you bottom out and capsize, concrete blocks on the streambed may do a lot of damage to you and your boat. At high water, a nice surfing wave forms.

One of Minnehaha's 101 bridges frames a pair of paddlers.

Heading under France Avenue (mile 1.8) feels like a journey into Middle Earth. As you enter the long, curving, corrugated metal culvert, buried far below the road, you can't see the light at the other end—truly spooky. Plus it's followed by a cemetery. After the parkway begins at Xerxes Avenue (mile 2.8), access is possible at any number of spots along the route. The bike trail now runs next to the creek.

Between Interstate 35-W and the Portland Avenue bridge (recently rebuilt), Minnehaha runs through several entertaining Class I drops. After the Cedar Avenue bridge and a pedestrian bridge, the creek flows left. To the right, the connecting stream to Lake Nokomis leads to an access and parking lot. Because of two very low bridges in the Hiawatha Golf Course downstream, many paddlers opt to take out here. For those enterprising souls who continue, lost golf balls may be salvaged from the streambed.

After exiting Lake Hiawatha, the creek flows another 1.2 miles to the Minnehaha Parkway bridge. Take out on downstream right, at a mowed parkway area along South 39th Avenue. **Warning: Don't go past the buoys; there's a lowhead dam at Hiawatha Avenue and the 53-foot-high falls is not far beyond.** To visit the spectacular falls, you can cross the bridge and go into Minnehaha Park.

Life jacket and helmet required for this stretch.

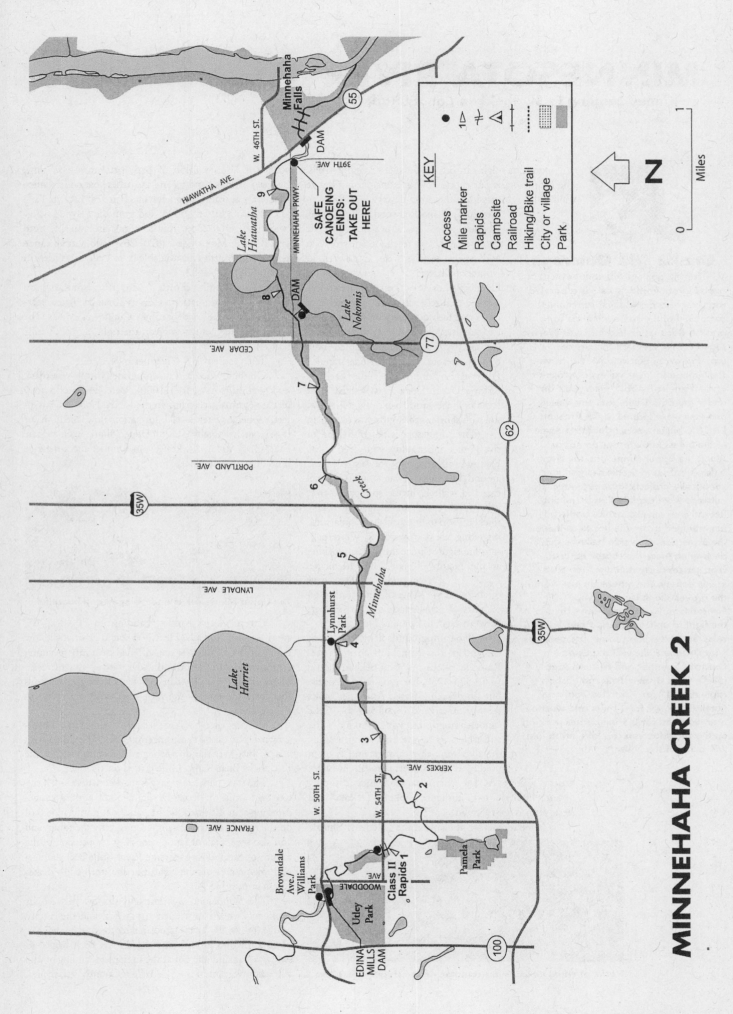

MINNEHAHA CREEK 2

MINNESOTA RIVER 1
Kinney Landing to Skalbekken County Park (9.3 miles)

Gneiss Old Outcrops

For the geologically uninformed, gneiss (pronounced "nice") is a banded rock, very hard and most commonly composed of the same minerals as granite. Back when Glacial River Warren raged across southern Minnesota, scouring away glacial drift and carving the Minnesota River valley, outcrops of ancient gneiss bedrock emerged from under the drift. Geologists say these gneisses were formed in the Archean Eon, 3.6 billion years ago. That's some of the oldest known rock on earth. Along the Upper Minnesota, the river valley's Wild and Scenic designation specifically protects these dramatic outcrops from exploitation by mining. Recently, an environmental battle has been waged over whether to continue the protection. One side believes that destroying these handsome natural features seriously damages the area's scenic beauty. The other side just wants the gravel. Clean Up the River Environment (CURE) has been active in the fight to uphold the Wild and Scenic rules. To hike among some nice outcrops near Granite Falls, visit the Gneiss Outcrops Scientific and Natural Area (SNA). From Granite Falls, go east on Highway 212 for 1.5 miles, south on County Road 40 for 1 mile, and west on a gravel road for 0.5 mile. After parking on the shoulder, you can hike north into 241 acres of the SNA.

From its origins in Big Stone Lake to Granite Falls, the Minnesota is impounded by six dams. From Granite Falls to the Mississippi, the river flows freely. Between Granite Falls and Redwood Falls, its wide, wooded valley has almost no riverside development. This reach, designated Wild and Scenic by the state, is covered in Minnesota Rivers 1, 2, and 3. Renville County's riverside campsites make possible a canoe-camping trip through an area that looks and feels quite remote. On this first trip, the river flows quietly, free of rapids. (Prospective canoe-campers should note that Minnesota River 2 includes rapids.) For several miles near the end of the trip, historic Upper Sioux Agency State Park lies along the south bank. Taking out at the park shortens the journey to 6.6 miles.

The Minnesota is a catfish kind of river: quiet and muddy, with deep holes. Flathead catfish, one of the largest catfish around, lurk in these waters, as do channel cats and walleye. In the spring, the river valley is alive with birdsong, and willow thickets seem to be especially popular with migrating flocks of warblers. White pelicans are sighted frequently, often flocking at the mouth of the Yellow Medicine. Eagles are also common. Paddlers have often found the bones of long-dead bison or parts of an elk rack on the sandbars between Granite Falls and New Ulm.

Two campgrounds flank the river at the end of this trip; both charge a fee. Renville County's Skalbekken Park, (320) 523-3768, has a shelter and toilets, but no drinking water. At Upper Sioux Agency State Park, (320) 564-4777, the canoe campground, with drinking water and toilets, is by the boat ramp. (When the river's up, this campground is often used by catfish anglers who fish at night: expect noise.) At the main campground, camping options include two authentic-looking Dakota tipis (reservations are required).

Canoe rentals are available at the state park. Shuttle

service is also available, if park personnel have time, between Kinney Landing and the park's boat ramp. Canoe rentals are available from Mitlyng's Bait near Lac Qui Parle State Park, (320) 269-5593, and from the Dawson Mini-Mall, (320) 769-2036. Kayak rentals are available from Java River in Montevideo, (320) 269-7106. Group canoe rentals and shuttles are available from Lentz Outfitters in Echo, (507) 925-4482.

The 8.2-mile shuttle route runs southeast on Highway 67 and north on County Road 21. After crossing the river, the road becomes County Road 10. The access is in the county park on the right, a quarter mile past the bridge.

The gradient is 0.6 feet per mile.

On the USGS gage at Montevideo (http://waterdata. usgs.gov/mn/nwis/uv?05311000), water levels of 5 to 9 feet are optimal, according to the DNR. Flood stage is 14 feet. General water level information (low, medium, or high) can be obtained from Upper Sioux Agency State Park, (320) 564-4777. Leave your number and a message if no one is in the office.

The Upper Minnesota is undeveloped and beautiful.

Put in at the Kinney Landing on Highway 67, south of Granite Falls. Heavily wooded at first, the low banks of the Minnesota are softened by a mix of young cottonwoods and willow thickets farther downstream. Hazel Creek (mile 1.3) comes in from the right. The hills that form the sides of the wide river valley are visible in the distance.

Halfway along a large island on the left, an overgrown DNR canoe campsite (mile 2.65) is marked with a sign. Just past the downstream end of the island, the Fredericks Boat Ramp (mile 3.0) is on river left.

The state park boundary is marked with a small yellow sign (mile 6.4) on the right. Soon after, a canoe-camping sign is posted by the park boat ramp (mile 6.6) on the right. The canoe campground is by the ramp, and you also see a rack of rental canoes. Just upstream of the mouth of the Yellow Medicine River (mile 8.2) there's a park picnic area on the right, but the steep bank makes access impossible.

The Minnesota runs fast and shallow between its confluence with Hawk Creek (mile 8.5) and the county bridge (mile 8.9). Curving north after the bridge, the river flows through a lovely wooded halfmile. As it begins to swing east again, take out at the unmarked landing on the left, just upstream of the Skalbekken County Park shelter.

Flocks of white pelicans are common on the Upper Minnesota.

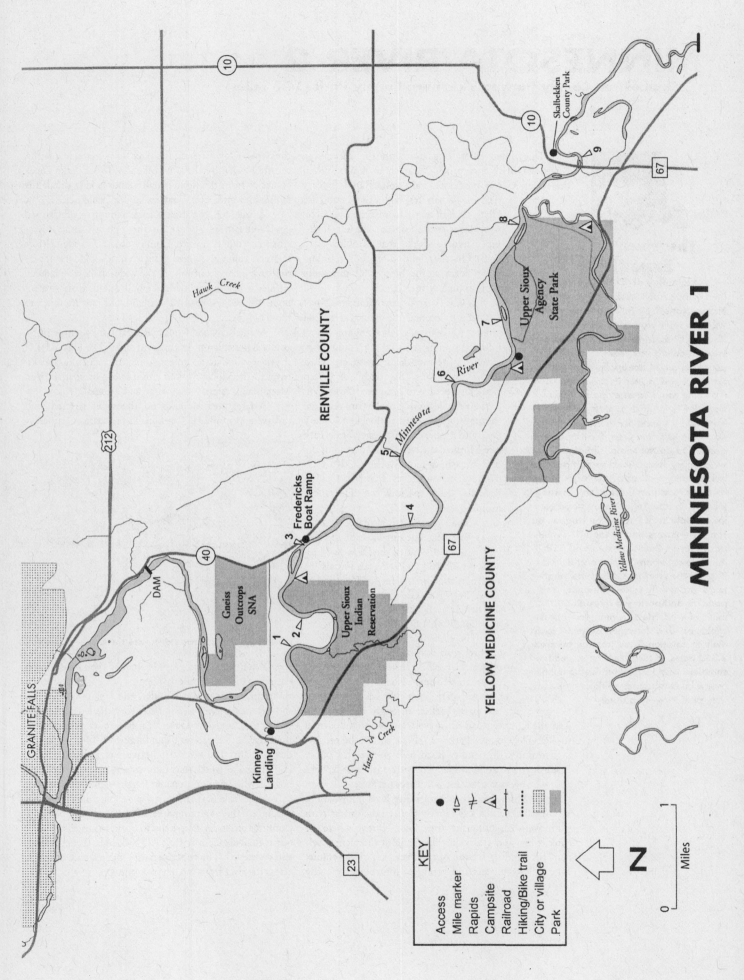

MINNESOTA RIVER 1

RENVILLE COUNTY

YELLOW MEDICINE COUNTY

Skalbekken County Park

Upper Sioux Agency State Park

Upper Sioux Indian Reservation

Gneiss Outcrops SNA

GRANITE FALLS

DAM

Kinney Landing

3 Fredericks Boat Ramp

Hawk Creek

Minnesota River

Yellow Medicine River

Hazel Creek

KEY

Access	●
Mile marker	1 ▷
Rapids	≠
Campsite	△
Railroad	
Hiking/Bike trail	⋯⋯
City or village	
Park	

N

Miles

0   1

MINNESOTA RIVER 2
Skalbekken County Park to Vicksburg County Park (14.3 miles)

The Hudson Bay Expedition

In late May of 2005, two young men camped at Vicksburg County Park. Minnesotans Scott Miller and Todd Foster were on their way up the Minnesota River, in flood at the time. (Yes, they were paddling *upstream*.) Seventy-five years earlier, Minneapolis teenagers Eric Sevareid and Walter Port had paddled the same route, journeying by canoe from the Twin Cities to Hudson Bay. Inspired by young Sevareid's book, *Canoeing with the Cree*, Scott and Todd decided to do the same. Although a bad wrist injury forced Todd to quit paddling in late June, Scott and new team member Matt Lutz finished this incredible journey. In late August, they paddled into remote York Factory on Hudson Bay. The adventurers had canoed 335 miles upstream on the Minnesota and 550 miles downstream (north) on the Red River of the North, paddled the length of huge and windy Lake Winnepeg, and paddled and portaged through 500 miles of wilderness, running countless rapids on wild Canadian rivers to reach their destination. Their journey covered 2,250 miles. A record of the expedition, complete with journal entries, is online (www.hudsonbayexpedition.com), and they plan to write a book.

This quiet, interesting route on the Minnesota River ends with a surprise—a stretch of rapids. When the water level is moderate, Patterson's Rapids rates a Class I. When it's high, the rapids are Class II and merit close attention. The river drops over a ledge on the left, forming a hydraulic like that of a low-head dam. On the right, three-foot standing waves form at the bottom of the rocky drop in high water.

Gneiss outcrops (see Minnesota River 1 sidebar) decorate the banks at several points. An especially large outcrop across from the landing at Vicksburg County Park creates a 22-foot-deep upstream eddy. Known locally as "Big Eddy" or "Deep Eddy," it's reputed to be a great fishing spot.

At the beginning of the trip, there are campgrounds at both Skalbekken County Park and Upper Sioux Agency State Park (see Minnesota River 1). At the end of the trip, Vicksburg County Park, (320) 523-3768, also known as Renville County Park #2, has a spacious riverside canoe-camping area.

Canoe rentals are available at Mitlyng's Bait near Lac qui Parle State Park, (320) 269-5593, and at the Dawson Mini-Mall, (320) 769-2036. Kayak rentals are available from Java River in Montevideo, (320) 269-7106. Group canoe rentals and shuttles are available from Lentz Outfitters in Echo, (507) 925-4482.

The 14.6-mile shuttle route is along a gravel road that offers panoramic views of the river valley. Instead of leaving the park on County Road 10, take the unpaved park road that leads east from the park shelter through the park to Renville County Road 81 (gravel). Go east to the turnoff to Renville County Park #2, about a mile before the intersection with County Road 6. If you reach County Road 6, you've gone too far. The park road is unpaved.

The average gradient is 1.6 feet per mile.

See Minnesota River 1 for water level information.

Skalbekken Park is a lovely place in the spring, with wildflowers carpeting the forest floor. Put in where the bank is low and grassy, just upstream of the picnic shelter. This winding section of the river feels quite remote, with willow thickets and young cottonwoods softening

the banks. Downstream, the river flows past a few farms, mostly hidden by trees. At mile 2.3, Wood Lake Creek comes in from the right. Small islands briefly divide the Minnesota into several narrow braided channels.

At mile 5.8, the ancient rock outcrops—grayish-red gneiss—begin to appear on the right. A mile downstream is the Redwood County Road 7 bridge. More bedrock follows. Large, glacial-erratic boulders appear midstream. At about mile 9, the wide, shallow streambed is filled with boulders and a small island. If the water's high and fast, go left of the island and pay attention to those boulders.

At the Redwood County Road 19 bridge (mile 10.5), access is possible on downstream right. The hilly sides of the river valley are no longer visible, and agricultural fields cover the floodplain behind a thin screen of riparian trees. More islands appear, some large and wooded.

A large rock outcrop on the right, covered with cedars, marks mile 12.3 and breaks the sense of flatness.

Ancient gneiss outcrops decorate the Upper Minnesota.

You'll hear the rapids before you see them. Patterson's Rapids (mile 13) begins at a rock outcrop on the right, a midstream boulder, and a sloping ledge on the left. Stay right of center to avoid the ledge. At high water, the rapids are Class II, a backroller forms below the ledge, and three-foot standing waves fill the channel downstream. The river drops five feet in a third-mile, including the riffles that follow. Several years ago, two boaters who were unprepared for the rapids drowned.

After little Sacred Heart Creek joins the Minnesota on the left, there's an unmarked canoe landing and a road. Continue around a sharp bend to the left to reach the takeout at Renville County Park #2 (Vicksburg County Park), also on the left. The concrete ramp, marked with a sign, is across the river from the big rock outcrop.

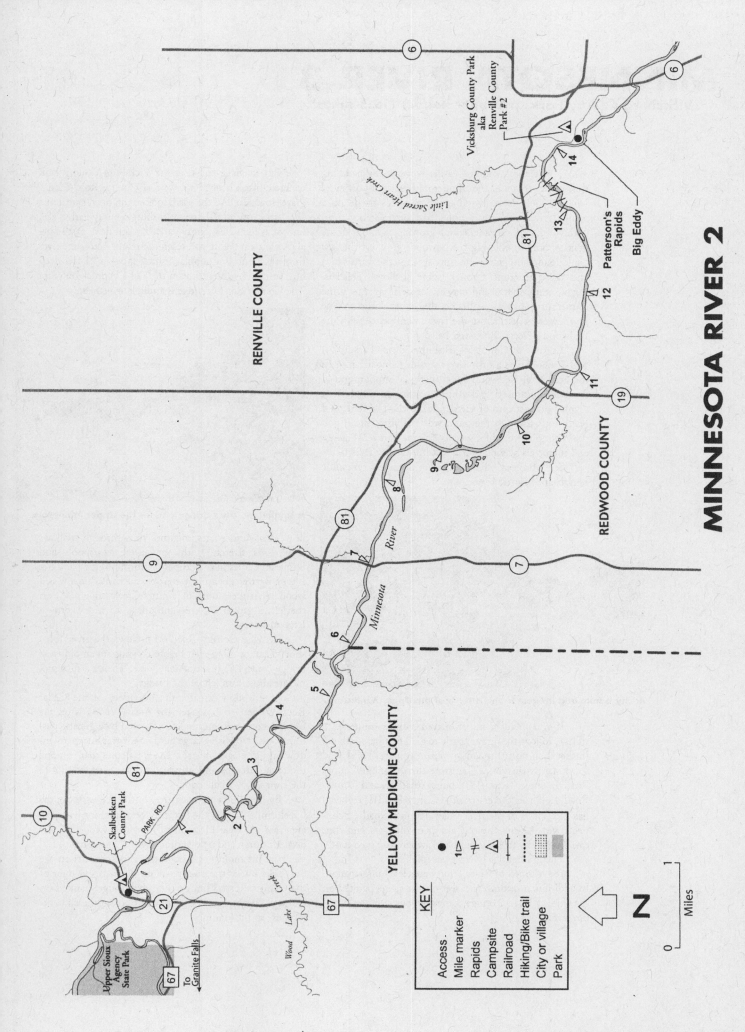

MINNESOTA RIVER 2

RENVILLE COUNTY

REDWOOD COUNTY

YELLOW MEDICINE COUNTY

Little Sacred Heart Creek

Vicksburg County Park aka Renville County Park #2

Patterson's Rapids

Big Eddy

Minnesota River

Wood Lake Creek

Skalbekken County Park

PARK RD.

Upper Sioux Agency State Park

To Granite Falls

KEY

- Access.
- 1△ Mile marker
- ≠ Rapids
- △ Campsite
- ┼ Railroad
- ···· Hiking/Bike trail
- ▦ City or village
- ▨ Park

N

0 — Miles — 1

MINNESOTA RIVER 3
Vicksburg County Park to County Road 1 (12.5 miles)

The recommended weather forecast for paddling this scenic stretch of the Minnesota River is a northwest wind: a cool, dry tailwind is the paddler's friend on a straight river. The river flows past bedrock outcrops, with weathered red cedars often growing right out of the granite. Some noble big cottonwoods grow on the low banks. Sand and gravel bars appear when the water's low, and the river runs through some shallows. Pelicans, eagles, kingfishers, and hawks, as well as the usual numerous songbirds, provide the entertainment. The journey ends just before the river's confluence with the Redwood River in Redwood Falls.

At Renville County's Vicksburg County Park, (320) 523-3768, there's a primitive riverside campsite next to the access. In Redwood Falls, there's a campground at Alexander Ramsey Park (http://www.rrcnet.org/~ramseypk/) downstream of the dam in town. The Redwood River runs through the park, worth a visit even if you don't camp there. Hiking trails lace the park's 217 acres, and there's an overlook for beautiful Ramsey Falls.

See Minnesota River 2 for information on canoe rentals and shuttle service.

Rocky banks add interest to this stretch of the Upper Minnesota.

If you prefer a mostly paved **shuttle route** (12.8 miles), follow the gravel park road 0.8 mile southeast (rather than north) to County Road 6 (paved) and head south across the river. The route then runs on County Road 9, County Road 17, County Road 25, and County Road 1. If you prefer scenic, County Road 15 (gravel) has nice views of the river valley. County Road 15 connects with County Road 6 north of the river and runs east all the way to County Road 1, where you turn south.

The **gradient** is 1.1 feet per mile.

See Minnesota River 1 for **water level** information. In addition, a reading of 5 feet on the gauge painted on the County Road 1 bridge at the take-out indicates medium water levels.

Put in on river left at the Vicksburg County Park concrete-plank boat ramp, west of County Road 6 on a gravel road. To find the road, look for an open gate and a sign listing opening dates. (Vicksburg County Park is also known as Renville County Park #2.) You drive past several picnic areas before you reach the ramp. Across the river from the ramp is a popular fishing spot—a 22-feet-deep hole formed by the upstream eddy of a bedrock outcrop. The County Road 6 bridge is a mile downstream.

A single-lane truss bridge crosses the Upper Minnesota.

The Minnesota sometimes runs through shallows along this stretch, with occasional whirlpools and upstream eddies in the deeper sections, but the paddling is easy. Between bedrock outcrops, the banks are low and wooded. At the mouth of Timm's Creek (mile 3.45) on the left, a gap in the tree line opens a window onto a large meadow.

Renville County Road 21 follows the river for a short distance on the left before crossing on an old truss bridge (mile 4.9) just one lane wide. There's a nice picnic area upstream left of the bridge.

A mile downstream, the boundary of the Cedar Rock Wilderness Management Area (WMA) is on the right. A corn field on the left, followed by a grazing pasture populated with a large herd of cows, is another window onto the agricultural scene. The cows roam among the rock outcrops and wander into the river, adding to the river's *E. coli* collection.

By the time you reach the confluence with Smith's Creek (mile 9.2) on the left, the rock outcrops have disappeared. At mile 11, signs of North Redwood appear: boulder riprap and a powerline. On the left at mile 11.7, you pass the mouth of a flood diversion channel on the left. **Take out** at the boat ramp on downstream right of the County Road 1 bridge. The river gauge, painted on a bridge pier, is visible from the ramp, and there's parking next to the landing.

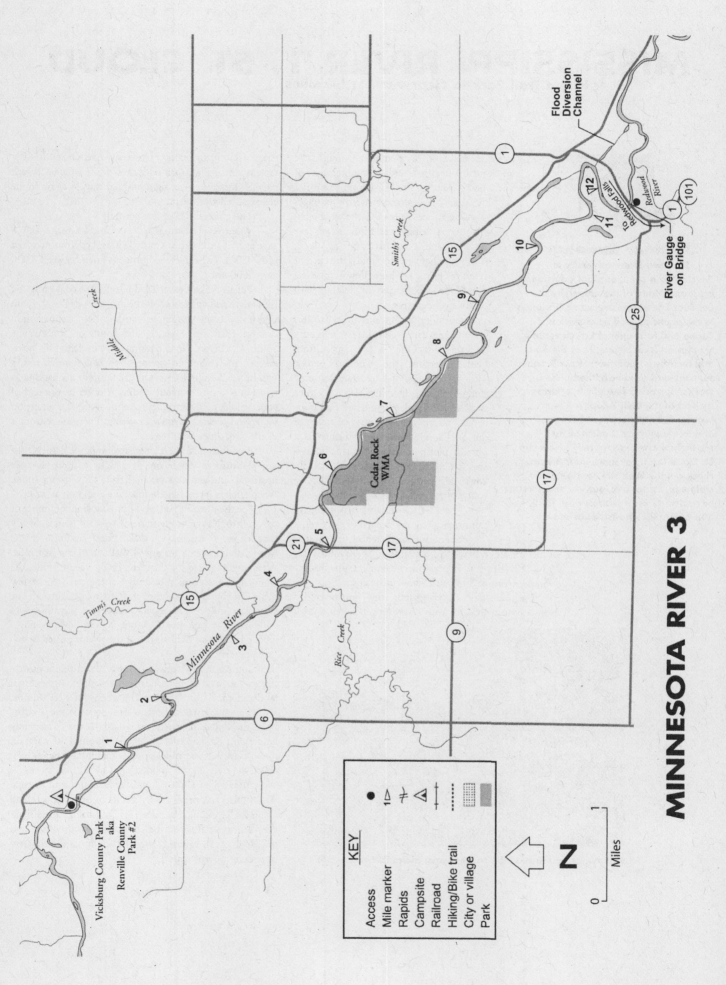

MINNESOTA RIVER 3

Flood Diversion Channel

River Gauge on Bridge

To Redwood Falls

Redwood River

Redwood Falls

Cedar Rock WMA

Smith's Creek

Rice Creek

Timm's Creek

Middle Creek

Minnesota River

Vicksburg County Park
aka
Renville County Park #2

KEY

- ● Access
- 1△ Mile marker
- ‡ Rapids
- △ Campsite
- ┼┼ Railroad
- ┈┈ Hiking/Bike trail
- ▦ City or village
- ▨ Park

N

Miles
0   1

MISSISSIPPI RIVER 1, ST. CLOUD
Beaver Island Trail Park to Clearwater (12.4 miles)

Outdoor Endeavors

St. Cloud State University is developing a great outdoor education program. Many of the university's Outdoor Endeavors programs are open to the public as well as to students. Canoe and recreational kayak rentals, shuttles on local segments of the Sauk and the Mississippi rivers, kayak pool sessions-and canoe-paddle building workshops are a few of the offerings. As part of the DNR Adopt-A-River program, the department holds an annual cleanup on 2 miles of the Mississippi River, above and below the St. Cloud Dam. For more information, check out the Web site (www.stcloud state.edu/campusrec/outdoorendeavors) or contact director Ivan Bartha, (320) 308-6691, ilbartha@stcloudstate.edu.

An intricate network of channels through the wooded and beautiful Beaver Islands is the highlight of this popular canoeing route on the Mississippi River. For the first 2 miles, these narrow passageways are a nice contrast to the wide open channel of the big river. More islands lace the channel downstream as well. Although there are no rapids, the current is quite strong at high flows; paddlers should be experienced in dealing with pushy river currents.

Considering its proximity to St. Cloud, the river corridor is relatively undeveloped. Only a few agricultural fields interrupt the wooded banks. Although clusters of houses are scattered along the route, there are also some nice stretches of completely undeveloped riverbank. The trip begins just downstream of the St. Cloud Dam, where fishing is a popular pastime. Anglers say smallmouth bass fishing is good all along this reach. You're likely to spot great blue herons, bald eagles, hawks, and wild turkeys.

The DNR maintains two primitive campsites along this stretch of the river.

Canoe and kayak rentals and **shuttle** service for are available from Outdoor Endeavors: (320) 255-3772; http://www.stcloudstate.edu/campusrec/out-doorendeavors, at St. Cloud State University.

The 12.8-mile **shuttle route** runs north on 3rd Avenue South, west on 15th Street South, north on 5th Avenue South, and east on University Avenue South. After crossing the bridge, turn right on County Route 8, which parallels the river. Turn right on Highway 24 to get to the access on upstream left.

The **gradient** is 2.1 feet per mile.

Water level readings are available from the USGS gage at St. Cloud (http://waterdata.usgs.gov/mn/nwis/uv?05270700). The DNR recommends levels between 3,000 and 9,000 cfs.

Put in at the Beaver Island Trail Park boat ramp, on river right downstream of the St. Cloud Dam. From University Avenue South, go south on 5th Avenue South, east on 15th Street South, and south on 3rd Avenue South. Just before the Q parking lot, turn left at the boat-access sign. There's no overnight parking here; in fact, a sign in the parking lot next to the ramp limits parking to two hours only. To avoid finding a ticket at the end of your paddle, park personnel recommend leaving a note on your windshield that you're canoeing. There are restrooms in the park office building.

As you launch, there's a great view of the dam. A fishing platform is visible on river right a short distance upstream, and you may see anglers on the opposite shore. Avian anglers (great blue herons) are common as well.

For the next 2 miles, you can choose any number of routes through the lovely maze of wooded islands. Sandy beaches on some islands make good landings. If the water's down, watch for gravel shallows in the first mile. After a golf course on the right in the second mile, the wooded banks seem pleasantly undeveloped for a few miles. If you plan to stop at Putnam's Pasture Canoe Campsite (mile 3.3) on the left, watch carefully: the river's wide and the sign small. About a mile downstream, a wooded island on the left side of the river is posted as private property.

You reach the halfway point of the trip as a power-line crosses and there's a farm on the right. Agricultural land and a few cabins replace the woods for a bit. Almost a mile after the woods return, Boy Scout Point is across from the downstream end of a large island. The sandy landing for the campsite (mile 9.6) is around the point on the left. In the next mile, several large houses perch high above the river on the wooded right bank.

After mile 11, the Clear Lake Scientific and Natural Area (SNA) comprises nearly a mile of undeveloped land along the left bank. At mile 12.1, old bridge piers flank the Clearwater River at the confluence on the right, and the Highway 24 bridge is ahead. **Take out** at the concrete boat ramp on upstream left.

Sometimes you find a little sandy beach along the Mississippi.

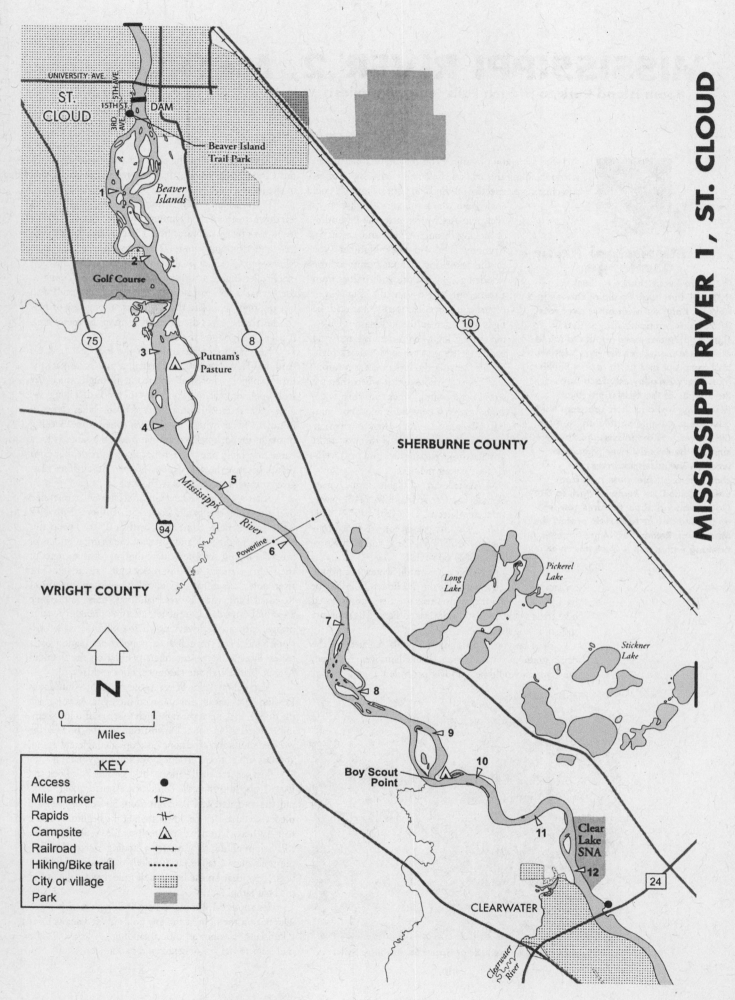

UNIVERSITY AVE.

ST. CLOUD

15TH ST.
5TH AVE.
3RD AVE.
DAM

Beaver Island Trail Park

Beaver Islands

1

2

Golf Course

75

3

Putnam's Pasture

4

8

Mississippi River

5

94

Powerline

6

SHERBURNE COUNTY

Long Lake

Pickerel Lake

Stickner Lake

WRIGHT COUNTY

N

0   1
Miles

7

8

9

10

Boy Scout Point

11

Clear Lake SNA

12

24

CLEARWATER

Clearwater River

KEY

Access	●
Mile marker	1▷
Rapids	⫢
Campsite	◬
Railroad	┼┼┼
Hiking/Bike trail	······
City or village	▦
Park	▨

MISSISSIPPI RIVER 2, METRO

Boom Island Park to Hidden Falls Park (8.4 miles)

The Mississippi River Challenge

Here's your chance to "lock through" in a huge flotilla of canoes and kayaks, hang out with other river rats (in 2006, Minneapolis Mayor Rybak signed up), learn more about the Mighty Miss, raise money for the river's future, and camp out and party at Fort Snelling (not otherwise allowed). Each August, the Friends of the Mississippi River (www.fmr.org) and their sponsors hold a two-day, 44-mile paddle on the Twin Cities stretch of the Mississippi River to support the Friends' river protection work (www.mississippiriver challenge.org). The route runs from Coon Rapids Dam Regional Park to Grey Cloud Island, and participants can sign up for one day or two. Help protect the Mississippi. Remember, Minneapolis's drinking water comes from this river.

Set aside any prejudices you may have about urban rivers. Paddling this trip on the Mighty Mississippi offers a fascinating perspective on the Twin Cities. From the cool angle from which you view Frank Gehry's Weisman Art Museum to the adventure of locking through Upper and Lower St. Anthony Falls and Lock Number One to the surprising natural beauty of the wooded gorge area, this is the Cities from a different angle—on the Big River. Negotiating the locks is easy; just read the signs and listen to the lockmaster. Unless the water is high, the current is lazy. Avoid paddling this trip when the river's high, because leaving the locks then is a turbulent project. Also avoid it when there's a strong east wind, since on this wide, straight river, a tailwind is a lot more fun. Fort Snelling State Park offers an alternate take-out. The downside is that you must portage to the parking area and pay a vehicle fee to enter the park.

Rentals are available from Aarcee Rental Center, (612) 827-5746, www. aarceerental.com; Hoigaard's, (952) 929-1351, www.hoigaards.com; REI Bloomington, (952) 884-4315; and REI Roseville, (651) 635-0211.

A **bicycle shuttle** works beautifully on this trip. Whether you take out at Hidden Falls Park or Fort Snelling, ride the metro area's great system of paved bike trails safely back to Boom Island Park. The trails are shown on the map.

Because you're paddling in "pools" created by the dams, **gradient** is not an issue. (If the dams were removed, the gradient would be 13.5 feet per mile.)

When **water flow** (http://www.mvp-wc.usace.army. mil/) is over 30,000 cfs, small watercraft are not allowed in the locks.

Put in at the Boom Island Park boat ramp, on river left downstream of the Plymouth Avenue bridge. There's a fee to park but the ramp is free. The park has shelters, toilets, and drinking water (as well as boat rides on the Mississippi Queen, a small sternwheeler). Go to the right of Nicollet Island, with its historic mansions. (Going to the left takes you too close to Upper St. Anthony Falls.) On the right, opposite the mansions, a long row of new condos characterizes the new urbanism of the metro area. A paved trail follows the river.

Keep right as you approach the lock at Upper St. Anthony Falls. Look for the signal, a pull cord, past the first stoplight. There's an intercom, through which the lock operator will tell you how to proceed. Filling the lock—that's nine million gallons of river—takes about 10 minutes. Even when there's just one canoe locking through, the lock is filled and emptied, the same as for a barge tow. Hold one of the ropes along the side, but don't tie up, because the water drops 50 feet. An air-horn blast gives you permission to leave the lock.

After you pass the new Guthrie Theater, cantilevered over the right riverbank, Lower St. Anthony Falls lock (mile 1.9) is next. Same drill, with a 25-foot drop this time. Out of the lock and just past the maroon girders of the Washington Avenue bridge, the improbable angles of the Gehry building top the rocky bluff on the left. The river now runs through Central Mississippi Riverfront Regional Park, with assorted landings, trails, and picnic areas on both sides. On the left after the Franklin Avenue bridge, intricate stairways down the bluff signal Mississippi Sand Flats (mile 3.9), a popular destination on a sunny day. (Note: the numbers painted on the Franklin Avenue Bridge indicate clearance, not depth.)

Just before Lake Street (mile 5), the Minneapolis Rowing Club has its clubhouse on the right. As you reach the bridge, look up at the right arch to see graffiti in a seemingly inaccessible spot. Downstream of the bridge, the wooded bluffs and sandstone outcrops are high and grand, and this urban river corridor looks amazingly natural.

Just past the Ford Parkway bridge (mile 7) is Lock and Dam 1, also known as the Ford Lock. As before, keep right, pull the cord, and wait. This one drops 30 feet. As you leave the lock, you're 105 feet lower than at the beginning of the trip. Where Minnehaha Creek (mile 7.8) joins the Mississippi on the right, there's a landing. Across the river, the trails, picnic tables, and shelters of Hidden Falls Park begin to appear on the left. A half mile down, **take out** at the boat ramp.

It's another 1.2 miles to Fort Snelling, where you can **take out** on the right at the low point of land across from Pike Island. (It's not an official landing.) A level 0.2-mile trail leads to the visitor center and parking lot.

A lone canoe waits in the lock at Upper St. Anthony Falls.

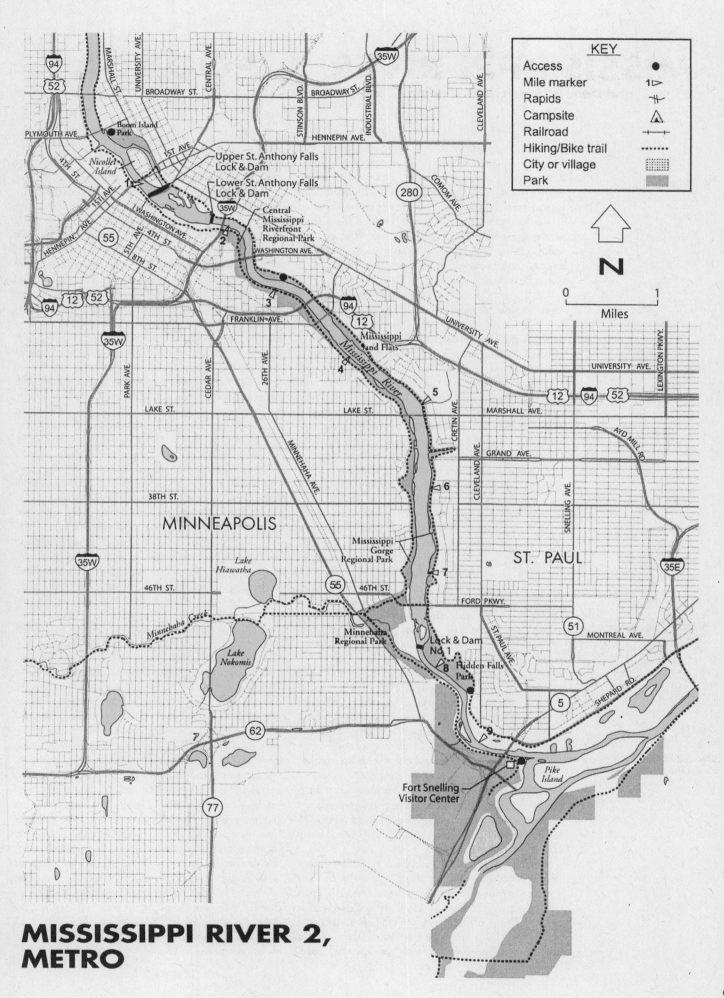

MISSISSIPPI RIVER 2, METRO

MISSISSIPPI RIVER 3, POOL 5A
Lock and Dam 5 to Verchota Landing (7.5 miles)

Unless the river's high, this is a good trip for beginning paddlers. Anyone who likes quiet water and abundant wildlife will enjoy it as well. As the journey begins, there's a pleasant tension between the wild beauty of the valley and various works of humans. Dramatic wooded bluffs faced with rock outcrops flanking the vast river valley contrast with Lock and Dam 5, the occasional motorboat or barge tow, the echoing rumble of an unseen train, and the Bass Camp Resort's campground.

Once past the resort, uninhabited wooded banks are edged with narrow sandy beaches.

A few miles down the main channel, the route flows into backwater sloughs and the Upper Mississippi River National Wildlife and Fish Refuge (www.fws.gov/mid west/winona) where there's a marked canoe trail. This lovely bottomland is home to amazing wildlife populations: songbirds, blue and green herons, white egrets, bald eagles, turkey vultures, ducks of all kinds, and many other species. Willow thickets, beds of rushes, American lotus, and arrowhead plants, and wild irises line heavily wooded banks. It's a popular area for anglers in shallow draft fishing boats.

Camping and **canoe rentals** are available at the Bass Camp Resort, (507) 689-2856. Another option is about 2 miles south of Verchota Landing on Prairie Island Road and just below the Dam 5A spillway: Winona's Prairie Island Campground, (507) 452-4501, has a tent area, canoe rentals, showers, and access to the river's Pool 5A.

There's primitive walk-in camping at John A. Latsch State Park, (507) 932-3007, just up U.S. Highway 61 from Lock and Dam 5. A half-mile park trail climbs to the top of Mount Charity, which affords great views of the valley from 500 feet above river level.

The 7.9-mile shuttle route runs south on U.S. Highway 61 to Minnesota City. Where Highway 248 turns right, go left on Bridge Street, left on Wenonah Road, left on Harbor Drive, and down Prairie Island Road.

Because the river is impounded, the **gradient** is negligible.

Wooded bluffs on the Wisconsin side rise above the Mississippi.

Water level information from Lock and Dam 5A is available online (http://waterdata.usgs.gov/mn/nwis/uv?cb_00065=on&format=gif&period=31&site_no=05378 490). At levels below 6 feet, the current will be moderate to slow.

Put in just below Lock and Dam 5. When you turn off U.S. Highway 61, the visitor parking is to the left. Turn right instead. About halfway down the short road, just past a line of posts on the left, is a rocky area that dam operators allow paddlers to use for access. You can park in the visitor parking lot. If you prefer an easier access, there's a boat ramp at the Bass Camp Resort just down the road.

Although the resort charges $7 to launch there, there are also bathrooms and a campground.

If there's any barge traffic on the main channel, stay between the buoys and the right shore. Between miles 1.5 and 3, there are five sloughs heading south. Depending how long you want to stay on the main channel, you may cut over on any of them to a backwater called Straight Slough. A navigational day mark (mile 2), a red and white checkerboard on the left, is located even with a green buoy in the channel. From there it's a half mile downstream to one of the entries into Straight Slough on the right. Watch out for shallows and the wing dam at the entry—whirlpools and eddies may form there.

In the slough, the sandy margins of the main channel disappear. Look for blue and white diamond signs on the right marking the refuge's Straight Slough Canoe Trail. Horseshoe Bend (mile 3.5) splits off to the left, leading back to the main channel and the north end of Fountain City. The canoe trail goes right. Depending on water levels, occasional sandbars provide places to stop.

At mile 6.3, the slough splits again. Pickerel Run heads left toward the distant bluffs on the Wisconsin side where you can see farm buildings perched on top. Several small sloughs that branch off to the left lead to Polander Lake. Crooked Slough flows ahead to the southeast, the canoe trail marked by a series of closely spaced signs on river right. After another half mile, follow the small secluded slough to the right for about 0.3 mile, ending in a junction with another slough. The Minnesota City Boat Club appears off to the right. Go left instead, following this slough to a tree line on the right that marks the entrance to the landing. Take out at the boat ramp.

Other trips: A nice variation on this trip is to go left at Horseshoe Bend and head back to the main channel. Cross the channel at Fountain City, Wisconsin, and stop at the upper Fountain City Landing for lunch or dinner. The Monarch Tavern, (608) 687-4231, is up the hill from the upper Fountain City Landing. The tavern's hours vary, so call ahead to see if it's open. If not, follow the main channel to the newer, more easily accessed lower Fountain City Landing. The Great River Café, a diner up by the highway, is another eating option, open only for breakfast and lunch. To return, cross the main channel from the lower landing into Pap Slough, the waterway that opens to the south of the lighted channel marker. This slough heads downstream and reconnects with the main channel above Polander Lake, a wide expanse on river right. At the end of the island on river right, head east toward the bluffs on the Minnesota side, crossing the north end of the lake. You see a series of small navigational markers heading across the lake; these lead boats through Polander Lake's underwater stump field, created by the installation of the lock and dam system. When you get across the lake, follow the navigation markers into the slough that heads northwest to the boat landing behind the line of trees.

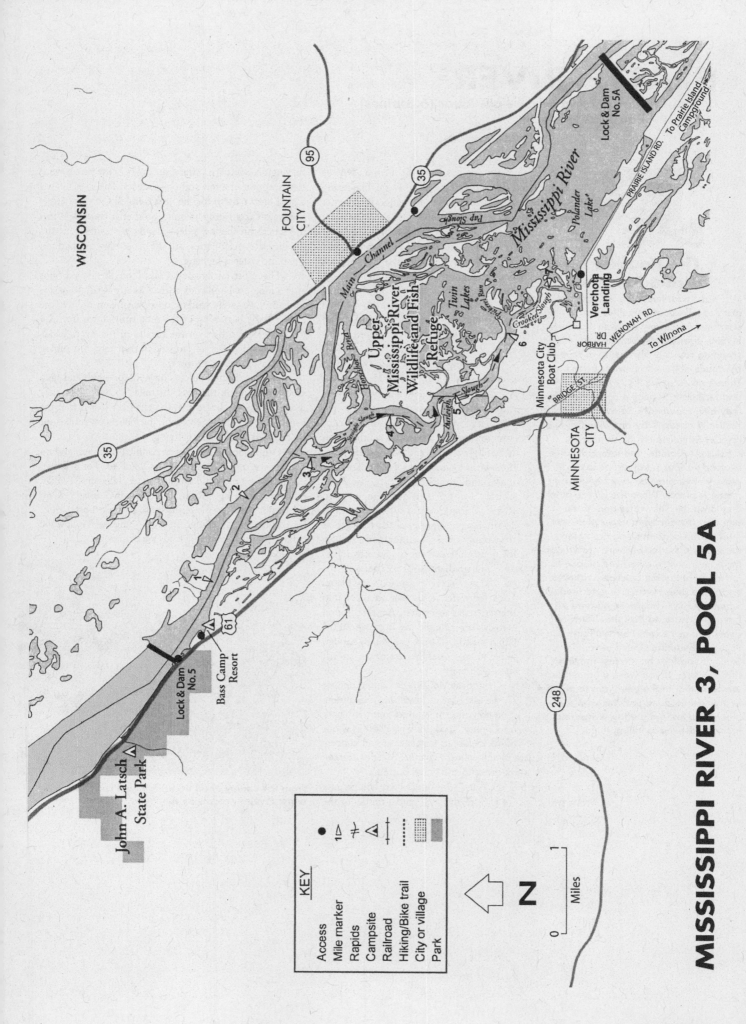

MISSISSIPPI RIVER 3, POOL 5A

WISCONSIN

FOUNTAIN CITY

Main Channel

Upper Mississippi River Wildlife and Fish Refuge

Horseshoe Bend

Mississippi River

Pup Slough

"Polander Lake"

Verchota Landing

Twin Lakes

Crooked Slough

Minnesota City Boat Club

Lock & Dam No. 5A

PRAIRIE ISLAND RD.

To Prairie Island Campground

HARBOR DR.

WENONAH RD.

To Winona

BRIDGE ST.

MINNESOTA CITY

Straight Slough

Straight Slough

John A. Latsch State Park

Lock & Dam No.5

Bass Camp Resort

KEY

Access
Mile marker
Rapids
Campsite
Railroad
Hiking/Bike trail
City or village
Park

N

Miles

0   1

95

PLATTE RIVER
County Road 26 to Mississippi River (6.3 miles)

The Paddler's Escort Service

Most paddlers have at least one story to tell about horseflies and deerflies. And many of these stories involve agonizing situations like paddling rapids whilst being assaulted by clouds of the carnivorous beasts. There's no escaping. They can fly faster and farther than people can paddle, and they bite, repeatedly. So the question naturally arises: Why do horseflies like rapids? Scientists call these nasty creatures tabanids, and tabanids have evolved various adaptations to the watery environment. They lay eggs on riverside plants. When the larvae hatch they drop into the water and nestle amongst the decaying vegetation and mud on the bottom, using breathing tubes. Once the females are grown and have their wings, they need blood—and lots of it—to lay the next generation of eggs. And their favorite time to feed is when the sun is brightest. So here we have bloodsucking flies that hatch on rivers and are excited by sunlight. Picture a beautiful stretch of rapids. Sunlight sparkles on the fast-moving, riffling water. If you were a horsefly, wouldn't that make you want to bite the first warm-blooded paddler who comes along? But lest we get too warm and fuzzy, Godspeed in killing them.

Early French fur traders gave the Platte River its name, meaning "flat and shallow." The Platte, like its big brother in Nebraska, is indeed flat and shallow in its upper reaches. Until it drops into the Mississippi River Valley, that is, racing through lots of rocky riffles and Class I rapids on its way. Paddlers enjoy this fun, fast run. Anglers like this segment for its smallmouth bass, northern and walleye pike, and channel cats. Groups of inner-tube riders float the last few miles on warm summer days. And one more group has an avid interest in this river: deerflies. (See the sidebar.)

Camping is available at Two Rivers Campground: (320) 584-5125; www.two riverscampground.net, a private campground at the take-out.

The 5.6-mile **shuttle** route runs west on County Road 26, southeast on U.S. Highway 10, and west at the junction with County Road 40. Cross the tracks and immediately turn south on County Road 73. At the sign for Two Rivers Campground, turn right onto 145th Street, a gravel road. Register at the campground office: there's a small fee for noncampers to use the landing.

The **gradient** is 7.1 feet per mile.

There's no river gauge on the Platte. Look for **water levels** that are at or into the terrestrial vegetation. Another option is to eyeball the rapid just upstream of the County Road 40 bridge. If there's enough water in that one, the rest of the stretch should be fine.

Put in at McGonagle Canoe Landing on the east edge of Royalton. The landing is on downstream left next to the city park on County Road 26. The Platte is about 80 feet wide, its waters clear and copper-tinted. Frequent islands split the channel. In late summer, river grasses streak the sand and gravel bottom.

At mile 0.8, the Platte runs under three bridges in a row: two spans for U.S. Highway 10 and a trestle for the Burlington Northern. After that, you're in the woods, with the exception of a few scattered houses. The river follows a pool-drop pattern for the next 6 miles. On this narrow river, the Class I drops require good boat control. When the water's on the low side, scraping is inevitable among the intricate rocky mazes; but the drops are wavy and fun when the water is higher.

The most challenging Class I on the river begins after a long pool and ends at the County Road 40 bridge (mile 3.9). A sandy landing on downstream right at the bridge is the beginning of the tube run. Downstream of the bridge, sand bars on the insides of the river's bends provide good places to stop. Unfortunately, the tubing crowd leaves their trash there.

By mile 5, the boulders have disappeared, and high sandy ridges flank the river. At mile 5.5, watch for submerged slabs of concrete in the channel. Just before the confluence with the Mississippi, the Platte slows. Take out on river left at the sandy landing.

Other trips: For a shorter paddle (4.9 miles) and no landing fee, take out at County Road 40. For a longer paddle (11.6 miles) and no landing fee, take out 5.3 miles down the Mississippi River at the Stearns County Park on river right. The Mississippi is quite pleasant upstream of the County Road 2 bridge. In the 2.5 miles that follow the bridge, power boats and jet skis are common.

From the County Road 40 bridge, you can check out water levels in rapids on the Platte.

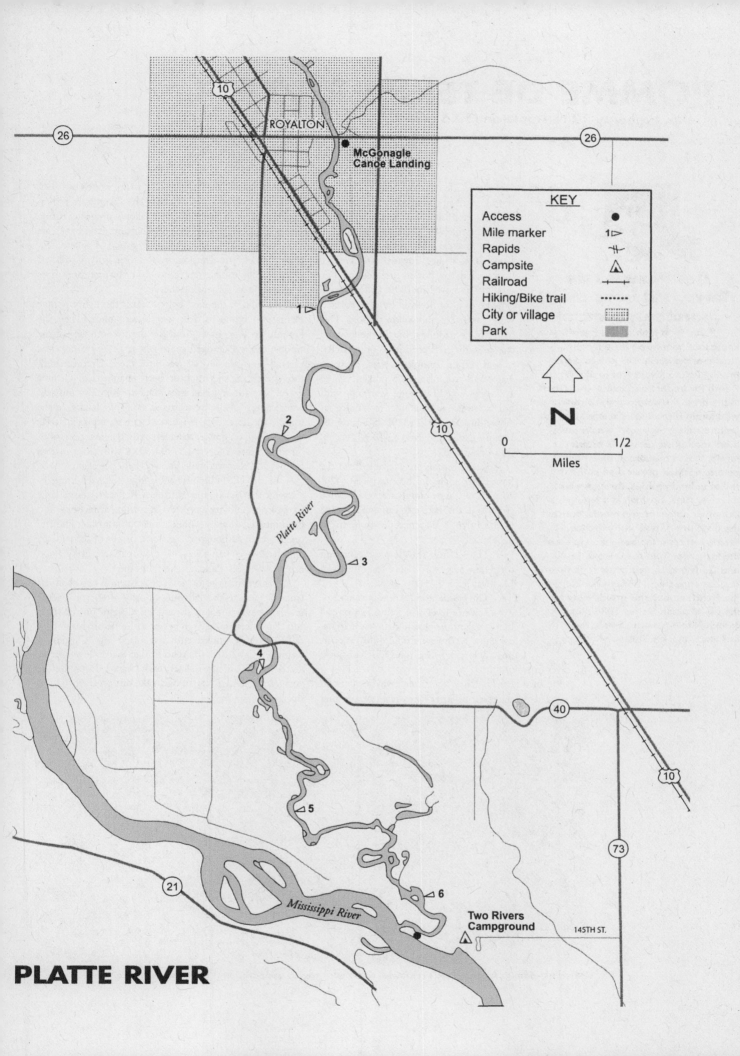

KEY

Access	●
Mile marker	1▷
Rapids	‡‡
Campsite	△
Railroad	+++
Hiking/Bike trail	········
City or village	▦
Park	▨

N

0   1/2

Miles

ROYALTON

McGonagle
Canoe Landing

Platte River

Mississippi River

Two Rivers
Campground

145TH ST.

PLATTE RIVER

POMME DE TERRE RIVER 1

U.S. Highway 12 to Appleton (10.6 miles)

Des Pommes de Terre, s'il vous plait (potatoes, please)

If you took high school French, you know that *pomme de terre* means "apple of the earth," or potato. So is this the Potato River? Not really. When French fur traders and explorers arrived in the area, the potato-shaped root of a wild turnip (*Psoralea esculenta*) that the Dakota called "tipsinah" was a favorite tribal food. Also known as prairie turnip, Indian breadroot, and Indian potato, tipsinah grows well in the dry soil of upland prairies, through which this river runs. Tipsinah is a legume, and like other native prairie plants, enriches the deep prairie soil with nitrogen. Prairie settlers often bought supplies of the tasty root from the Dakota. Lewis and Clark and company ate it on their famous expedition. Both the Dakota and the French named this prairie river for the useful plant. On his 1838 map, Joseph Nicollet inscribed only the Dakota name, the Tipsinah River.

On this reach, the prairie river Pomme de Terre presents some interesting contrasts. Long, winding stretches overhung with dense stands of silver maples share the river with a popple tree plantation laid out in straight rows on grassy banks. Little Class I rapids now race down a stretch once impounded for power production. The dam was removed in 1999, and the wide expanse of a former mill pond is covered with grass, trees, and willow thickets. This isn't remote paddling, but in the wooded stretches, the river corridor is quite pretty.

Riverside **camping**, with drinking water and an outhouse, is possible at the U.S. Highway 12 wayside. Camping with hot showers is available for a fee at Appleton City Park, (320) 289-1363; or Lac qui Parle State Park, (320) 752-4736, west of Watson.

Kayak rentals are available from the Java River Cafe in Montevideo, (320) 269-7106. **Canoe rentals** and rental canoe pickup at the take-out can be arranged with Mitlyng's Bait near Watson, (320) 269-5593.

The 4.8-mile **shuttle route** runs west on U.S. Highway 12 and south on Highway 119.

The **gradient** is 2.4 feet per mile.

A **water level** of 4.5 to 6 feet on the USGS gage at Appleton (http://waterdata.usgs.gov/mn/nwis/uv?05294000) is optimal. Below 3.5 feet, the DNR considers the river uncanoeable.

Put in at U.S. Highway 12, at a nice wayside park on the east side of the river. It's just downstream of a former mill dam, but all that remains is a rocky stretch of riffles, which gets you off to a fast start. The Pomme de Terre is narrow, about 75 feet wide. Its shallow, somewhat turbid water flows swiftly over a sandy bottom. The banks are low, grassy, and sometimes heavily grazed. A mile downstream, an electric fence crosses the river, forcing paddlers to duck. Big deadfalls are common in the first three miles of the wooded, serpentine channel.

At mile 3, the river begins a trip through a popple plantation, home to deer and lots of birds. Then the Pomme de Terre flows from the narrow intimacy of the woods into a wide-open space where it's easy to imagine the tall-grass prairie that was once there. Unfortunately, this stretch appears to have been channelized. Shallow gravel bars and a gravel streambed are home to mussels, whose empty shells are scattered along the banks. In the middle of this stretch is Larson Landing, a public access with parking on downstream left at the Highway 36 (60th Street) bridge. A lovely island covered with silver maples follows and the riverbanks are wooded once again.

At the U.S. Highway 59 bridge, followed immediately by the Burlington Northern Railroad trestle, large piles of deadfalls are a preview of coming attractions. You head into 1.5 heavily wooded miles of fast water and frequent snags. Although the massive trunks of some deadfalls have been cut away to allow passage, every flood brings new trees. Paddlers should be alert.

Where the Pomme de Terre splits into two channels (mile 8.5), take the left one. Shortly after, you paddle under a powerline and see a grain elevator on the horizon. You meet some stretches of riffles before reaching a railroad trestle posted with signs that say "Caution—Rapids." Right after the road bridge that follows immediately, you run three short, easy Class I drops. Before you reach the highway bridge, **take out** on river right at Appleton Ciry Park.

When the dam in Appleton was removed, these easy rapids appeared on the Pomme de Terre.

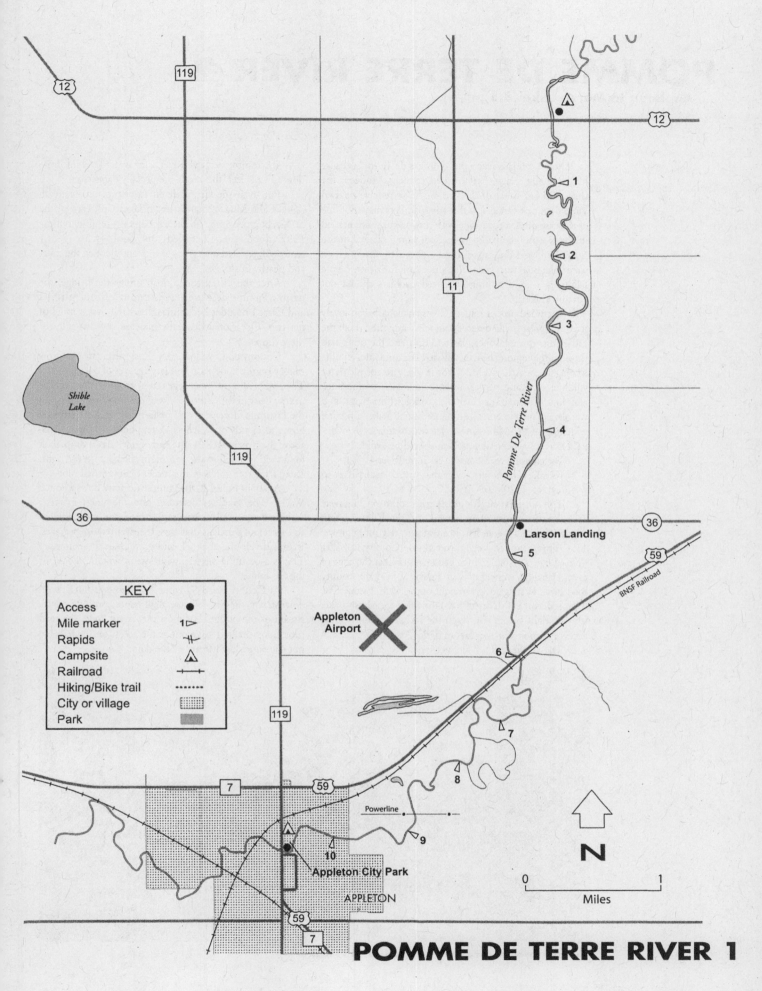

KEY

Access	●
Mile marker	1▷
Rapids	╫
Campsite	⛺
Railroad	┼┼┼
Hiking/Bike trail	┈┈┈
City or village	░░░
Park	▓▓▓

Shible Lake

Pomme De Terre River

Larson Landing

Appleton Airport

BNSF Railroad

Powerline

Appleton City Park

APPLETON

N

0   1
Miles

POMME DE TERRE RIVER 1

POMME DE TERRE RIVER 2

Appleton to Marsh Lake (8.5 miles)

Some call this reach the "Pomme de Terror" because of the many snags that threaten canoeists. Indeed, the snags and fast water of the Pomme de Terre have claimed more than one canoe. On this trip, paddlers may spot one of the casualties: a red canoe with rotting gunwales nestled in the weeds. The paddlers made it home safely, but the river swallowed the canoe. Later spit out by spring's high water, the boat was wedged in a tree fork for a time before falling to a sandbar. Inexperienced paddlers should not attempt this trip.

Accorded proper respect for its challenges, this lovely stretch of river richly deserves canoeists' attention. Half the route runs through open pastoral land and the other half through the remote, heavily wooded Lac qui Parle Wildlife Management Area (WMA). You're likely to see plenty of wildlife: snapping turtles, owls, bald eagles, cormorants, and lots of songbirds, including orioles, kingbirds, and warblers. The trip ends just before Marsh Lake, a natural widening of the Minnesota River with water levels maintained by a lowhead dam, which should be avoided.

For **camping**, see Pomme de Terre River 1.

Kayak rentals are available from Java River in Montevideo, (320) 269-7106.

The 4.8-mile **shuttle route** runs south on Highway 119 (South Munsterman Street). At the Y-intersection where Highway 7 goes left, bear right to stay on Highway 119. Almost immediately, turn right on County Road 51 (West Reuss Avenue), which becomes gravel at the edge of town, heading west and then south. Where the county road turns west again, go straight onto 240th Avenue SW. Turn right on 100th Street SW at the sign for Marsh Lake. On the right before you reach the lake, the public canoe access has room for two cars to park.

The **gradient** is 5.9 feet per mile.

See Pomme de Terre River 1 for **water level** information. Over 6 feet, this reach is especially dangerous.

Put in at the City Park in Appleton, on upstream right at the Munsterman Street bridge. Upstream of the bridge, boulder riprap on the left bank is a reminder of the 1997 flood that damaged the dam (subsequently removed), covered the campground, and flooded the street and nearby businesses.

After the initial rocky drop under the bridge, the narrow Pomme de Terre speeds through frequent riffles and Class I boulder beds throughout the first 5 miles of the trip. Occasional deadfalls increase the difficulty of these drops.

Cottonwood, willow, ash, and silver maple grow thickly on the floodplain and large groves of oaks, upland. The riverbanks, soft with vegetation, are lower than on the nearby Lac qui Parle River. Between two railroad bridges in the first mile, dozens of nest holes in the vertical bank are home to clouds of swallows. A few human homes perch above the river as well. At the end of one Class I drop, look for an old wooden rowboat sunk in the river on the right. Later, a tall tree grows in the center of an unused silo.

At about mile 4.2, the Pomme de Terre flows into the WMA. The gradient decreases and the snags increase. Although the boulder-bed rapids are gone, the current's still swift and deadfalls that cross the river require portages. Islands divide the channel, and gravel bars are common. This is a beautiful stretch, with lots of wildlife. Look for the red canoe.

At County Road 51 (mile 6.7) access is possible on downstream right or left. Deadfall issues continue downstream of the bridge. For most of the last mile, the road runs along the left. **Take out** at the access on the left. Do not continue downstream to the dam.

The fast-moving Pomme de Terre is plagued with snags.

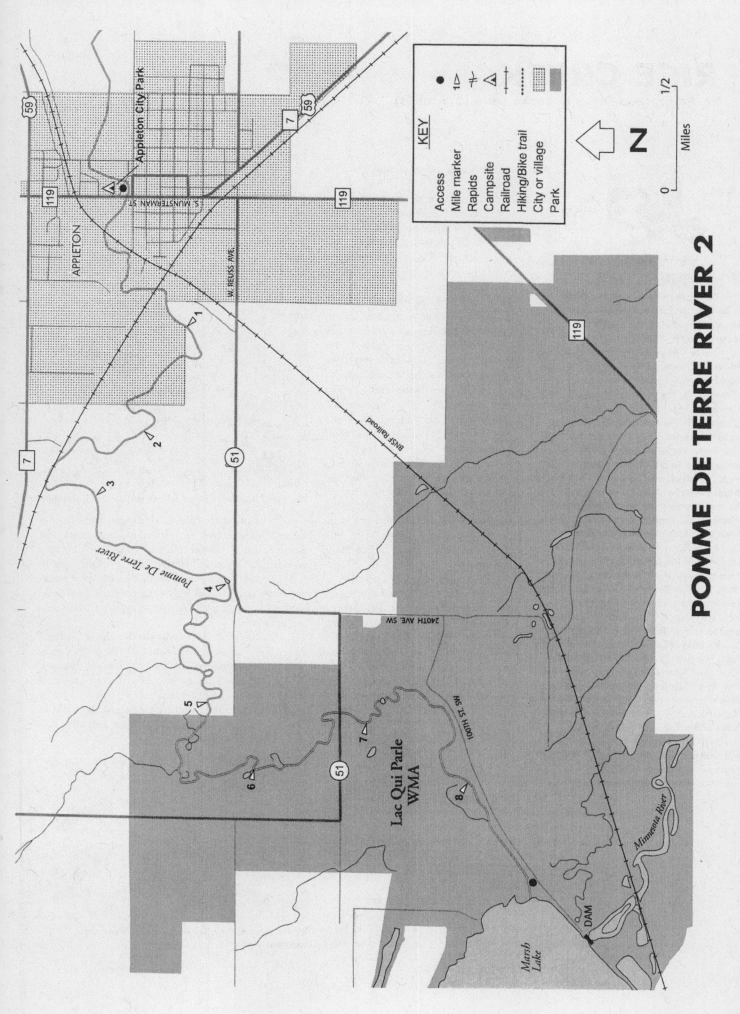

POMME DE TERRE RIVER 2

RICE CREEK
Poppyseed Drive to Locke Lake (6.5 miles)

A Wealth of Bike Trails

Bicyclists can ride miles of trails in Ramsey and Anoka counties. A wonderful network connects the counties' extensive green spaces. It's possible to ride paved trails along the Mississippi River all the way from Coon Rapids Dam Regional Park to Minneapolis. The route is through Riverfront Regional Park, where trails connect with Minneapolis Park System trails. Ramsey County trails include the Rice Creek Regional Trail, the Central Lakes trails, Battle Creek Regional Park trails (which also has a mountain-biking loop), the Keller Lake/Lake Phalen trails, the McCarrons/Trout Brook/Reservoir Woods trails, and, in the northeast, the Birch Lake Regional Trail. In Anoka County, parks with bike trails include Bunker Hills Regional Park, Coon Rapids Dam Regional Park, Riverfront Regional Park, Kordiak County Park, Lake George Regional Park, Locke County Park, Manomin County Park, Martin/Island/Linwood Lakes Regional Park, Rice Creek Chain of Lakes Regional Park Preserve, Rum River Central Regional Park, Rum River North County Park, and Rum River South County Park. On its Web site (www.anokacountyparks.com/qlinks/trails.htm), Anoka County has maps and additional information. Ramsey County Parks, (651) 748-2500, will mail out a booklet of trail maps. The maps are also on a Web site (www.co.ramsey.mn.us/parks.)

Fast-moving Rice Creek offers exciting paddling adventures in suburban New Brighton and Fridley. Woods and backyards, bridges and culverts, riffles and Class I rapids, culvert backrollers, twists and turns, and plenty of deadfalls: This creek has it all. If you want to paddle with a group, join the River Ramblers annual spring trip (river-ramblers.org). When it's not passing numerous backyards, the creek runs through Creekview Park, Rice Creek Trail West Park, and Locke County Park, where paddlers can stop for lunch. Rice Creek West Regional Trail and other recreational trails follow the creek, crossing repeatedly on arched truss bridges.

The 4.2-mile **shuttle route** runs west on Poppyseed Drive, south on Long Lake Road for 0.25 mile, and west on Mississippi Street for 3.1 miles. After crossing the tracks, turn right on Hickory Street and right on Rice Creek Way, where a narrow park runs between the street and the lake. For the intrepid, a bicycle shuttle is possible on the paved Rice Creek West Regional Trail. Detailed trail maps are available from Anoka, (763) 757-3920, and Ramsey, (651) 748-2500, county parks.

The **gradient** is 6.5 feet per mile.

For **water level** information, check the culvert at the put-in. If less than 1.5 feet of water stain shows on the downstream side, the water's high enough. If the water's quite high, the backroller in the culvert at mile 6.0 may be 2 feet high. In early spring, Long Lake may be ice-covered. If the dam at Locke Lake is undergoing maintenance, the lake will be drawn down, with class II rapids under the railroad trestles. By midsummer, the creek is generally too low to paddle.

Put in at the Ramsey County Long Lake Regional Park in New Brighton. From Interstate 694 west, go 2 miles north on Long Lake Road. After crossing the tracks, turn right on Poppyseed Drive and go to the end of the street. From the sign reading "Ramsey County Open Space Site Boundary," a short trail leads to a bridge over the creek. Put in downstream right. (Private land abuts the access: please don't trespass.)

After you enter Long Lake, the creek's exit is off to the right. There's a short, rocky drop under the Long Lake Road bridge; stay left of center to avoid most of the boulders. If the water's high, clearance under the bridge will be tight, so pick your route first and then duck. Rice Creek races and twists through wooded ravines, and downed trees are the inevitable result of all that woodsy beauty. Some deadfalls have been cut to allow passage; others remain to challenge paddlers. Frequent sharp bends (we're talking 180-degree angles) demand good boat control in this narrow channel. Boulders streaked with bright canoe tracks litter the winding streambed. Be alert at every bend.

The River Ramblers head out on a Rice Creek expedition.

In addition to nature's challenges, paddlers run through bridge culverts at Mississippi Street, Silver Lake Road, Central Avenue, Highway 65, and University Avenue. The Highway 65 culvert (mile 3.4) is fairly long. In the University Avenue culvert (mile 6.0), a backroller forms, and waves can be 2 feet high when the creek is really up. When the water's low, you may scrape on a barely submerged pipe.

After the creek flows under the Burlington Northern & Santa Fe trestle and into Locke Lake, the journey ends. Take out on the south (left) shore at an unofficial access. It's a short, steep climb up the bank and across two recreational trails to Rice Creek Way.

Rice Creek, impounded by a dam at the outlet of Locke Lake, joins the Mississippi River a quarter mile downstream of the lake.

Rice Creek's fast water and deadfalls require constant vigilance.

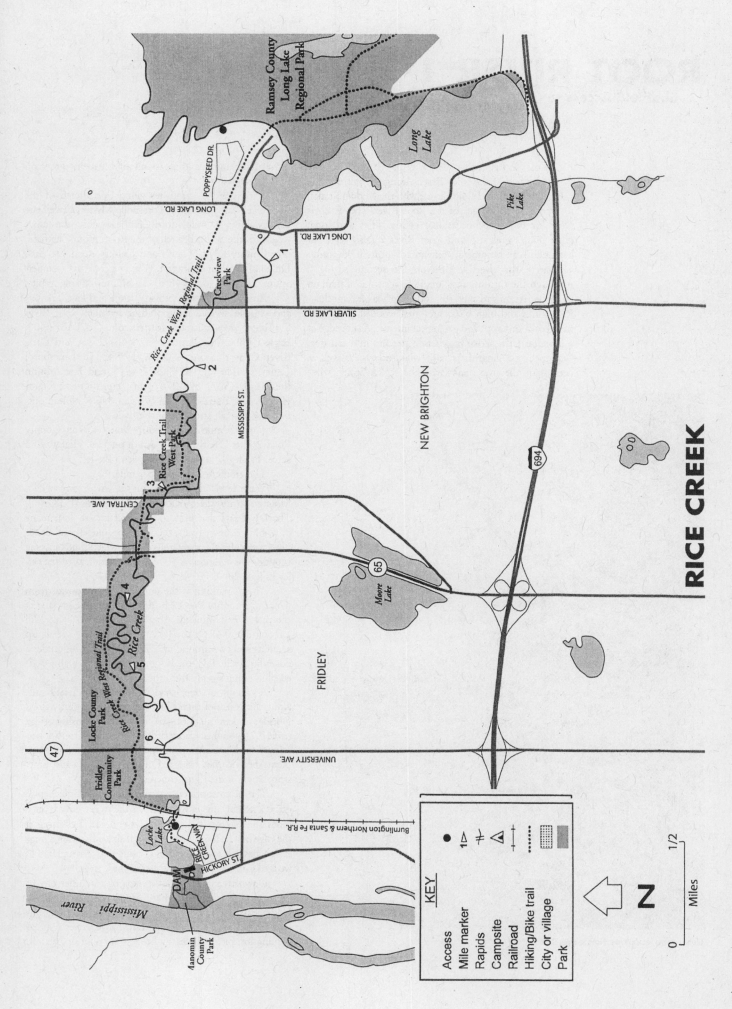

RICE CREEK

KEY

- ● Access
- 1△ Mile marker
- ⌁ Rapids
- ⬯ Campsite
- Railroad
- ⋯⋯ Hiking/Bike trail
- City or village
- Park

N

0   1/2

Miles

Mississippi River

Manomin County Park

DAM

Locke Lake

RICE CREEK WAY

HICKORY ST.

Burlington Northern & Santa Fe R.R.

Fridley Community Park

Locke County Park West Regional Trail

Rice Creek West Regional Trail

Rice Creek

Rice Creek Trail West Park

Creekview Park

Ramsey County Long Lake Regional Park

POPPYSEED DR.

LONG LAKE RD.

LONG LAKE RD.

SILVER LAKE RD.

MISSISSIPPI ST.

CENTRAL AVE.

UNIVERSITY AVE.

FRIDLEY

NEW BRIGHTON

Long Lake

Pike Lake

Moore Lake

47

65

694

ROOT RIVER 1
Chatfield Access to Parsley Bridge (8.9 miles)

This short bluff-country cruise begins on the North Branch of the Root River. Along the journey, the narrow North Branch joins forces with the Middle Branch to form the main stem of the Root River. This reach is great for beginners: occasional gentle riffles and long, quiet pools. This trip and Root River 2 (also good for beginners) can become a weekend adventure if you camp at one of the riverside sites on the second segment. Although the surroundings are more agricultural than on the downstream stretches, this is definitely a pleasant float. Riverbanks and high bluffs are often wooded, and occasional rock outcrops add geological interest. At the edge of a farm field, an active eagle's nest perches in a tall tree. Woodpeckers, kingfishers, and wild turkeys, as well as deer, share the river banks with the eagles. Spring wild-flowers, including a thick stand of bluebells, grow on wooded slopes.

There are no campsites along this stretch of the Root. For nearby **camping**, Forestville/Mystery Cave State Park is about 20 miles from Chatfield, along the upper reaches of the South Branch of the Root. From Chatfield, take County Road 5 south and County Road 118 east. On a hot summer afternoon, visiting a cool cave (temperatures may be as low as 48°F) can be a revitalizing respite.

Area outfitters who provide **canoe and kayak rentals** and **shuttle service** on the Root include: Root River Outfitters, www.rootriveroutfitters.com, (507) 467-3400, Eagle Cliff Canoe Rental, (507) 467-2598, and Little River General Store, (800) 994-2943, in Lanesboro; Geneva's Hideaway, (877) 727-4816, and Just Around the Bend, (507) 875-2767, in Peterson; and Gator Greens, (507) 467-3000, in Whalan. Note: Not all outfitters service all stretches of the river.

The 4.5-mile **shuttle route** runs east on County Road 2 into Chatfield, then south on U.S. Highway 52 across Parsley Bridge. The access is on the left.

The **gradient** is 3.8 feet per mile.

Water levels are measured on the USGS gage at Pilot Mound (http://waterdata.usgs.gov/mn/nwis/uv?05383950). The DNR says that 8.25 to 9.25 feet is best. Like many other bluff country rivers, the Root rises quickly and floods in a spectacular and dangerous way, at which time canoeing is out of the question. A 500-year flood inundated the valley in June 2000.

There's parking at the public access on downstream left at the County Road 2 bridge. A flurry of fast water at the **put-in** ends quickly. After the confluence with Mill Creek (mile 0.4) on the left, the river briefly speeds up again as it curves around an island. After flowing under a powerline (mile 1.1), the Root heads toward a high wooded bluff rising steeply from the edge of the river.

A canopy of trees shades the river for a half mile along the 260-foot-high bluff. Between the County Road 5 bridge and an interesting old truss-style township bridge (mile 3.2), you meet more riffles. About a half mile downstream of the township bridge are the crumbling abutments of a former bridge. On the left is dry-laid limestone, and on the right, concrete.

The quiet confluence with the Middle Branch produces a notably bigger Root. Across the river from a layered limestone outcrop (mile 6.4), a cluster of tall trees stands at the edge of a field on the right. High above the river, a huge eagle's nest—active when this guide was researched—is wedged into the branches of one of these trees.

Downstream, the Root swings past another one of those steep wooded bluffs that make this area so beautiful. Under Parsley Bridge and around a bend, the river runs fast to just before the landing. **Take out** on river right. A parking lot, picnic tables, and toilets are right up the hill.

Limestone outcrops flank the Root.

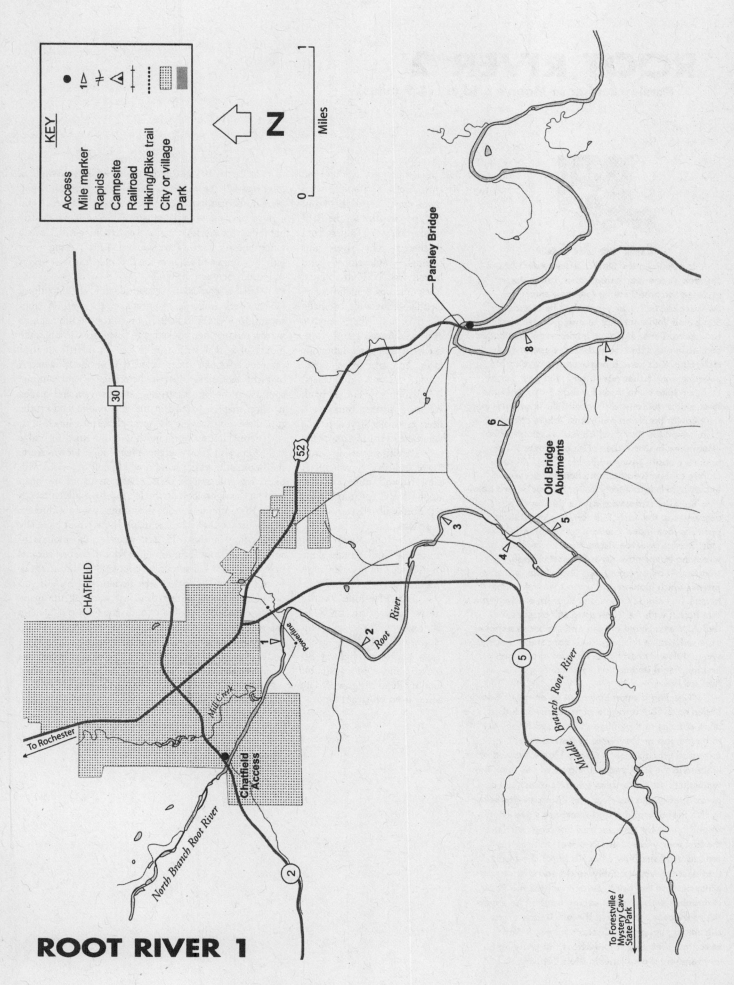

ROOT RIVER 1

ROOT RIVER 2
Parsley Bridge to Moen's Bridge (14.9 miles)

Call to Action

Joe Deden is the Bluff Country's new Richard J. Dorer. (A one-man conservation army, Dorer reversed the area's earlier environmental catastrophe.) In the 25 years since he founded Eagle Bluff Environmental Learning Center near Lanesboro, Deden has seen environmental attitudes change in ways that he finds both hopeful and disturbing. Kids have a better understanding of environmental issues now than in the past. Eagle Bluff can take some credit for that: Students from three states get some dirt under their fingernails in the popular hands-on programs. Adults attend "Dinners on the Bluff," which feature lectures like "Hormones in Our Waters: Fish on Prozac." The center's website (www.eagle-bluff.org) will soon feature real-time data on the Root River's water quality, which is definitely better than in Dorer's time.

But after almost destroying this sensitive ecosystem in the early 20th century, agricultural practices that ended then are creeping back into play. Erosion was the villain then, and erosion is wreaking havoc now. Over the past decade, a steady shift away from crops like alfalfa and small grains, which blanket and protect the vulnerable topsoil, has already done damage. An erosion cycle that began with the 2000 flood still plagues the region. Vast acreage of corn and soybeans expose bare soil, and in this hilly land, bare soil is quickly washed downstream. "The amount of erosion is sinful," said Deden, "and you never get that soil back."

"Flooding is often looked at as an act of God," Deden said, "But agricultural methods—including tiling of fields and planting of bare-soil crops—are to blame, just as they were in Dorer's time." Increased urbanization is also to blame. Instead of infiltrating the land and seeping slowly through the watershed, the water runs off acres of asphalt and pours directly into the river. The Root can rise four to five feet overnight, and riverbanks are often ripped away by such sudden flooding. Just in the last four years, over 260 feet of bank have eroded. Add the flow of agricultural chemicals that destroy water quality, and you have an ecosystem on the brink. Deden can tell the Root is flooding without even seeing it when he smells the rootworm pesticide in the air. Deden urges citizens to support the Center's research and to contact their legislators about the growing environmental problems in Bluff Country.

A swift current, spectacular high wooded bluffs with bold rock outcrops, wildlife and birds, trout streams, riverside camping: what more could a paddler want? This popular run on the Root is also only 20 miles from Rochester. The river runs through undeveloped and heavily wooded bluff country. Rock outcrops, sometimes layered like stone walls, overhang the river, and lichens, mosses, and wildflowers grow from cracks in their damp limestone faces. You may spot eagles, hawks, herons, kingfishers, woodland songbirds, bank swallows, turtles, otters, and deer, especially if you paddle when the river isn't crowded.

Primitive riverside camping is available at two DNR Pilot Mound campsites. See Root River 1 for information on Forestville/Mystery Cave State Park.

See Root River 1 for canoe and kayak rentals, shuttle service, and water level information.

The 11.6-mile shuttle route runs north on U.S. Highway 52 and east on County Road 40 (gravel). Turn south on Highway 30 (paved) and south again on County Road 21 (gravel). The access is on upstream right.

The **gradient** is 4.2 feet per mile.

At Parsley Bridge 2 miles south of Chatfield on U.S. Highway 52, the public access is on downstream right. Next to the parking area are picnic tables, outhouses, and a gravel path down to the **put-in**. The Root flows quickly but quietly here, with occasional entertaining riffles, over a sandy bottom streaked with gravel. After passing a few farm buildings and fields in the first mile, the river begins its journey between the bluffs.

After a particularly beautiful cliff, the mouth of Lynch Creek (mile 2.7) appears on river left. A trout stream, Rice Creek (mile 3.5), flows in from the right, its narrow mouth often choked with fallen trees. Just past the mouth of a small stream (mile 5.6) on the left, the first campsite is located under willow trees on the left bank. A high cliff looms over the river before the second campsite appears on the left, bordering a small stream and shaded by silver maples. Nestled in the only public land on the trip, these campsites are also great places for a lunch stop.

Several houses surround the County Road 11 bridge (mile 9.3), also known as the Allen Bridge. Downstream, the Root riffles past a handsome big cliff decorated with old cedars and swallow nests. After a stretch of low, open land on the right, look on the left for the confluence with Trout Run, a premier trout stream that also runs through Bucksnort County Park (see map). Brown trout especially like feeding in the cold, fast water at the mouths of streams, and Trout Run, considered one of the best streams in the area, has a self-sustaining population of brown trout. In the Root itself, anglers seek smallmouth bass. If you don't care about catching fish, just watching the many groups of fish that dart past you in the Root can be quite entertaining.

As the Root makes a sharp bend (mile 13.2), a house and road are visible high up the bluff. The next houses you see are at the **take-out**. The Moen's Bridge public landing is on upstream right. A steep gravel path with timber steps at the bottom leads to the parking area and a toilet.

ROOT RIVER 2

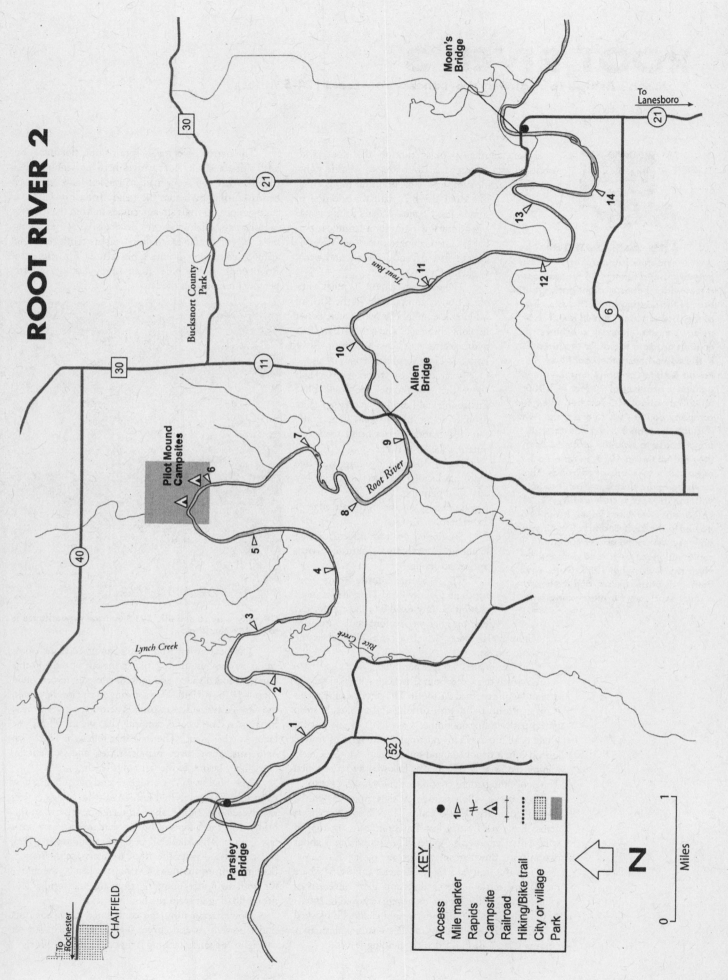

Moen's Bridge

To Lanesboro

Bucksnort County Park

Trout Run

Allen Bridge

Root River

Pilot Mound Campsites

Lynch Creek

Rice Creek

Parsley Bridge

CHATFIELD

To Rochester

KEY

Access
Mile marker
Rapids
Campsite
Railroad
Hiking/Bike trail
City or village
Park

N

Miles

ROOT RIVER 3
Moen's Bridge to Highway 16/Lanesboro Access (14.5 miles)

The Bat Tunnel

Behind the disintegrating riverside powerhouse, a tunnel—10 feet tall and 8 feet wide—heads straight back into the rock of the soaring bluff. The other end of the thousand-foot tunnel is 3.5 river miles upstream. In order to achieve enough gradient to power the turbines in the powerhouse, the Root River Power & Light Company dug the tunnel, gaining a gradient of 20 feet in 1,000 feet (that's about 100 feet per mile). The company built a dam to divert the river through the tunnel and a neoclassical powerhouse to hold the turbines. And they did all this in 1915, in an area inaccessible by roads or railroads. This amazing hydroelectric project, bought with the labor of a crew of fifty Bulgarians over three years, brought power to the Bluff Country. For 13 years, anyway. When the power company could no longer meet area demand for electricity, it closed in 1928. Gates cover both ends of the tunnel, and it's become a quiet sanctuary for hibernating bats.

Here's another popular run on the Root, with wooded bluffs, outcrops, a trout stream, wildlife sightings, and riverside campsites. This beautiful trip is much like Root River 2, with the addition of some Class I rapids. Moen's Bridge is also a good starting point for a 16-mile trip to Eagle Cliff Campground (Root River 4) on the first day of a paddle and pedal weekend.

The river runs almost 12 miles without a bridge, and portions of the Richard J. Dorer Memorial Hardwood State Forest lie along this reach. The remains of a 1915 hydroelectric project—the Root River Power & Light Company's powerhouse—quietly crumble on river's edge. High above the powerhouse, the Eagle Bluff Environmental Learning Center has miles of hilly forest hiking trails. The softly rounded shapes of weathered sandstone outcrops flank the river.

Four DNR primitive campsites (see map) are located on the river. Highway 250 Campground, (507) 467-3395, is a private facility on the northeast edge of Lanesboro.

See Root River 1 for information on canoe and kayak rentals, shuttle service, and water levels.

The 9.5-mile shuttle route goes south on County Road 21 (gravel at first), east on County Road 8 to Lanesboro, and east on Highway 16 for about 3 miles to the Highway 16 access, which a DNR sign labels the Lanesboro Access.

The gradient is 5.0 feet per mile.

To reach the access from Chatfield, take Highway 30 east and County Road 21 south. The public canoe access is on upstream right, with parking and a toilet. A steep gravel path ending in timber steps leads to the put-in. Quiet until it passes a big outcrop, the Root riffles around a bend into a floodplain and quiets again. Money Creek, joining the Root at mile 0.7, is followed by more riffles. The pool-drop pattern continues the length of the trip.

Just past a yellow state forest sign (mile 5.1) on the right is the first DNR campsite, Whispering Pines, across the river from a low limestone outcrop topped with white (whispering) pines. The second site is about two minutes downstream, also on the right.

The Root carves a sharp left bend (mile 6.3) where the hydroelectric project's diversion dam once stood. (The remains of the broken dam were removed in 2004.) At the bend is an island, and the right channel is blocked by rocks and logs. Follow the left channel through a curving Class I drop filled with standing waves.

The narrow river valley sprawls out, floodplain on both sides, and the Root weaves between sandbars and islands. After you see a road on the left bank, the river bends south. Just before the bend, Torkelson Creek, a state-designated trout stream, comes in from the left. (Its mouth may be jammed with deadfalls.) You run a long series of riffles and easy Class I rapids, both here and again as you swing around a big island. Just before the Root bends south at mile 10, an osprey-nesting platform perches on a pole on the left.

The only way to see this 1915 vintage powerhouse is to paddle the Root.

The neoclassical Root River Power & Light Company's powerhouse (mile 10.1) seems out of place in this remote wooded valley, and indeed its useful life was quite short—1915 to 1940. Downstream on the low left bank, the first Powerhouse campsite is across the river from a metal gate. The second campsite, also on the left, is just before a large island. The mile that follows is filled with sand bars, gravel bars, islands, riffles, and, sometimes, cows. They belong to the farm on the left.

The Highway 250 bridge recently acquired a new paint job. This lovely old-fashioned truss bridge crosses the river about 2 miles above the take-out. Between this bridge and the bike-trail bridge that follows, you see a few houses. The bike-trail bridge extends from a long spit that also divides the Root from its South Branch, flowing in from the right. On hot weekends, watch out for both swimmers jumping from the trail bridge and tubers floating in from the South Branch.

Downstream from the confluence, the Root runs under powerlines and curves slightly east. Take out on the right; the sandy landing is marked with a DNR sign.

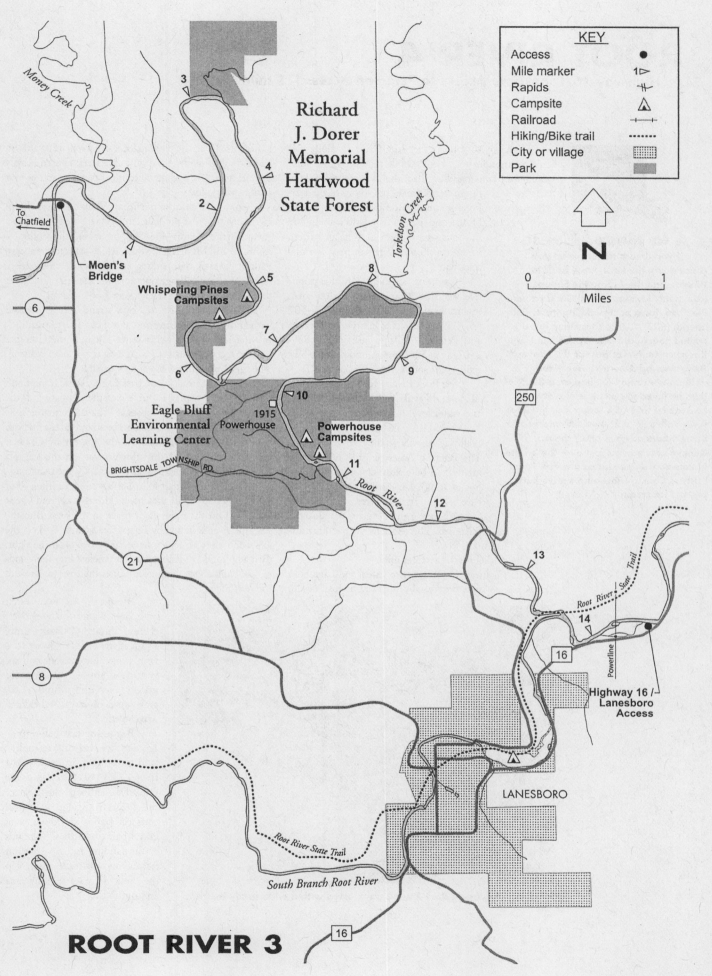

KEY

Access ●
Mile marker 1▷
Rapids ⊢⊬⊣
Campsite △
Railroad ⊢⊦⊦⊣
Hiking/Bike trail ┈┈
City or village
Park

N

0   1
Miles

Richard
J. Dorer
Memorial
Hardwood
State Forest

Money Creek

To Chatfield

Moen's Bridge

Whispering Pines Campsites

Eagle Bluff Environmental Learning Center

BRIGHTSDALE TOWNSHIP RD.

1915 Powerhouse

Powerhouse Campsites

Torkelson Creek

Root River

Root River State Trail

Powerline

Highway 16 / Lanesboro Access

LANESBORO

Root River State Trail

South Branch Root River

ROOT RIVER 3

6

21

8

250

16

16

ROOT RIVER 4
Highway 16/Lanesboro Access to Peterson Access (15 miles)

À la Mode, Please

If you dream about pie as you cruise down the Root, head back to Whalan and the Aroma Pie Shoppe (commonly known as The World Famous Pie Shop) for a post-paddling treat. Call ahead, (507) 467-2623 as they have limited hours on weekdays. When Dan Kaercher, author of *Best of the Midwest: Rediscovering America's Heartland*, visited the Aroma Pie Shop on a 2005 tour, he loved the pie. It is one of the reasons he told *USA Today* that the Root River valley is "a Midwest Shangri-La." Dessert hounds have other choices: Geneva's Hideaway, just over the bridge in Peterson, serves ice cream. The Pedal Pushers Café in Lanesboro serves both pie and ice cream.

Highway 16 follows the Root River all along this route. Although you might think that the road noise would ruin your paddling fun, the lively, burbling, riffling river balances the sound of the traffic quite nicely. Add in the beauty of the bluffs, and it's quite possible to ignore the road. A pie shop in Whalan and an ice cream shop in Peterson may also distract you.

Camping possibilities include primitive riverside campsites with their own beach; Eagle Cliff Campground, (507) 467-2598, a private facility on the river; and Peterson Village Park, (507) 875-2587, a city RV campground near the bike trail on the south edge of Peterson.

See Root River 1 for information on canoe and kayak rentals, shuttle service, and water level information.

The 11.4-mile **shuttle route**, all on Highway 16, follows the river to Peterson. The Peterson Access is right next to the highway. A bike shuttle works well if you put in at Whalan instead. Ride the Root River State Trail between the Whalan Canoe Landing and Peterson and cross the bridge to reach the access. This shortens the paddling distance to 11.8 miles.

The **gradient** is 3.4 feet per mile.

The Highway 16 Access, also called the Lanesboro Access on the sign next to the highway, is just east of Lanesboro. From the parking lot, carry about 150 yards on a level trail to the river. Because this access is used heavily by outfitters, you find rental canoes piled next to the river at the level, sandy **put-in**.

For a bike shuttle, **put in** at Whalan instead. From Highway 16, cross the Whalan Bridge, turn right at 2nd Avenue (the Aroma Pie Shoppe is on the corner—mmmm) and left on New Street, which leads to the access. Park in the state trail parking area farther down the road. As you read the mileage notations for this trip, remember that mile 3.2 is your starting point from Whalan.

The Root runs quickly over a sand bottom overlaid with gravel patterns. Sand and gravel bars lace the channel, moving and shifting with water levels. If the river has flooded recently, watch for snags, especially near Peterson. The DNR clears those as soon as possible.

Within 1.5 miles, you pass Eagle Cliff Campground on the right. Another 1.1 mile past the campground, the County Road 36 bridge crosses at Whalan. A quarter mile downstream, you see the remains of an old bridge on both banks. After these abutments, the mouth of Gribben Creek is on the right. Just downstream on the left is a hand-painted sign for the sandy Whalan Canoe Landing.

In the 5 miles that follow, the winding, riffling Root is fed by several small streams, including Diamond Creek (mile 6.8) on the right. As it makes a sharp bend to the east, the river is joined by Raaen Creek (mile 8.4) on the left. Soon after, you see a large sandy beach on the right. Two adjoining DNR campsites are tucked into the woods on the bank above. Public land lines the river for most of the next mile.

Two campsites along Root River 4 are blessed with a wide sandy beach.

At mile 9.7, the Root is split by a large island; follow the left channel through a Class I drop. As the island ends, Highway 16 is visible on the right, but you see very few houses. On an old unused truss bridge (mile 11.6), grass grows on a roadbed riddled with holes.

Beginning just before mile 13, another half mile of public land lines the right bank of the river. This stretch has some beautiful sandbars. Just before the Peterson Bridge, the river runs through a shallow area of gravel bars and riffles. **Take out** at the landing for the Peterson Access on upstream right. Up the bank there's a parking area and outhouse.

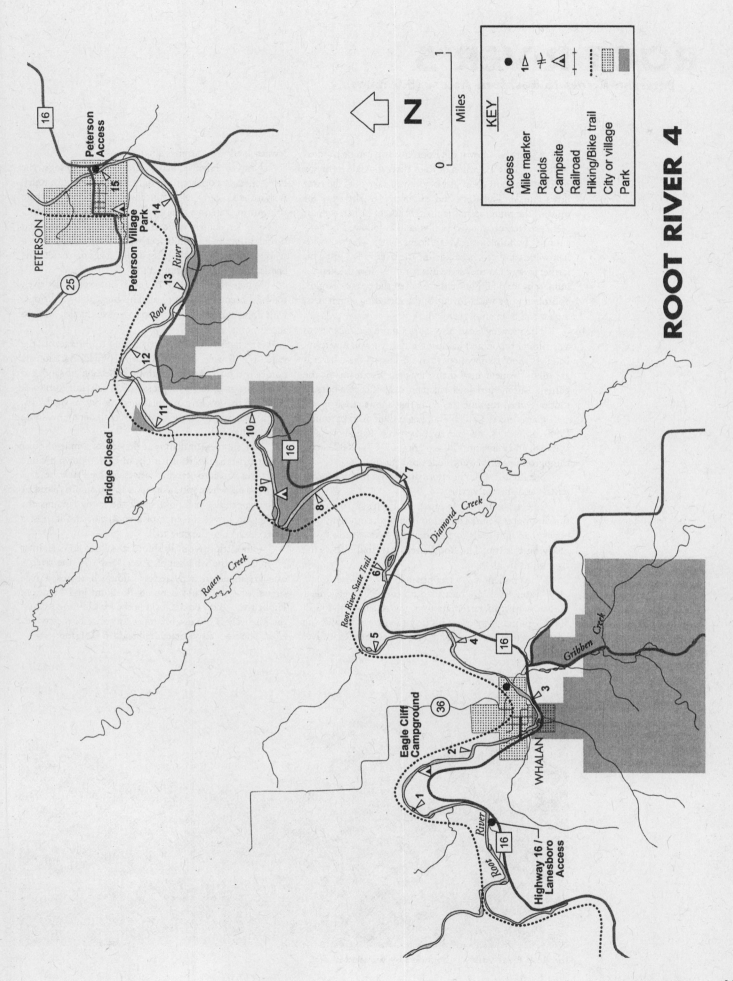

ROOT RIVER 4

KEY

Access
Mile marker
Rapids
Campsite
Railroad
Hiking/Bike trail
City or village
Park

Miles
0   1

N

16
Peterson Access
PETERSON
25
15
Peterson Village Park
14
Root River
13
12
11
Bridge Closed
10
16
9
Raaen Creek
8
7
6
Root River State Trail
Diamond Creek
5
4
16
Gribben Creek
36
Eagle Cliff Campground
3
2
WHALAN
1
Root River
16
Highway 16 / Lanesboro Access

ROOT RIVER 5
Peterson Access to Rushford Access (5.9 miles)

A short float down the Root, this trip can be paddled by itself or as an extension of Root River 4. Aside from few riffles and a short drop just before you take out, the river flows quietly. The Root and Highway 16 part ways for most of the route, so traffic noise is absent or barely audible. A stretch of wooded public land is followed by agricultural bottomlands. Magnificent bluffs covered with hardwoods and cedars still define the river valley, just a bit farther away than they were upstream. Willow thickets on numerous sand and gravel bars soften the river's margins. You often spot water-loving birds, including kingfishers, eagles, and even an osprey.

The growing Root now carries more sediment from agricultural runoff and has lost the clarity it had upstream. Paddlers should know how to avoid snags—these hazards are more frequent now than they were upstream. At the partially submerged lowhead dam near the take-out, be cautious when running the chute that allows passage.

Camping is available at Eagle Cliff Campground, (507) 467-2598, on the river between Lanesboro and Whalen; and Peterson Village Park (507)875-2587, a city campground on the south edge of Peterson.

See Root River 2 for information on **canoe and kayak rentals** and **shuttle service**.

The 4.3-mile **shuttle route**, on Highway 16, crosses the river once. Before you get to Rushford, turn right on a gravel road that leads to the access. A **bike shuttle** works nicely on this trip. The Root River State Trail follows the river on its north bank.

The **gradient** is 2.9 feet per mile.

Water levels are measured on the USGS gage near Houston (http://waterdata.usgs.gov/mn/nwis/uv?0538 5000). Although the river is rarely too low to paddle, the DNR says that between 3 and 5 feet is best. See Root River 1 water levels for warnings about floods.

Next to Highway 16 at the Peterson Bridge, the Peterson Access on upstream right has parking and a toilet. A short, steep carry takes you down to the landing where you **put in**. Peterson disappears quickly and more than a mile of quiet, densely wooded land follows. The somewhat turbid Root, at least 200 feet wide, flows swiftly over a sandy bottom. You'll probably dodge snags on the outside bends throughout the trip.

Where the Highway 16 (mile 2.6) crosses the river, the land becomes agricultural. This busy highway bridge, with long guard rails and snag-strewn banks, has no access point.

The banks are wooded again after the bridge, but the valley is still wide and open. Farmers' fields occasionally border the river. An ever-shifting collection of sand and gravel bars provides good rest stops. As you near Rushford, you'll see the town's name blazoned on one of the bluffs. Occasional rip-rap on the banks is a reminder of the Root's flooding habits.

The submerged dam is at the end of a mile of quiet wooded riverbanks. Run it right of center, down a chute that takes you into standing waves. Immediately head to the left bank where you **take out** at the Rushford Access. A gravel bar and several posts mark the sandy landing; the parking area is at the edge of a cornfield; and it's just a short distance to the bike trail.

Other trips: From Rushford, the Root flows another 35 miles to the Mississippi. After Rushford, the river is often channelized and treeless, although there's a nice stretch of public land between Rushford and Houston. Public river access points include the Houston Access and the Highway 26 access, 3.2 miles upstream of the confluence. The Root River State Trail ends in Houston.

The Root River valley is bounded by wooded bluffs.

ROOT RIVER 5

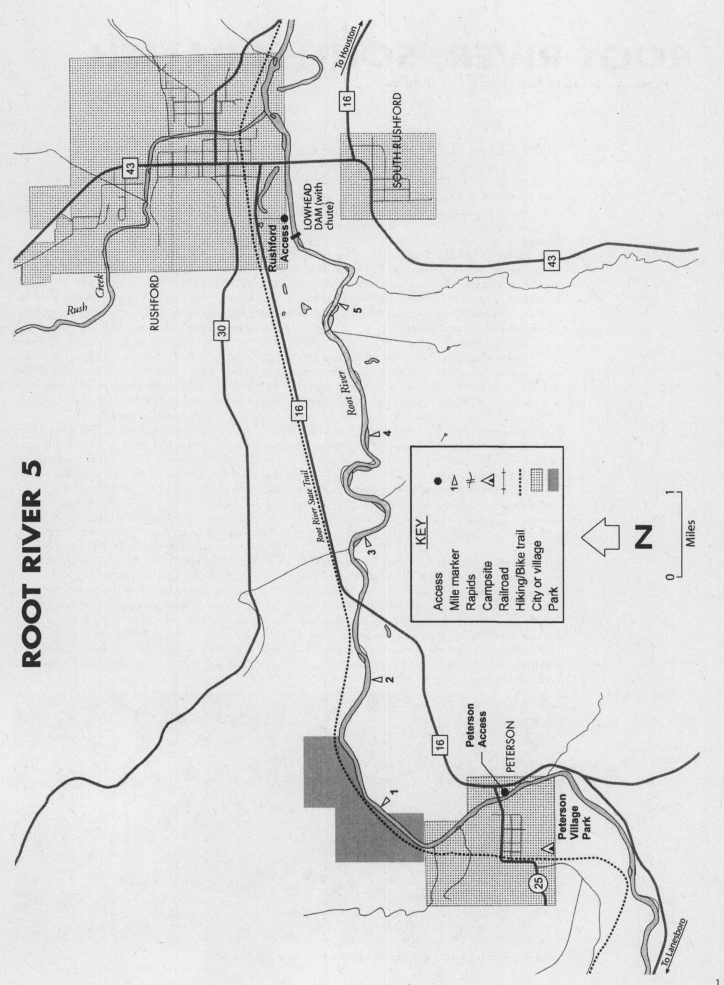

KEY

- • Access
- 1△ Mile marker
- ≠ Rapids
- ◁ Campsite
- ┼ Railroad
- ⋯ Hiking/Bike trail
- ▦ City or village
- ▓ Park

N

Miles
0 — 1

RUSHFORD

Rush Creek

SOUTH RUSHFORD

To Houston

Rushford Access

LOWHEAD DAM (with chute)

Root River

Root River State Trail

Peterson Access

PETERSON

Peterson Village Park

To Lanesboro

16
43
30
25

5
4
3
2
1

ROOT RIVER, SOUTH BRANCH

Preston Access to Lanesboro (15.3 miles)

The South Branch of the Root is a pretty stretch of river running through beautiful bluff country. Although water levels aren't as reliable as they are on the main stem, many entertaining riffles in the first half of the trip make it well worth paddling when the water's up. In the second half of the trip, the flow gradually slows as the river feels the effects of the Lanesboro hydroelectric dam. Taking out at the Old Barn Resort eliminates the slow stuff and shortens the trip to 8 miles. Because the South Branch is a noted trout stream, paddlers often pass anglers wading in the river. The Preston to Lanesboro and Root River state trails, used by bicyclists and hikers, follow the river on an old railroad grade, crossing several times.

Camping is available at the Old Barn Resort: (800) 552-2512; www.barnresort.com), a private facility with a canoe landing, restaurant, golf course, and swimming pool in addition to the campgrounds. There's camping at the Lanesboro City Campground at the take-out. Along County Road 17 west of the river, the state's Isinours Forest Management Unit has several hike-in campsites.

Canoe and kayak rentals and **shuttle service** are available from the Old Barn Resort (see above) and Just Around the Bend in Peterson, (507) 875-2767.

The 9-mile **shuttle route** from Preston runs on County Road 12, U.S. Highway 52, and Highway 16 to Lanesboro. Turn left on Highway 250 in Lanesboro. At the Thompson House B&B, turn left into the city campground.

For a **take-out at the Old Barn Resort**, go north from Preston on County Road 17 and turn right on the gravel road that leads to the resort. If you're not camping there, stop at the barn to ask permission to park and land. There's no fee, and they'll give you directions to the landing. The resort asks that you park up at the barn, not at the turnaround. Because the landing is unmarked, it's a good idea to drive down and look at the landing when you run the shuttle so you recognize where to take out.

Whichever take-out you use, this trip is a natural for a **bicycle shuttle** on the state trail.

The **gradient** is 5.0 feet per mile.

Water levels, best between 2.2 and 4 feet, are measured on a gauge below the Lanesboro dam. Real-time readings are available on the DNR Web site (http://www.dnr.state.mn.us/river_levels/index.html).

Put in at the Preston Access at the County Road 12 bridge. From U.S. Highway 52 in Preston, turn south on St. Paul Street (County Road 17) and west on Fillmore Street (County Road 12). The canoe landing on downstream left has parking. The river speeds through town, passing junk-covered, riprapped banks on the left and some very pretty rock cliffs on the right. There's a river gauge painted on the County Road 17 bridge, but readings are not reported. From the landing to a half mile past the U.S. Highway 52 bridge, the South Branch is a state-designated trout stream. Please be courteous to anglers by giving them plenty of room as you pass.

The South Branch flows under U.S. Highway 52 and out of town, the state trail runs along the left bank, crossing four times in the next 8 miles. Limestone outcrops rise above the river. The swiftly flowing river riffles through many little drops. At low water levels, dragging and scraping are inevitable.

As the river runs through the Old Barn Resort golf course (starting at about mile 7.8), watch for an inconspicuous, unmarked access (mile 8.3) on the right, upstream of the resort's "River's Bend" bridge. If you're stopping at the Old Barn, take out here.

After the resort bridge, the South Branch races through a riffly S-curve. Downstream, as the state trail crosses on a railroad trestle next to a log shelter, it speeds up again, briefly. In the last 3 miles, the flow is quiet and slow as the river wanders into Lanesboro. Take out on the right at the Lanesboro city campground upstream of the dam.

Riffles and rapids on the South Branch of the Root offer a fast, fun ride.

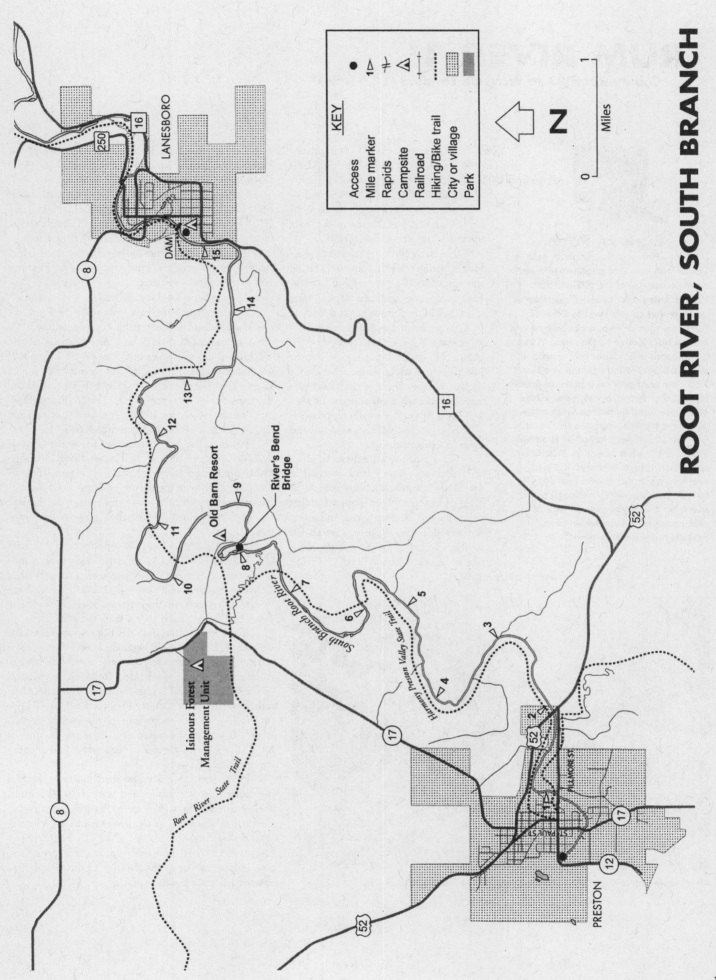

ROOT RIVER, SOUTH BRANCH

KEY

- Access ●
- Mile marker 1△
- Rapids ≠
- Campsite △
- Railroad ┼
- Hiking/Bike trail ⋯
- City or village
- Park

N

Miles
0 — 1

LANESBORO

250
16

DAM

8

16

17

52

Isinours Forest
Management Unit

Old Barn Resort

River's Bend
Bridge

South Branch Root River

Harmony Preston Valley State Trail

Root River State Trail

17

52

PRESTON

All Route St.

RUM RIVER 1
County Road 27 to Wayside Landing (14.5 miles)

Park to Park

For off-river entertainment, you can bicycle between two popular state parks on Mille Lacs Lake. From Mille Lacs Kathio State Park, it's just 7 miles on a quiet, paved county road to Onamia. (Within a year or two, a paved trail will extend from Kathio to Onamia.) In town, the restored train depot has restrooms and parking. From there, the Soo Line Trail runs northeast on a railroad grade for 11 miles to Isle, passing the village of Wahkon and numerous wetlands with abundant birdlife. From the trailhead in Isle, city streets lead to Father Hennepin State Park, with a beach on Mille Lacs Lake. **Two things to note:** The trail provides a parallel gravel lane for all-terrain vehicles (ATVs), although use is sporadic. And if you plan to stay at either park on a summer weekend, definitely make reservations.

The Rum, a state-designated Wild and Scenic River, begins its 145-mile journey to the Mississippi as it flows from Mille Lacs Lake and wanders through Kathio State Park, feeding three lakes linked by channels filled with wild rice in late summer. This first trip begins as the river leaves the last lake, Lake Onamia.

The lively Rum runs clear and shallow: sometimes quietly, sometimes racing through riffles and various Class I rapids. One exception, Bradbury Rapids, rates Class I-II in medium water and Class II in high water. In the first 6 miles, U.S. Highway 169 is the Rum's constant companion. Whether it's crossing the river or just generating traffic whine, it's there. In the last 8 miles, the river and road part ways and the whine disappears. In May and June, fishing for smallmouth bass is said to be good in pools below rapids and holes by bridge crossings.

For a two-day adventure, combine this stretch with Rum River 2, camping at the DNR campsite just downstream of Wayside Landing. Note: Wayside Landing requires a long carry up a steep and sometimes eroded trail. When you set up the shuttle, check out the trail; If you don't like it, use the County Road 19 (250th Street) bridge instead.

Car camping is available at Mille Lacs Kathio State Park, (320) 532-3523, northwest of Onamia. There's a DNR canoe campsite near Wayside Landing.

Canoe rentals (no shuttle service) are available at Mille Lacs Kathio State Park. Country Camping in Isanti, (763) 444-9626, offers canoe rentals and shuttle service for the Rum from Onamia to Isanti (107 river miles).

The 11-mile shuttle route runs east on County Road 27, right on Pine Street, and south on Highway 169 to the highway rest area.

The gradient is 5.3 feet per mile.

Because huge Mille Lacs Lake feeds the Rum, the river's water level is fairly stable, usually sufficient for canoeing from April through June. After that, a good rain will bring it up. The gauge at County Road 25 south of Onamia should read at least 0.5 feet. Above 1 foot is high water, a low bridge (mile 4.5) may have to be portaged and Bradbury Rapids becomes Class II. The DNR posts readings weekly, when available: http://www.dnr.state.mn.us/river_levels/levels.html?id=rum; (888) 646-6367.

Put in at the public access just below the Onamia dam, on upstream right at the County Road 27 bridge. Two more bridges follow in quick succession. The current can be pushy in the narrow opening under the railroad trestle. Avoid the submerged pilings on the left. Under County Road 25, the river gauge is on downstream right.

The next 2 miles seem like a bridge tour. The twin U.S. Highway 169 bridges are rather decorative. A mile downstream, a prosaic single span carries County Road 22. After another mile and another pair of highway bridges, the river leaves the scattered houses behind. The clear Rum flows quickly over a sand and gravel bed.

In the fourth mile, boulders begin to appear on the streambed. If the water's high, duck under or portage around the low wooden County Road 19 bridge. Another pair of highway bridges (mile 5.4) is followed by the County Road 7 bridge (mile 5.8). Less than a half mile downstream of County Road 7, Bradbury Rapids (mile 6.1) is a steep, rocky drop in two separate pitches. Class I-II at medium water, at high water the drop is filled with two- to three-foot-high waves and a pushy current, rating Class II.

In the remaining 8 miles, the Rum races through intermittent rocky riffles and easy Class I rapids. Sheltered from highway noise by its wooded corridor, the river is a peaceful place. Take out on river left at Wayside Landing, downstream of the U.S. Highway 169 bridge. A 200-yard trail leads up to the highway rest area, indoor restrooms, and parking. County Road 19 is another 1.6 miles downstream.

After leaving Lake Onamia, the Upper Rum is free-flowing and quick.

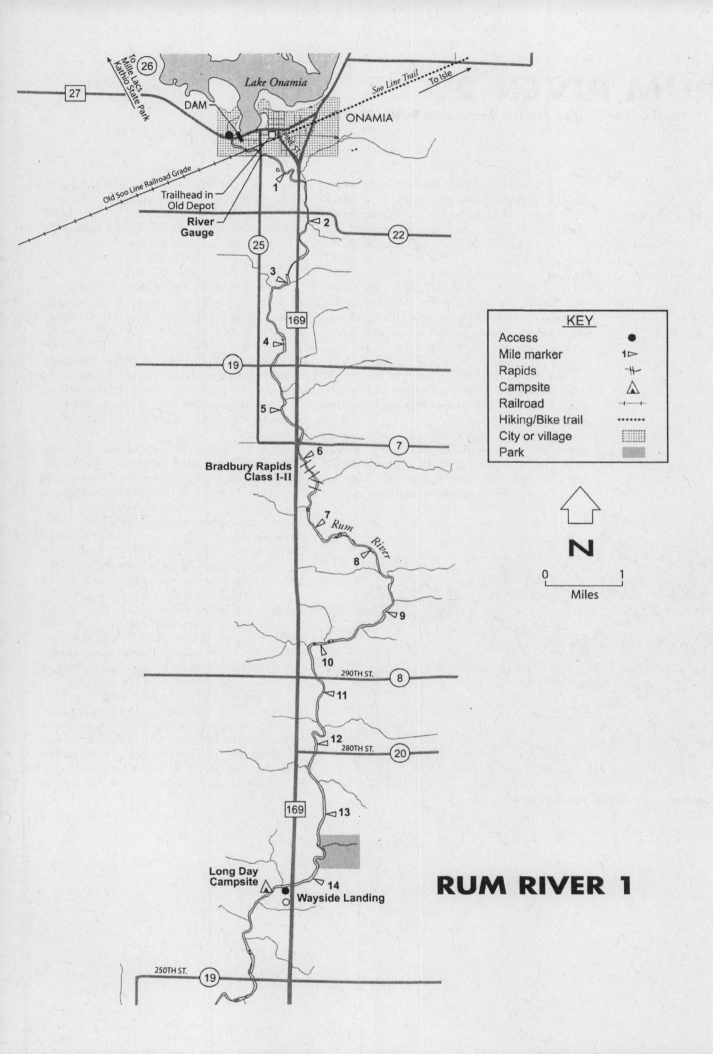

KEY

Access	●
Mile marker	1▷
Rapids	╫
Campsite	⛺
Railroad	┼─┼
Hiking/Bike trail	••••
City or village	▦
Park	▨

Lake Onamia

DAM

ONAMIA

To Mille Lacs Kathio State Park

Soo Line Trail   To Isle

Old Soo Line Railroad Grade

Trailhead in Old Depot

River Gauge

N

0   1
Miles

Bradbury Rapids Class I-II

Rum River

290TH ST.

280TH ST.

Long Day Campsite

Wayside Landing

250TH ST.

RUM RIVER 1

RUM RIVER 2
Wayside Landing to Milaca Recreation Park (16.3 miles)

This stretch of the Rum is even prettier than the first. The river's narrow, rocky nature and the combination of wooded banks and frequent islands make the trip visually appealing. Easy Class I rapids alternate with quiet pools in an entertaining rhythm that characterizes the whole journey. With no U.S. Highway 169 crossings and only four county bridges, there's little traffic noise. Until you reach the outskirts of Milaca, there are few houses. For a 9.7-mile trip that ends before Milaca's presence is apparent, take out at the County Road 11 bridge. A two-day, 31-mile trip between Onamia and Milaca combines this stretch with Rum River 1 and a night at the canoe campsite just downstream of Wayside Landing.

Mountain-biking enthusiasts will be interested to know that Milaca has 14 miles of single-track bike trails across the river from Recreation Park on the walking bridge.

See Rum River 1 for information on **camping**, **canoe rentals**, and **shuttles**. In addition, overnight car camping is also available at Recreation Park in Milaca with prior permission. The park has public restrooms and drinking water. There's also a band shell and two

The Upper Rum runs through a wooded corridor.

shelters, so it can be a busy place. Call the City of Milaca, (320) 983-3141, for permission to camp.

The **shuttle route** runs south on U.S. Highway 169 to Milaca. Go southwest on Highway 23, north (right) on County Road 36 (Central Avenue), and west (left) on NW 2nd Street to Recreation Park.

The **gradient** is 7.9 feet per mile.

See Rum River 1 for **water level** information.

Put in at Wayside Landing. From the parking lot of the U.S. Highway 169 rest area, the 200-yard portage trail down to the river is steep and sometimes eroded. Just downstream of Wayside Landing, the DNR's "Long Day" campsite is on the right. The Rum is rather uniform at first, its even width flanked by lightly wooded banks and a few cabins. The river's gravel bottom is visible in the clear, shallow water. Upstream left at the County Road 19 bridge (mile 1.6) is an unofficial, but good, access.

After the bridge, the river corridor feels more remote, and frequent islands make the journey interesting. The woods give way to meadows for a bit at the County Road 16 bridge (mile 5.5). After Tibbet's Brook, on the right at mile 6.9, the Rum winds through a long, scenic stretch with many islands and light rapids. There's a canoe rest area on the right at (mile 7.2). An occasional deadhead (a partly submerged log left over from the logging era) is a reminder of the past. Avoid these North Woods crocodiles; they can tip a canoe.

On upstream left at the County Road 11 bridge (mile 9.7), you find a short, well-used trail to the road. Soon after, signs of Milaca begin to appear: an industrial building and groups of houses. The riffles and islands that make the Rum fun to paddle continue all the way through town. The County Road 19 Bridge (mile 14) crosses. A golf course follows, and more houses.

Just past the WPA-era walking bridge (mile 16.1) in Recreation Park, **take out** anywhere along the grassy left bank. Orange buoys warn paddlers not to go over the lowhead dam just downstream. Below the dam is a popular fishing spot. Paddlers who plan to continue past Milaca can easily portage the lowhead dam and paddle the 1.5 miles through Milaca to Riverview Park, the start of Rum River 3.

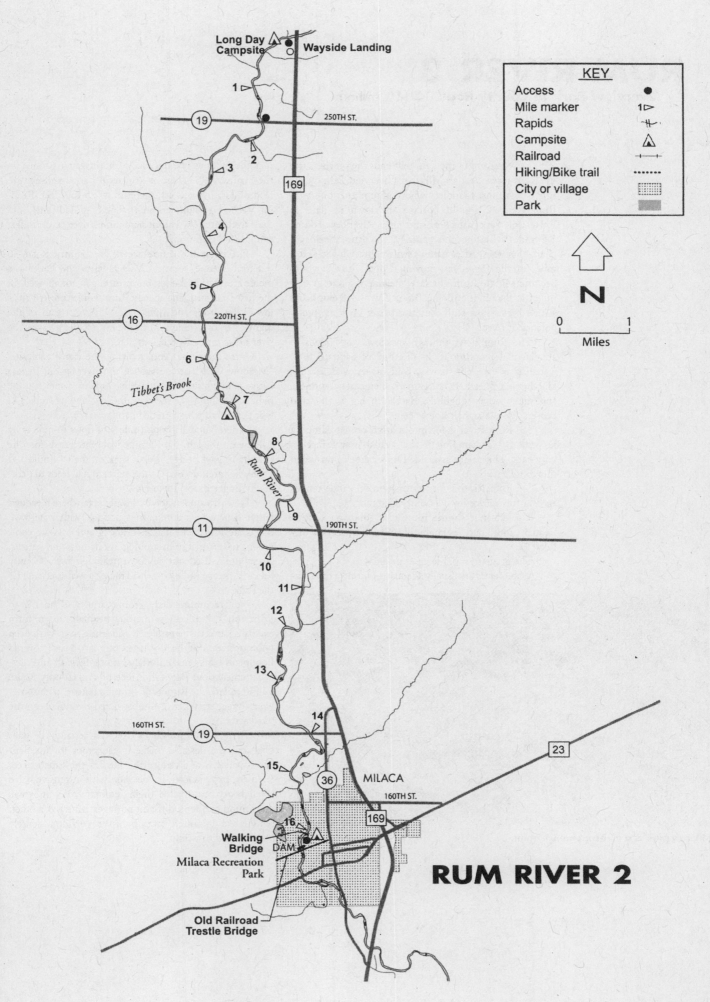

Long Day Campsite

Wayside Landing

1

19 250TH ST.

2

3

4

5

16 220TH ST.

6

Tibbet's Brook

7

8

Rum River

9

11 190TH ST.

10

11

12

13

14

23

160TH ST.

19

15

36 MILACA

160TH ST.

169

16

Walking Bridge

DAM

Milaca Recreation Park

Old Railroad Trestle Bridge

Access

Mile marker 1

Rapids

Campsite

Railroad

Hiking/Bike trail

City or village

Park

N

0   1
Miles

RUM RIVER 2

RUM RIVER 3
Riverview Park to County Road 12 (10 miles)

Downstream of the dam that ends the previous trip the Rum races through Milaca to Riverview Park, where this trip begins. (Paddlers who combine this one with Rum River 2 should portage the lowhead dam in Recreation Park instead of starting at Riverview, adding 1.5 miles.) During this journey, the Rum begins to change its ways. After riffling swiftly through the first 5 miles of the route, fast-moving Upper Rum slows to become Middle Rum, the lazy, meandering one. A 6.4-mile trip that ends at Bogus Brook Town Hall eliminates a little bit of slow stuff, but also passes up some pretty patches of river.

The Rum flows through meadows and woods in about equal proportions. In this mix of habitats, bird-watching is excellent: hawks, bald eagles, wild turkeys, blue herons, pheasants, kingfishers, mergansers, warblers, and many other songbirds. Raccoons, big turtles, and beavers also make their homes here.

See Rum River 2 for information on **car camping** in Milaca. Car camping is also available at Princeton City Park. There's one riverside DNR canoe campsite on this route.

See Rum River 1 for information on **canoe rentals** and **shuttle service** from Country Camping.

The 8.6-mile **shuttle route** runs south on County Road 36, south on U.S. Highway 169, and east on County Road 12.

The **gradient** is 5.3 feet per mile.

Water levels are usually adequate. During a dry sum-mer, the riffles will be too rocky. On the gauge painted on the Highway 95 bridge at Princeton (faded and hard to read on last inspection), medium is 2.5 to 4 feet. Readings taken by volunteers are available, sporadically, from the DNR: http://www.dnr.state.mn.us/river_levels/index.html; (888) 646-6367.

Put in at the canoe access on County Road 36 (Central Avenue) south of Milaca. Riverview Park has a picnic area with a shelter, but camping is not allowed. In the first few miles, the speedy Rum winds through shallow rocky drops and quiet pools. Downstream of the highway bridge (mile 1.1) traffic noise fades away as the river flows into a wooded stretch.

After the woods end, look for the canoe campsite. "Meadow Gem" perches above the river in an 18-acre native prairie restoration accessible only by canoe. On the right at the end of the meadow, the low landing (mile 3.2) is at the end of a high eroded bank.

Where Vondell Brook (mile 5.5) flows in quietly by a house on the left, the Rum bends right. Just before the County Road 4 bridge, timber steps on the left (mile 6.4) signal the canoe access. A short portage trail leads to parking by Bogus Brook Town Hall.

Downstream, a wide backwater area where meadows rather than woods dominate is popular with waterfowl. Banks are lower and marshier, and gravel bars are common. The channel splits and rejoins, detours and returns, several times. **Take out** on downstream left at the County Road 12 Bridge (mile 10) where there's a well-used trail up the bank.

Not recommended: From County Road 12 to Princeton (12 miles) numerous deadfalls often form extensive jams that completely block the river, with deep pools upstream of the blockages. Slippery, brush-covered floodplain banks make portages quite difficult and travel extremely slow. Between Princeton and County Route 14 (36 miles), the Rum is of a similar nature, with somewhat longer stretches of unobstructed river between the blockages.

This 48-mile stretch of river can certainly be paddled, but the obstacles make it dangerous for inexperienced paddlers and reduce the fun for the experienced. Paddlers experienced in dealing with extensive jams (French explorers called them "embarrasses") and who don't mind frequent, difficult portages can travel a quiet, remote-feeling, often swampy river corridor, densely populated with wildlife.

Milaca's park is a pleasant launch point.

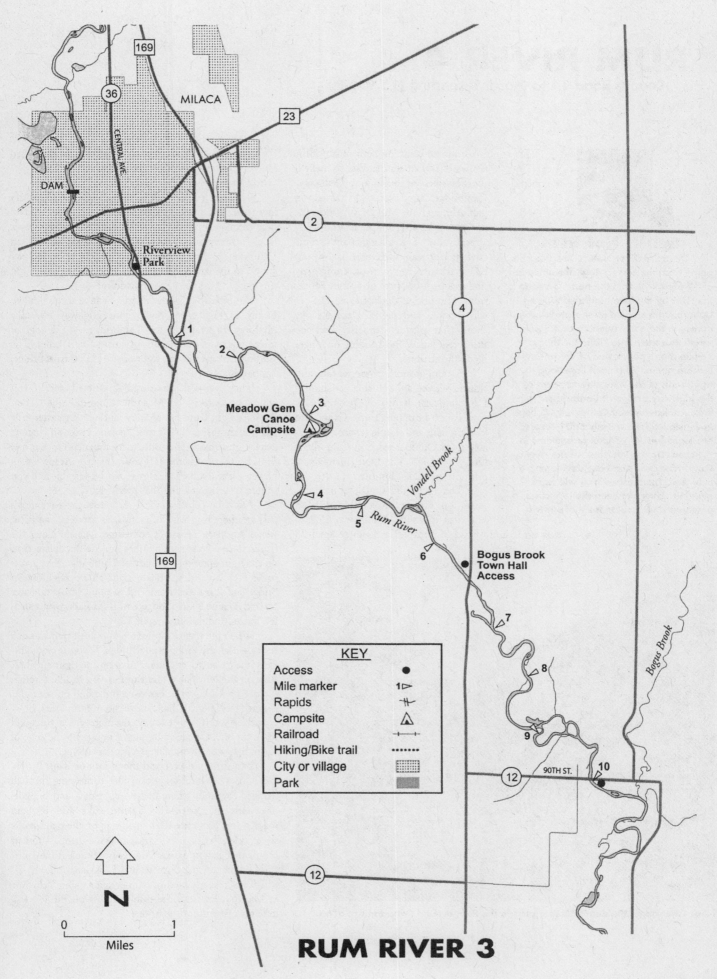

KEY

Access   ●

Mile marker   1▷

Rapids

Campsite   △

Railroad

Hiking/Bike trail   ·········

City or village

Park

Meadow Gem
Canoe
Campsite

Bogus Brook
Town Hall
Access

Riverview
Park

MILACA

DAM

Rum River

Vondell Brook

Bogus Brook

N

0   1

Miles

RUM RIVER 3

RUM RIVER 4
County Road 14 to Martin's Landing (15.9 miles)

Spirit, Not Rum

The Spirit River Nature Area gets its name from the correct English translation of "Watpa Wakan," the name given to the river by the Isanti Indians. Warren Upham, who studied Minnesota place names in the early twentith century, wrote that the name "Rum" is the "white men's perversion of the ancient Dakota name." The park lies along the right bank of the river downstream of the highway bridge at Cambridge. The local Anoka-Ramsey Community College has installed hiking trails and interpretive signs for the various ecosystems in the area. On the left bank of the river, Cambridge and Isanti are developing a bike trail. The finished trail will run along the river between the two cities, a potential shuttle route for that stretch.

This popular Rum run is just an hour north of the Twin Cities. Quiet water and an alternate access make it a good choice for families or beginners: Using the Cambridge canoe access cuts the trip in half. Although the Middle Rum lacks the narrow upper river's intimate and lively appeal, this is a pleasant and scenic stretch. Upstream of Cambridge, wooded riverbanks are almost completely undeveloped. Clusters of houses appear from Cambridge downstream, but it's still forested and pretty. Deadfalls like those that plague canoeists between Princeton and Walbo Landing no longer block the channel.

A campground, canoe rentals, and shuttle service are available at Country Camping near Isanti, (763) 444-9626; www.country-camping.com). Canoe and kayak rentals and shuttle service are available from Outdoor Edge in Cambridge, (763) 552-3343. The DNR maintains a primitive riverside campsite.

The 11.8-mile shuttle route runs south on County Road 14, east on Highway 95, south on Highway 65, and west on County Road 5. Turn left at County Road 23 (Whiskey Road), and right at Martin's Landing Road (gravel). There's parking at the public access.

The gradient is 0.8 feet per mile.

This reach is usually passable, but when the river's low (common in late summer) canoeists may need to drag through some shallows. See Rum River 3 for water level information from the Princeton gauge. In Cambridge, a river gauge is painted on the bridge pier closest to the landing, but readings are not reported. On this gauge, 3.0 to 5.5 feet is medium.

Put in at the County Road 14 canoe access, known locally as High Meadows. From Highway 65, take Highway 95 west through Cambridge. At the edge of town, take County Route 14 north for 3 miles. The landing, on downstream right of an old iron truss bridge, has parking.

The Rum is shallow, sandy-bottomed, and 90 feet wide. The DNR's High Meadows campsite (mile 1.7) on the high right bank has a sandy landing. A quarter mile past the campsite, the Rum splits, and a second channel heads right. Taking this route (a meander cutoff channel) slices a rather lovely mile off your river trip. At low water, however, the main channel may not be passable and you should take the channel that heads right.

After the cutoff channel reappears, the Rum flows past an interesting array of islands, backwaters, and occasional sandbars. Deadfalls sometimes pile up along the banks. A few houses visible through the floodplain trees on the right announce the city of Cambridge. The access (mile 8.1) is on downstream right at the Highway 95 bridge and is reached from 2nd Avenue. Across the river on 2nd Avenue is Cambridge East River Park, with a shelter, toilets, and drinking water.

When the water's low, watch out for the remains of a rock dam at the 2nd Avenue Bridge. Wooded city parkland, the Spirit River Nature Area on the right and East Park on the left, flanks the Rum as you paddle through town. At a DNR canoe campsite (mile 8.9) on the right, a picnic table perches high above the river. In 2005, however, there was no way to climb the high vertical bank and reach the site. Of the scattering of houses on the edge of town, the most memorable is a geodesic dome.

Between mile 11.1 and the mouth of Isanti Brook, the houses all but disappear. The Rum runs through wooded lowland, where occasional cedars and big cottonwoods mix with the upland oaks and lowland maples. Just past mile 13, a small sign on the right marks the Hidden Prairie picnic area, a pleasant stop. A row of cabins that begins across from Isanti Brook (mile 14.6) ends before the County Route 5 bridge (mile 15.4), which has a sandy landing on upstream right. Take out at Martin's Landing, the public access on the left 0.3 mile downstream of the bridge.

Near Cambridge, the deadfalls that plague the Rum around Princeton are gone.

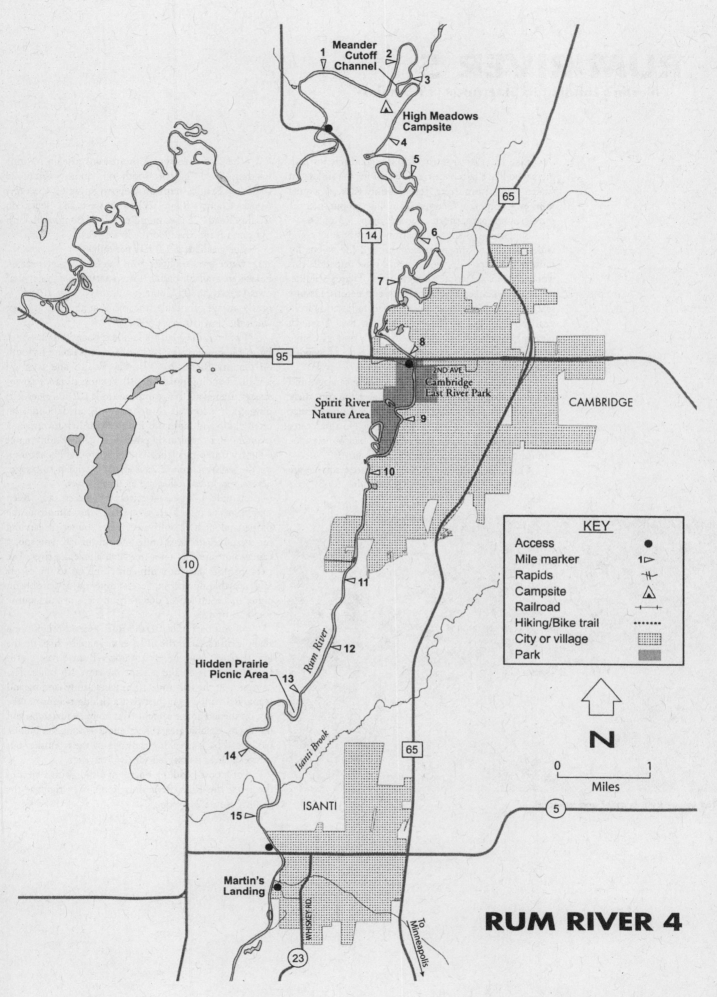

Meander
Cutoff
Channel

High Meadows
Campsite

2ND AVE.
Cambridge
East River Park

Spirit River
Nature Area

CAMBRIDGE

KEY

Access	●
Mile marker	1▷
Rapids	
Campsite	△
Railroad	
Hiking/Bike trail	·········
City or village	
Park	

N

0   1

Miles

Rum River

Isanti Brook

Hidden Prairie
Picnic Area

ISANTI

Martin's
Landing

WHISKEY RD.

To
Minneapolis

RUM RIVER 4

RUM RIVER 5
Martin's Landing to St. Francis (11.5 miles)

Like Rum River 4, this trip is a good one for paddlers who like a laid-back river. Except for the riffles that waken you at Rum River North County Park, it's a quiet journey. Campers at Country Camping can put in at the campground ramp, shortening the trip to 9.3 miles.

Sometimes shady and narrow, mostly sunny and wide, the quiet Rum meanders through the woods for most of the trip. Fall color is a nice time to paddle this wooded (and sometimes buggy) river. There's wildlife, often hawks, eagles, sandhill cranes, and herons. Despite scattered development and occasional traffic noise from nearby roads, a dense band of riparian trees creates a pleasant sense of isolation. The trip ends on a nice note at Rum River North County Park, 80 acres of wooded land bordering the river.

In addition to the Country Camping **campground** (see Rum River 4) near the beginning of the trip, there is a primitive, no-fee **canoe campsite** a short distance upstream of the take-out in Rum River North County Park: (763) 757-3920; http://www.anokacountyparks. com/qlinks/Parks/RumNorth/rumnorth.htm).

Canoe and kayak rentals and **shuttle service** are available from Outdoor Edge in Cambridge, (763) 552-3343.

The Lower Rum is quiet and wooded.

The 11.3-mile **shuttle route** runs east on Martin's Landing Road (gravel), south on County Route 23 (Whiskey Road), south on County Route 69 (becomes Anoka County Route 72), and west and south on County Road 725 (becomes Rum River Boulevard). Turn right into Rum River North County Park.

The **gradient** is 1.0 feet per mile.

Water level readings from the USGS gage near St. Francis are available online (http://waterdata.usgs.gov/usa/ nwis/uv?site_no=05286000). Although this stretch is nearly always canoeable, the riffles at the end are best when the flow is at least 500 cfs.

Put in at the Martin's Landing boat ramp in Isanti. From Highway 65, go west on County Route 5, south on County Route 23 (Whiskey Road), and west on Martin's Landing Road (gravel). A short distance downstream, there's a DNR campsite (mile 0.2) on river left; however, it's located in a heavily wooded floodplain, often damp and mosquito-infested. Farther downriver, a swinging rope at a sandy point signals the beginning of Country Camping's land. The campground's boat ramp, on the right at mile 2.2, is marked with a stop sign. Several tent sites are located along the river.

At mile 4, an east–west power line crosses. "Keep Out" signs at mile 5 are a reminder that almost all the property along here is private. Before you see the landing for the DNR rest area (mile 5.6) on the left, you spot a canoe-campsite sign on a tree high above the river. The steep bank makes for a difficult climb up to the picnic table. Farther downriver, access (mile 6.8) is possible on either upstream left or downstream right at the County Road 10 bridge.

As you pass mile 10, the Rum races through some shallow riffles. After the riffles end, a sign by steps on the left reads, "Campsite 300 Yards." Rum River North County Park is on the left for the next 1.5 miles. The campsite on the left (mile 10.8) has a sandy landing and is marked with a sign. Just past a fishing platform, **take out** on the left at the cement boat ramp. A few steps lead up to a nice picnic area, toilets, and a parking lot. Hiking paths lead back up along the river to the campsite, but camping there is reserved for river travelers.

For a post-paddling burger at a spot with a view of the river, the Rum River Inn is on river right at the County Route 24 bridge.

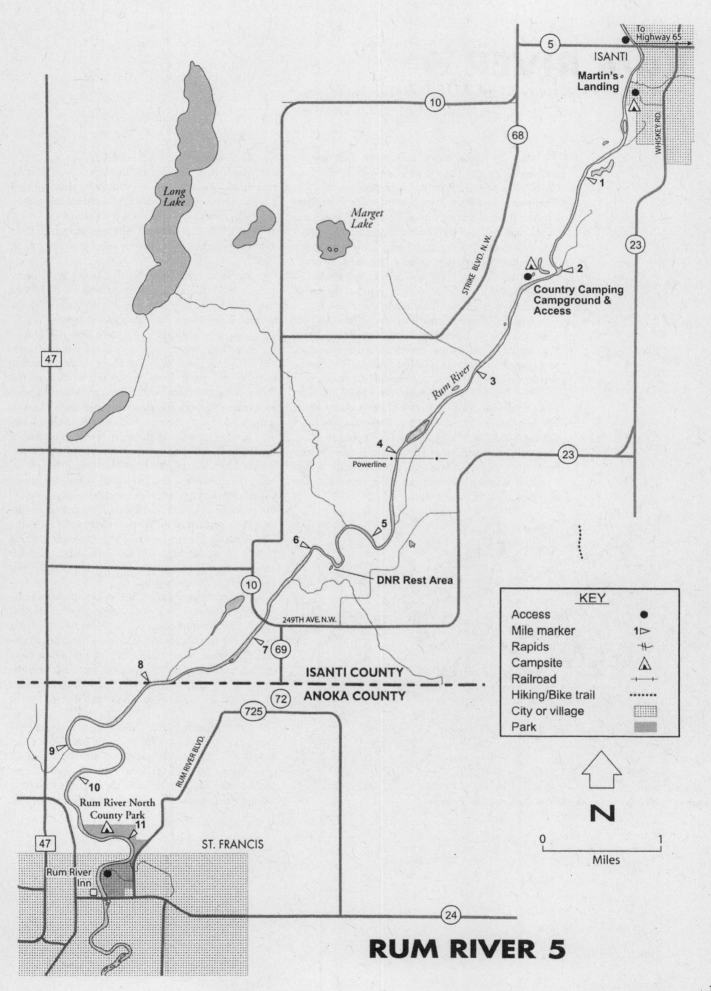

To Highway 65

5

ISANTI

Martin's Landing

10

68

WHISKEY RD.

23

1

Long Lake

Marget Lake

STRIKE BLVD. N.W.

2

Country Camping
Campground &
Access

47

Rum River

3

4

Powerline

23

5

6

DNR Rest Area

10

249TH AVE. N.W.

7 69

8

ISANTI COUNTY

ANOKA COUNTY

72

725

RUM RIVER BLVD.

9

10

Rum River North
County Park

11

ST. FRANCIS

47

Rum River
Inn

24

KEY

Access	●
Mile marker	1▷
Rapids	╫
Campsite	⛺
Railroad	┼┼
Hiking/Bike trail	·····
City or village	▦
Park	▨

N

0 _____ 1
Miles

RUM RIVER 5

RUM RIVER 6
St. Francis to County Road 7 (13 miles)

Like the Upper Rum, this reach races through assorted riffles and Class I rapids. Close to the Twin Cities, it's a popular Rum run with paddlers who like faster water than Rum River 5 has to offer. (The River Ramblers have an annual trip on this route.) Canoes and kayaks share the river with small fishing boats, as another attraction is good fishing in the deep pools between the drops, where it's common to see anglers catching small-mouth bass. Although the area is feeling considerable development pressure, 4 miles of parkland at the end of the route help ameliorate the effect on the river.

Primitive riverside **campsites** are available at both Rum River North County Park and Rum River Central Regional Park. (Entry to the north park is free; the central park charges a vehicle fee.) See Rum River 4 for information on Country Camping, northeast of St. Francis.

The 8.4-mile **shuttle route** runs south on Rum River Boulevard, west on Bridge Street (County Route 24) and south on Rum River Boulevard (becomes County Road 7 at Viking Boulevard). If you are taking out at the park, turn left at 179th Lane; there's a vehicle fee to enter the park. Otherwise, continue to the bridge, where an unofficial access is on downstream left. The only parking is on the shoulder.

Anglers in a canoe enjoy the Lower Rum near St. Francis.

The **gradient** is 2.5 feet per mile.

Water level readings on the USGS gage near St. Francis are available online (http://waterdata.usgs.gov/usa/nwis/uv?site_no=05286000). Because of the numerous rocky riffles and rapids, look for a minimum flow of 500 cfs. 1,100 cfs is better. If the river's really high (over 2,500 cfs) you may take on some water in the drop at St. Francis.

Put in at Rum River North County Park's canoe access in St. Francis, 14 miles north of Anoka. There's a large parking lot, a picnic area, and toilets next to the landing. Timber steps lead down to the river.

Right after the County Road 24 bridge (0.1 mile) the Rum drops through the remains of a broken dam. You'll have no problem in this short patch of standing waves if you run it down the center. In the next few miles, riffles alternate with quiet pools, and wooded islands are common. You pass some unobtrusive houses, some not so unobtrusive, and one that is absurdly huge.

In a big meadow on the right, there's an unmarked landing (mile 2.9) just upstream of a row of wood-duck houses. Downstream, the Rum runs quietly for several miles before starting to riffle again. A long stretch of Class I rapids starts upstream of the County Road 22 bridge (mile 6.9) and continues downstream. At the bridge, an access trail on upstream left runs next to the USGS gaging station. Starting at a cable-car crossing (mile 7.2) just downstream, the Rum dances through another half mile of entertaining riffles and Class I rapids alternating with short pools.

As you approach mile 9, the regional park lies along the right bank. You have three choices of where to **take out**. A concrete boat ramp (mile 9.4) on the right has a road to the parking lot and is close to the canoe camp-sites. The canoe access (mile 12.5) requires a long carry up to a parking area but gives you more time on the river. On downstream left at the County Road 7 bridge (mile 13) is an unofficial landing with a dirt road up to the road.

Other trips: From Rum River Central Regional Park, the Rum runs 8 miles to the Northern States Power dam in Anoka. Take out a mile upstream of the dam, at the boat ramp on river right in Rum River South County Park, next to the county fairgrounds. Below the dam, the river flows one more mile to its confluence with the Mississippi River.

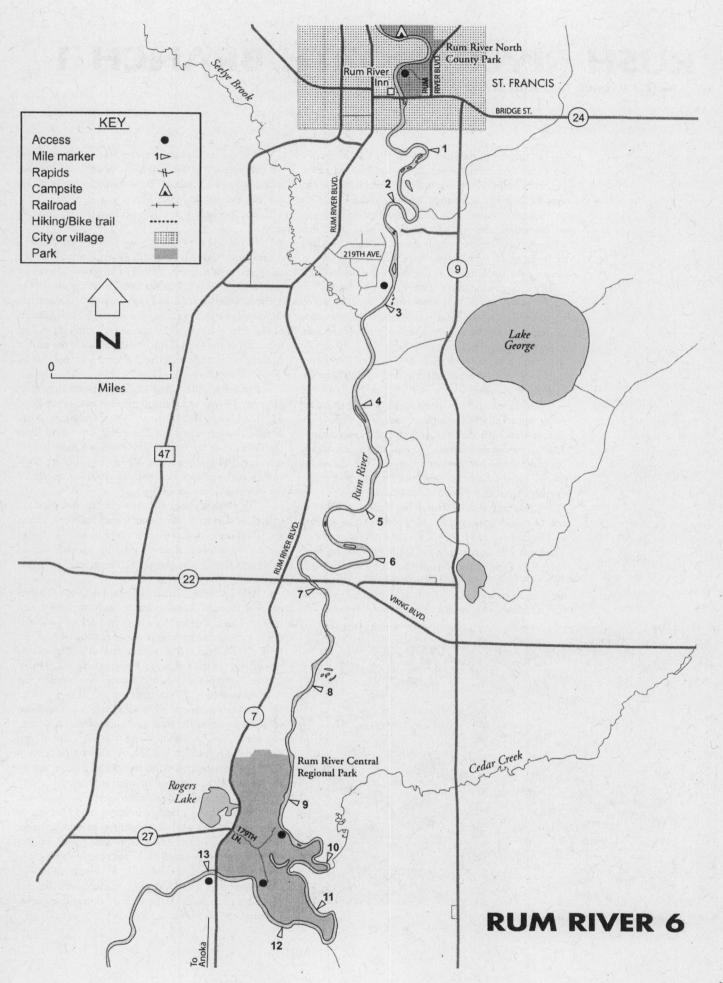

KEY

Access ●
Mile marker 1 ▷
Rapids ≠
Campsite ⚠
Railroad ┼┼┼
Hiking/Bike trail ·····
City or village
Park

N

0 ——— 1
Miles

Rum River North County Park

ST. FRANCIS

Rum River Inn

BRIDGE ST.

24

RUM RIVER BLVD.

219TH AVE.

9

Lake George

Rum River

RUM RIVER BLVD.

22

VIKNG BLVD.

Cedar Creek

7

Rum River Central Regional Park

Rogers Lake

27

179TH LN.

To Anoka

RUM RIVER 6

RUSH RIVER, NORTH BRANCH 1

401st Avenue to 300th Street (9.6 miles)

In this reach, the Rush is definitely a rushing river, which at first glance seems to account for its name. However, in the 1830s, mapmaker Joseph Nicollet noted that Rush is the translation of "Wanyecha Oju," the river's Dakota name. The Dakota referred to rushes in wetlands along the river, not the flow. Today, the rushes are gone and heavy runoff from excessive wetland drainage leads to fast flow, especially in the spring. Leaving the surrounding agricultural land behind, this speedy stream rushes down a lovely, heavily wooded valley on its way to the Minnesota River. Maneuvering on Class I rapids and long wave chains in the narrow channel requires good boat-control skills. Deadfalls are common, adding to the difficulty of negotiating the rapids, and there's a barbed-wire fence near the end of the run. Intermediate to expert paddlers will enjoy both the challenges and the view.

Red-tailed hawks and bald eagles, soaring above the valley, apparently like the place, too. Wild turkeys are common on both the riverbanks and the shuttle route. The valley sides are steep and wooded, and a dramatically high hogback of land, known locally as "The End of the World," looms over the river near the end of the trip. Frequent sandbars are good for rest stops.

Camping, with electrical hookups, hot showers, and flush toilets, is available for a fee at Allanson's Park in Henderson; call (507) 248-3234 for reservations. There's also rustic camping at Rush River Park, on Rush River Park Road west of Henderson, along Rush River 2. This park is quite popular with groups of horseback riders. The Friends of Rush River, who maintain both the park and road, request that users leave a donation.

The 4.8-mile **shuttle route** runs south on 401st Avenue, east on 310th Street, north on 390th Avenue (County Road 17), east on 306th Street, north on 371st Avenue, and east on 300th Street.

The **gradient** is a rapids-generating 10.1 feet per mile.

Water levels: A small gauge, visible from downstream river right, is fastened to a County Road 17 bridge pier. At 0.5 feet, there's barely enough water to paddle. Optimal is 1.5 to 3.0 feet. The gauge tops out at 3.3 feet, which is high and fast. Another indicator is a culvert on upstream right at the Highway 93 bridge south of Henderson. If the culvert opening is completely visible, this reach of the Rush is too low to paddle. If the culvert is completely underwater and thus no longer visible, there's enough flow.

Put in on 401st Avenue. From Henderson, take Highway 19 west of town and turn left on County Road 62. Take County Road 62 west (mostly gravel) and 401st Avenue south (gravel too). The Kelso Town Hall is on the right before the bridge. There's an outhouse behind the town hall and a parking lot in front, but it's more convenient to park on the shoulder as the best choice for the put-in is across the bridge.

The Rush is about 40 feet wide, fast and winding, with chains of waves and the occasional boulder. Cliffs of glacial till rise high and sheer above the river. The banks are mostly wooded, interspersed with occasional farm fields and field drains. An isolated dumpsite (mile 2.6) temporarily spoils the view.

At the **County Road 17 bridge**, a hard-to-read river gauge is mounted on downstream right of the wooden trestles. This bridge isn't a good access because the shoulder is too narrow for safe parking. Downstream of the bridge, the corridor feels remote and wild. Big cottonwoods, red cedars, and oaks forest the steep valley walls. Eroded canyons sometimes score the banks. The riverbed is filled with boulders now.

At a cable-car crossing (mile 8) watch out for a low rope strung across the river under the cable. Soon after, you reach "The End of the World"—a long ridge of high land, the end of which is accessible only from the river. After the river loops around this ridge, a gravel bar on the left makes a good spot for a lunch break.

Watch carefully for the barbed-wire fence (mile 9.3) at the beginning of a field of heavily grazed land on the right. The Rush is relatively quiet here, so ducking under works at most water levels. Some years there's another strand at the bridge as well. **Take out** on upstream right at the 300th Street Bridge, dubbed the Poison Ivy bridge by Mankato Paddling and Outings Club members who discovered a large patch of the stuff on downstream right. Downstream left may be infested, too.

A solo paddler enjoys the fast water of the Rush.

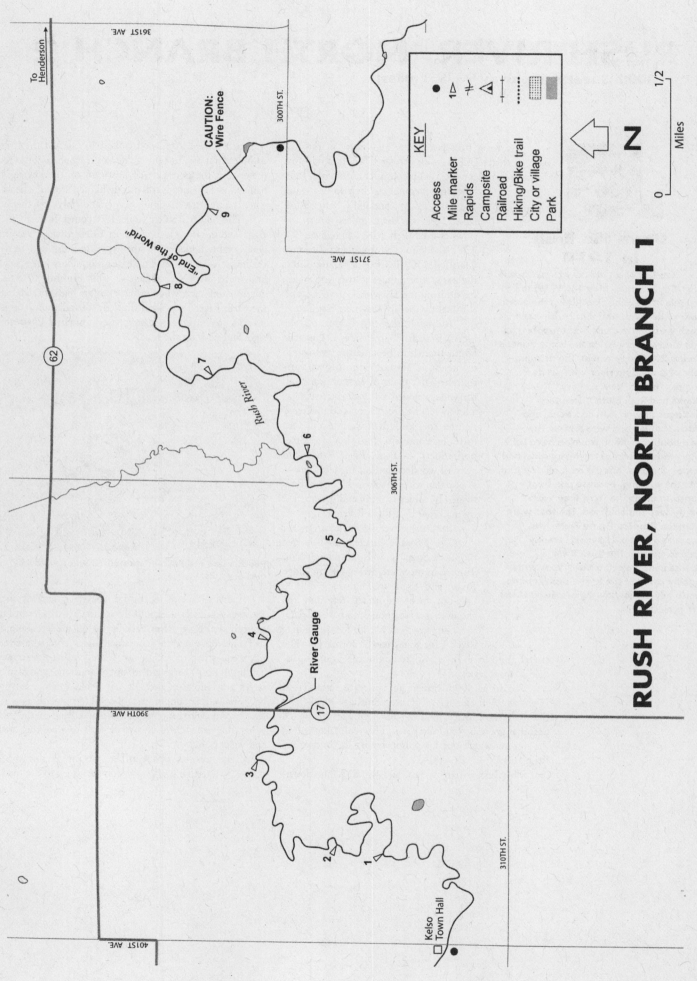

RUSH RIVER, NORTH BRANCH 1

KEY

- Access
- Mile marker
- Rapids
- Campsite
- Railroad
- Hiking/Bike trail
- City or village
- Park

N

Miles

0   1/2

CAUTION:
Wire Fence

"End of the World"

Rush River

River Gauge

To Henderson

36TST AVE.

300TH ST.

371ST AVE.

306TH ST.

390TH AVE.

310TH ST.

401ST AVE.

62

17

Kelso
Town Hall

RUSH RIVER, NORTH BRANCH 2

300th Street to Highway 93 (9.3 miles)

Down the Rush in 1919

Readers of an old newspaper article (*The Gaylord Hub*, May 16, 1919) telling the tale of a spring float down the North Fork of the Rush find that cruising the Rush was pretty much the same then as it is today. Reprinted in the same paper's Spring 2006 supplement, the account tells of a winding river with pretty rapids, "magnificent scenery," "cut banks and high bluffs," frequent portages around downed trees, and occasional barbed-wire fences. The two-boat expedition traveled from Lake Titloe to just short of the Minnesota, and it took the four intrepid men all day and into the evening. Because one boat capsized along the way, they were pretty wet and cold, too. The four were from the Gaylord Game Protective League, a group that most recently helped sponsor the Rush River Assessment Project, a three-year water-quality study of the Rush (http://mrbdc.mnsu.edu/major/lowminn/subshed/rush/rr_project.html).

The Rush runs fast, steep, and rocky in the first part of this segment, with strong Class I rapids that demand excellent boat control. Occasional deadfalls block the channel, as they do upstream, and may require portaging. After Rush River Park, the river quiets down and flows at a leisurely pace to Highway 93. The Mankato Paddling and Outings Club (MPOC) is fond of taking out at the park, shortening the trip to 6 miles, maximizing the fast-water quotient, and eliminating the highway take-out.

Although the trip begins on the North Branch, after 2 miles it joins the South Branch to become the main stem of the Rush. Carved deep into the surrounding flat plain of agricultural land, the wide, wooded valley of the Rush has a lovely feeling of isolation and unaltered nature. You see lots of wildlife and very little development. You also see horseback riders, as Rush River Park—296 acres of wooded land on the left bank—is popular with equestrians. The park is owned by Sibley County and maintained by the Friends of Rush River.

See Rush River 1 for **camping**.

The 7.8-mile **shuttle route** runs east on 300th Street (gravel) into Henderson. Turn right on South Street, left on Ridge Road, and right on Highway 93. The take-out is on upstream left and the shoulder is wide enough to park safely.

The **gradient** is 12.0 feet per mile. See Rush River 1 for **water level** information. The stretch from Rush River Park to Highway 93 can be paddled at most levels.

Put in at 300th Street, on upstream right. From Highway 93 in Henderson, go west on Ridge Road. Turn right on South Street and left on 300th Street, which becomes gravel as you leave town. This road takes you to the put-in. Watch out for poison ivy by the bridge (see Rush River 1).

The Rush is narrow, fast, and winding. Just downstream, a huge cottonwood (mile 0.9) blocked the river completely at the time this guide was researched. If it's still there, start the portage well upstream on the low right bank, where the tree is still mostly hidden around a bend. After the tree, the drops are steeper and closer together.

The South Branch (mile 1.7) comes in from the right, and the Rush is now almost 100 feet wide. Despite considerable added flow, the river runs through some shallows. A pair of huge midstream boulders (mile 3.4), known by MPOC paddlers as Old Faithful, forms a good surfing wave when water levels are high enough. At the Rush River Park Road (mile 6), the adjacent land is private. If you take out here, use immediate upstream right and park on the road.

Paddlers on the Rush in springtime wear wetsuits and drysuits.

Downstream of the bridge, the valley sprawls out, the river's much quieter, and the scenery's just as beautiful as upstream. Rush River Park begins on the left about a half mile downstream. The small signs along the river mark equestrian crossings, not landings. The first canoe landing (mile 7) isn't marked, but an outhouse and picnic tables are visible on the low left bank. Often used by equestrians, this camping area is open to canoeists as well. The second canoe landing, also unmarked and on the left, is just downstream. A short trail leads to a parking area and water pump.

Take out on upstream left at the Highway 93 bridge, where a gentle, grassy slope leads up to the road.

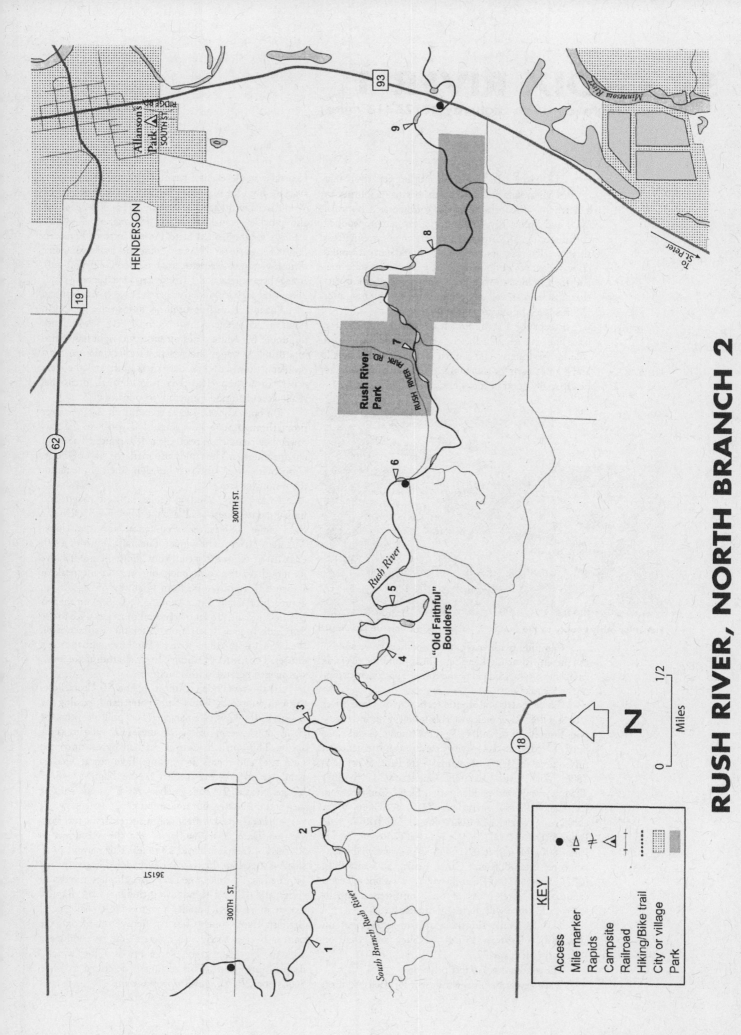

RUSH RIVER, NORTH BRANCH 2

KEY

Access	●
Mile marker	1△
Rapids	≠
Campsite	△
Railroad	┼┼
Hiking/Bike trail	····
City or village	
Park	

N

0   1/2

Miles

"Old Faithful" Boulders

Rush River

South Branch Rush River

Rush River Park

RUSH RIVER PARK RD.

HENDERSON

Allanson's Park

RIDGE RD.

SOUTH ST.

300TH ST.

300TH ST.

361ST

Minnesota River

To St. Peter

93

19

62

18

ST. CROIX RIVER 1
Wisconsin Highway 35 to Highway 48/77 (13 miles)

The St. Croix, the beautiful border river that divides Minnesota and Wisconsin, begins its journey in a northern Wisconsin flowage. Protected as a National Wild and Scenic River since 1968, the remote wooded corridor of the St. Croix is a premier canoe-camping destination. The first journey in this book starts 23 miles downstream of the flowage, quickly crosses the state line, and then follows the border. There's good paddling farther upstream as well (see Other Trips below), but, after all, this is a Minnesota paddling book.

Except for a short stretch of Class I rapids at the state line, this reach of the river runs quietly and is suitable for beginners. This stretch and St. Croix Rivers 2 and 3 are known for smallmouth bass fishing, which can be especially good in rocky areas.

Fall color adds beauty to the St. Croix valley near Riverside Landing.

Camping (with water and outhouses) is available at the put-in, Riverside Landing. Three primitive riverside campsites are located along the route. There is no camping at the take-out.

Canoe rentals and shuttle service for St. Croix River 1 to St. Croix River 6 are available from (by outfitter location, from north to south): Pardun's Canoe Rental, Danbury, (715) 656-7881, www.pardunscanoerental.com; Adventures—St. Croix, St. Croix State Park, (320) 384-7806; Wild River Outfitters, Grantsburg, (715) 463-2254, www.wildriverpaddling.com; Ekdall Country Store and Canoe Rental, Grantsburg, (715) 463-3686, www.ekdall.com; Wild River Canoe Rental, Wild River State Park, (651) 465-3127; Taylors Falls Canoe Rental, Taylors Falls, (800) 447-4958, (651) 465-6315, www.wildmountain.com; Eric's Bike and Canoe Rental, St. Croix Falls, (651) 270-1561, (715) 483-9007, www.ericsbikeandcanoe.com. Note: Most of these outfitters also rent kayaks and some will shuttle nonrental boats.

The 12.6-mile shuttle route runs southwest on Wisconsin Highway 35 to Danbury and west on Wisconsin Highway 77.

The gradient is 1.3 feet per mile.

Water levels are usually sufficient for good paddling.

General water-level information (high, medium, low) is available from the National Park Service, (320) 629-2148. Wild River Outfitters at Grantsburg, (715) 463-2254, will also provide general water-level information. Real-time readings for the United States Army Corps of Engineers (USACE) gauge at Norway Point are available online (http://www.mvp-wc.usace.army.mil/dcp/GTBW3.html). A stage between 4.4 and 10 feet is considered good for paddling. Above 10 feet (flood stage) the river is dangerous.

Put in at Riverside Landing, next to the Wisconsin Highway 35 bridge. A new National Park Service landing under big white pines on upstream right has camping, drinking water, and toilets. (Traffic noise can be a problem, however.) The current is swift and the clear water, fairly deep. The river runs through occasional shallows and around numerous wooded islands.

On both sides of a large island (mile 2.2) the river drops through State Line Rapids. If you take the narrower left channel, expect Class I-II rapids. The right channel is easier. The rapids also mark the start of the St. Croix State Forest land that lies along the right bank for the rest of the trip.

From Pansy Landing (mile 3.8), a rough and unmaintained forest road leads to Highway 35. On the right (mile 3.8) is the confluence with the Upper Tamarack River. (The Upper Tamarack provides a fun Class II-III whitewater run from about 11 miles above its mouth to the confluence, but only at the peak of snowmelt.) Traffic noise from Highway 35 signals the approach of Yellow River Landing (mile 8.2) on the left behind an island. To land here, you must pay a fee to the St. Croix Indian Reservation. After the confluence on the left with the Yellow River, a Soo Line railroad trestle crosses. The town of Danbury, just a short distance away, was started because of this rail line.

In the remainder of the trip, the St. Croix flows through remote St. Croix State Forest land, passing the mouth of the Lower Tamarack River (mile 11.5) on the right, downstream of which there's a walk-in canoe access. This small landing is reached by an unnamed sand road and there's no parking. Take out at Thayers Landing, on downstream left at the Highway 48/77 bridge. Next to the concrete boat ramp is a big parking area and outhouses, but no camping.

Other Trips: Upstream of this stretch, the run from Gordon Dam at the outlet of the flowage down to Riverside Landing is about 23 miles. This narrow, often shallow stretch of the river is best paddled in the spring. For the first 20 miles, the river races through numerous riffles and Class I-II rapids, including Scott Rapids, Coppermine Dam Rapids, and the most challenging, Big Fish Trap Rapids (Class II). Between the rapids the narrow river is shady and quiet. Below its confluence with the big Namekagon River, the St. Croix widens, deepens, and slows. This section is described in Mike Svob's book *Paddling Northern Wisconsin*.

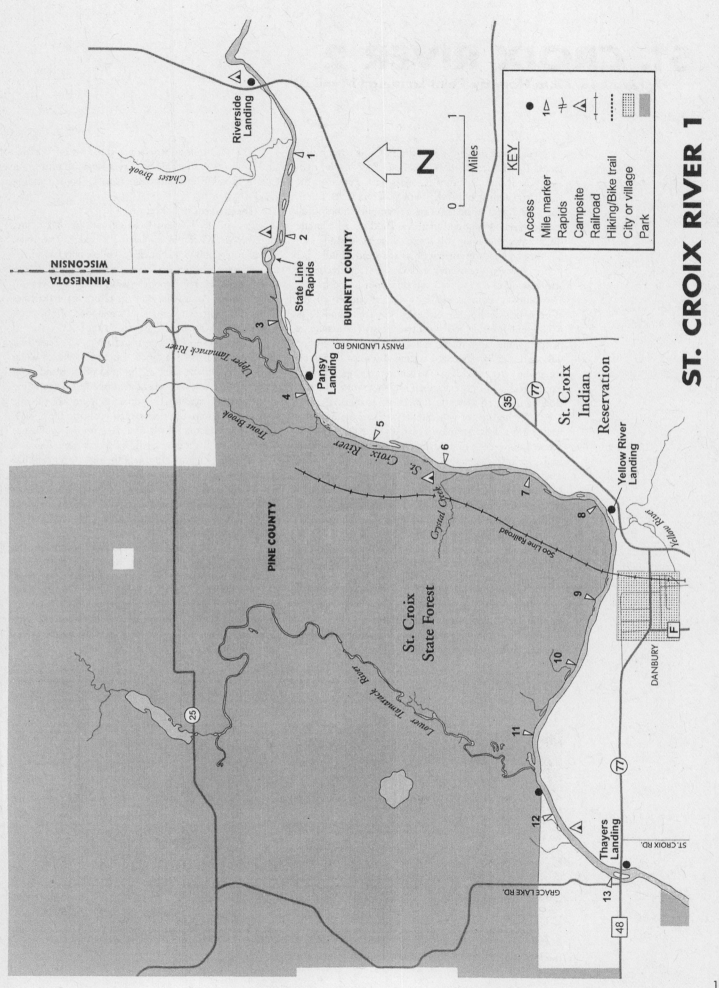

ST. CROIX RIVER 1

ST. CROIX RIVER 2
Highway 48/77 to Norway Point Landing (14 miles)

For nearly this entire trip, the St. Croix River is protected by Minnesota's St. Croix State Park on the right and Wisconsin's Governor Knowles State Forest on the left. If you combine this trip with St. Croix River 1 or 3, you have a great weekend of canoe-camping in beautiful, remote, heavily wooded country. Paddlers who prefer quiet water will enjoy this stretch. The paddling is usually easy because the current flows at a steady 3 miles per hour; however, occasional shallows and the frequently strong wind of a wide river can slow your progress.

Norway Point Landing, the take-out, is on the Wisconsin side. To take out at Sand Creek Landing in Minnesota instead would subtract less than a mile of paddling and add many miles to the shuttle route. Taking out at Sand Creek Landing also means a vehicle fee at the state park. If you're canoe-camping, however, Sand Creek will be quieter than Norway, which is accessible by road and may attract weekend partiers.

Whether or not you camp, St. Croix State Park is well worth a visit. Minnesota's largest state park (34,000 acres) has over a hundred miles of hiking and biking trails, including a stretch of the Willard Munger State Trail. There's swimming in Lake Clayton and a fire tower to climb. Along the Kettle River, which flows through the park and into the St. Croix, dramatic bedrock outcrops are visible from a trail overlook. The park also has several canoe landings on the Kettle River (Class II through the park). See the Trails Books guide *Paddling Northern Minnesota* for information on four trips on the Kettle, Minnesota's first State Wild and Scenic River.

Camping is possible at five primitive riverside campsites and at Norway Point Landing. There's also car camping at St. Croix State Park, (320) 384-6591.

See St. Croix 1 for information on **canoe and kayak rentals, shuttle service,** and **water levels.**

The 17.3-mile **shuttle route** runs east on Wisconsin Highway 77, south on St. Croix Road, southwest on County Road F, and north on Norway Point Landing Road.

The **gradient** is 0.9 feet per mile.

Put in at Thayers Landing, at the Minnesota Highway 48/Wisconsin Highway 77 bridge, 23.6 miles east of Interstate 35 at Hinckley. Unless rain has stirred up sediment, the water's clear and the sandy bottom often visible. Heavily wooded banks make the river feel quite remote. After mile 0.6, St. Croix State Park lies along the right bank for the remainder of the trip. Governor Knowles State Forest is on the left.

Downstream of a large island (mile 4.5) Pease Hill rises on the left; there's a canoe campsite on the left along this stretch. On the right at the head of an island is an access, Little Yellow Banks Landing (mile 7.0). The landing is in a backwater, and there's another campsite here, this one with a water pump. The next campsite, also on the right, is a mile downstream. Shortly after, next to the confluence with the Clam River on the left, is a fourth campsite.

The park's main landing on the right (mile 9.8) has drinking water and flush toilets just a short hike up the hill. These little luxuries are to be found at St. Croix Lodge, a log and stone building that overlooks the river. (The lodge also has exhibits about the prehistory, history, and plants and animals of the area.)

The St. Croix now flows southwest. After 3 miles, the channel is split by a large island and then bends sharp left. Just past the confluence with Sand Creek on the right are Sand Creek Landing and the fifth campsite. As of 2005, there's a drinking-water well at the landing. In less than a mile, **take out** on the left where the river bends sharp right. Norway Point Landing has campsites and drinking water near the parking area.

The landing at Little Yellow Lakes is along a backwater.

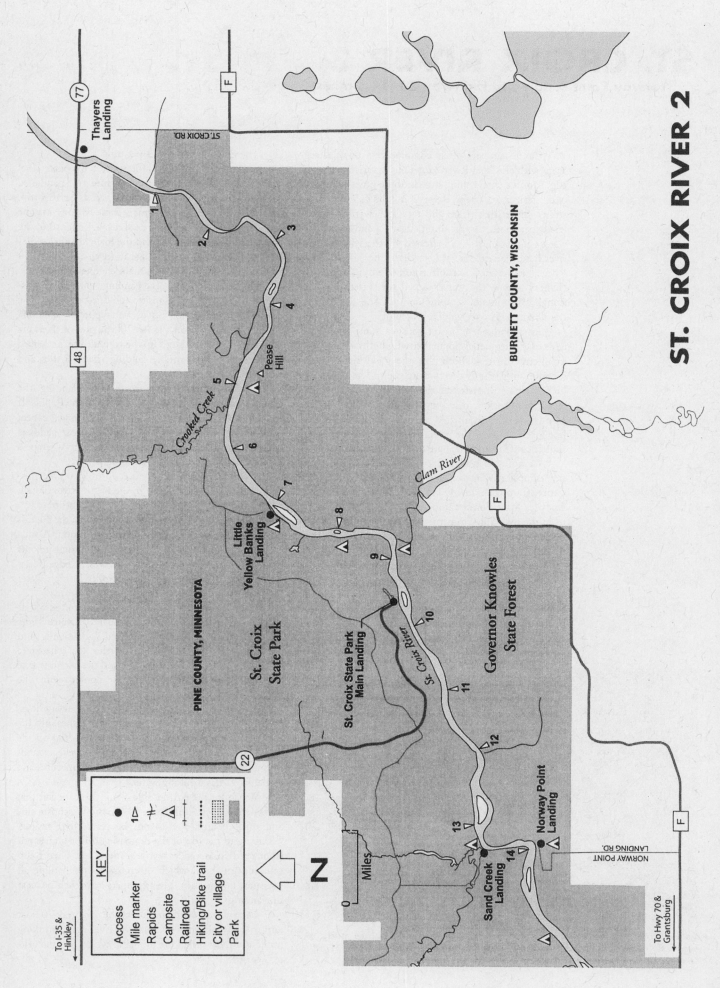

ST. CROIX RIVER 2

Thayers Landing

To I-35 & Hinkley

ST. CROIX RD.

PINE COUNTY, MINNESOTA

St. Croix State Park

Crooked Creek

Pease Hill

Little Yellow Banks Landing

St. Croix State Park Main Landing

St. Croix River

Governor Knowles State Forest

Clam River

BURNETT COUNTY, WISCONSIN

Norway Point Landing

NORWAY POINT LANDING RD.

Sand Creek Landing

To Hwy 70 & Grantsburg

KEY

- Access ●
- Mile marker 1△
- Rapids ⚲
- Campsite △
- Railroad
- Hiking/Bike trail
- City or village
- Park

N

Miles

ST. CROIX RIVER 3
Norway Point Landing to Highway 70 (14.5 miles)

Canoe-campers often combine this popular segment with St. Croix River 2 for a nicely varied overnight trip. On this trip, a short stretch of the quiet water that characterizes St. Croix River 2 is followed by a long stretch of exciting riffles and rapids. A warning to the less experienced: if you dump in the rapids when the water's up, your risk is increased by the width of the river here. For experienced paddlers, the 5-mile Kettle River Slough (Class I-II) offers some fun in a secondary channel—when the water's up. If the water's low, the slough offers lots of scraping and walking. Either way, the slough has better wildlife watching.

An abundance of nice campsites, some on islands, adds to this segment's popularity with both paddlers and small-craft boaters. Both like the good fishing, too. (Smallmouth bass is the favorite prey.) The banks rise higher along this stretch than upstream. From atop scenic Sandrock Cliffs, there's a grand view. On the Minnesota side, dominated by many acres of state land, few roads run near the river. The put-in, take-out, and shuttle route for this trip are thus in Wisconsin.

Camping is available at numerous primitive riverside campsites. Car-camping is available for a fee at St. Croix Campground, (715) 463-2898, a Governor Knowles State Forest campground across Highway 70 from the take-out. From the road wayside, turn left up the hill and into the campground, which has drinking water and toilets. The Wood River Interpretive Trail, a 1-mile loop that starts and ends in the campground, has great views of the Wood River.

See St. Croix 1 for information on **canoe and kayak rentals, shuttle service, and water levels.**

The 14.2-mile **shuttle route** is on Norway Point Landing Road, County Road F, Bistram Road, Soderbeck Road and Highway 70.

The **gradient** is 4.4 feet per mile.

See St. Croix River 1 for sources of **water level** information. Check water levels before you paddle so you know what to expect from the rapids on this trip. Below 4.4 on the USACE gauge, some walking may be necessary in both channels. Between 4.4 and 10.0, the slough rapids are Class I-II and the main channel, riffles to Class I. Above 10.0, the ledge at the end of the slough approaches Class III and the main channel, Class II.

Put in at Norway Point Landing, north of Grantsburg. The landing has campsites and drinking water. The quiet St. Croix speeds up as you approach Nelson's Landing (mile 2.5) on the left. If you stop at Nelson's Landing when the water's up, be careful. Inexperienced paddlers have had trouble landing there. Riffles and rapids follow the landing.

Less than a mile downstream of the landing, the channel splits at a fork known as Head of the Rapids. If you continue down the main (left) channel, expect entertaining riffles and Class I rapids. (Most paddlers take the main channel.) In low water, expect to scrape a lot. Fox Landing (mile 4.6) is on the left.

If you go right instead, expect 5 miles of intermittent rocky rapids (Class I-II) in the Kettle River Slough at medium to high water (or at low water, lots of scraping and walking). The state park's Head of the Rapids Canoe Access on the right has drinking water. A mile past the confluence with the Kettle, the slough rejoins the main channel in a flurry of big waves. A ledge (Class I-II) forms a wide, three-foot backroller in high water that you should avoid.

After the two channels rejoin, adding in the waters of the Kettle, the St. Croix is almost 200 yards wide. This lovely stretch of river is dotted with islands, and wooded bluffs flank the river on the left. There are numerous campsites between here and the take-out; one is at the tip of the island where the slough rejoins the main channel.

Just upstream of a matched pair of boat landings, the fast-moving Snake River (mile 10.4) rushes into the St. Croix from the right. Snake River Landing on the right and Soderbeck Landing on the left were ferry landings until the 1920s. Both landings have outhouses and Snake River has drinking water.

Watch for the narrow side channel on the left that leads to Sandrock Cliffs (mile 13) on the Wisconsin side and duck behind the islands to reach the landing. Climbing to the top of the dramatic 60-feet-high sandstone cliff yields a view worth working for. There's also camping up there, which of course means hauling all your gear up the path. Most campers leave their boats at the landing.

Take out on upstream left at the Highway 70 boat ramp. At the Marshland Center on river right, drinking water and flush toilets are available even when the center's closed.

As the Water Rat said, "...there is *nothing*—absolute nothing—half so much worth doing as simply messing about in boats. Simply messing..." (*The Wind in the Willows*, Kenneth Grahame)

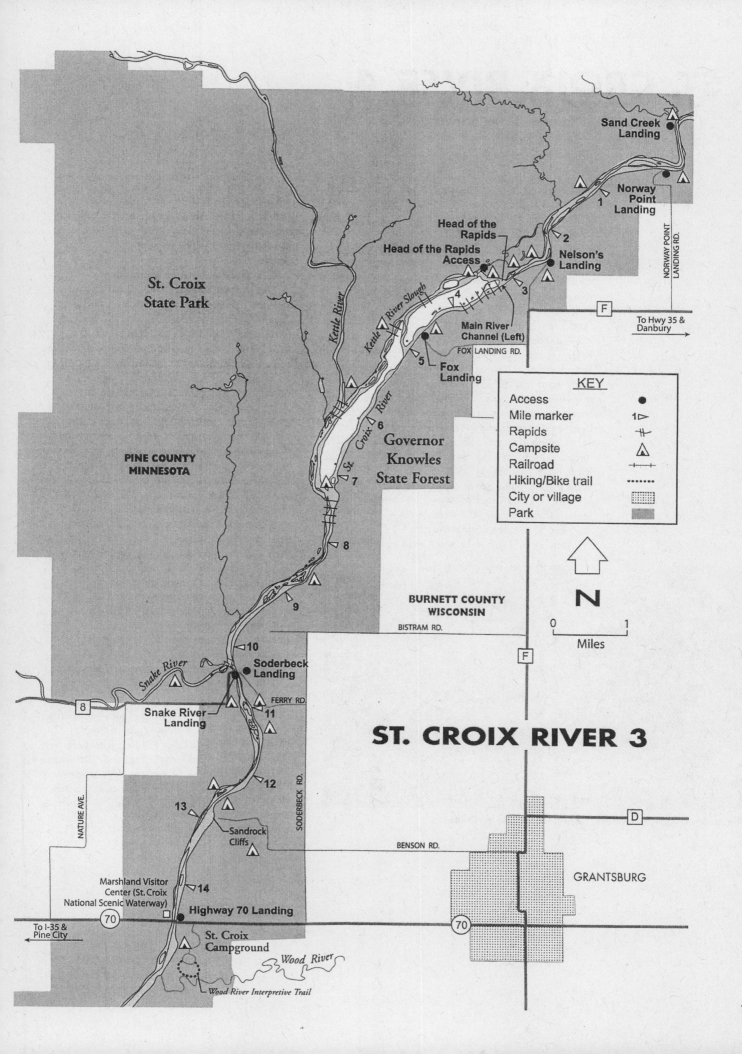

Sand Creek Landing

Norway Point Landing

NORWAY POINT LANDING RD.

Head of the Rapids

Head of the Rapids Access

Nelson's Landing

Main River Channel (Left)

FOX LANDING RD.

Fox Landing

St. Croix State Park

PINE COUNTY MINNESOTA

Kettle River

Kettle River Slough

St. Croix River

Governor Knowles State Forest

F

To Hwy 35 & Danbury

KEY

Access ●
Mile marker 1▷
Rapids
Campsite 🏕
Railroad
Hiking/Bike trail ······
City or village
Park

N

0   1
Miles

BURNETT COUNTY WISCONSIN

BISTRAM RD.

F

ST. CROIX RIVER 3

Snake River

Soderbeck Landing

FERRY RD.

Snake River Landing

8

SODERBECK RD.

NATURE AVE.

Sandrock Cliffs

BENSON RD.

D

GRANTSBURG

Marshland Visitor Center (St. Croix National Scenic Waterway)

Highway 70 Landing

70

To I-35 & Pine City

70

St. Croix Campground

Wood River

Wood River Interpretive Trail

ST. CROIX RIVER 4
Highway 70 to Sunrise River Landing (17.3 miles)

Downstream of Highway 70, the rocky rapids that paddlers enjoy upstream are gone. The St. Croix still moves swiftly, occasionally riffling just a little when the water's up. The river's wide and straight, however, and a headwind can really slow you down. With the St. Croix's sandy bottom and oft-shallow water, swimming is a great option on this quiet trip. Public land, heavily wooded with hardwoods and white pines, flanks much of the river. Chengwatana State Forest and Wild River State Park are on the Minnesota side and Governor Knowles State Forest is in Wisconsin.

To shorten the shuttle and avoid the fee for Sunrise River Landing, paddlers can use Wisconsin's Sunrise Ferry Landing. However, Wild River State Park is definitely worth visiting. The park's 6,800 acres lie along 18 miles of the St. Croix and include large parcels of prairie restoration, 35 miles of hiking trails, and 18 miles of horse trails (with horses for rent).

Camping is available at nine primitive riverside campsites. Car-camping is available for a fee at Wild River State Park, (651) 583-2125, or Wisconsin's St. Croix Campground (see St. Croix River 3).

See St. Croix 1 for information on **canoe and kayak rentals, shuttle service, and water levels.**

The 30.3-mile **shuttle route** runs 4.5 miles west on Highway 70 and 5.7 miles south on Highway 361 to Rush City. Stay straight to continue on County Road 30 for 7 miles to Harris. Turn left on Sunrise Road (County Road 9 and 44th Street). Before reaching the town of Sunrise, turn left on Ferry Road (gravel) and drive 1.5 miles to the landing. The state park charges a fee to park at the landing.

The **gradient** is 1.7 feet per mile.

Put in at the Highway 70 Access, 10.8 miles east of Interstate 35 and 4.5 miles west of Grantsburg, Wisconsin. The National Park Service landing is on upstream left. The St. Croix's clear waters flow over a sandy bottom, soon passing the mouth of the Wood River on the left. Soon after, Raspberry Landing (mile 1.4) is also on the left. Downstream, a group of islands dots the river. There's an occasional cabin now.

Stevens Creek Landing (mile 4.6) is on the right at the end of some riffles. After several cabins, Rock Creek (mile 6.3) comes in from the right. Interesting rock outcrops appear along this stretch, and the heavily wooded banks are beautiful in the fall. At Old Railroad Bridge Landing (mile 7) on the right, a railroad bridge crossed until 1951. There are toilets at the landing, and just downstream, a nice grassy campsite.

County O Landing (mile 8.7), a boat ramp on the left, has campsites with drinking water and toilets. Directly across the river (making another one of those matched sets of old ferry landings) Rush City Ferry Landing is tucked into a cluster of cabins. It's just a dirt road to the river, with no room for parking. To the right of two long, slender islands (mile 11.1) a big new house right next to the river stands where Landers Landing once was. Soon after, yellow signs on the right (mile 12) mark the boundary of Wild River State Park.

A mile farther, there's a campsite (mile 13) on the left with timber steps up the hill. The next campsite, which has drinking water, is at Goose Creek (mile 16) on the right as the river begins to bend left. Look for a group of big white pines up the hill. Another mile brings the Sunrise Campground (mile 17) on the left.

Take out at Sunrise River Landing, a boat ramp on the right, upstream of the confluence with the Sunrise River. There's no camping at this landing, but across the river, Sunrise Ferry Landing has campsites. If you need a burger, the Sunrise River Pub and Grill in Sunrise is right on the river.

The St. Croix valley is wooded, undeveloped, and peaceful.

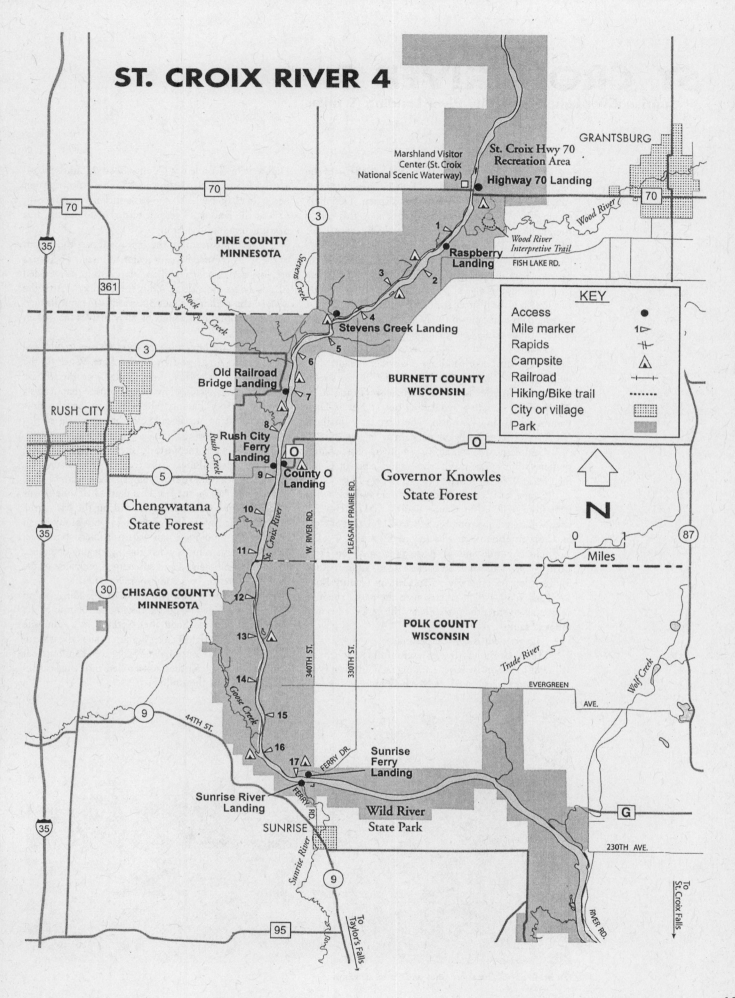

ST. CROIX RIVER 4

GRANTSBURG

Marshland Visitor Center (St. Croix National Scenic Waterway)

St. Croix Hwy 70 Recreation Area

Highway 70 Landing

Wood River

70

PINE COUNTY MINNESOTA

Stevens Creek

Rock Creek

1

Raspberry Landing

Wood River Interpretive Trail

FISH LAKE RD.

3

2

4

Stevens Creek Landing

5

6

BURNETT COUNTY WISCONSIN

KEY

Access	●
Mile marker	1▷
Rapids	╫
Campsite	⚠
Railroad	┼┼
Hiking/Bike trail	------
City or village	▦
Park	▨

Old Railroad Bridge Landing

7

RUSH CITY

Rush Creek

8

Rush City Ferry Landing

O

County O Landing

9

O

Governor Knowles State Forest

N

0   1
Miles

87

Chengwatana State Forest

10

St. Croix River

11

W. RIVER RD.

PLEASANT PRAIRIE RD.

POLK COUNTY WISCONSIN

30

CHISAGO COUNTY MINNESOTA

12

13

Trade River

14

EVERGREEN

Goose Creek

15

340TH ST.

330TH ST.

Wolf Creek

9

44TH ST.

AVE.

16

17

FERRY DR.

Sunrise Ferry Landing

G

Sunrise River Landing

FERRY RD.

Wild River State Park

RIVER RD.

SUNRISE

Sunrise River

230TH AVE.

9

To St. Croix Falls

95

To Taylor's Falls

ST. CROIX RIVER 5
Sunrise River Landing to Wild River Landing (9 miles)

The swift St. Croix begins to feel the effects of the big hydroelectric dam at Taylor Falls by the end of this trip. The current slowly begins to slacken. Definitely earning its Wild and Scenic designation, this lovely stretch of river is bounded completely by state land: Minnesota's Wild River State Park and Wisconsin's Governor Knowles State Forest. There's not a house to be seen. Both the put-in and the take-out are in the state park, making this a great paddle for park visitors. Along this stretch is the historic site of Nevers Dam, the biggest logging dam ever built in the North Woods. In the park is an outdoor exhibit on the logging era.

Paddlers should be aware that strong headwinds or crosswinds can make paddling this wide, straight river quite a project. Those who want to avoid the park's vehicle fee can paddle this same stretch by putting in at Sunrise Ferry Landing and taking out at Nevers Dam Landing, both in Wisconsin. The next (and final) St. Croix segment begins below the dam at Taylors Falls.

Camping is available at five primitive riverside campsites, including one across the river from the put-in. Camp for a fee at Wild River State Park, (651) 583-2125.

Canoe rentals and **shuttle service** are available in the park from Wild River Canoe Rental, (651) 465-3127, www.wildrivercanoe.com. See St. Croix 1 for a list of more St. Croix River outfitters who service this route.

The 9.5-mile **shuttle route** runs south on Ferry Road (gravel) and south on Sunrise Road (County Road 9). Turn left on Highway 95 and left on County Road 12 (Park Trail), which takes you to the park. There's a vehicle fee to enter the park. Follow the park road east to the boat ramp.

The **gradient** is 0.4 feet per mile.

See St. Croix 1 for **water level** information.

Put in at Sunrise River Landing in Wild River State Park. From Interstate 35 at North Branch, go east on Highway 95. Turn left at County Road 9 (Sunrise Road and 44th Street). At the town of Sunrise, turn right on Ferry Road (gravel). A state-park sticker is required to park at the landing. There's a nice riverside picnic area near the cement boat ramp.

Just downstream on the right, you pass the mouth of the lively Sunrise River, a major tributary. The banks are low and wooded and a pretty group of wooded islands makes the wide St. Croix seem intimate. After the islands, the channel's about 300 yards wide and flanked by dense, continuous stands of silver maples that soften the banks.

Because the St. Croix is so wide, it's easy to miss seeing campsites unless you're near the shore. Watch for the mouth of the little Trade River (mile 5) on the left. By the confluence, there's a low-lying campsite that makes a good picnic spot if empty. The right bank is higher now and a big island lies ahead. On the right side of this island is a sandy beach.

Approaching the historic site of Nevers Logging Dam, the wooded sides of the river valley gradually rise. Along this beautiful stretch, you pass the mouth of Wolf Creek (mile 7.6) on the left. Less than a half mile downstream, around a bump-out of land on the left, is the boat ramp at Nevers Dam Landing. On a sandy beach opposite the landing, a sign warns paddlers about hazardous currents. This is where the big logging dam once stood. Half-submerged and submerged remnants of the dam structure can create unexpected eddies.

On an island downstream of the landing, a "no camping" sign may be posted because restoration of the island is in progress. Soon after, Spring Creek Campsite is located on the right bank. A quarter mile downstream on the right, **take out** at the Wild River Landing boat ramp. There's a picnic area and a toilet, and rental canoes are piled high by the landing.

On St. Croix 5, the river runs wide and straight.

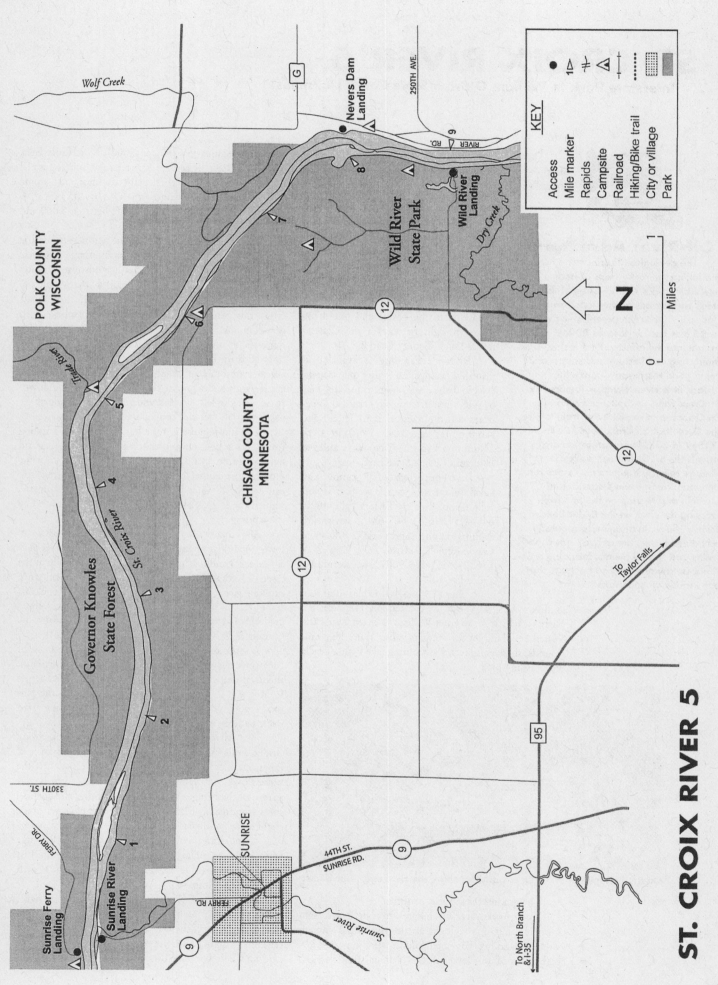

KEY

Access
Mile marker
Rapids
Campsite
Railroad
Hiking/Bike trail
City or village
Park

N

Miles

Wolf Creek

POLK COUNTY
WISCONSIN

Governor Knowles
State Forest

Trade River

St. Croix River

Sunrise Ferry Landing

Sunrise River Landing

330TH ST.

FERRY DR.

CHISAGO COUNTY
MINNESOTA

SUNRISE

FERRY RD.

44TH ST.
SUNRISE RD.

Sunrise River

To North Branch
& I-35

Nevers Dam Landing

250TH AVE.

RIVER RD.

Wild River
State Park

Wild River Landing

Dry Creek

To Taylor Falls

ST. CROIX RIVER 5

ST. CROIX RIVER 6
Interstate Park to William O'Brien State Park (14.7 miles)

Off-River Adventures

The geologically curious can have fun hiking the rocky trails of both Interstate Parks. Grand vistas of the steep rocky walls of the Dalles and close-up visits to the potholes—as wide as 25 feet and as deep as 80 feet—offer insight into the effects of the last ice age. Interesting architecture and shops, and some good restaurants, make the historic little river towns of Taylors Falls, St. Croix Falls, Osceola, and Marine on St. Croix fun to explore. For train lovers, the Osceola & St. Croix Valley Railway [715]-755-3570, www.trainride.org) travels the St. Croix River valley in vintage railway equipment. Routes run between Dresser and Osceola, and Osceola and Marine on the St. Croix, crossing the river on the Cedar Bend Swing Bridge. In addition to regularly scheduled trains, the railway has food trains and special events, including a St. Croix Getaway weekend package that can include a canoe rental.

This great trip, suitable for beginners, is also one of the most popular on the St. Croix. Beautiful rock cliffs, lots of sandbars, island campsites, and good landings are just a few of the draws. In the fall, the color show put on by hardwood-covered bluffs towering over the broad river valley makes this area a destination for more than just paddlers. Best of all, this beautiful area is only an hour from the Twin Cities. For a shorter paddle, use Osceola Landing. Whitewater enthusiasts carry upstream on the Minnesota side to the bridge and put in on upstream right to play in the Class II rapids under County Road 8.

Riverside **camping** is available at primitive campsites, some on islands. (Note: If the river's high, campsites may be under water. Campsites are also sometimes closed for restoration.) There's also camping at Interstate Park, in both Minnesota and Wisconsin, and at William O'Brien State Park.

Two outfitters offer **canoe and kayak rentals** and **shuttle service:** Taylors Falls Canoe Rental, Taylors Falls, (800) 447-4958, (651) 465-6315, www.wildmountain.com; and Eric's Bike and Canoe Rental, St. Croix Falls, (651) 270-1561, (715)-483-9007, www.ericsbikeandcanoe.com.

The 17.7-mile **shuttle route** runs south on U.S. Highway 8 and left on Highway 95. There's a vehicle fee to enter William O'Brien State Park. Near the parking lot for the boat ramp, there are picnic grounds, shelters, toilets, a swimming lake with a beach, and a fishing pier.

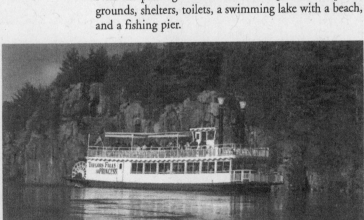

On the first mile of St. Croix 6, paddlers share the river with tour boats.

The gradient is 0.5 feet per mile.

Water levels vary with releases from the power dam at Taylors, but this segment almost always has enough water for paddling. For general information on water levels (high, medium, low) call the National Park Service's Riverway headquarters (new in 2006) in St. Croix Falls, (715) 483-3284. Real-time water level readings for the USGS gage at St. Croix Falls are available online (http://waterdata.usgs.gov/wi/nwis/uv?05340500). Recommended flows for paddling are between 5,000 and 11,000 cfs.

Put in at Interstate Park, at the Minnesota landing or the Wisconsin landing. Both parks charge a vehicle fee. Wisconsin's is a half mile farther upstream. (Note: The mile markers for this trip begin at the Minnesota landing.) Tour boats that look like historic steamboats cruise this part of the St. Croix, turning around at an island in the first mile. You also share the river with motorboats, and traffic noise from the highway on the right adds to the din. The wide St. Croix is beautiful—an intricate braid of channels, islands, and backwaters, always with a clear main channel. About a mile downstream on the left, lichens, mosses, and ferns adorn the basalt of a 50-feet cliff topped with white pines.

The traffic noise is gone before Franconia Landing (mile 2.1), a boat ramp on the right where landing and parking is free. Just downstream on the left, look for the mouth of a channel leading to a backwater lake that you can explore if water levels allow. A mile farther on the right is the Eagle's Nest (mile 3) with a campground by the landing.

As you pass a long, slender island, the Osceola water tower and bridge appear in the distance. There's a nice park at Osceola Landing (mile 6.0) on downstream right at the Osceola Bridge. By the boat ramp, you'll find a picnic area, drinking water, and toilets. Across the river, limestone cliffs rise high. Cut into the side of cliffs downstream, a railway grade blasted out for the Soo Line now also carries the Osceola & St. Croix Valley Railway's tourist train.

A series of big islands on the right hides a maze of backwater channels. On the upstream end of one island, there's a campsite (mile 8); another (mile 8.5) lies across from a wall of slate-grey riprap that reinforces the railroad grade. On the next island, a "No Trespassing" sign guards a little cabin on stilts.

The railway crosses on historic Cedar Bend Swing Bridge (mile 10.2), which is mounted on piers built of limestone block; the center pivot-pier is circular. If the water's high, whirlpools and strong eddies form downstream of the bridge. Right after the bridge, the channel splits around a big island. To the left, the shallower canoe channel has sandbars. To the right are the deeper motorboat channel and a row of vintage cabins under huge white pines. At mile 11.8, the two channels rejoin. Just past a log house (mile 12.4) is Log House Landing, with a public boat ramp.

After you pass the state park signs on your right, follow the low stone bank on the right. A hiking trail at river's edge goes all the way to the landing. At the top of Greenberg Island, go right. A short channel leads to the landing where you **take out.**

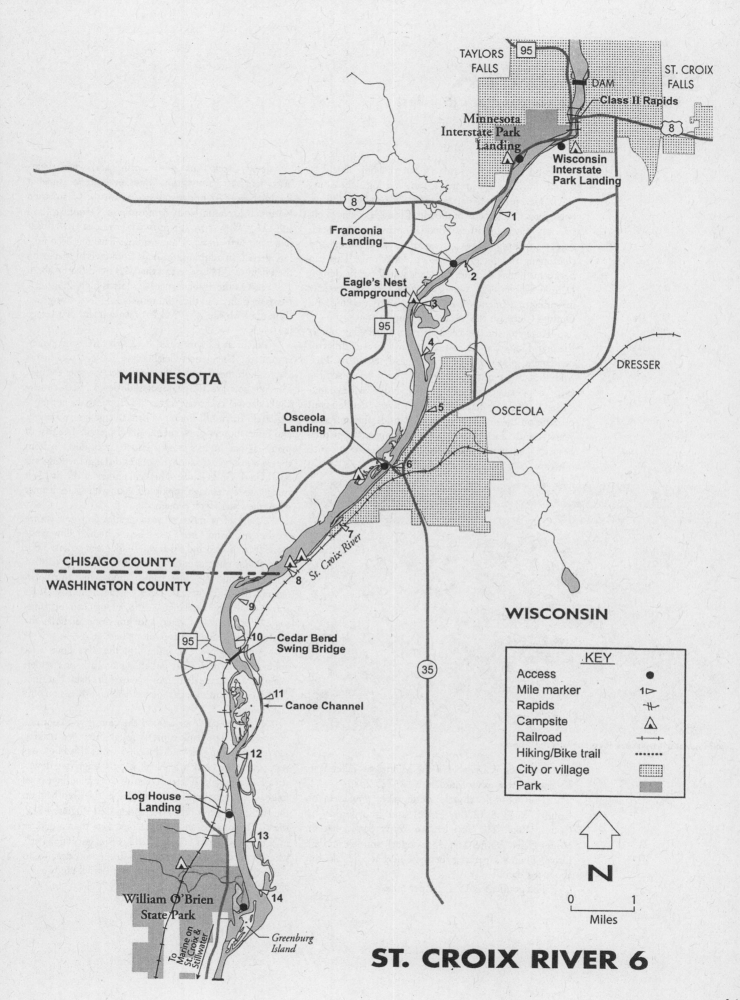

TAYLORS FALLS

95

ST. CROIX FALLS

DAM

Class II Rapids

8

Minnesota Interstate Park Landing

Wisconsin Interstate Park Landing

1▷

Franconia Landing

2▷

Eagle's Nest Campground

3▷

95

4▷

MINNESOTA

5▷

Osceola Landing

OSCEOLA

DRESSER

6

7▷

CHISAGO COUNTY

WASHINGTON COUNTY

8 St. Croix River

WISCONSIN

9▷

95

10▷ Cedar Bend Swing Bridge

35

11▷ ← Canoe Channel

12▷

Log House Landing

13▷

KEY

Access ●
Mile marker 1▷
Rapids
Campsite △
Railroad
Hiking/Bike trail ......
City or village
Park

14▷

William O'Brien State Park

To Marine on St. Croix & Stillwater

Greenburg Island

N

0   1
Miles

ST. CROIX RIVER 6

SAND CREEK
County Road 8 to Lagoon Park (5 miles)

Sand Creek's a fast ride. When you hop aboard at County Road 8, the stream's already moving right along, and it rarely rests until you take out. The paddling difficulty escalates near the end of the trip. Class I-II chains of big standing waves; a narrow, winding channel; and enough sweepers to make things dicey add up to an exciting and challenging run for experienced paddlers only. This trip begins just outside Jordan and ends just above the Jordan Dam in Lagoon Park. Whenever the water's up, especially in springtime, members of the Mankato Paddling and Outings Club visit the creek to play on the waves.

Portaging the 14-feet-high dam and taking out at Riesgraf Lion's Park yields an additional 1.3 miles of excitement, plus a chance to wave at diners in the Feed Mill Restaurant on Water Street. (For a post-paddling treat, stop in later for one of their tasty Reuben sandwiches.) While it's hardly a pristine river—development pressure on the area has increased considerably in recent years—Sand Creek definitely has its moments of natural beauty, racing past high wooded cliffs and interesting rock outcrops.

Whitewater kayakers love surfing the Sand.

Camping is available in the Minnesota Valley State Recreation Area west of Jordan, (612) 725-2389.

The 4.8-mile **shuttle route** takes you west on County Road 8 (220th Street) and into Jordan on County Road 21. Turn left on Water Street, left on Sunset Drive (Varner Street goes right), and left on Park Drive. There's a parking lot right next to the take-out above the dam.

The **gradient** is 15.4 feet per mile.

Sand Creek runs in the spring and when there's heavy rain near Farmington. **Water levels** are measured at the Highway 282 bridge and posted on the Chanhassen National Oceanic and Atmospheric Administration (NOAA) Web site (http://www.crh.noaa.gov/ahps2/index.php?wfo=mpx). These readings have not been fully interpreted. In addition, readings from a visible gauge on the Highway 282 bridge and the Web site differ by about 1.5 feet. On the visible gauge, 5.5 feet is high, 2.5 to 3.5 feet is medium, and the minimum is 1.35 feet. Using data from the Web site, 4 to 5 feet is medium and flood stage is 10 feet.

Put in at County Road 8 (220th Street) on downstream left. There's no official access. You can park across the road on the shoulder of a side street, Camber Avenue. Lift your boat over the guardrail; slide down a steep, brushy bank; clamber over some rocks; and drop into the fast-moving creek. Right off, riprapped banks, large houses, fences, and other niceties of suburban sprawl prevail. The first of many railroad bridges crosses. Porter Creek flows in from the right just before Sand Creek races through the Ridges at Sand Creek Golf Course. The steel girders of the first golf bridge are low enough to clip off your whitewater helmet when the water's high enough.

After a few more railroad trestles and golf course footbridges, Sand Creek races beside high, yellow-sandstone cliffs topped and sided with dark green cedars. Steep wave chains punctuate the fourth mile. After the railroad bridge at mile 3.8, the banks are heavily riprapped. Sawmill Road follows the creek on the right as it drops through the most challenging drop, a long chain of standing waves. Layers of shale and limestone underlie the banks in intriguing outcrops along here.

After Highway 21 (mile 4.7) the river slows as it approaches the dam. **Take out** at Lagoon Park, on river left just upstream of the dam. Don't go over the dam. **Caution:** there are no warning signs for the dam and there's no official landing.

A paved trail leads around the dam if you continue downstream. The bank is pretty rough, however, making access somewhat awkward. In 2006 when this book was researched, the creek was blocked by a huge tree downstream of the dam. A stretch of truly large standing waves follows. Be sure to wave to the folks in the Feed Mill on the right, just before the street bridge. At Highway 282, the visible gauge is on the right pier. Less than a quarter mile downstream of Highway 282 is Riesgraf Lion's Park, where you **take out** on the left. It's just a short distance to the Feed Mill and that Reuben. (The Rachel sandwich is another good bet.)

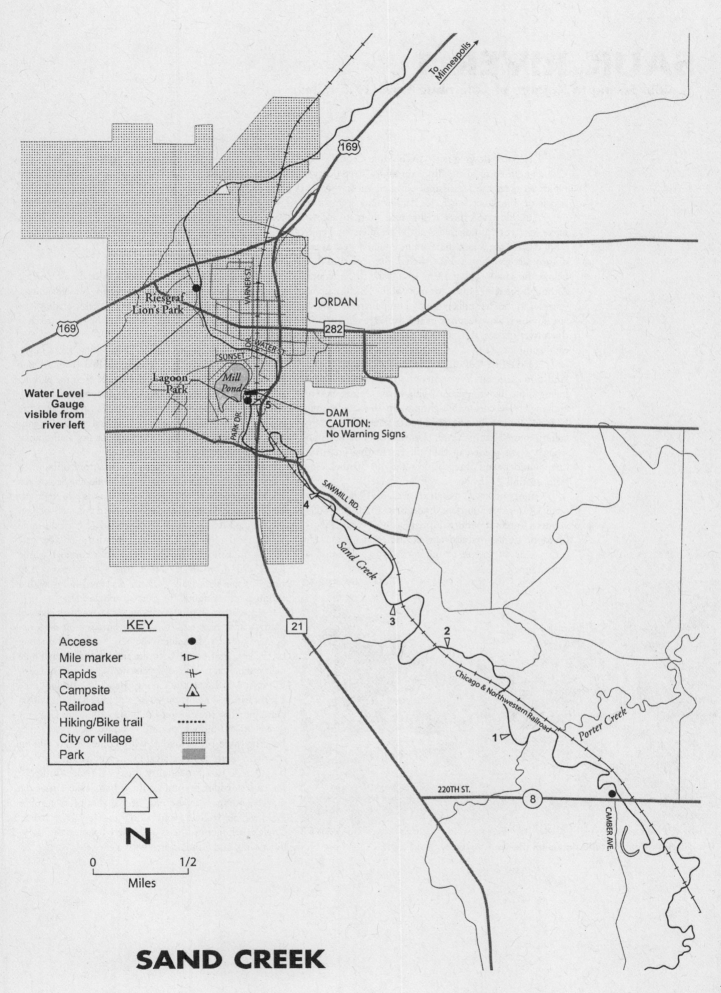

KEY

Access	●
Mile marker	1▷
Rapids	‡
Campsite	△
Railroad	┼┼
Hiking/Bike trail	········
City or village	▦
Park	▨

N

0   1/2
Miles

SAND CREEK

SAUK RIVER 1
Cold Spring to Knights of Columbus Park (17.5 miles)

The Sauk flows quietly from Sauk Centre to St. Cloud and then suddenly drops through a steep flurry of rapids to meet the Mississippi River. Because this first trip is on the quiet water, 17.5 miles may seem like a long haul. However, three well-spaced alternate accesses make shorter trips possible. And for paddlers who enjoy a full day on the water, there are nice picnic areas at two of those access points. This stretch of the Sauk runs from below the Cold Spring Dam to a park in St. Cloud. Although the river's quiet for most of the reach, a stretch of riffles in the first mile requires a little maneuvering. In late summer, slow sections of the Sauk are choked with thick river grasses, thus it's best paddled in the spring or early summer.

For the first half of the trip, a mix of woods, farmland, and scattered development borders the river. River-loving birds like kingfishers, blue herons, green herons, and eagles are common sightings. In the Cold Spring Heron Colony Scientific and Natural Area (SNA) a large colony nested until 1989. Downstream, a tamarack swamp glows golden in the fall. Fascinating groups of huge boulders and outcrops decorate the channel, especially around Rockville.

Canoe and kayak rentals are available from St. Cloud State University's Outdoor Endeavors, (320) 308-6691, www.stcloudstate.edu/campusrec/outdoorendeavors. Outdoor Endeavors also has **shuttle service** (from the access near St. Joseph to the park) for a minimum of three canoes.

The 15-mile **shuttle route** runs west on 2nd Street and south on Red River Avenue (County Road 2). Turn left and follow Highway 23 for 12.5 miles to 10th Avenue (County Road 138) where you turn left; 10th Avenue becomes 54th Avenue. Before you reach 8th Street (Veterans Drive/County Road 4), turn left into the Knights of Columbus Park.

The **gradient** is 2.4 feet per mile.

Real-time **water level** information for the USGS gage near St. Cloud is available online (http://waterdata.usgs.gov/usa/nwis/uv?site_no=05270500). Weekly readings are available from the DNR, (888) 646-6367. This stretch is passable as low as 300 cfs.

Put in at Frogtown Park in Cold Spring. From Highway 23 at Cold Spring, go north on Red River Avenue (County Road 2) and east on 2nd Street. Near the parking for the boat ramp are drinking water and toilets. The Sauk starts out about 100 feet wide and fast. The banks are heavily wooded with willows, and several wooded islands split the channel. As you head downstream, traffic noise from Highway 23 comes and goes.

A bouldery stretch at mile 1 varies from riffles to an easy Class I rapid. On its way to Rockville, the Sauk flows quietly around numerous wooded islands, through the heron rookery SNA, and past an elevated tamarack bog on the left bank. The channel splits around a big island (mile 5), followed a half mile later by a wonderful boulder garden in midstream. (Not to worry, the current's gentle here.) On downstream left at the County Road 139 bridge, Eagle Park (mile 5.7) has a shady landing with a fishing platform (good for picnics) and parking.

Downstream of the landing, the wooded channel narrows and snags tend to collect. There's a bit of development on the right bank in the next 4 miles and nothing on the left. Traffic noise becomes audible about a half mile before the twin bridges of Interstate 94 (mile 10.8) cross. On upstream left at the County Road 121 Bridge (mile 11.9) near St. Joseph, there's an unmarked access with a gravel parking circle. After the bridge, the Sauk flows for several miles through peaceful wooded land. At Miller Landing (mile 14.4), marked with a canoe access sign on the right, there's a picnic area, toilet, and parking.

A mile past the County Road 75 bridge (mile 15) the river corridor becomes quite urban. **Take out** at the gravel landing near the end of Knights of Columbus Park, which stretches out along the low right bank. There's parking near the street, a paved path to the carry-in landing, and a picnic area with a shelter.

This dramatic boulder collection is on the Sauk River.

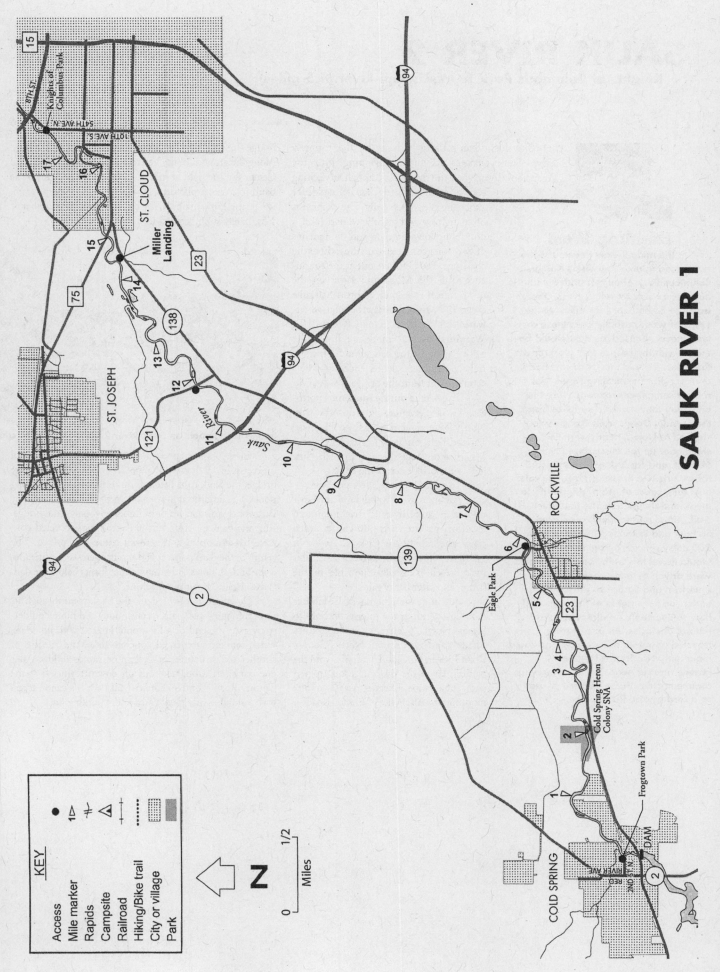

SAUK RIVER 1

KEY

Access
Mile marker
Rapids
Campsite
Railroad
Hiking/Bike trail
City or village
Park

N

Miles

0   1/2

ST. CLOUD

Miller Landing

ST. JOSEPH

Sauk   River

ROCKVILLE

Eagle Park

Cold Spring Heron
Colony SNA

Frogtown Park

COLD SPRING

DAM

Knights of
Columbus Park

SAUK RIVER 2

Knights of Columbus Park to Mississippi River (4.5 miles)

Heading West

In the mid-nineteenth century, the river crossing now known as Knights of Columbus Park often resounded with the noise of oxcarts traveling west. Oxcart trains could be heard for miles. Made solely of wood, usually oak, these carts were never greased, as dust would have mixed with the grease and worn down the axles. It's said that each cart had its own peculiar penetrating shriek. For remote settlements, oxcarts were the only way they received supplies from the outside. Goods from Europe were shipped to New Orleans, sent by steamboat up the Mississippi River to St. Paul, and carried over land in Red River Carts. On the return trip, the carts held furs, sacks of grain, dried buffalo meat, and pemmican. The Red River Trail, rutted and tangled, connected St. Paul and Winnipeg. Trains of up to 200 noisy oxcarts (imagine the noise!) would travel this trail. The oxcart trains were driven by Métis (people of Native American and European descent) who understood the rigors of the trails and how to overcome breakdowns and natural obstacles. An oxcart train traveled about 20 miles a day and could make only two trips a summer. A granite marker near the canoe landing commemorates Waite's Crossing, used as a ford by Red River Carts.

On this urban-paddling adventure, the formerly sedate Sauk changes its tune. Dropping into the Mississippi River valley, the river races through an exciting series of boulder-filled Class I-II rapids for experienced paddlers only. The channel is often narrow and tightly wound, and a crumbling lowhead dam and the remains of two other concrete structures add to the challenge. Paddlers take out at the confluence with the Mississippi River on the north side of St. Cloud. Another half mile down the Mississippi is a popular whitewater run, the Sauk Rapids (Class I-III). Warning: even at moderate flows, the Sauk Rapids are too dangerous for inexperienced paddlers. Experienced paddlers should scout from the bridge.

The 4-mile **shuttle route** runs northeast on 54th Avenue, right on 8th Street North (Veterans Drive), left on Highway 15, and right on County Road 1. Heim's Mill Canoe Access is on the left, just before the bridge across the Sauk.

The **gradient** is 9.3 feet per mile.

For sources of **water level** information, see Sauk River 1. The minimum level for this stretch is 300 cfs, at which point the rapids are Class I. At about 1,100 cfs, the rapids become Class II. This rocky reach is usually runnable in the spring and after heavy rains.

Put in at the Knights of Columbus Park, just south of the intersection of 8th Street North (Veterans Drive/County Road 4) and 54th Avenue North (County Road 138) in St. Cloud. Carry in from the parking lot to the river on a long, paved path. The canoe access is near a granite monument. After the County Road 4

bridge (mile 0.2) the Sauk weaves quietly through islands. Along the grounds of the Veterans Administration Medical Center (on the right at mile 1.3), there are stairs down the bank to a stone platform. A short distance downstream, watch for the remains of an old concrete structure (mile 1.5), barely submerged at low water.

In one of the pools on Sauk River 2, geese watch the canoes

Class I rapids appear now, followed by a long pool upstream of Highway 15 (mile 2.1). Downstream of the bridge, the Sauk runs through more short drops and long pools. The hazardous lowhead dam (mile 3.3) in Whitney Park is easy to spot: It's right under a wooden trail bridge. Run the dam on river left where the moss-covered concrete has crumbled and a rocky chute has formed. The center of the dam is intact and too dangerous to run, especially at high flows. A hydraulic that forms below the dam is the classic "drowning machine."

Downstream of the dam, the Sauk races through its most difficult rapids, more continuous and more boulder-strewn. At the end of a long pool littered with boulders, watch out for submerged concrete slabs, the remains of another old structure. Several more rapids follow. After one last short drop, **take out** on downstream left at the County Road 1 bridge. Heim's Mill Park is a canoe access with a small, shady picnic area and a parking lot.

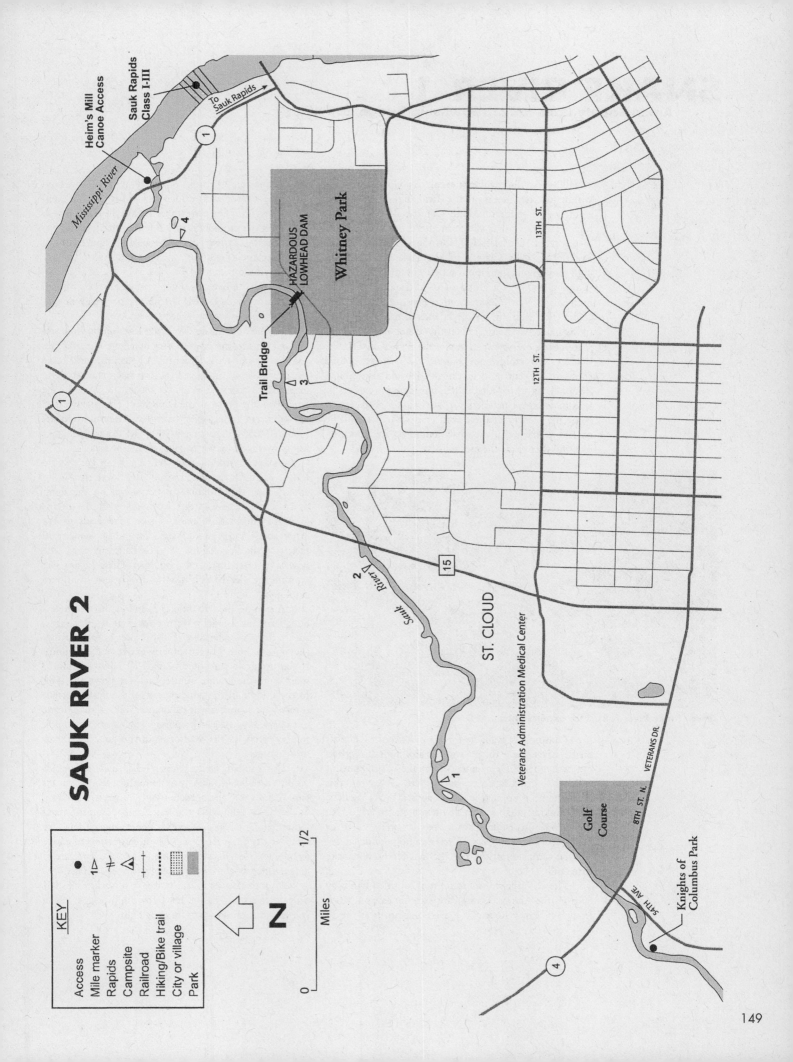

SAUK RIVER 2

KEY

Access	●
Mile marker	1△
Rapids	≠
Campsite	△
Railroad	┼
Hiking/Bike trail	·······
City or village	▦
Park	▨

N

Miles

0   1/2

Mississippi River

Heim's Mill
Canoe Access

Sauk Rapids
Class I-III

To
Sauk Rapids

1

1

4

Trail Bridge

HAZARDOUS
LOWHEAD DAM

Whitney Park

13TH ST.

12TH ST.

3

2

Sauk River

15

ST. CLOUD

Veterans Administration Medical Center

VETERANS DR.

8TH ST. N.

1

Golf
Course

Knights of
Columbus Park

54TH AVE.

4

SNAKE RIVER 1
Aitkin County Park to Ford Township Bridge (5.9 miles)

The exciting whitewater of the Upper Snake is within just two hours of the Twin Cities, in wooded country just south of Aitkin County. Best in spring's high water, this run is also great after a heavy rain. Most of the rapids are Class I-II. On the Upper and Lower Snake River Falls, Class II-IV, the Snake roars between high pink-granite outcrops capped with old white pines. If you're not with a group of paddlers experienced in both Class IV whitewater and rescues, don't run these "falls." The Web site for the Friends of the Snake River (www.snakerivermn.org) notes that canoes are destroyed there nearly every year. (Despite the names of the falls, they're steep rapids, not waterfalls.) There's no road access to the falls and getting help could take hours. Both falls have well-established, but long, portage trails. Less-than-expert paddlers are advised to portage and enjoy the scenery of these wild gorges. Anglers will be pleased to know that the smallmouth bass are reportedly plentiful (but so are the mosquitoes).

Lower Snake River Falls is for experts only.

Camping is available for a fee at Aitkin County's Snake River Park (http://www.co.aitkin.mn.us/departments/Land%20Dept/land-dept/snake%20river.htm), which has drinking water and toilets. (A caveat: this campground is popular with and abused by ATV riders: think muddy ruts.) Father Hennepin State Park, (320) 676-8763, on Mille Lacs Lake, 10 miles west of Highway 65 on Highway 27, has a campground. There's a canoe campsite on the portage trail for Lower Snake River Falls.

The 8.7-mile **shuttle route** runs south on Highway 65 from the Aitkin County Park exit. Go east on 360th Avenue (County Road 82, gravel) and north at the T-intersection on Olympic Street (gravel) to the Ford Township (Woodland) bridge. An unmarked but well-used access is on downstream right, and the only place to park is on the shoulder. The painted bridge gauge is visible from the landing. **Note:** Because the Snake runs in the spring and after a rain, the road into Aitkin County Park may be too mucky for most vehicles. In this case, start the trip 2.8 river miles upstream at Silver Star Road.

The average **gradient** is 15.5 feet per mile; the gradient in the falls area is 30 feet per mile.

Be sure to get up-to-date **water level** information, and find out whether the water is rising or falling. The river rises and drains as much as a foot in 24 hours; the rocks make this stretch almost impassable at low water; and there's no intermediate access. A volunteer reports the level on the Ford Township bridge to the DNR most Thursdays: http://www.dnr.state.mn.us/river_levels/levels.html?id=snake, (888) 646-6367. A reading at 1.2 to 3.5 feet is medium; 3 feet or over is best if you're going to run the falls.

Put in at Aitkin County's Snake River Park. From Mora, go north on Highway 65. Just over the Aitkin county line, the entrance to the park is on the right, down a long one-way dirt road. Just past the campground's information kiosk, a side road leads to the canoe access and a parking area. The Snake is about 80 feet wide. Its bog-stained water is dark but clear. The flow is quiet at first, and a bouldery Class I waits just around the bend. This pool-drop pattern continues throughout the run.

A sign on the left (mile 3.3) marks the well-maintained and occasionally steep portage trail (300 yards) for the Upper Snake River Falls. (**Note:** In early spring, the signs for both falls are sometimes flat on the ground.) If you decide to run these Class II-III rapids, definitely scout from the granite outcrop halfway down the trail. In the middle of the winding gorge, the pushy current throws you against a vertical granite wall on the outside of a curve. If you decide to portage, blueberries (and poison ivy) grow on the outcrops and you get a great view of the gorge.

Downstream of the Upper Falls, Class I-II rapids resume. The Snake races by a cabin, the only one on this trip. At mile 4.8, the portage trail (900 yards) for Lower Snake River Falls is on the left. At the campsite that's located along the trail, there's a good vantage point for scouting the Class III-IV rapids: three-quarters of a mile of boulders, ledges, steep gradient, and a deep, narrow gorge. Open-boaters will probably want to portage.

After the Lower Falls, a half mile of rocky Class I-II drops delivers you to the Ford Township bridge, where you **take out** on downstream river right.

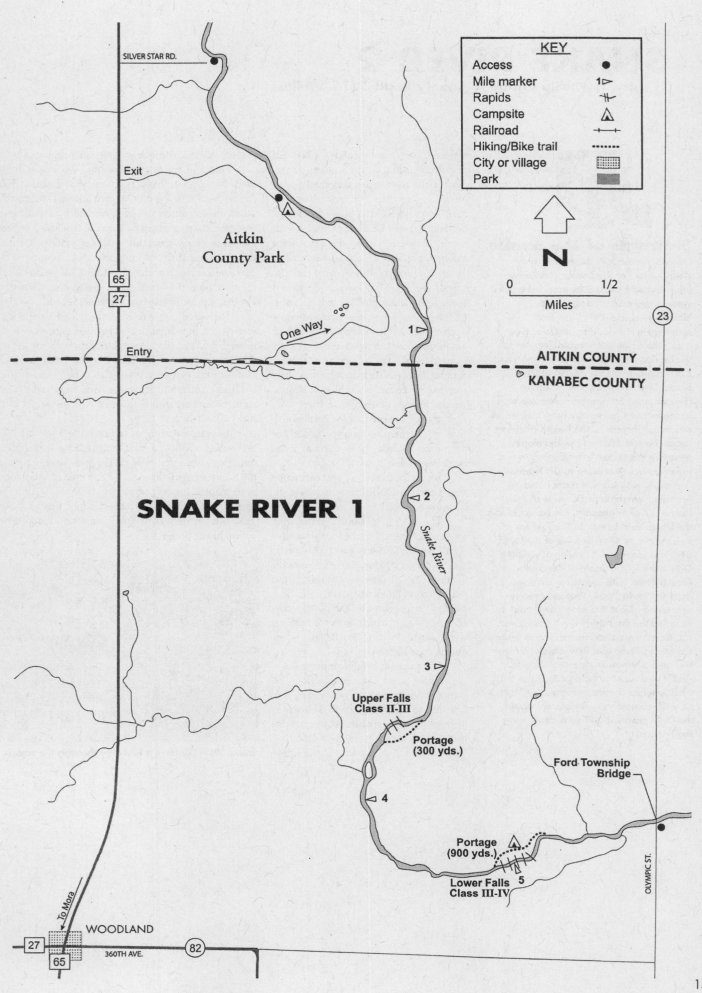

SILVER STAR RD.

Exit

Aitkin
County Park

65
27

One Way

1 ▷

Entry

AITKIN COUNTY
KANABEC COUNTY

SNAKE RIVER 1

◁ 2

Snake River

3 ▷

Upper Falls
Class II-III

Portage
(300 yds.)

Ford Township
Bridge

◁ 4

Portage
(900 yds.)

5

Lower Falls
Class III-IV

23

KEY
Access   ●
Mile marker   1▷
Rapids
Campsite   △
Railroad
Hiking/Bike trail   - - - -
City or village
Park

N

0   1/2
Miles

OLYMPIC ST.

To Mora

WOODLAND

27
65

360TH AVE.

82

SNAKE RIVER 2
Ford Township Bridge to County Road 3 (14.3 miles)

Stewards of the Snake

As you paddle the remarkably clean waters of the Snake, just imagine what would be lost if its wooded banks were rutted and eroded by off-highway-vehicle (OHV) use and sediment were clouding its flow. (For help visualizing what could happen to the banks, check out the photo in "The ATV Problem" on the Friends of the Snake River Web site, www.snakerivermn.org.) Stream-bank erosion and sedimentation caused by man's activities are major threats to the health of rivers today. Even a relatively undeveloped river like the Snake is beginning to feel the pressure. According to Dr. Thomas F. Waters, well-known author and professor emeritus of fisheries at the University of Minnesota, the banks along the Upper and Lower Falls could be threatened by OHV use. As of 2006, the DNR has identified 51 miles of existing OHV trails in the Snake River State Forest, some with extensive damage from OHVs. In 2000, Waters, greatly concerned about this emerging problem, founded the Friends of the Snake River, a citizens' organization striving to protect the Snake River and its watershed from this and other environmental threats. And if you want to help protect the wild and beautiful Snake from man's abuse as well, contact your legislators about the OHV problem and consider joining the Friends.

Riffles, frequent Class I rapids, and a Class I-II as well, make for a lively paddle on the winding Snake. The gradient is lower, the river wider, and the wooded land along the river a bit more developed than on Snake River 1, but just as lovely. Scribing a large horseshoe as it flows east, south, and then west, the river races through portions of Snake River State Forest land for about 6 miles of the trip. Handsome big oaks, lowland deciduous trees, some white pines, stands of ferns, and wild roses line the river. Meadow openings are home to many warblers, and kingfishers, owls, hawks, and eagles are common sightings all along the river. Although early settlers caught huge lake sturgeon in the Snake (for historic photos, see the Friends of the Snake River Web site), today's anglers cast for smallmouth bass, northerns, and walleyes. Clouds of dragonflies feed on the burgeoning mosquito population.

See Snake River 1 for area car camping. There's a DNR canoe campsite on this stretch.

The 12.5-mile **shuttle** route runs south on Olympic Street (gravel), west on 360th Avenue (County Road 82, gravel), and south on Highway 65. Go east on County Road 3 (Hinckley Road) to the public access on downstream right. The painted bridge gauge on the downstream center piling isn't visible from the landing; you have to be next to the bridge on downstream right to see it.

The gradient is 5.6 feet per mile.

Water level information for the painted bridge gauge at County Road 3 is reported to the DNR most Thursdays, http://www.dnr.state.mn.us/river_levels/levels.html?id=snake; (888) 646-6367. Medium is 1.2 to 5.0 feet. If the gauge reads below 1.2, you'll be wading and dragging.

Put in at the Ford Township (Woodland) bridge. From Mora, go north on Highway 65 and east on 360th Avenue, and turn left on Olympic Street. The unmarked access on downstream right is reached by a short gravel road, and there's room to park on the shoulder. The Snake gets off to a quiet start, and it's almost a mile before it settles into the pattern of long drops and long pools that characterizes much of the trip. After Chelsey Brook joins the river from the left, there's a pretty stretch where the channel divides, braided around small islands.

The canoe campsite is on the left where the Snake sprawls out in a large pool. The river narrows, running through a Class I drop. A jumble of rocks on the left is all that remains of the Old Bean Logging Dam (mile 4.3). Downstream, you see a few cabins, a farm, and a rickety old bridge (mile 5.7) across the river. To avoid the remnants of another rock dam (mile 6.3), stay right in the rocky Class I-II drop.

Alongside a string of cabins (mile 9) on the right, the river drops over a low, straight ledge into a pile of standing waves. After mile 12, the lively water quiets and the Snake wriggles through a shady mile of overhanging silver maples. Expect some deadfalls in this section. The river's quiet all the way to the County Road 3 bridge. **Take out** on river right, just past a tiny island downstream of the bridge.

Snake River 2 offers a fast ride through the rapids.

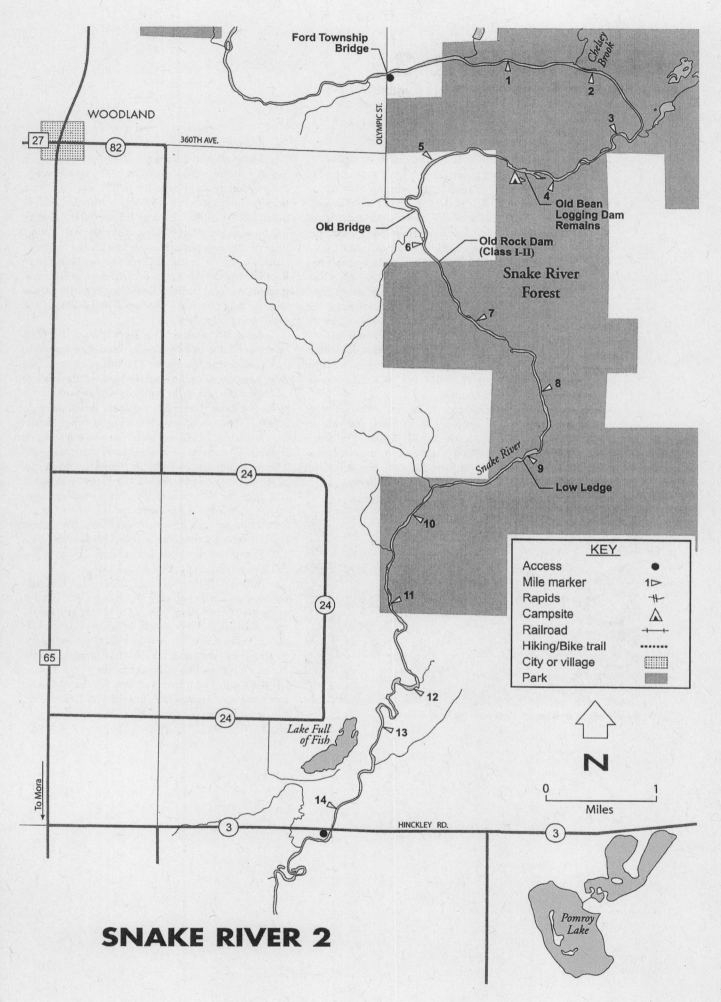

Ford Township Bridge

Chelsey Brook

1

2

3

WOODLAND

27

82

360TH AVE.

OLYMPIC ST.

5

4

Old Bean Logging Dam Remains

Old Bridge

6

Old Rock Dam (Class I-II)

Snake River Forest

7

8

Snake River

9

Low Ledge

24

10

24

65

11

KEY

Access ●

Mile marker 1▷

Rapids

Campsite △

Railroad

Hiking/Bike trail ......

City or village

Park

24

12

Lake Full of Fish

13

N

0   1
Miles

To Mora

3

14

HINCKLEY RD.

3

Pomroy Lake

SNAKE RIVER 2

SNAKE RIVER 3
County Road 3 to County Road 6 (15 miles)

Class I rapids and shallow riffles strung loosely together with long pools add interest to this route. The Snake's width varies considerably, ranging from narrow and intimate to wide and sunny. There's more development—several rows of cabins—than on the Upper Snake. Herons, eagles, and owls don't seem to mind the people. Nor do the large turtles that inhabit the river. And despite the development, it's a nice paddle down a wooded river. This is also the route of Mora's Snake River Canoe Race (www.snakerivercanoerace.org) sponsored annually by the Snake River Canoe Club since 1980. The finish line is downstream of County Road 6, at a landing by the Kanabec History Center (www.kanabechistory.org).

The Snake River Canoe Club **rents aluminum canoes** and trailers when paddling conditions are right. Contact Bob Lindig, (320) 679-1081 or lindiglaw@ncis.com, for more information.

The 14.5-mile **shuttle route** runs west on County Road 3, south on Highway 65 to Mora, and west on County Road 6 (Maple Avenue). At the landing on downstream left, there's a shady picnic ground next to the parking area. To view the gauge on the bridge pier, walk down to the landing and follow a short trail to the right.

Gentle riffles and rapids characterize Snake River 3.

The **gradient** is 3.8 feet per mile.

A volunteer reports the **water level** on the Hinckley Bridge (County Road 3) to the DNR most Thursdays, http://www.dnr.state.mn.us/river_levels/levels.html?id= snake, (888) 646-6367. Between 1.2 and 5.0 feet is medium. In addition, daily readings of the gauge at County Road 6 are also posted online (http://www.snakeriver canoerace.org) for several weeks before the Mora Canoe Race in May. On this gauge, between 3.0 and 6.5 feet is medium. As noted on Snake River 1 and 2, the river drains quickly. On a river reach with rapids and shallows, "low water" translates to "wading."

Put in at County Road 3. From Mora, go north on Highway 65 and east on County Road 3 to the public access on downstream right. The bridge gauge on the downstream center piling isn't visible from the landing; you have to be next to the bridge on downstream right to see it. For about three miles, the Snake flows quietly. At mile 0.7, the channel opens into an oxbow on the left.

A Class I rapids begins as the Snake narrows at about mile 3 and ends as the river flares into a long pool. This pool-drop pattern continues through the remainder of the trip. As you pass the most developed area on the trip, note the collection of 28 "No Trespassing" signs (mile 4.5) in front of a house on the left. At the County Road 19 bridge (mile 8) access is possible on downstream right. A farm on the right at mile 10.8 features about 1,000 feet of shoreline trampled and eroded by cattle, but this is the only such example on this trip.

After the Highway 65 bridge at mile 11.9, the Snake flows around a cluster of small islands. More islands follow as the wide Knife River (mile 12.6) speeds in from the right. **Take out** at the County Road 6 bridge. As you paddle under the bridge, look for the river gauge on the center pier. The landing is on the left, a bit downstream of the bridge. Hungry paddlers can head for the Crystal Bar and Grill on North Union Street in Mora. Go east on County Road 6 (Maple Avenue) and turn right on Union Street. The Union Burger is a great choice.

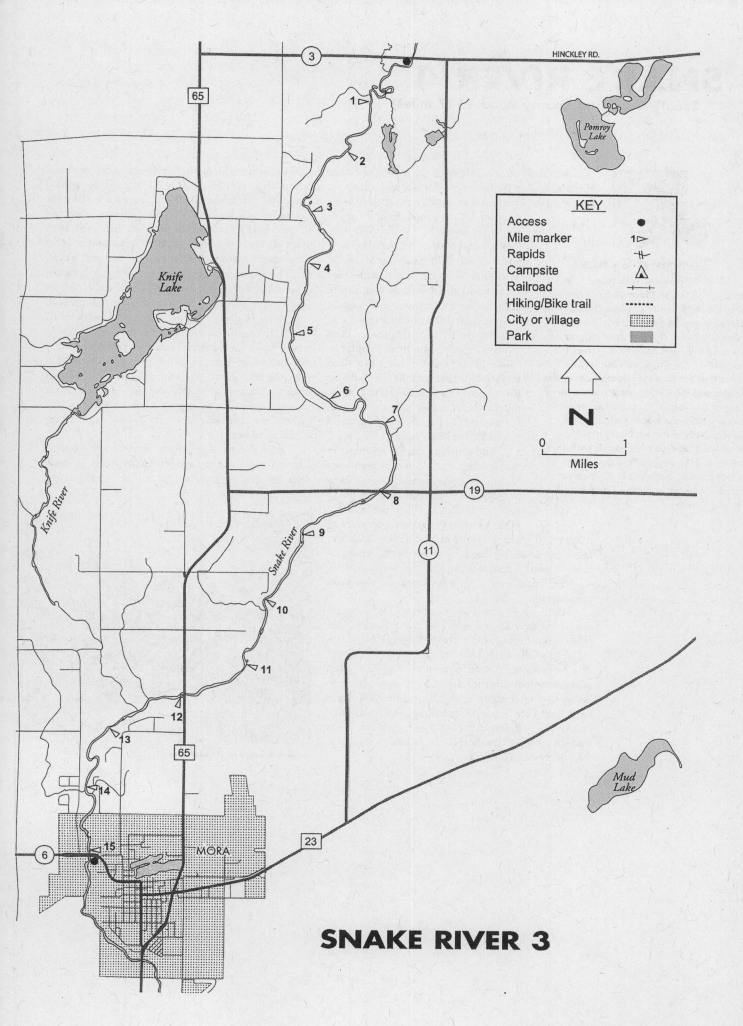

SNAKE RIVER 3

SNAKE RIVER 4
County Road 6 to County Road 11 (7 miles)

Logging Boom

The Snake River watershed is in an area called the St. Croix Delta, a region once rich with white pine. In *The Streams and Rivers of Minnesota*, Dr. Thomas Waters tells the story of how loggers stripped this land of its timber over the last half of the nineteenth century. He notes that the logs that floated down the Snake and the Kettle rivers were a large part of that logging production. In the century since the boom ended, steady new growth of aspen, birch, maple, basswood, and oak has successfully reforested the region. To learn more about logging in Kanabec (Ojibwe for "snake") County, visit the Kanabec History Center.

A peaceful stretch—although the traffic noise from Highway 65 is a bit intrusive—this is a nice midseason float when the water's too low to paddle the upper or lower segments. It's also a good choice for beginning river paddlers. The formerly fast-moving Snake slows considerably as it reaches Mora and enters an area of low, flat floodplain. Winding slowly south from Mora, under dense cover of overhanging silver maples and between small islands, the river at first has an intimate feeling that belies its width. The Snake grows in these 7 miles, picking up three tributaries: Spring Brook, the Ann River that flows through Fish Lake, and the Groundhouse River at the take-out. By the end of the trip the river's too wide to be roofed by silver maples. Occasional deadfalls are easy to avoid in the gentle current.

Bird watching can be rewarding in this wooded river corridor. Numerous blue herons, green herons, kingfishers, hawks, and owls live here. You pass the 37 acres of land on which the Kanabec History Center (www.kanabechistory.org) is located. If you're interested in local history exhibits or just want to walk the center's wooded riverside trails, the center is worth a post-paddling visit.

See Snake River 3 for information on **aluminum canoe rentals.**

The 7.4-mile **shuttle route** is east on County Road 6, east on Highway 23, and south on County Road 11. The public access has plenty of parking by the sandy landing.

The **gradient** is 1.3 feet per mile.

From County Road 6 to the Cross Lake Dam (downriver from this trip) the Snake is usually passable. **Water level** information is available for the USGS gage near Pine City (http://waterdata.usgs.gov/mn/nwis/uv?05338500). A reading of 3.0 to 6.5 feet is medium. These readings correspond to those on the painted river gauge at the County Road 6 bridge.

Put in at the Mora Municipal public access on downstream left at the County Road 6 bridge. There's a shady picnic area next to the parking. If you want to check the river gauge, walk down to the landing and take a short trail to the right. After one last burst of fast water from upstream, the river quickly quiets. Just downstream of the bridge, islands divide the wide channel. The banks are carpeted with ferns and forested with a silver-maple monoculture. Many trees are canted at 45-degree angles over the river. On the left bank is the Kanabec History Center land.

Noisy Highway 65 crosses (mile 1.8), adjoined by several riverbank houses. Downstream, the highway retreats behind wooded banks, but the traffic whine persists for a while. At mile 2.8, tiny Spring Brook comes in from the left. Shortly after, the Ann River—free of its upstream impoundment in Fish Lake—joins the Snake from the right. The Snake's wider and deeper now, and without the upstream islands, its channel is no longer overhung by trees.

Take out on downstream right at Twin Bridges Landing, the County Road 11 public access. A sandy delta has formed on the right at the mouth of the Groundhouse River.

Snake River 4 is a quiet one.

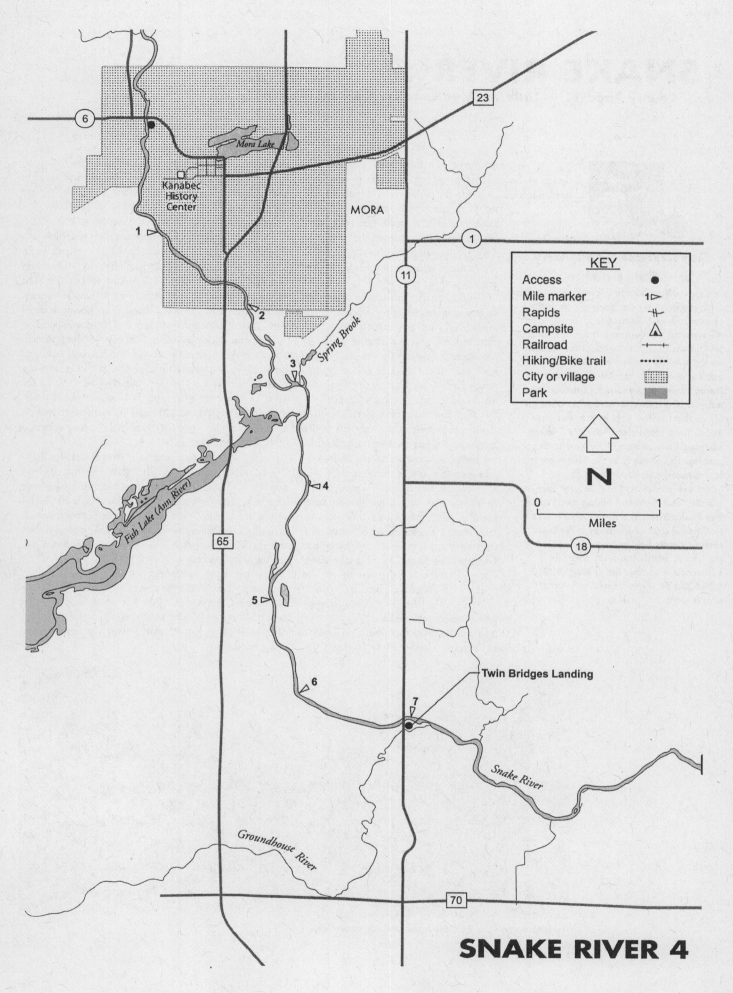

KEY

Access	●
Mile marker	1▷
Rapids	⌗
Campsite	△
Railroad	+—+
Hiking/Bike trail	·····
City or village	▦
Park	▨

N

0   Miles   1

Kanabec History Center

MORA

Mora Lake

Spring Brook

Fish Lake (Ann River)

Twin Bridges Landing

Snake River

Groundhouse River

SNAKE RIVER 4

SNAKE RIVER 5
County Road 11 to Little Walleye Landing (12.7 miles)

Northwest Company Fur Post

Just off Interstate 35 at Pine City, you can visit the early nineteenth century. Almost. Authentic looking re-creations of a wintering fur post and an Ojibwa encampment that once stood on the site are staffed by costumed guides, quite skilled in reenactment. During tours, these colorful characters tell you about the fur trade and about life at this trading post in the winter of 1804. They also relate how the Ojibwa adapted their seasonal rhythms to the trading. The exhibits in the visitor center are detailed and fascinating (a real birchbark canoe and real beaver furs to handle) and there are hiking trails along The Snake River. The center also offers traditional craft workshops and the Historic Crafts Fair in August.
For hours, admission fees, and more information, contact the center: (320) 629-6356 or www.mnhs.org/places/sites/nwcfp.

As on Snake River 4, a float down this peaceful stretch of the Snake takes you through quiet wooded bottomland. It's a good trip for families and beginners. The woods are interrupted occasionally by scattered houses and farm field openings. Midway along the journey, the river runs through the village of Grasston, where a bridge access makes it possible to shorten the trip at either end.

With the river quieter and somewhat deeper than on its upper reaches, small motorboats use this stretch. However, there generally isn't much motor traffic. At low water, a few stretches of sandy shallows may mean wading and dragging. About halfway to the village of Grasston, the Snake sprawls out in a wide pool, 10 feet deep. You may meet anglers fishing for channel catfish along this segment of the Snake. Eagles, herons, songbirds, kingfishers, mergansers, and squadrons of dragonflies provide wildlife entertainment.

Two adjoining DNR canoe campsites (mile 0.9) are in a low wooded area, popular with mosquitoes especially in midsummer. These sites are best used on a cool-weather trip. For car camping, Chengwatana State Forest's Snake River Campground is at the mouth of the Snake, 11 miles east of Pine City.

See Snake River 3 for information on aluminum canoe rentals.

The 11.2-mile shuttle route runs south on County Road 11, east on Highway 70, and north on Highway 107 through Grasston. North of the river, turn east (right) on County Road 7. As County Road 7 curves north, go right onto Canary Road (gravel). Parking for Little Walleye Landing is at the end of the road.

The gradient is minimal: 0.6 feet per mile.

See Snake River 3 for information on water levels.

Put in at the Twin Bridges Landing boat ramp. From Highway 65 south of Mora, take Highway 70 east and County Road 11 north. There's parking at the access. The Snake is wide and quiet, punctuated with wooded islands. Where the banks rise above floodplains heavily forested with silver maples, groves of oaks and meadows appear.

Chipmunk Hollow campsite (mile 0.9) is on the left, across the river from a house with a green roof. Although the site is unmarked, the picnic table is visible from the river. Watch for a mysterious stairway (mile 1.6) on the right. On a stretch where the Snake bends several times, there's a big pool, about 150 feet wide and 10 feet deep. At a Grasston bridge (mile 6.4) a red-sand landing is located on downstream left.

Highway 107 also crosses the river at Grasston (mile 7.7) followed quickly by the Burlington Northern Railway trestle, still in use. After a handsome old truss bridge (mile 8) crosses, the riverbanks are wooded and undeveloped for several miles. After mile 10.7, you see scattered cabins, including one with a powerboat dock. Take out on the left at Little Walleye Landing. There's no sign at the access, but the big gravel parking area is hard to miss.

Other trips: Downstream of Little Walleye Landing, you can paddle 6.3 miles to a pier that is the landing of the Northwest Company Fur Post Historical Site, 1.5 miles west of Interstate 35. Motorboat traffic increases on this often-wide river route that passes the entrance to Pokegama Lake.

From Mora to Pine City, the Snake winds peacefully.

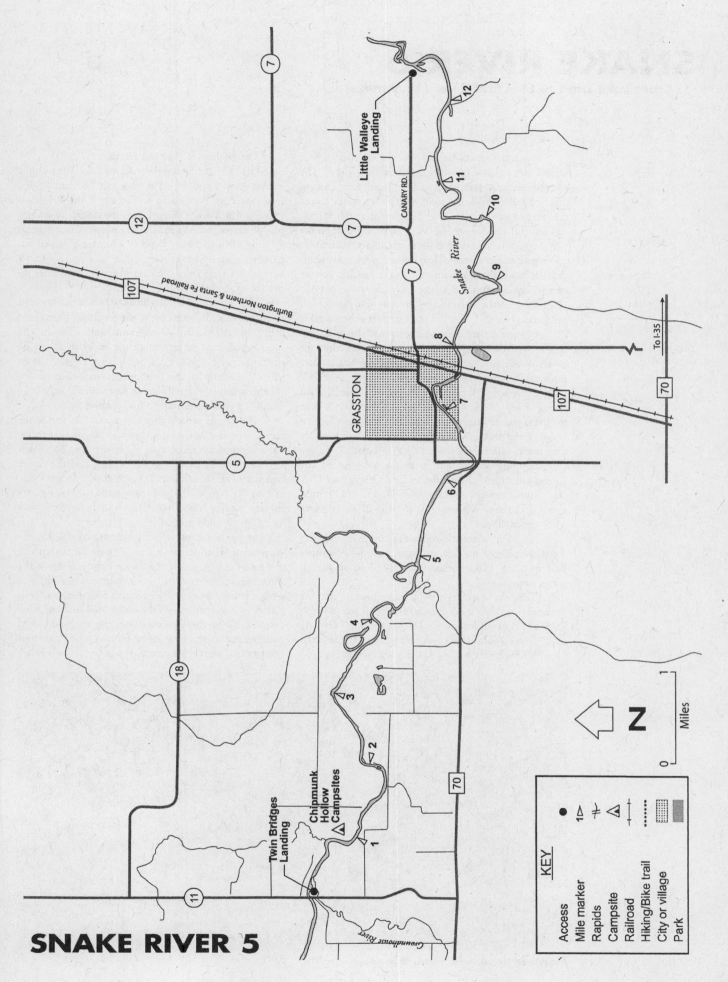

SNAKE RIVER 5

Little Walleye Landing

CANARY RD.

Snake River

Burlington Northern & Santa Fe Railroad

GRASSTON

To I-35

Twin Bridges Landing

Chipmunk Hollow Campsites

Groundhouse River

KEY

Access

Mile marker

Rapids

Campsite

Railroad

Hiking/Bike trail

City or village

Park

Miles

N

SNAKE RIVER 6
Cross Lake Dam to St. Croix River (11.9 miles)

When the Lower Snake's running, it offers a nice whitewater run just 65 miles from the Twin Cities. The river rushes through one rocky Class I rapids after another, quieting briefly at Bear Creek. At high water, it's full of standing waves up to three feet high, and the run edges up to Class II. Launching at high water (over 3,000 cfs on the USGS gage) is challenging in a non-whitewater boat. Don't try to paddle this stretch at low water, however: the boulder bed makes the route frustrating to impassable. A **note of warning:** Recreational kayakers have drowned trying to run the lowhead dam at the put-in. Lowhead dams form dangerous hydraulics that can trap paddlers underwater.

An eclectic assortment of cabins, made less obtrusive by the heavily wooded banks, decorates the riverbanks for much of the run. In the last 2 miles, the Snake races through Chengwatana State Forest. Throughout, the floodplain is forested with silver maple and ash. Upland, thick stands of second-growth white pine and hardwoods echo the river's past as a highway for the St. Croix Delta logging boom of the 1800s. Members of the River Ramblers say that smallmouth fishing is good along this reach.

Camping is available near the take-out at the Chengwatana State Forest River's End Campground.

Shuttle service is available from Wild River Outfitters near Grantsburg, Wisconsin, (715) 463-2254, or www.wildriverpaddling.com.

The 11-mile **shuttle route** runs south on County Road 9 and east on County Road 8, which becomes County Road 118 to Snake River Landing on the St. Croix River.

Check the **water level** right before heading out: the Snake rises and falls quite quickly. The DNR recommends levels of 3.3 to 6.3 feet on the USGS gage near Pine City (http://waterdata.usgs.gov/mn/nwis/uv?05338500). Over 3,000 cfs on the USGS gage is high water.

The **gradient** is 10.0 feet per mile.

Put in at the Snake River Cross Lake Dam public access. From Interstate 35W, take exit 169 and go east into Pine City, then north on County Road 361. Turn right on 8th Avenue SE and cross the tracks. Turn right on 2nd Street SE and head out of town on County Road 8. Turn left on County Road 9. The access, which has parking, is on upstream river left at the County Road 9 Bridge. Readings from the river gauge on the bridge do not correspond to the USGS readings.

The Snake is relatively shallow below the lowhead Cross Lake Dam. From here to the St. Croix, its riverbed is littered with rocks of all shapes and sizes. Choosing the most expeditious path through the rocky maze can be challenging. At mile 4, Bear Creek flows in quietly from the left. Once past this confluence, the Snake takes a short rest from the rapids and in less than a mile, a large island is a good place to stop for lunch.

The rapids return after the island. As the Snake closes in on the St. Croix, it carves an ever-deeper gorge. Tall, red-sand cliff faces tower above the river. The channel narrows, the current grows swifter, and the rapids become more continuous. The Willard Munger State Hiking Trail (mile 10.5) arches over the river on a graceful iron bridge. Soon after, you see a landing for River's End Campground on the right.

As the Snake swoops through the confluence, the curve of its faster current is clearly drawn on the smooth surface of the St. Croix. On river right just down the shore, Snake River Access (also known as Snake Bit) is at a historic ferry crossing. (Wisconsin's Soderbeck Access is directly across the river.) **Take out** at the concrete plank ramp. You'll find outhouses, drinking water, and lots of parking, but no camping at the landing. The state forest campground entrance is one mile back on St. Croix Road.

Man's best friend doesn't have to paddle.

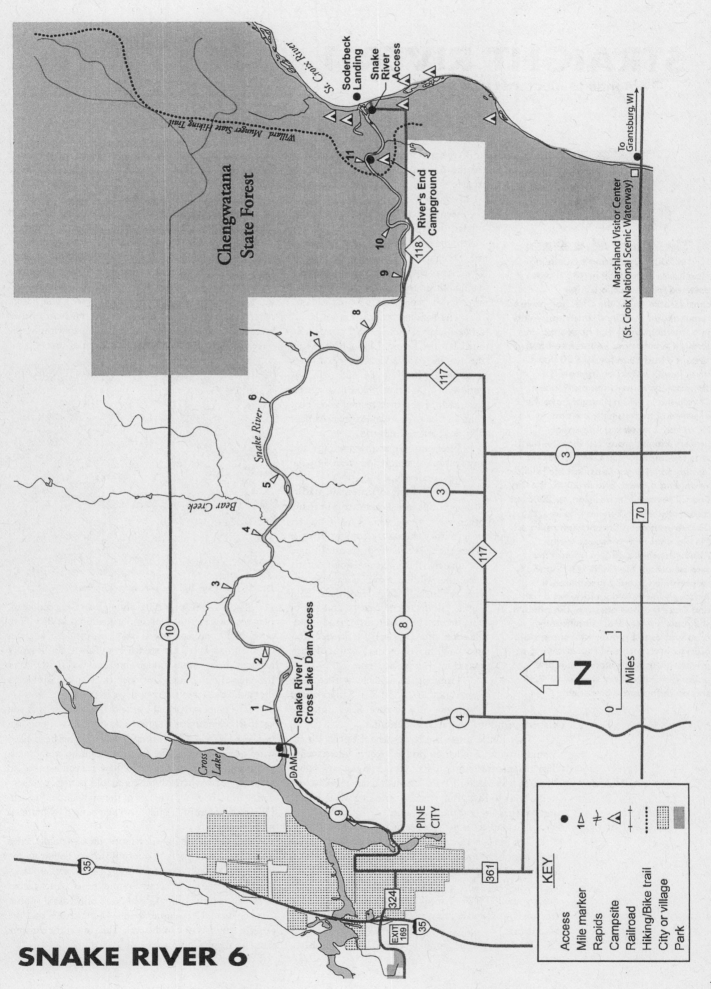

SNAKE RIVER 6

KEY

- Access ●
- Mile marker 1△
- Rapids ╪
- Campsite △
- Railroad ┼┼┼
- Hiking/Bike trail ·······
- City or village
- Park

Chengwatana State Forest

Willard Munger State Hiking Trail

St. Croix River

Soderbeck Landing
Snake River Access

River's End Campground

Snake River

Bear Creek

Snake River /
Cross Lake Dam Access

Cross Lake

DAM

PINE CITY

To Grantsburg, WI

Marshland Visitor Center
(St. Croix National Scenic Waterway)

N

0   1
Miles

EXIT 169

STRAIGHT RIVER 1
Owatonna to Medford (10.7 miles)

The Cost of a Dam

In 2002, Owatonna's crumbling Morehouse Dam (built in 1859) was destined for destruction. After considerable study, the DNR had advised removal and the City Council had voted in agreement. Had that happened, the Straight would now be the free-flowing stream it had been for 10,000 years. River health would be improved significantly, rather than marginally. Owatonna would no longer have the expense of maintaining the dam. However, a small but influential preservationist group felt that the dam was too important to Owatonna's identity to let it go. Considerable political wrangling ensued, and in 2005, the City Council reversed its decision. In 2006, at a cost of about 1.2 million dollars, the Dam Preservation Corporation replaced the old dam with a pseudo-dam. Although private dollars bought the reconstruction, the city is still financially responsible for daily maintenance. Although the new dam includes a fish and Class II canoe passage, river health still pays a price. Most significantly, area watershed groups and some state officials are concerned that allowing a private group with money to make policy decisions about the public trust sets an unfortunate precedent.

The Straight River has its marshy beginnings south of Owatonna, where the restoration of the Straight River Marsh is a great success story in wetlands reclamation. Many species of waterfowl that hadn't been seen there in decades are now regular migratory visitors. Once it leaves the marsh, the fast, riffling, northward flow of the Straight is interrupted only once: Owatonna's Morehouse Dam is a lowhead dam modified to allow fish and canoe passage. This trip begins just above the dam.

The winding Straight has a Class II canoe passage, a few Class I rapids, and one Class II-III rapid, Clinton Falls. Here, the river roars around a steep, rocky horse-shoe bend where an old mill dam was removed. In addition, frequent snags on this reach of the river require good boat control. If you're not an experienced paddler, don't attempt this trip.

Interstate 35 parallels the river and any illusion of remoteness created by the wooded, undeveloped corridor is lessened by the drone of interstate traffic. Although this is a pleasant trip in many other ways, those who want a quieter river journey should try Straight River 2, where the river and the interstate diverge. Fortunately, the interstate noise doesn't keep the wildlife away. Creatures you may see include deer, kingfishers, bald eagles, pileated woodpeckers, and lots of blue herons. One last caveat: if you paddle soon after the river has flooded, you may be dismayed by the amount of trash snared by riverbank brush.

Camping is available at Rice Lake State Park, (507) 455-5871, 8 miles east of Owatonna. Across Rice Lake from the main campground are canoe-in campsites.

The **shuttle route** is east on School Street, left on Walnut Avenue, and left on Bridge Street to Interstate 35. Take the interstate north to Exit 48 and go east on County Road 23 into Medford. Turn left on 2nd Street NW to get to the Straight River Park. Parking, drinking water, toilets, and a shelter are near the boat ramp.

The **gradient** is 4.5 feet per mile.

The Straight rises and falls quickly, so check **water levels** right before you paddle. The river can be dangerous at high water, especially at Clinton Falls. On the USGS gage near Faribault (http://waterdata.usgs.gov/usa/nwis/uv?site_no=05353800), medium is 4.5 to 6.5 feet. At 7 feet or above, the river is fast and exciting but may be filled with debris.

Put in at the asphalt ramp in Owatonna's Morehouse Park. From Interstate 35W, go east on Bridge Street, right on Walnut Avenue, and right on School Street into the park. Just downstream of the ramp, you run the planned new canoe passage (Class II) to the left of the new dam. Scout first, and put in below the dam if necessary. Paddling through Owatonna, a city of bridges, you'll pass under a railroad trestle, the West Street bridge, the Highway 14 Bridge, the Rose Street bridge, and a steel truss footbridge. The river is overhung with a canopy of silver maples and willows that screens and muffles the urban bustle. You may even see a blue heron. More bridges—a railroad trestle and the North Street bridge—are followed by the confluence with Maple Creek on the right. After that you're out of town.

The Straight's a tightly wound, riffly river.

The Straight soon riffles through an S-shaped bend. Between County Road 34 and a township bridge (36th Street NW) you pass several big glacial boulders and run more riffles. There are stretches of easy Class I rapids between the township bridge and a railroad trestle. After the railroad trestle, a high wooded ridge on the left blocks the traffic noise and the river flows in peace.

The quiet is replaced by the roar of the rapids as you approach Clinton Falls. (There may not be a warning sign posted.) This Class II-III drop is a steep, tight bend filled with large boulders where the current pushes you against the outside wall. Experienced whitewater paddlers should scout from river left. All others should portage by clambering over the rocky remains of the mill dam on the left. Historic Clinton Falls Bridge, no longer used by traffic, is just downstream.

Less than a half mile downriver, there's a public access on downstream right at County Road 45. Following the bridge, the Straight meanders through a big lazy loop westward and Crane Creek comes in from the left. After a series of easy little Class I drops, the houses of Medford appear, County Road 12 (Central Avenue West) crosses and the Straight riffles its way to the park. **Take out** at the concrete ramp on the right.

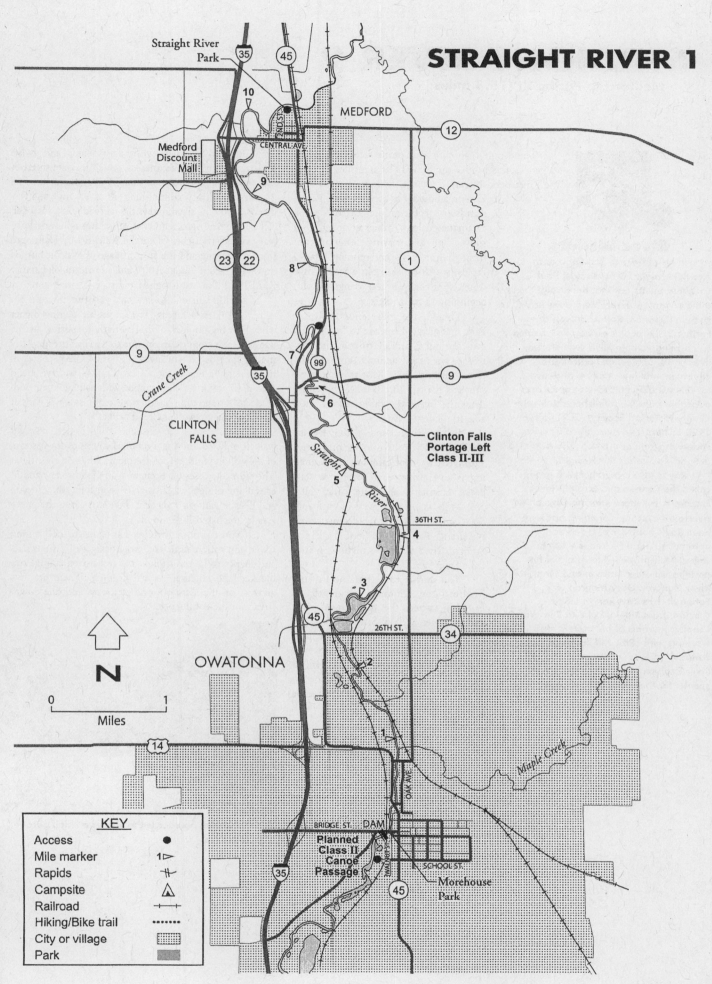

STRAIGHT RIVER 1

Straight River Park

10

MEDFORD

Medford
Discount
Mall

CENTRAL AVE.

2ND ST.

12

9

23 22

8

1

9

7

99

9

Crane Creek

35

CLINTON
FALLS

6

Clinton Falls
Portage Left
Class II-III

Straight   River

5

36TH ST.

4

3

45

26TH ST.

34

OWATONNA

2

14

1

N

0   1
Miles

BRIDGE ST.   DAM

Planned
Class II
Canoe
Passage

WALNUT AVE.

OAK AVE.

Maple Creek

SCHOOL ST.

Morehouse
Park

35

45

KEY

Access	●
Mile marker	1 ▷
Rapids	⫢
Campsite	⚠
Railroad	┼┼┼
Hiking/Bike trail	····
City or village	▦
Park	▨

STRAIGHT RIVER 2
Medford to Faribault (15.8 miles)

River Writers

In his preface to *The Saga of the Not-So-Straight River*, essayist Paul Gruchow points out that the Straight isn't a big or famous river, but it does have its own historian. Roy Anderson of Faribault, the book's author, has written a charming volume filled with stories, interviews, photos, geological and environmental information, and love for this winding little river. Copies are available from the publisher, the Steele County Historical Society: (507) 451-1420 or http://www.steelecohistorical society.org/emporium.php. This book's a delightful voice for the Straight.

Roy is also a member of a group called the Cannon and Straight River Explorers. For more information, contact riverroy@msn.com. Canoeing has long been Roy's hobby (he's a retired optometrist), and he keeps what he calls a "self-propelled journal" of his paddles. Another Cannon and Straight River Explorer, Gary Mogren of Faribault, has kayaked the entire Cannon (from Shields Lake to Red Wing), keeping journals of his travels. He's working with artist Jeff Jarvis of Faribault (also a Cannon and Straight River Explorer) to create a book that speaks for the Cannon River watershed.

Handsome high cliffs with stone faces streaked by mineral stains border the Straight as it rushes through the River Bend Nature Center. Upstream of the Nature Center, a boulder as big as a small garage stands in the middle of the river. Dramatic geology is the star of this river show. The fast-moving Straight runs through numerous entertaining Class I rapids, which develop big waves at high water. This trip is too dangerous for beginning river paddlers.

Though the route ends at Teepee Park, paddlers who want to keep going can take out 2 miles farther at the confluence with the Cannon. Another variation—putting in at Krogh's Landing—shortens the trip to 8.6 miles and eliminates the interstate traffic noise noticeable in the first 2 miles.

In the River Bend Nature Center, (507) 332-7151 or www.rbnc.org, there's a primitive riverside **camping** area. Camping is also available at three area state parks. Sakatah Lake State Park, (507) 362-4438, is 14 miles west of Faribault. See Cannon River 1 for information on Nerstrand Big Woods State Park and Straight River 1 for information on Rice Lake State Park.

The **shuttle route** goes north from Medford on County Road 45 to Faribault, where the road angles right and becomes Willow Street. Turn right on Highway 60, cross the bridge, and take the first right on 5th Avenue NE. Go right on Division Street East, which curves left into Mott Avenue, right on 1st Street NE, and left across a small bridge into Teepee Park.

The **gradient** is 6.4 feet per mile.

See Straight River 1 for **water level** information.

Straight River Park is north of County Road 12 on 2nd Street NW in Medford. **Put in** at the boat ramp next to the shelter. The park has drinking water and toilets. The first half mile takes you under County Road 45 and two railroad trestles. The 270th Street East bridge (mile 2) may be choked with debris, especially after a flood.

Although the narrow Straight winds and twists under a canopy of silver maples, which insulate the river somewhat, the noise of Interstate 35 intrudes for the first 2 miles, gradually diminishing as river and highway diverge. After the river follows the railroad tracks for a half mile, it curves right, and you drop through two short, wavy Class I-II pitches where the Walcott Mill Dam once stood. (The mill and the entire village of Walcott burned down in 1895.) About 100 yards upstream of County Road 19 (240th St), Krogh's Landing is on the right.

Downstream of the landing, you run intermittent riffles and Class I rapids. The banks are getting higher when that big boulder, a glacial erratic (deposited by the last glacier far from its origin), appears in midstream. After the Straight bends southwest and Falls Creek comes in from the right, expect more Class I rapids. In River Bend Nature Center, high cliffs topped with oaks alternate with wooded bottomland. Another piece of fast water ends at the tall stone piers of a railroad bridge.

Downstream is an old steel truss bridge, now for walkers only. To find the unmarked campsite downstream of the walking bridge, look for picnic tables on river right. The railroad crosses the Straight again, followed by another walking bridge (watch your head at high water levels!) and Teepee Park on river left. Take out along the grassy area by the baseball diamond.

If you continue through Faribault to the Cannon River, you paddle under six more bridges of various sizes and shapes. When this guide was researched, a huge tree blocked the channel on this stretch. There are two accesses on the Cannon: one upstream and one downstream of the confluence.

This midstream boulder is the size of a small garage.

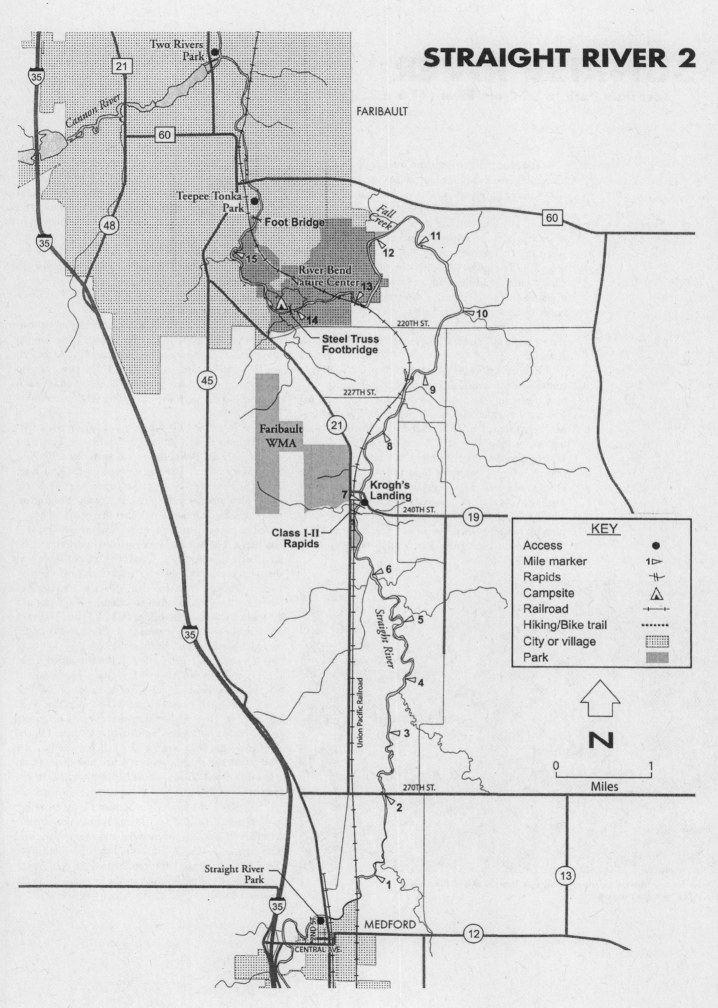

STRAIGHT RIVER 2

FARIBAULT

Two Rivers Park

Cannon River

Teepee Tonka Park
Foot Bridge

Fall Creek

River Bend Nature Center

Steel Truss Footbridge

220TH ST.

227TH ST.

Faribault WMA

Krogh's Landing

Class I-II Rapids

240TH ST.

Union Pacific Railroad

Straight River

270TH ST.

Straight River Park

MEDFORD

2ND ST.
CENTRAL AVE.

KEY

Access	●
Mile marker	1▷
Rapids	╫
Campsite	△
Railroad	┼┼┼
Hiking/Bike trail	····
City or village	▦
Park	▨

N

0   1
Miles

SUNRISE RIVER

Kost Dam Park to St. Croix River (11.5 miles)

The wooded and intimate Sunrise River offers a nice springtime paddle for experienced paddlers who like fast water and rapids and don't mind maneuvering around numerous deadfalls. In the last 3 miles, the state park and a tubing outfitter clear the jams. To avoid the more snag-afflicted upper section, put in at the public access right below the County Road 11 bridge for a 3.5-mile run. The quick current is livened by riffles and Class I rapids, and the gradient increases as the Sunrise nears the St. Croix. You run a short wavy Class I-II drop under County Road 11 and a long drop in the last mile that can also edge into Class II. The trip ends with a very short paddle up the St. Croix to the state park's Sunrise River Landing.

In addition to being home to plentiful wildlife—turtles, deer, beavers, otters, dragonflies, herons, warblers, owls, and eagles—to spy on, local anglers say that the river has great smallmouth bass fishing. Mussel fans will be interested to know that naturalists have found pigtoes, washboards, pimplebacks, muckets, and monkeyface mussels in the Sunrise. Disturbing or collecting mussels is illegal, but trying to identify them is fun. The DNR sells a great little guidebook, *A Field Guide to the Freshwater Mussels of Minnesota*, by Bernard Sietman, which also explains the valuable role these simple creatures play in water quality.

There's a **campground** at Wild River State Park, (651) 583-2125.

The 7.5-mile **shuttle route** runs northeast on Kost Trail (County Road 15) and north on County Road 9. Just past the town of Sunrise, turn right on Ferry Road (gravel), which leads to the parking area and landing on the St. Croix. A state-park vehicle sticker is required to park here.

The **gradient** is 6.9 feet per mile.

Water levels are best in the spring. A good rain will bring the level up later in the season, but it won't ever be as high as in the spring. The Wild River State Park office can give you a general idea of the level.

If the water's too low to paddle and you want to tube the last 2.2 miles of the river, Sunrise River Tubing, (651) 674-2157, operates out of the Sunrise River Pub and Grill (think hamburger rest stop). The pub is housed in a classic 1919 vintage bank building on Sunrise Road right next to the river, with a landing for pub and tube-rental customers.

Put in at the Kost Dam Park. From Interstate 35, take Highway 95 east through North Branch. Turn right on County Road 9 and right on County Road 15 (Kost Trail, 375th Street). Turn left at the sign for Kost Dam Park. There's parking by the shelter (where you can also see an old dam turbine) and a picnic area (with toilets) across the bridge. You can **put in** on either side of the bridge.

The narrow Sunrise runs swiftly between low, red-clay banks. The water is tannin-stained but clear, and the sand bottom is heavily freckled with mussel shells and shell fragments and lightly laced with river grasses. Expect deadfalls from the dam down to the town of Sunrise. After a trio of bridges—County Road 15 (mile 1.5), a low-clearance footbridge (mile 4.3), and Highway 95 (mile 4.8)—the river runs through a stretch of tight meanders, some cut off by breakthroughs.

The North Branch (mile 7.2) flows in quietly from the left, followed shortly by Hay Creek. The Sunrise is 80 feet wide now. Under County Road 11 (Wilcox Road) at mile 8.8, you run a wave-filled drop that edges up to Class II at high water: the remains of an old Northern States Power Company hydro dam. On the right below the drop, Sunrise City Park has a good access with toilets and a picnic shelter. A half mile downstream is Sunrise Road (County Road 9) with access to the Sunrise River Pub and Grill on upstream river right.

The last 2.2 miles of the Sunrise are the most fun and the most scenic: riffles and rapids (including a quarter mile of Class I-II), white pines and swamp oaks, and state-park land. Just downstream of the park footbridge, there are steps on the left up to the parking area. At the confluence, paddle 0.05 mile up the St. Croix and take out on the left.

At the former site of a power dam, the Sunrise drops through a flurry of standing waves.

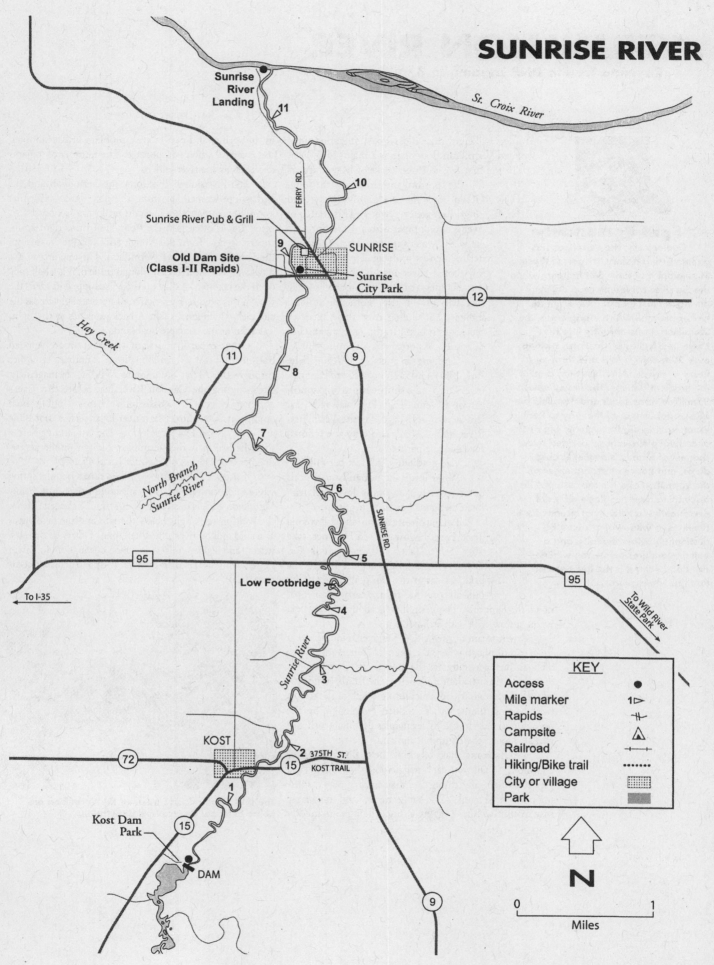

SUNRISE RIVER

Sunrise River Landing

11

St. Croix River

FERRY RD.

10

Sunrise River Pub & Grill

9

Old Dam Site
(Class I-II Rapids)

SUNRISE

Sunrise City Park

12

Hay Creek

11

9

8

7

North Branch
Sunrise River

6

SUNRISE RD.

95

5

95

To I-35

To Wild River State Park

Low Footbridge

4

Sunrise River

3

2 375TH ST.

KOST

KOST TRAIL

72

15

1

Kost Dam Park

15

DAM

KEY

Access	●
Mile marker	1▷
Rapids	⫲
Campsite	△
Railroad	┿
Hiking/Bike trail	·······
City or village	▦
Park	▬

N

0 _____ 1

Miles

VERMILLION RIVER

Ravenna Trail to DNR Landing (6.8 miles)

Split Personality

Geologically, the Vermillion has an interesting history. It's one of those Mississippi tributaries left hanging when the big river carved its deep valley during the last glacial melt. From the higher plain on which it originates, the Vermillion drops abruptly into the Mississippi Valley at Hastings, roaring over 20-feet-high falls and through a flurry of rapids. After less than a mile, the gradient flattens. The newly quiet Vermillion turns south and parallels the Mississippi almost all the way to Red Wing, wandering through the big river's wide floodplain, a huge braided river channel of islands, sloughs, closing dams, and backwaters: a merger of the Vermillion and the Mississippi. This fascinating river has three different personalities: a riffly trout stream above Hastings, a whitewater-kayaking destination below the falls, and a quiet meanderer across the wildlife-rich floodplain. It is the last persona that this trip explores.

Birders will enjoy this quiet trip. At migration time, the wooded Vermillion floodplain is a major bird destination. In the first two to three weeks of May, warblers fill the bottomland forest with song. Heron rookeries are another draw and kingfishers are everywhere. This stretch of river is also popular with anglers. Spring is when the water's up and when riverbank nettles aren't a problem. Deadfalls—shallow-rooted silver maples that fall across the channel—can be a nuisance in the first half of the trip. Portaging around rather than hauling over these unstable blockages is best. (In this case, an absence of nettles on portages is a definite plus.)

Camping is available at Afton State Park, (651) 436-5391, northeast of Hastings.

The 5-mile **shuttle route** runs southeast on Ravenna Trail (Highway 54.) Turn left at the DNR sign for the Vermillion River Public Access and cross the railroad tracks to the parking area.

The **gradient** is 0.7 feet per mile.

Water levels are not an issue on this quiet river, but autumn's low levels can make the jams harder to negotiate.

Put in on upstream left at Ravenna Trail. From Highway 61 in Hastings, take 10th Street (a.k.a. Ravenna Trail and County Road 54) east. Just before the bridge, a car or two can park in the utility pull-off on the right. Carry your boat down the faint trail. The Vermillion is about 60 feet wide, its quiet flow dark with sediment.

Downstream of the bridge, the river wanders into a huge cattail marsh where the channel splits and rejoins. The left fork generally has the most flow. The railroad is visible for almost a half mile before the trestle (mile 0.6) crosses. Although it's possible during much of the trip to hear passing trains, they're hidden from view by the dense floodplain forest. Silver maples dominate; ash and elm also forest the damp bottomland.

Deadfalls and snags blocking the channel are pretty common. When you can't wiggle your boat through a gap, it's much safer to portage than to drag over a shifting pile of tree trunks. The banks are low and reasonably easy to climb while dragging a canoe. Things are muddy in the spring, and nettles are a problem in late summer, so be careful when you portage. The number of logjams decreases as the river widens.

The first slough that joins the Vermillion and the Mississippi comes in from the left (mile 0.9); the Vermillion turns right. The current in the second slough (mile 2.8) is often fast; the Vermillion turns right again. Incoming flow from this slough adds opaque Mississippi mud to the already dark Vermillion. The opening to the quiet water of the Truedale Slough (mile 6.3) is a half mile from the take-out. A dike on the Mississippi end stems the flow in this slough. Turn right and head straight across the channel, which curves left. A backwater lies to the right. Take out at the concrete boat landing.

Other trips: If you want to explore more wooded bottomland, the Vermillion flows another 12 miles through the Gores Pool State Wildlife Management Area, joining the Cannon River just before that river's confluence with the Mississippi. There's a public boat landing at 200th Street East near Etter, access is possible at County Road 18 by Eggleston. The last landing before the Mississippi is the Vermillion Slough public access, northeast of Harliss on County Road 47.

If you want to explore your wild side, a popular spring whitewater run down the sandstone gorge just below Vermillion Falls is upstream of this trip. The access is from the park on river right below the falls and the take-out is at an old mill on river left. A half mile of Class III-V holes, waves, and ledges, this is a major destination for Twin Cities whitewater play-boaters (http://trucurrent.com/maps.htm).

The thick bottomland forests of the Vermillion are home to large, diverse bird populations.

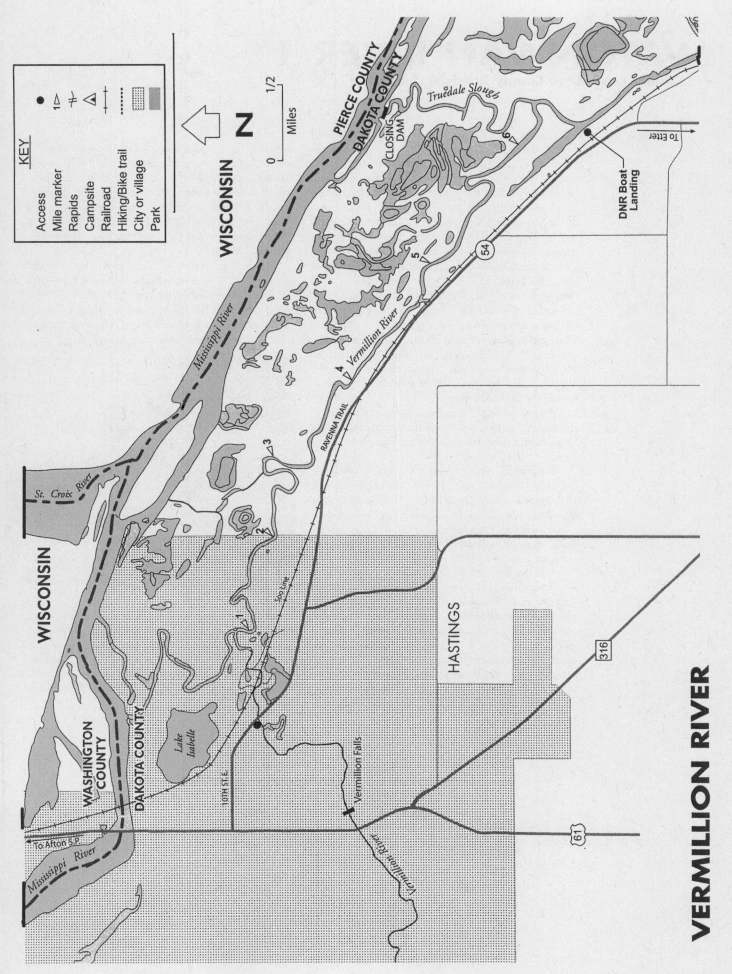

KEY

Access ●
Mile marker 1△
Rapids ≠
Campsite △
Railroad ┼
Hiking/Bike trail ┄┄
City or village
Park

N

0   1/2
Miles

WISCONSIN

WISCONSIN

Mississippi River

St. Croix River

PIERCE COUNTY
DAKOTA COUNTY

Truedale Slough

CLOSING DAM

6

5

4 Vermillion River

Vermillion River

RAVENNA TRAIL

To Etter

DNR Boat Landing

54

3

2

Soo Line

1

WASHINGTON COUNTY
DAKOTA COUNTY

Lake Isabelle

10TH ST E.

HASTINGS

Vermillion Falls

To Afton S.P.

Mississippi River

Vermillion River

61

316

VERMILLION RIVER

169

WATONWAN RIVER 1
County Road 32 to County Road 20 (5.5 miles)

A short trip down the Watonwan offers quiet, wooded sanctuary from the vast, flat farmland that surrounds the river. A lovely tangle of trees—oaks and cedars mixed with floodplain elm, silver maple, and cottonwood—borders this prairie river. The banks are low at the put-in, exposing mostly topsoil, but rise much higher after the first two miles. Bright-orange iron deposits sometimes stain the steep clay banks. Although there are no riffles or rapids, the current is swift, even at low water. Deadfalls are less common and easier to avoid than on the nearby Big Cobb River. The Watonwan provides good bird- and animal-watching, with kingfishers, swallows, herons, owls, and river otters in residence. There are birdsongs of all kinds in the willow thickets.

Sadly, the Watonwan has water-quality issues. Phosphate levels are high, cows are allowed to wander into the water, and the smell of agricultural chemicals sometimes floats over the river.

Minneopa State Park, about 18 miles northeast of the take-out, has a **campground**. In the park, Minneopa Creek (which flows out of Lake Crystal) cascades over a beautiful pair of waterfalls.

Aluminum canoe rentals are available from A-Z Rental in Mankato, (507) 388-1677, and Mankato State University's Maverick Game Room, (507) 389-1321. On Watonwan River 2, aluminum canoes aren't a good idea.

The 5.1-mile **shuttle route** runs north on County Road 32 (paved), east on County Road 128 (gravel), and south on County Road 20 (paved).

The **gradient** is 3.3 feet per mile.

Water level readings on the USGS gage near Garden City are available online (http://waterdata.usgs.gov/usa/nwis/uv?site_no=05319500) or from the DNR, (888) 646-6367. The DNR says the river is impassable below 2 feet; medium levels are 3.5 to 4.5 feet; above 5.25 feet, caution is advised. A minimum of 1 foot on the painted bridge gauge at the take-out means the river is canoeable.

Put in at the County Road 32 access on downstream right. From Mankato, take Highway 60 southeast toward Madelia and County Road 32 south. A gravel road leads down to the concrete ramp and there's room for a few cars to park off the road. The Watonwan is narrow here, only 60 feet wide. The flow is fast and often muddy. Exposed gravel bars, sprinkled with mussel shells, are common at low water levels. Perch Creek (mile 0.4) flows in from the right and the Watonwan widens to about 100 feet.

In the first 2 miles, the banks are low and a border of riverbank trees is sometimes interrupted by farm fields. A long wooded island (mile 1.9) divides the river. In the third mile, cliffs of sand and clay begin to change the pattern of low banks. In late spring, look for wild roses and phlox blooming on their sandy faces.

The wooded Watonwan offers peaceful respite from the surrounding farmland.

At about mile 4, the river begins to wind and twist, the riverbanks are consistently higher, and the wooded buffer is wider. From here until the landing, the river is scenic and remote. Take out on downstream right at the County Road 20 bridge. Up the hill from the boat ramp, a picnic shelter and parking area comprise "The Watonwan Stop."

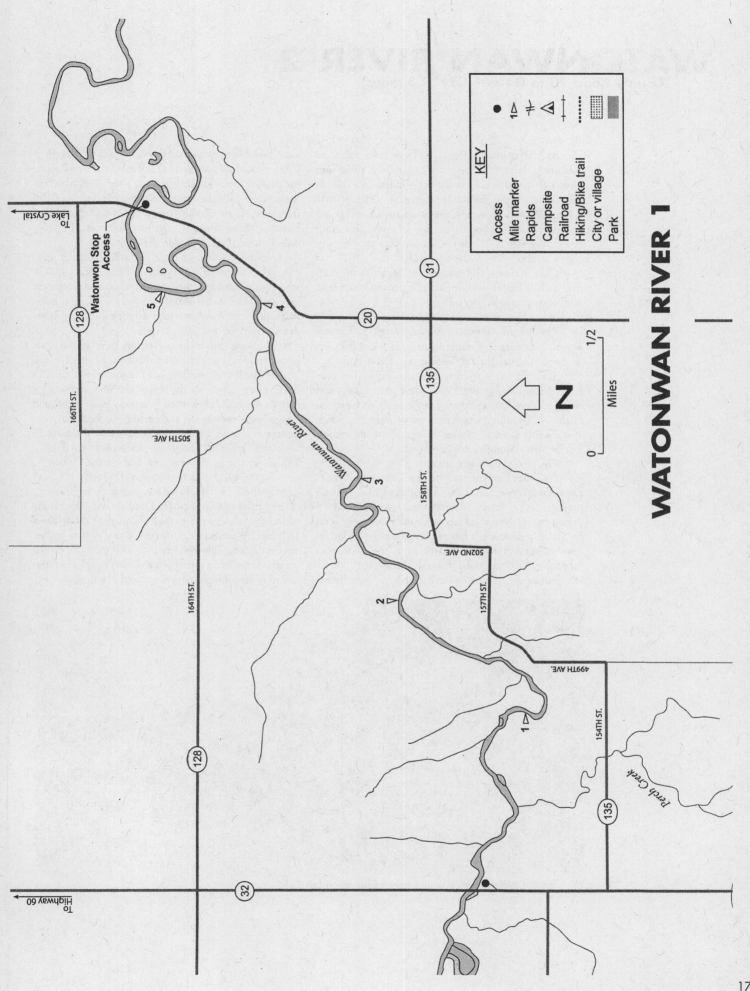

WATONWAN RIVER 1

KEY

Access
Mile marker
Rapids
Campsite
Railroad
Hiking/Bike trail
City or village
Park

N

Miles

0   1/2

To Lake Crystal

Watonwan Stop Access

Watonwan River

Perch Creek

To Highway 60

166TH ST.
164TH ST.
158TH ST.
157TH ST.
154TH ST.
205TH AVE.
502ND AVE.
499TH AVE.

128
128
20
31
32
135
135

1
2
3
4
5

WATONWAN RIVER 2
County Road 20 to Garden City (9.3 miles)

As it drops into the deep Blue Earth River valley, the Watonwan races through many entertaining riffles and Class I rapids, especially in the last 4 miles. Two alternative accesses make shorter trips possible. Putting in at County Road 13 shortens the route to 3.6 miles and includes most of the rapids. Taking out at the boat ramp at the Highway 169 bridge in Garden City shortens any trip by a mile, most of which is rapids.

Oaks, walnuts, and scattered cedars forest the deep river valley. There's wildlife, including many varieties of birds and occasional river otters.

For information on **camping**, see Watonwan River 1.

The 5.2-mile **shuttle route** runs north on County Road 20 and east on County Road 13 into Garden City. In town, go straight on Washington Street and then Fairground Street. The carry-in landing is in the Blue Earth County Fairgrounds, near some picnic tables and benches. If you want to take out at the public access by the Highway 169 bridge, watch for a public water access sign after County Road 13 crosses the river. Turn left and follow the signs through a neighborhood.

The **gradient** is 4 feet per mile.

For **water level** information, see Watonwan River 1. Local kayakers say that 4 to 5 feet on the USGS gage are the best "play" levels. **Note:** At the County Road 13 bridge, where the optical sensor for the USGS gage is on the downstream side, a gauge painted on the bridge on downstream left reads the same as at the Watonwan Stop, about 1.8 feet lower than the USGS gage.

Put in at the County Road 20 bridge. From Man-kato, take Highway 60 southwest to Lake Crystal, then County Road 20 south to "The Watonwan Stop." From the parking area and picnic shelter, a road leads down to the concrete-plank boat ramp. The Watonwan, about 150 feet wide, flows quickly through a wooded corridor. Frequent riffles punctuate the first few miles. Just past mile 4, there's a steep, boulder-filled pitch.

At County Road 13 (mile 5.5) where access is difficult, the best choice is downstream right. Local paddlers who want to maximize their rapids quotient usually put in here instead of at the Watonwan Stop. In the 3.6 miles that follow, the Watonwan races through numerous boulder-strewn riffles and Class I rapids.

A pair of old bridge abutments built of limestone blocks (mile 7.3) is followed by a sedan-sized glacial erratic boulder. You hear the traffic noise of Highway 169 (mile 8.1) before you get there. At the bridge, the Watonwan curves past a little island and through a rocky drop. A painted bridge gauge–reading the same as the previous two–is on upstream center. The public landing on downstream left–almost under the bridge–isn't accessible from Highway 169. To drive to it, you have to go into Garden City.

In the quarter mile between Highway 169 and County Road 13, the Watonwan rushes through a long, curving series of Class I rapids. Deadfalls and little islands add to the fun, and more rapids follow the County Road 13 bridge. As you pass the remains of an iron truss bridge, the river quiets. **Take out** less than a quarter mile downstream, on the left at the fairgrounds boat ramp. The ramp is hard to spot if high water has coated it with mud.

The wooded Wantonwan is a nice break from open farmland.

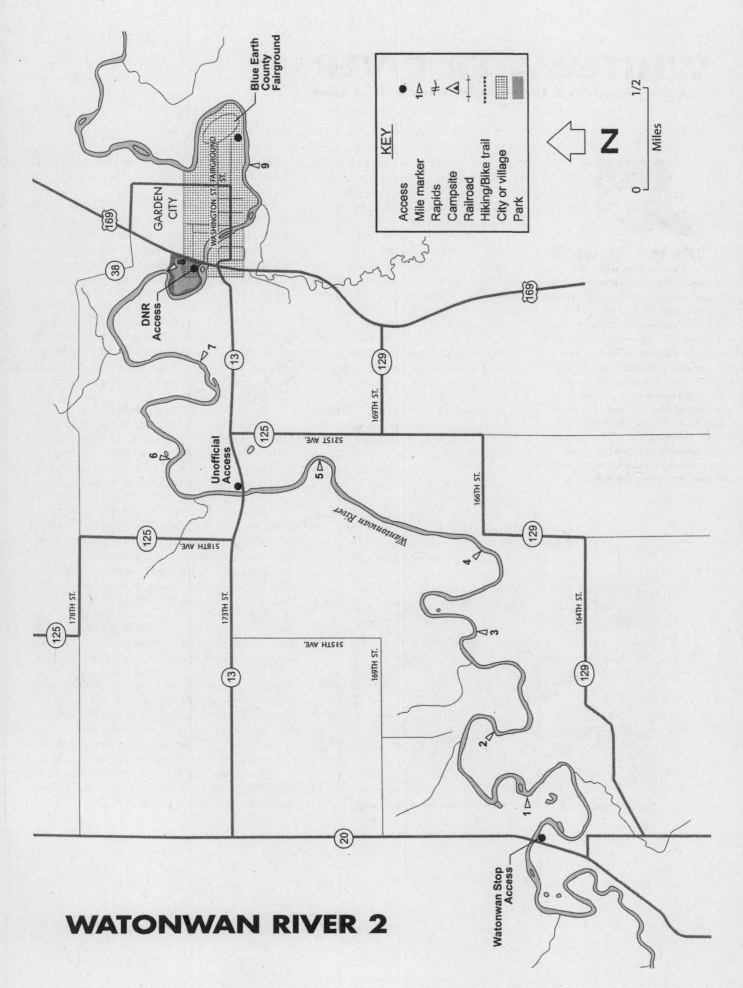

WATONWAN RIVER 2

Blue Earth County Fairground

GARDEN CITY

DNR Access

Unofficial Access

Watonwan River

Watonwan Stop Access

KEY

Access
Mile marker
Rapids
Campsite
Railroad
Hiking/Bike trail
City or village
Park

N

0   1/2
Miles

WHITEWATER RIVER
County Road 26 to Highway 74 Landing (10.4 miles)

Where's Beaver?

There was a time when the Whitewater River valley was in deep trouble, literally. Flooding and erosion from bad land use had caused catastrophic damage. Whole towns in the valley were abandoned. The old site of the town of Beaver now lies completely buried under 12 feet of eroded soil deposited by floods. Not even a chimney cap is visible. The residents of Beaver moved their town away from the river. Beginning in the 1940s, Richard J. Dorer's revolutionary environmental work slowly ended destructive agricultural practices and did much to restore the valley.

The good news is that the Whitewater's a beautiful river. Its many riffles, broad sand bars, sense of isolation, and glimpses of distant bluffs all make for a good paddle. Birds appreciate it, too. Marshy areas in the bottomland attract large flocks of ducks and geese. During spring migration, warblers, flickers, and orioles abound. Sandpipers and killdeer hang out on the sandbars. Swallows nest in holes in the clay banks. A bald eagle's nest is wedged into a riverside tree and wild turkeys roam the banks.

For all that, the Whitewater is not a popular canoe route. Its deep, narrow channel sometimes feels like a tunnel. Deadfall jams often complicate the paddling. For the whole trip, the river runs through the Whitewater Wildlife Management Area (WMA) where the DNR leaves most deadfalls in place for wildlife habitat. During the spring turkey-hunting season, you may want to avoid paddling. Hunting is allowed throughout the WMA, so check with the WMA office, (507) 932-4133, for the dates. A short boulder-filled drop created by a rock weir is the only "whitewater" on the river. (Taking out at the access upstream of the rapids shortens the trip to 6.25 miles.)

The Whitewater is a fast little river through the driftless area.

Even though it isn't one of the popular rivers, the Whitewater is well worth paddling. The beauty definitely outweighs the pesky details.

Camping is available at Whitewater State Park, (507) 932-3007, on Highway 74 south of Elba. The Middle Fork of the Whitewater, a popular state-designated trout stream, runs through the campground. Hiking trails lead to blufftops with great views of the wooded river valley. On this trip, the Whitewater runs through a WMA, where camping is not allowed.

The 8.25-mile **shuttle route** runs west on County Road 26 and north on Highway 74 (gravel after County Road 30) to the unofficial landing on the right, 3 miles past the intersection with County Road 30. Here, the road runs next to the river, there's room to park on the wide shoulder, and the bank is low. (If you see a small road sign for "Mile 51," you passed it.)

The **gradient** is 4.8 feet per mile.

The river is usually canoeable. For general water levels (high, medium, or low), call Whitewater State Park. The USGS gage at Beaver was removed.

Put in at County Road 26 by Elba. From Interstate 90, take Highway 74 through St. Charles, where the highway jogs west. Continue on Highway 74 north to the town of Elba, and turn right on County Road 26. Use downstream right for access. The Whitewater runs fast and shallow over its sandy, gravel-streaked bottom. Numerous riffles alternate with long pools.

A half mile downstream, the South Fork, considered to be an excellent trout stream, flows in from the right. High in a deciduous tree (mile 2.3) on the left is an eagle's nest, occupied when this guide was researched. If you don't want to run the drop that begins under County Road 30, take out at the canoe landing on upstream left. A rock weir creates two tricky Class I rapids, short and steep. Scout from upstream of the bridge.

After this momentary mayhem, the Whitewater gradually slows, flowing through real bottomland now. The deadfall quota increases as the gradient decreases. Although the road runs close to the river at mile 8.4, access here is difficult. **Take out** instead at a sloping sandy spot on the left (mile 10.4) where the road again runs close.

Not recommended: On the final 6 miles to the Mississippi, jams block the Whitewater so frequently that paddling this stretch isn't much fun.

WHITEWATER RIVER

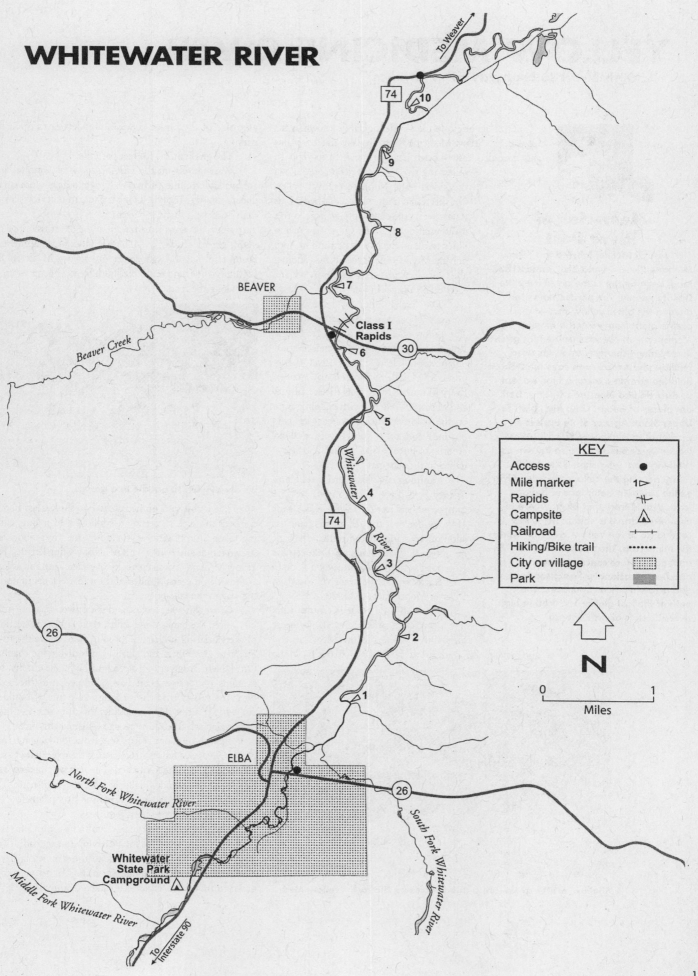

To Weaver

74
10

9

8

BEAVER

7

Class I
Rapids

6

30

5

Beaver Creek

Whitewater

4

74

River

3

26

2

1

KEY

Access	●
Mile marker	1 ▷
Rapids	╫
Campsite	⚠
Railroad	┼┼┼
Hiking/Bike trail	····
City or village	▦
Park	▨

N

0   1
Miles

ELBA

North Fork Whitewater River

26

South Fork Whitewater River

**Whitewater
State Park
Campground** ⚠

Middle Fork Whitewater River

To Interstate 90

YELLOW MEDICINE RIVER
560th Street to Highway 67 (7.5 miles)

Memories of River Past

Joseph Nicollet labeled the Yellow Medicine River "Pejuta Zizi" on his 1838 map, keeping the name given it by the Dakota people. The phrase refers to digging the bitter yellow root of a prairie plant (some say the moonseed, *Menispermum canadesnse*), which grows thickly along the river and was used medicinally. A local man says the Dakota hold the river in the same high esteem as they do Red Pipestone Quarry: both are places of peace. On a high bluff in Upper Sioux Agency State Park is a memorial to Wahpaton Sioux (Dakota) leader Maz-zo-ma-nee, also known as Walking Iron, who signed the 1858 treaty naming the Yellow Medicine River as the southern boundary of Indian land. Visible from that bluff, where his unmarked grave is said to lie, is the confluence of the Yellow Medicine with the Minnesota. The past sometimes appears in more concrete ways: paddlers occasionally find bison bones and arrowheads on sandbars. The path of the last glacier is traced in high riverside cliffs of drift deposit.

From its origin in the prairie highlands known as the Coteau, the Yellow Medicine River drops to the low plains and meanders east through flat farm land. In its final 10 miles, the river carves a deep gorge down the side of the Minnesota River valley. On this reach, frequent boulder-bed rapids (Class I-II) and chains of standing waves mean exciting paddling. Quick to rise and quick to drain, the river is best run in April or May. Members of the Mankato Paddling and Outings Club run the Yellow Medicine early each spring—in wet suits.

The last 3 miles of the route are through Upper Sioux Agency State Park. The Yellow Medicine is one of six Prairie Rivers designated by the conservation organization Clean up the River Environment (CURE, www.curemnriver.com). Every May, the group hosts River, Culture, and History Weekend, with paddling trips on the Yellow Medicine (water levels permitting) and other local rivers, and an evening of history talks, music, and storytelling at the state park.

Camping is available at Upper Sioux Agency State Park, (320) 564-4777. The campground is just off Highway 67, west of the bridge over the Yellow Medicine. In addition to standard campsites, the park rents two authentic-looking Dakota tipis (equipped with unauthentic wood floors).

Kayak rentals are available from Java River in Montevideo, (320) 269-7106.

The 6.8-mile **shuttle route** runs north on 560th Street (gravel), northeast on 240th Avenue (Yellow Medicine B1, also gravel), and southeast on Highway 67 (paved). On the

west side of the bridge, a wide shoulder leaves room for parking.

The **gradient** is 11.4 feet per mile.

Water levels on the USGS gage near Granite Falls are available online (http://waterdata.usgs.gov/usa/nwis/uv?site_no=05313500). Don't try to run it at flows lower than 360 cfs; 500 cfs is better.

Put in on downstream right at the old truss bridge on 560th Street. (Sorlien's Mill once stood just upstream.) From Highway 67, go south on Yellow Medicine B1 (240th Avenue) and south on 560th Street. There's room to park along the road.

It's always fun to paddle in a group.

The rapids start immediately. Two short Class I boulder beds in quick succession are followed by a long, curving Class I drop. And so on down the river—boulder-strewn rapids alternating with pools of varying lengths. The Yellow Medicine is a steep, rocky river here. You run at least 10 drops in the first 2 miles, and this pattern continues all the way to the take-out.

Groves of oaks, cedars, and cottonwoods, some quite big, soften the banks. High cliffs, their faces cross-sections of the glacial till under the topsoil, tower above the river. Frequent gravel bars and small islands divide the channel. On the left, along a long stretch of high, sheer cliffs, big mounds of loose subsoil have slumped into the river. Near the top of that cliff, a long, clear line of boulders embedded in the cliff face marks the time that the most recent glacier—10,000 years ago—visited this area.

Near the end of the trip, watch out for dangerous single-wire livestock fences strung across the river (hard to see) when this guide was researched. The first was marked with tiny flags and extended halfway from the right bank. The second was unmarked and crossed the river just before the bridge. They may have been removed.

The **take-out** is over rocky flats on upstream left at the Highway 67 bridge. It's a long carry up to the road. If you go all the way through the park to the Minnesota River, two more miles, there's an access on the Minnesota, a mile downstream on the left at Skalbekken County Park.

Shallow draft kayaks are a good choice on the rocky Yellow Med.

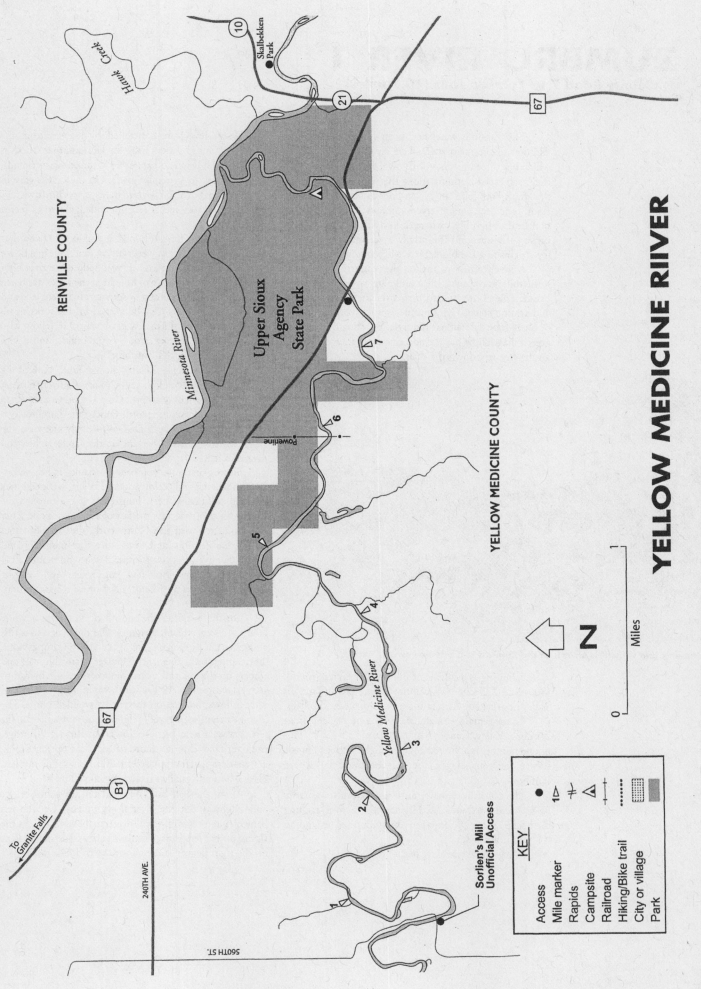

YELLOW MEDICINE RIVER

KEY

- Access ●
- Mile marker ¹△
- Rapids
- Campsite △
- Railroad
- Hiking/Bike trail
- City or village
- Park

N

Miles

0   1

RENVILLE COUNTY

Skalbekken Park

Hawk Creek

10

21

67

Upper Sioux Agency State Park

Minnesota River

Powerline

7

6

5

YELLOW MEDICINE COUNTY

4

Yellow Medicine River

3

2

B1

To Granite Falls

67

240TH AVE.

Sorlien's Mill Unofficial Access

560TH ST.

ZUMBRO RIVER 1
County Road 7 to Zumbro Falls (10.7 miles)

The Zumbro watershed is an intricate system. In addition to the main stem, there are three forks, one of which has three branches of its own. Just to confuse you, they're all called Zumbro. Along this popular canoe route, the South Fork joins the North Fork to become the main stem, and the main river rambles through scenic blufflands. High hills, where turkey vultures, hawks, and eagles soar, surround the narrow river valley. Hardwood forests covering the bluffs blaze with color in the fall.

A lively current makes the canoeing fun, and numerous gravel-bar riffles alternate with quiet pools. Paddlers need the skill to maneuver in a quick current and around snags. On a warm summer weekend, flocks of inner-tube riders float the river. Paddling during fall's great foliage show has the additional advantage of being a tube-free trip down the river.

Winding and riffly, this stretch of the Zumbro is a popular run.

Camping is available at Bluff Valley Campground, (800) 226-7282 or www.campbvc.com, and at Zumbro Valley Sportsman's Park at the take-out in Zumbro Falls.

Canoe rentals with shuttle service are available from Zumbro Valley Canoe Rental, (507) 753-2568. This phone number is activated May through October. Shuttle service for your own canoe may be available; call to inquire.

The 6.4-mile **shuttle route** runs south on County Road 7 and north on U.S. Highway 63. Before reaching the bridge, turn right into the campground. The landing is a public access.

The **gradient** is 3 feet per mile.

Water levels are controlled by releases from the dam at Zumbro Lake. Even in late summer, there is often enough water to canoe the Zumbro on weekends, when releases are generally made. On the USGS gage in Zumbro Falls (http://waterdata.usgs.gov/mn/nwis/uv? 05374000) 7 to 9 feet is recommended; above 12 feet is flood stage.

When the Zumbro floods, it rises quickly and dramatically, sweeping away everything that's not tied down (and some things that are). If you paddle the river after a flood, you see evidence of how high the water has risen: dead tree branches, garden hoses, Styrofoam coolers, and runaway lawn chairs may be lodged in tree forks up to 12 feet above the normal water level. One fellow who loves to paddle the river said, "I could build a house with stuff salvaged from the Zumbro."

Put in at County Road 7 on the South Fork of the Zumbro. From U.S. Highway 52, take Highway 60 East through the town of Mazeppa. Go south on County Road 7, which first crosses the North Fork of the Zumbro. Two miles farther is the Green Bridge (formerly known as the Black Bridge). There's parking at the sandy landing on upstream left.

For the first mile, you pass low banks, lightly wooded with willows and cottonwoods. The big, wooded bluffs are in the distance. A few houses are visible through the trees. This short reach is the last of the South Fork. After its confluence with the North Fork, the river becomes simply the Zumbro and heads into the hills. The land along the river is private, posted with numerous "No Trespassing" signs, but few houses are even visible. Paddlers can stop on island gravel or sand bars without trespassing.

On the left after the mouth of a creek is a sandy landing. Downstream, a sign on the right identifies this stretch as the "tube run" for Bluff Valley Campground. The campground ends with a cluster of small houses and trailers on the left and a carry-in access for use by campground customers. A beautiful, often riffly, stretch of river follows, flanked on the left by wooded bluffs. The Zumbro swings east and Highway 60 is visible on the left. Between here and the Township Road 124 bridge, the river races through more riffles. Cold Spring Brook, a state-designated trout stream, flows in from the left. Gravel bars and islands weave several channels.

Along the half mile between the township bridge and Highway 63, the river flows quietly. On the left bank a riprap retaining wall protects the highway. As the riprap on the left ends, Zumbro Valley Sportsman's Park on the right begins. **Take out** at the concrete ramp.

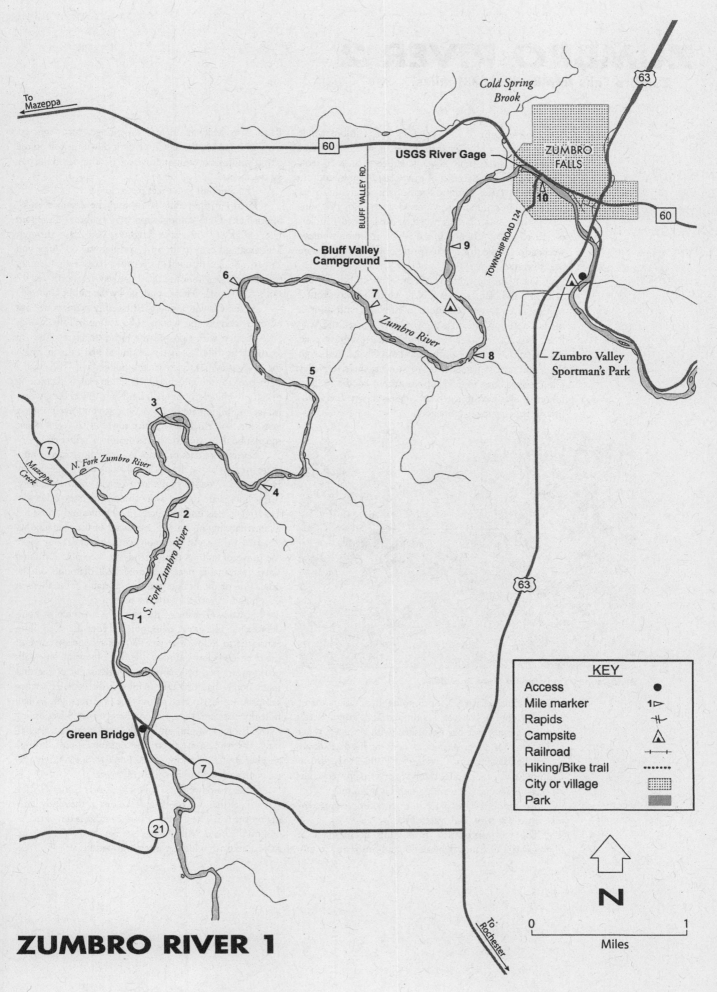

To Mazeppa

60

Cold Spring Brook

63

USGS River Gage

ZUMBRO FALLS

60

10

Bluff Valley Campground

9

6

7

Zumbro River

8

BLUFF VALLEY RD.

TOWNSHIP ROAD 124

5

Zumbro Valley Sportman's Park

7

N. Fork Zumbro River

3

Mazeppa Creek

2

4

S. Fork Zumbro River

1

63

Green Bridge

7

21

To Rochester

KEY

Access	●
Mile marker	1▷
Rapids	╫
Campsite	⚠
Railroad	┼┼┼
Hiking/Bike trail	·······
City or village	▦
Park	▬

N

0 — 1

Miles

ZUMBRO RIVER 1

ZUMBRO RIVER 2
Zumbro Falls to Millville (13.3 miles)

Downstream of Zumbro Falls, the Zumbro winds swiftly down its bluff country valley, now narrower and deeper than on Zumbro River 1. Expect a brisk current, frequent riffles, one stretch of easy Class I rapids, and the snags that are the Zumbro's trademark. Beginning river paddlers who can maneuver around snags enjoy this popular DNR canoe route as much as experienced paddlers do. To avoid the tubing traffic that's common on summer weekends, paddle this one in spring or fall. It's even more beautiful then.

The highlight of the trip is the Zumbro Falls Woods Scientific and Natural Area (SNA), which borders about 2 miles of river. Dense deciduous forest blazes with color in the fall, spring wildflowers grow in thick stands, and Wall Rock rises 200 feet. Few cars travel the narrow gravel road that parallels the river all the way to Millville. Although the Zumbro also passes two little towns, the river valley often feels remote. In deference to current flooding habits, no one builds next to the river. Anglers report that small-mouth bass fishing is quite good.

Bluff Country's a beautiful place to paddle.

See Zumbro River 1 for **camping**. In addition, there's a canoe campsite between Hammond and Jarrett. Read's Park at the take-out has campsites (with drinking water and toilets) for a fee. Permits to camp at Read's Park are sold at Beckland's Auto Center, (507) 798-2441, just up County Road 11, and sites can be reserved. On weekends, especially in August, the campground is often full.

See Zumbro River 1 for information on **canoe rentals**, **shuttle service**, and **water levels**.

The 9.6-mile **shuttle route** runs north on U.S. Highway 63, east on Highway 60, and south on County Road 2 to Millville. Before the bridge, turn right on County Road 11. Read's City Park is down the hill on the left. If you park overnight, leave the parking fee in the box by the toilets.

The **gradient** is 4.4 feet per mile.

Put in at the public landing in the Zumbro Valley Sportsman's Club campground by Zumbro Falls. From U.S. Highway 52, take Highway 60 East through Mazeppa and turn south on U.S. Highway 63. After you cross the bridge, turn left at the canoe access sign. Coming from Rochester, follow U.S. Highway 63 north for 17 miles to the park. There's parking by the public landing.

As soon as you round the first riffly bend, you're out of town and in the woods. The Zumbro Falls Woods SNA, posted with signs on the right, begins at mile 1.5 and ends at mile 3.5. After the initial half mile in which the SNA straddles the river, the public land is all on the right bank. Although the DNR doesn't allow picnicking or camping here, stopping on sand- and gravel bars, swimming, and hiking are fine—as long as you leave no trace. Look for Wall Rock, a cliff face towering 200 feet above the east bank as the river heads around a riffly bend.

Several stretches of riffles and standing waves punctuate the flow along the SNA and along the 3 miles before Hammond. Wooded bluffs increasingly enclose the river. A few houses are tucked away among the trees; otherwise this stretch feels undeveloped. The Hammond access has a sandy landing on the left, upstream of the blue County Road 11 bridge. An enormous cottonwood, rising above the grove of walnut trees, stands in the park. Drinking water is available next to the baseball diamond on the other side of the bridge; there's a portable toilet there in season and a grocery across the road.

Just downstream of the bridge is a stretch of bouldery riffles. The gravel road, notched into the steep bluff, continues to follow the river. Where an outside curve of the river lies below the road, the first of several long walls of riprap topped by guardrails is a reminder of the dramatic floods that the Zumbro loves to dish out. The canoe campsite (mile 10) is in a low area on river right. A half mile downstream, the quiet confluence with Silver Spring Creek is on the right, after riffles and a sandbar. A half mile downstream at Jarrett, the Zumbro speeds through another stretch of rocky riffles. Look for a strikingly tidy car junkyard as you leave the tiny town.

After the powerlines (mile 13), Read's County Park is 0.3 mile farther downstream. **Take out** at the sandy landing on the left. The County Road 2 bridge is downstream, around the bend. Millville has two bars that serve burgers, so you needn't go hungry after your paddle.

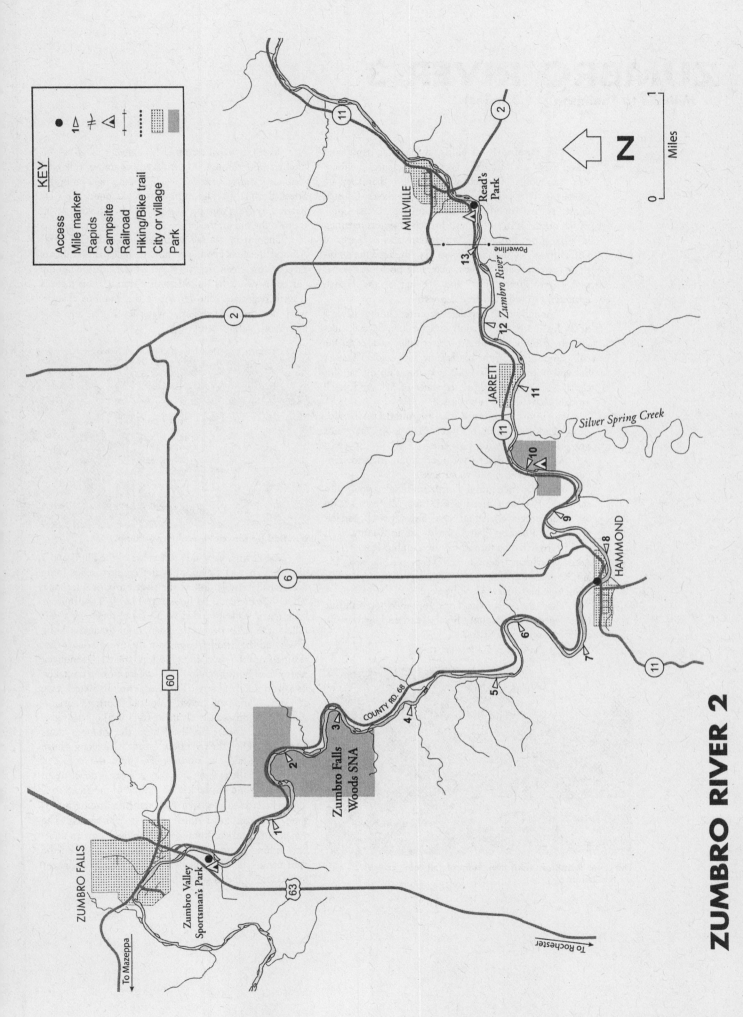

ZUMBRO RIVER 2

KEY

Access ●

Mile marker 1△

Rapids ≠

Campsite △

Railroad ┼

Hiking/Bike trail ┊┊┊

City or village ▦

Park ▩

ZUMBRO FALLS

Zumbro Valley Sportsman's Park

To Mazeppa

To Rochester

Zumbro Falls Woods SNA

COUNTY RD. 68

Silver Spring Creek

Zumbro River

Powerline

MILLVILLE

Read's Park

JARRETT

HAMMOND

N

Miles

0   1

ZUMBRO RIVER 3
Millville to Theilman (11.3 miles)

The Zumbro is all bluffs, swift water, sand- and gravel bars—and deadfalls. Deadfalls and snags are more common along this reach of the Zumbro than they are upstream, recalling the origin of the river's unusual name. Native Americans called the river "Wazi Oju," which means "Place of Pines." French explorers renamed it "Rivière des Embarras," which translates as "River of Difficulties," for the many snags that hindered the ambitious traveler. Later settlers, mangling both pronunciation ("day-zahmbahrah") and spelling of the French moniker, evolved the name Zumbro.

Although not as popular a route as Zumbro River 1 or 2, this journey is certainly as appealing. Several miles into the trip, the deep, narrow river valley widens. In the fall, dense forests on the bluffs glow with color. The river bottom, painted in gravel paisley patterns on the sand, is clearly visible in the algae-free water of fall. And you'll probably have the river to yourself.

For information on the **campground** at Millville's Read's Park, see Zumbro River 2. The DNR maintains one primitive canoe-camping site.

See Zumbro River 1 for information on **canoe rentals**, **shuttle service**, and **water levels**.

The 10.4-mile **gravel shuttle route** takes you south across the river on County Road 2 (paved). Turn left on 592nd Street (gravel), left on 609th Street (gravel), and left on County Road 86 (gravel). Follow 86 to County Road 4 and turn left. The turnoff for the Zumbro River Public Access Theilman (pronounced "Tileman") Site is on the left, just past the bridge. Note: Some of the roads on this route look like driveways, so be alert!

That's the short route. For a 16.9-mile **paved shuttle route**, go north on County Road 2, east on Highway 60, and south on County Road 4.

The **gradient** is 3.3 feet per mile.

The River Ramblers take their annual fall color cruise on the Zumbro.

To reach Millville from U.S. Highway 52, go east on Highway 60 through Mazeppa and Zumbro Falls and south on County Road 2 to Millville. Turn right on Bridge Street. Before the bridge, turn right onto County Road 11. Read's City Park, with parking, toilets, and drinking water, is down the hill on the left.

The **put-in** is a sandy landing in Read's City Park. Around the first bend, a jumble of rocks and sandbars precedes the green County Road 2 bridge. Although the current is swift, the sinuous course through this maze is easy to negotiate. The terrain of the Zumbro changes with each flood. At different water levels, this area may be smooth sailing.

Bundled up for cool-weather paddling.

Just downstream are great views of the bluffs and a pleasant sense of isolation. Quiet country roads, only occasionally visible, follow the river on both sides for a while, but there are no houses visible. Willow thickets back gravel bars sprinkled with mussel shells. At about mile 4, the valley begins to widen, quite gradually. Long Creek and the Middle Creek join the river in quick succession from the right, their mouths choked by sandbars. A stretch of bottomland follows, where erosion has taken its toll on the riverbanks. The river is up to 150 feet wide at times. If you pass the wide mouth of Spring Creek on the left, you missed the campsite (mile 7.5) on the right.

Houses appear on the left as the Zumbro nears Theilman. When the river bends sharply left along a huge sandbar, one **take-out** is on the left. Climb the mound of sand to reach the parking area. A new access is downstream around the bend on the left, at the end of the access road that once crossed the river. Although the landing isn't as good, you can drive much closer to this access. The remaining abutment from that old bridge is now an unofficial fishing platform next to the township road on the right bank. The DNR plans to build a more permanent access close to the County Road 4 bridge.

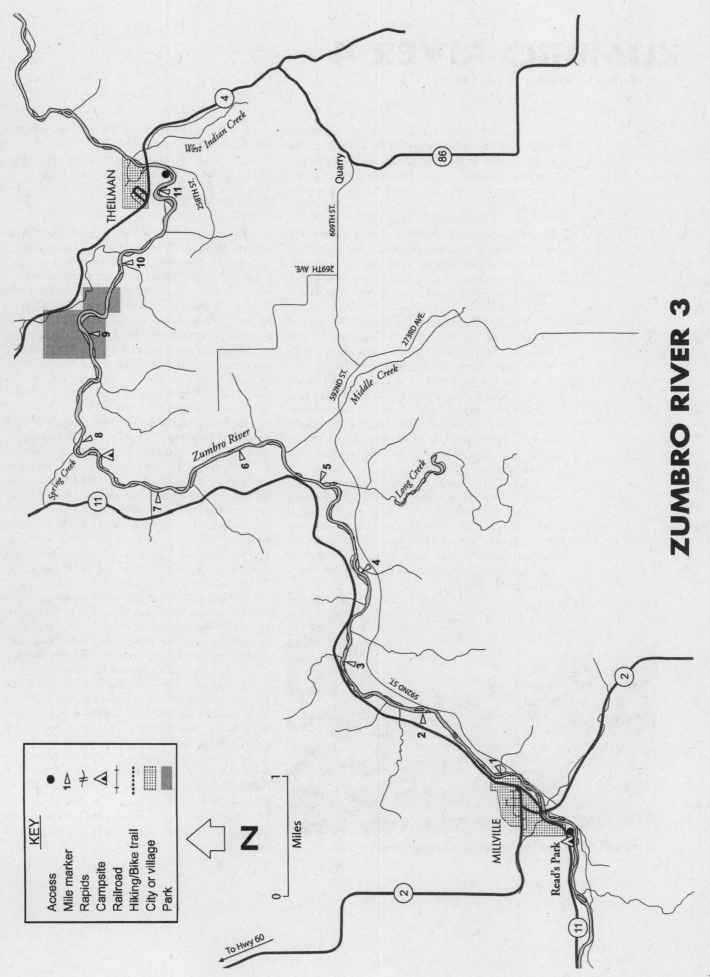

ZUMBRO RIVER 3

KEY

- Access
- Mile marker
- Rapids
- Campsite
- Railroad
- Hiking/Bike trail
- City or village
- Park

N

Miles

0   1

To Hwy 60

THEILMAN

West Indian Creek

258TH ST.

Quarry

609TH ST.

269TH AVE.

273RD AVE.

592ND ST.

Middle Creek

Long Creek

Zumbro River

Spring Creek

MILLVILLE

592ND ST.

Read's Park

ZUMBRO RIVER 4
Theilman to Kruger (11.3 miles)

The Zumbro still has a lively current, but it's not as riffly as upstream. Because the DNR doesn't clear this stretch as often as the more popular stretches, snags are common. A wide expanse of bottomland with beautiful distant views ends the trip. The bluffs may be farther away on much of this trip, but they're still a central and beautiful feature of the landscape. Hiking trails on the bluff at Kruger Campground, although overgrown at times, lead to good views of the river valley. Taking out at the Funk Ford access, reached by a dirt forest road from the north, shortens the trip to 6.5 miles, but the road is sometimes washed out and the access is hard to spot. The historic truss bridge at Funk Ford is closed to vehicles.

The river flows through the Zumbro Bottoms and Kruger Unit, two large tracts of Richard J. Dorer Memorial State Forest. Paddlers share this wealth of public land with several other groups. Horse trails, 48 miles in all, are the most popular recreational trail in the Zumbro Bottoms, attracting up to 20,000 riders a year. Motorcycle riders are allowed to use the trails two weekends a year: the weekend before Memorial Day and the weekend after Labor Day. If you want a quiet paddle, avoid those two weekends. Wild turkeys and deer hunters also roam the woods.

The DNR maintains three primitive riverside campsites. In addition, the Zumbro Bottoms Horse Campground North is located a quarter mile north of the Funk Ford access. Accessible by car, the small campground is open to all campers. Across the road from the take-out is the Kruger Campground, managed by Frontenac State Park, (651) 345-3401. Car camping is available here for a fee.

See Zumbro River 1 for information on canoe rentals, shuttle service, and water levels.

The 13.3-mile shuttle route runs north from Theilman on County Road 4 and east on Highway 60. Turn right on County Road 81. The access is on the right, a half mile down.

The gradient is 2.6 feet per mile.

Put in at the Theilman access. From Wabasha, go west on Highway 60 and south on County Road 4 through Theilman. A sign for the access is on the right, before the bridge. The old Theilman access was washed out in 2004, so you have two options: (1) Carry through the woods from the parking area to a big sandbar; or (2) drive straight to the end of the access road that once crossed the river. Although the landing isn't as good, you can drive closer to this access. The remaining abutment from that old bridge is now an unofficial fishing platform next to the township road on the right bank. The DNR plans to build a more permanent access close to the County Road 4 bridge.

As the trip begins, the Zumbro is running through agricultural bottomland. After County Road 86 appears briefly on the left at the bottom of a bluff, the river and the road diverge. The river flows into the state forest. Downstream of a small tributary on the left, a campsite (mile 4) is on the wooded right bank, across from a bluff that rises 300 feet above the river.

Apart from the one near the put-in, the only other bridge on this trip is at Funk Ford (mile 6.4). The Zumbro Bottoms Road crosses the river on a spindly old truss bridge, closed to vehicles. The canoe access is on the left, about 100 yards upstream of the bridge.

The second campsite (mile 6.9) is accessed by timber steps up the steep right bank. Because of frequent flooding, the DNR has cabled the picnic table to the ground. Downstream of the site, a high, steep, eroded bank contributes its sediment to the river. The third campsite (mile 7.5) is on the right, at the bottom of a ravine.

Downstream, the bluffs beat a steady retreat and the river valley sprawls out in both directions. The banks are low and the Zumbro is about 300 feet wide, shallow and silty. The clearer waters of Trout Brook flow in from the left, its confluence (7.9 miles) marked by a trailer, the first house since entering the Zumbro Bottoms. A signal tower is visible on a distant ridge. Above farm buildings clustered at the base of a bluff, the traffic on Highway 60 moves up the steep slope. Take out on river left at the Kruger Canoe Access (mile 11.3). The Kruger Campground is across County Road 81, up the hill from the picnic area.

At the Funk Ford Bridge, the Zumbro is a peaceful river.

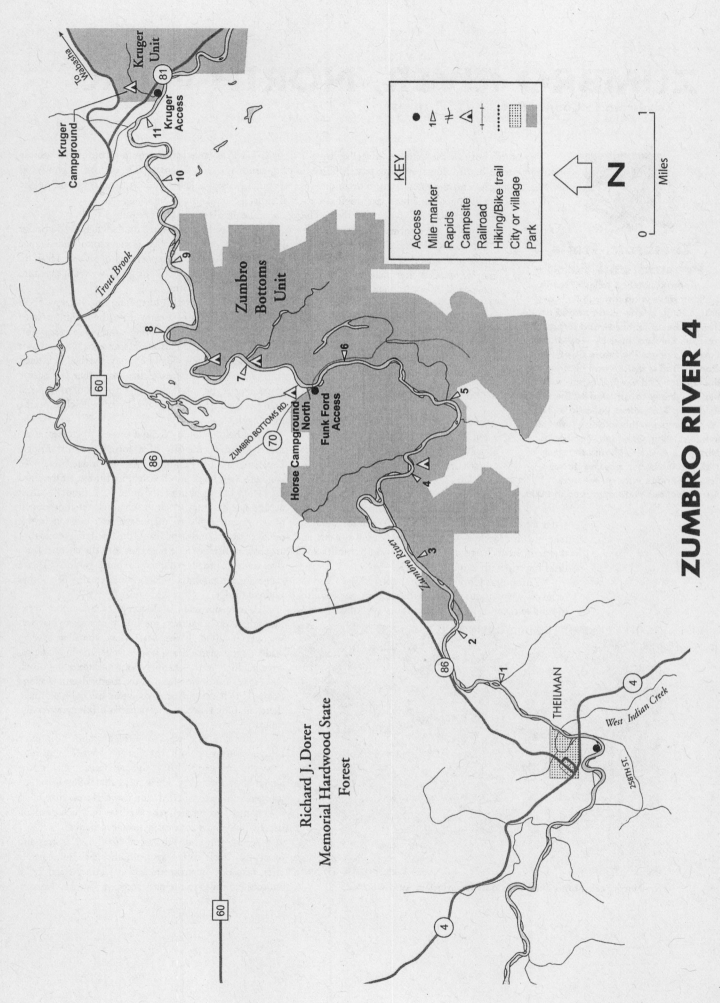

ZUMBRO RIVER 4

KEY

- Access
- Mile marker
- Rapids
- Campsite
- Railroad
- Hiking/Bike trail
- City or village
- Park

N

Miles

Kruger Unit

Kruger Access

Kruger Campground

To Wabasha

Trout Brook

Zumbro Bottoms Unit

ZUMBRO BOTTOMS RD.

Horse Campground North

Funk Ford Access

Zumbro River

Richard J. Dorer Memorial Hardwood State Forest

West Indian Creek

THEILMAN

258TH ST.

ZUMBRO RIVER, NORTH FORK
Zumbrota to County Road 7 (15.1 miles)

Zumbrota Trails, Present and Future

Approximately 5 miles of scenic walking trails wind through the Covered Bridge Park, over an old railroad trestle, through beautiful hardwood forest, and over the Zumbro River by way of the Covered Bridge. The future Goodhue Pioneer Trail is a state trail planned for the Chicago and Great Western railway bed, originally constructed by the Duluth, Red Wing & Southern Railroad in 1888. When complete, this exciting trail will link Red Wing, Goodhue, Zumbrota, Mazeppa, Pine Island, and the Douglas Trail into Rochester, passing through Covered Bridge Park on the way. Appropriations were approved in 2006.

The North Fork of the Zumbro River has been a popular place to build bridges over the past 150 years. Between Zumbrota and the main stem, nine bridges—including Minnesota's last original covered bridge—still cross the river. The remains of seven former bridges crumble on its banks. Despite all these man-made crossings, a float down the riffly Zumbro's narrow wooded river valley is a pleasant journey. Other than in the towns of Zumbrota and Mazeppa, few houses are visible. The river's wooded margin and high bluffs hide much of the agricultural land. Bird and wildlife sightings may include screech owls, kingfishers, songbirds, wood ducks, geese, river otters, groundhogs, and deer.

Water levels are not as consistently canoeable on this fork as on the main stem. Paddlers must dodge snags and the occasional remains of bridges. The DNR doesn't maintain this stretch as often as the more popular main stem, and downed trees sometimes completely block the narrow channel until high water moves them again. To shorten the trip to 10 miles, take out in Mazeppa. Continuing to Zumbro Falls, on the main stem, lengthens the paddle to 23.5 miles and links the trip with Zumbro River 2.

Zumbrota's Covered Bridge Park, (507) 732-7318 or http://www.zumbrota.com/art&rec.htm, has a **campground** and an Olympic-sized outdoor swimming pool.

The 11.8–mile **shuttle route** is south on Highway 58, south on U.S. Highway 52, east on Highway 60 through Mazeppa, and south on County Road 7 to the first bridge across the Zumbro.

The **gradient** is 7 feet per mile.

Water levels are measured on the Highway 58 bridge in Zumbrota. From 1 to 3 feet is the recommended range for paddling. A volunteer reports readings to the DNR on Thursdays, (888) 646-6367, or http://www.dnr.state.mn.us/river_levels/index.html.

Put in at Covered Bridge Park, on Highway 58 in Zumbrota. It's a bit of a carry from the parking area to the left side of the covered bridge, the best access point. The Zumbro makes a narrow, fast, and shallow start as it races under Highway 58. The sandy riverbed is littered with sharp-edged chunks of limestone that will scrape your canoe if you're not alert. The trip out of town is less than pristine: a large scrap-metal yard is perched on the right bank.

Just before County Road 4 (mile 2.4) crosses, abutments stand at the site of a former railroad bridge. Downstream of the County Road 10 bridge (mile 3.4), concrete slabs mark another defunct bridge. At the third set of old bridge abutments (mile 4.1), deadfalls often accumulate and may block the channel. Yet another pair of abutments (mile 6) marks where a railroad bridge once crossed. Just downstream, the low-lying remains of an old iron bridge (mile 6.25) jut into the channel from river right. Partially submerged posts (mile 6.7) at a curve are the potentially hazardous remains of another railroad bridge.

A mile upstream of Mazeppa, the Zumbro flows through several shallows, the legacy of a dam that was removed in 2000. If the water's low, you may have to wade. At the Maple Street bridge (mile 9.5) in Mazeppa, large boulders in the channel create an interesting obstacle course. Just downstream of the footbridge in Walking Bridge City Park, you can take out on the right, although there's no official access. The park has drinking water and toilets.

After the Highway 60 bridge (mile 9.8), more bridge abutments join the list of historic crossings. Downstream, a row of new, upscale houses perches atop a high bluff on the left. The 4 miles that follow are undeveloped and quite wooded, and downed trees may block the channel. Fortunately, the shallows in which deadfalls usually lodge have low, easily portaged banks.

As the trip ends, Township Road 123 crosses and Mazeppa Creek comes in from the left. Immediately after, **take out** on upstream left at County Road 7. It's another 8.5 miles to the next access in Zumbro Falls.

The North Fork of the Zumbro is narrow, winding, and wooded.

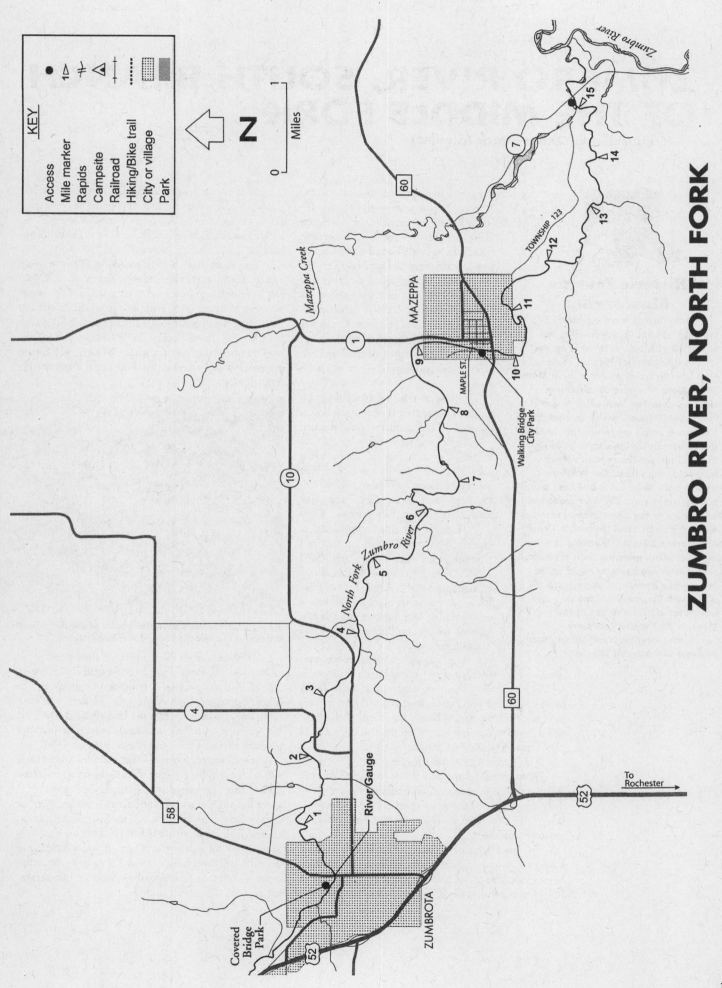

ZUMBRO RIVER, NORTH FORK

KEY

- Access
- Mile marker
- Rapids
- Campsite
- Railroad
- Hiking/Bike trail
- City or village
- Park

N

Miles

0 1

Zumbro River

Zumbro River

15

14

7

13

60

TOWNSHIP 123

12

11

MAZEPPA

1

9

10

MAPLE ST.

8

Walking Bridge
City Park

7

10

6

North Fork Zumbro River

5

4

3

4

10

2

58

River Gauge

1

52

60

To
Rochester

52

Covered
Bridge Park

52

ZUMBROTA

Mazeppa Creek

ZUMBRO RIVER, SOUTH BRANCH OF THE MIDDLE FORK

Mantorville to Oxbow Park (8 miles)

Historic Tour de Mantorville

Many towns have a historic building or two. In Mantorville, the whole 12-block downtown is on the National Register of Historic Places. Stop into Riverside Mercantile on Main Street for a brochure describing a walking tour. The best place to eat is the Hubbell House, which started life in 1854 as a small log hotel. The three-story Mantorville-limestone building that still houses the restaurant was built two years later. The hotel and saloon once did a brisk business as a stagecoach stop. On your placemat are copies of the signatures of famous visitors, like General Ulysses S. Grant and Horace Greeley. If you're in town on a Saturday morning, you can watch Stagecoach Ale being brewed at the Mantorville Brewing Company, (507) 635-5404. To round out the day, get tickets for a performance of the Mantorville Theatre Company (www.mantorvillain.com) during their Summer Melodrama Season.

This charming but little-traveled route is on the Zumbro's Middle Fork. Downstream of the Mantorville dam, the swift South Branch has carved a deep, winding valley. Paddlers should be comfortable maneuvering in riffles and Class I rapids and around deadfalls and boulders. In this heavily wooded valley, deadfalls may create an obstacle course for paddlers. As part of the DNR's Adopt-a-River volunteer program, the Zumbro River chapter of Minnesota Bowhunters, Inc., holds an annual spring cleanup. Contact Ivan Diderrich (ijdiderrich@msn.com) if you want to help.

Spring and fall are likely times for this trip, as the river is often quite low in summer. In spring, many of the wooded river banks are blanketed with delicate wildflowers, including bluebells, wood anemones, and marsh marigolds. The hardwood forests are beautiful in fall. Paddlers often spot eagles, great blue herons, kingfishers, and pheasants.

There's a riverside campground at Oxbow Park as well as hiking trails and a nature center with a small zoo, (507) 775-2451, or http://www.co.olmsted.mn.us/index.php?loc=55. Rice Lake State Park, 15 miles west of Mantorville, has a campground. Rice Lake is the shallow, marshy source of this strand of the Zumbro network.

The 7.8-mile **shuttle route** runs north on Highway 57, east on County Road 16, and south on County Road 5. From the intersection with County Road 4, go north on County Road 105 and turn left into the Oxbow Picnic Area. There is no official landing; the easiest place to take out is between the two shelters. The picnic area has toilets and drinking water.

The **gradient** is 8.4 feet per mile.

Water level information is not available. You can make a reasonable assessment of conditions by comparing the water level with the water stains on the Highway 57 Bridge in Mantorville. If it's down more than a foot, it's too low to paddle.

To reach Mantorville from Rochester, take U.S. Highway 14 west to Kasson and Highway 57 north to Mantorville. The easiest place to **put in** is on downstream left below the dam. Park in the lot at the Sinclair Station (be sure to ask permission) and slide your canoe down the grassy slope. Another option is to park in the public park across the highway and carry your canoe along the sidewalk under the highway bridge, away from the dam's turbulence.

The South Branch is 40 feet wide, the water clear, and the sandy bottom littered with limestone, from pebbles to boulders to huge mossy slabs. Layered limestone outcrops protrude from some of the bluffs. As the trip begins, the river runs through almost continuous gravel-bar riffles. At the golf course (mile 1.8), an island occupied by one of the greens divides the river, which runs shallow and rocky under two footbridges that cross the right channel.

Spring wildflowers adorn the banks of the riffly South Branch of the Middle Fork of the Zumbro.

A mown area on the right with a shelter and picnic tables (mile 3.8) looks at first like an excellent picnic spot. Like all land along the river, however, this is private. The Byron Sportsmen's Club provides the site for a Boy Scout camp and asks that canoeists not land. In 2001, the Club did extensive riverbank restoration along its property, restoring eroded areas in cooperation with the DNR.

Just downstream of the bridge at 272nd Avenue (mile 4.5), a big gravel bar is a good place to stop, if it's still there. (Gravel bars often move with spring floods.) The river is wider and quieter now, and the bottom is sandier. After the County Road 5 bridge (mile 6.9) the South Branch enters Oxbow Park. In another mile, take out on the right anywhere along the oxbow picnic area. If you're camping in the park, you can paddle another 1.5 miles to the campground. The banks are steeper there, so scout the best **take-out** point as you run the shuttle.

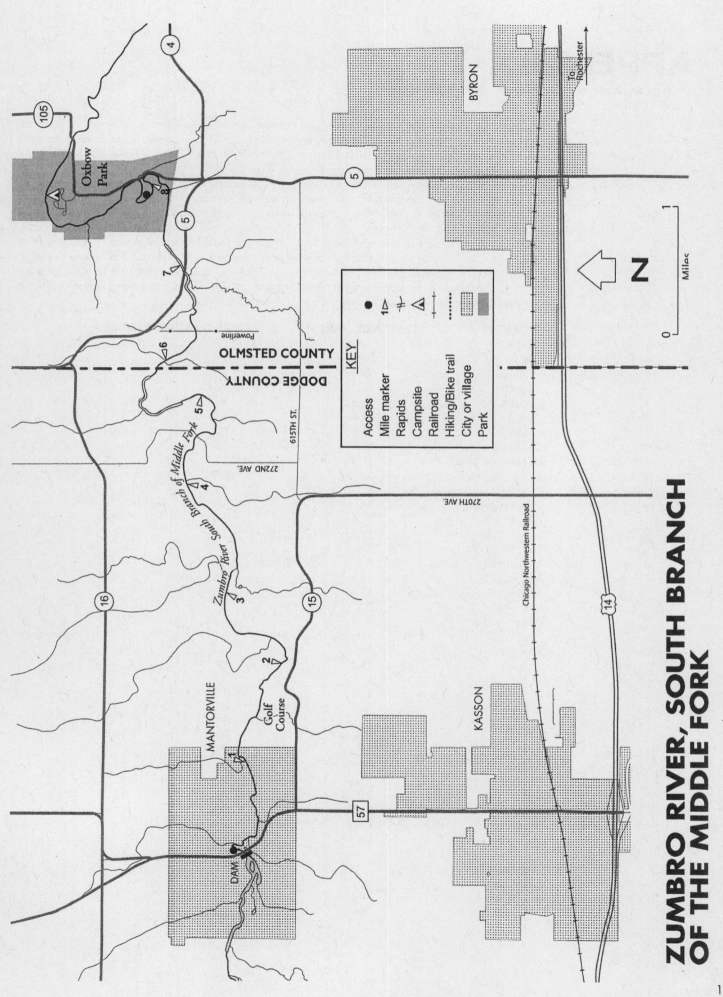

ZUMBRO RIVER, SOUTH BRANCH OF THE MIDDLE FORK

APPENDIX 1
Trip Distances, Gradients, and Skill Levels

Use this chart to choose trips suited to your skill level. Beginner trips are on generally quiet water, broken occasionally by riffles or easy rapids. This guide defines a beginner as someone who has basic river-paddling skills, NOT someone who has never paddled before. Those new to canoeing or kayaking should always take a class from an accredited instructor or paddle with an experienced paddler before attempting a river trip.

Under optimal conditions (proper equipment, low to medium water levels, warm air and water temperatures, short distances), beginners can take intermediate level trips, IF accompanied by experienced paddlers. However, even beginner-level trips can be dangerous in some situations, like icy water, high water, fallen trees, bad weather, or long distances, to name a few. NO BEGINNER SHOULD PADDLE ANY RIVER AT HIGH WATER.

An **intermediate** trip is characterized by moderate challenges that may include frequent strainers or other obstacles; a narrow, winding channel with a fast current; or long stretches of standing waves or Class I boulder rapids. Many trips could be classified as either beginner or intermediate. In those cases, I chose the intermediate rating.

The four trips labeled **expert** involve significant challenges (Class II rapids and above, numerous difficult obstacles, remote locations).

SEGMENT	DISTANCE (MILES)	AVERAGE GRADIENT (FPM)
BEGINNER		
Cannon 2	9.2	2.5
Chippewa 1	20.6	1.9
Chippewa 2	9.5	2.5
Cottonwood 2	13.9	4.7
Crow 1	12.4	1.4
Crow 2	15.3	2.7
Des Moines, West Fork 1	16.1	1.4
Des Moines, West Fork 2	10.8	1.2
Le Sueur 2	8.7	6.0
Long Prairie 1	8.2	1.8
Long Prairie 2	9.1	1.4
Long Prairie 3	14.6	1.7
Long Prairie 4	11.2	1.3
Long Prairie 5	9.4	1.5
Minnesota 1	9.3	0.6
Minnesota 3	12.5	1.1
Mississippi 1, St. Cloud	12.4	2.1
Mississippi 3, Pool 5A	7.5	0
Pomme de Terre 1	10.6	2.4
Root 1	8.9	3.8
Root 2	14.9	4.2
Rum 4	15.9	0.8
Rum 5	11.5	1.0
St. Croix 1	13.0	1.3
St. Croix 2	14.0	0.9
St. Croix 4	17.3	1.7
St. Croix 5	9.0	0.4
St. Croix 6	14.7	0.5
Sauk 1	17.5	2.4
Snake 3	15.0	3.8
Snake 4	7.0	1.3
Snake 5	12.7	0.6
Vermillion	6.8	0.7
Watonwan 1	5.5	3.3
INTERMEDIATE		
Big Cobb 1	12.2	5.9
Blue Earth	11.8	5.0
Cannon 1	17.8	3.1

Cannon 3	20.3	4.8
Cannon 4	11.6	1.2
Cottonwood 1	6.8	6.2
Crow, North Fork 1	11.2	2.3
Crow, North Fork 2	11.9	3.4
Elk	9.0	3.7
Hawk	9.0	10.2
Lac qui Parle	12.9	3.6
Le Sueur 1	10.8	7.7
Maple 1	12.4	6.9
Maple 2	8.4	9.0
Minnehaha 1	11.2	3.6
Minnehaha 2	9.8	7.6
Minnesota 2	14.3	1.6
Mississippi 2, Metro	8.4	0
Platte	6.3	7.1
Pomme de Terre 2	8.5	5.9
Rice	6.5	6.5
Root 3	14.5	5.0
Root 4	15.0	3.4
Root 5	5.9	2.9
Root, South Branch	15.3	5.0
Rum 1	14.5	5.3
Rum 2	16.3	7.9
Rum 3	10.0	5.3
Rum 6	9.4	2.5
Rush, North Branch 1	13.0	10.1
Rush, North Branch 2	9.3	12.0
St. Croix 3	14.5	4.4
Sauk 2	4.5	9.3
Snake 2	14.3	5.6
Snake 6	11.9	10.0
Straight 1	10.2	4.5
Straight 2	15.8	6.4
Sunrise	11.5	6.9
Watonwan 2	9.3	4.0
Whitewater	10.4	4.8
Yellow Medicine	7.5	11.4
Zumbro 1	10.7	3.0
Zumbro 2	13.3	4.4
Zumbro 3	11.3	3.3
Zumbro 4	11.3	2.6
Zumbro, Middle Fork	8.0	8.4
Zumbro, North Fork	15.1	7.0

EXPERT

Big Cobb 2	6.4	12.1
High Island Creek	12.4	15.7
Sand	5.0	15.4
Snake 1	5.9	15.5

APPENDIX 2
Resources for Paddlers

INSTRUCTIONAL BOOKS

American Canoe Association. *Introduction to Paddling: Canoeing Basics for Lakes and Rivers.* Birmingham, AL: Menasha Ridge Press, 1996.

Jacobson, Cliff. *Canoeing & Camping: Beyond the Basics.* 2nd ed. Guilford, CT: Globe Pequot Press, 2000.

Landry, Paul, and Matty McNair. *The Outward Bound Canoeing Handbook.* New York: Lyons Press, 1992.

Lessels, Bruce. AMC *Whitewater Handbook: Third Edition.* Boston: Appalachian Mountain Club Books, 1994.

McGuffin, Gary, and Joanie. *Paddle Your Own Canoe.* Erin, Ontario: Boston Mills Press, 1999.

McNair, Robert E., Paul A. Landry, and Matty L. McNair. *Basic River Canoeing: Complete Instructional Guide to Whitewater Canoeing.* American Camping Association, 1985.

INSTRUCTIONAL VIDEOS

Essential Boat Control. 58 min., 1996. Waterworks, P.O. Box 190, Topton, NC 28781.

Heads Up! River Rescue for River Runners. 29 min., 1993. American Canoe Association, 7432 Alban Station Boulevard, Suite B-232, Springfield, VA 22150.

Path of the Paddle: Doubles. 55 min., 1983. National Film Board of Canada, 1123 Broadway, Suite 307, New York, NY, 10010; (800) 267-7710; http://www.nfb.ca.

RECOMMENDED READING
Rivers and River History

Anderson, Roy. *The Saga of the Not-So-Straight River.* Owatonna, MN: Steele County Historical Society, 1997. Also see "River Writers," Straight River 2.

Bray, Martha Coleman. *Joseph Nicollet and His Map.* Philadelphia: American Philosophical Society, 1980. Joseph N. Nicollet's 1843 map, *Hydrographical Basin of the Upper Mississippi River,* was reprinted from original copperplates in 1965 by the Minnesota Historical Society. For information on obtaining a copy, see Appendix 3.

Diebel, Lynne Smith. *Paddling Northern Minnesota.* Madison, WI: Trails Books, 2005.

Featherstonhaugh, George W. *A Canoe Voyage up the Minnay Sotor.* 1835, 2 vols. Reprint. St. Paul: Minnesota Historical Society, 1970. Also see Appendix 3.

Fremling, Calvin R. *Immortal River: The Upper Mississippi in Ancient and Modern Times.* Madison, WI: University of Wisconsin Press, 2005. Calvin Fremling has written a Mississippi masterpiece, merging history and science in an eminently readable book.

Gilbertson, Victor C. *Watercolors of Bridges over Minnehaha Creek.* Lakeville, MN: Galde Press, 2002. Paddlers on Minnehaha Creek may be surprised to learn how many bridges cross this short stream. Also see Minnehaha Creek 1 and 2.

Gruchow, Paul. *Grass Roots: The Universe of Home.* Minneapolis, MN: Milkweed Editions, 1995. *The Necessity of Empty Places.* Minneapolis, MN: Milkweed Editions, 1999. Paul Gruchow, who grew up on a small farm in Chippewa County and whose father was an organic farmer before anyone even knew the term, wrote eloquently about his own sense of place and need for nature.

Hoogeveen, Nate. *Paddling Iowa.* Madison, WI, 2004.

Johnson, Steve and Ken Belanger. *Minnesota Waterfalls.* Madison, WI: Trails Books, 2007.

Jones, Evan. *The Minnesota.* Reprint. Minneapolis: University of Minnesota Press, 2001. The Minnesota river valley's tumultuous settlement history is portrayed with fascinating stories of exploration and warfare.

MacGregor, J. *A Thousand Miles in the Rob Roy Canoe.* 21st ed. Reprint. Murray, UT: Dixon-Price Publishing, 2000. Although he never made it to Minnesota, MacGregor's 1866 account of his paddling journey on European rivers is a great read for river rats.

Nicollet, Joseph N. *The Journals of Joseph N. Nicollet: A Scientist on the Mississippi Headwaters with Notes on Indian Life.* Trans. André Fertey, ed. Martha Coleman Bray. St. Paul: Minnesota Historical Society Press, 1970. The journals from Nicollet's expeditions on the Mississippi and the St. Croix are annotated in this book. Also see Appendix 3.

Joseph N. Nicollet on the Plains and Prairies: The Expeditions of 1838–39 with Journals, Letters, and Notes on the Dakota Indians. Trans. and ed. Edmund C. Bray and Martha Coleman Bray. St. Paul: Minnesota Historical Society Press, 1993. This book covers Nicollet's explorations of the Minnesota and its tributaries, the Cannon and the Zumbro. Also see Appendix 3.

Sevareid, Eric. *Canoeing with the Cree.* 1935. Reprint. Minneapolis: Borealis Books, 2005. In 1935, two 17-year-olds canoed from Minneapolis to Hudson Bay. Young Sevareid's amazing account inspired a similar voyage in 2005 (see "The Hudson Bay Expedition," Minnesota River 2).

Sietman, Bernard. *A Field Guide to the Freshwater Mussels of Minnesota.* St. Paul: State of Minnesota, Department of Natural Resources, 2003.

Svob, Mike. *Paddling Northern Wisconsin.* Madison, WI: Trails Books, 1998.

Waters, Thomas F. *The Streams and Rivers of Minnesota.* Minneapolis: University of Minnesota Press, 1977. This is an absolutely invaluable resource for anyone interested in Minnesota's waterways. Waters's classic describes every aspect of the state's rivers and streams, and his final chapter about stewardship is an inspiration.

Wildstream: A Natural History of the Free-flowing River. St. Paul, MN: Riparian Press, 2000. Waters explains stream ecology in terms that a nonscientist can understand, offering detailed and fascinating insights into river science.

FISHING

Ross, John. *Trout Unlimited's Guide to America's 100 Best Trout Streams.* Rev. ed. Guilford, CT: Lyons Press, 2005.

APPENDIX 3

On the Rivers with Joseph N. Nicollet and George W. Featherstonhaugh

Heading out on a river can take you to a different time and place. Slip into the unending flow, and you find history lurking in the currents, ghosts of paddlers of times past. For the average Minnesotan on an average day, the name Nicollet calls up images of Nicollet County, Nicollet Avenue, Nicollet Island, and Nicollet Mall. Few think about the Frenchman, Joseph N. Nicollet, whose nineteenth-century explorations and map influenced the state's history. Unless, of course, that average Minnesotan's a river explorer, as Nicollet was. Nicollet's survey of the Upper Mississippi valley, his 1843 map, and information from his extensive journals helped the U.S. government open the land between the Mississippi and the Missouri rivers to settlers. His detailed and accurate maps of rivers and land forms dramatically changed cartography in the United States. Drawing from the close relationships he developed with tribal members whom he met on his explorations, Nicollet also wrote extensively and eloquently about traditional Dakota and Ojibwa cultures and languages.

Like most nineteenth-century explorers, Nicollet traveled on foot, by oxcart, and, most notably for readers of this guide, by river. His journals contain detailed descriptions of many Minnesota rivers, offering great reading for paddlers with a historic bent.

In their books, *Joseph N. Nicollet on the Plains and Prairies* and *The Journals of Joseph N. Nicollet,* Edmund C. and Martha Coleman Bray (with André Fertey) translate and annotate the explorer's journals. It's interesting to see familiar rivers through Nicollet's nineteenth-century eyes. Discovering that the oft-muddy Cottonwood once ran clear enough that he could "see many little objects at the bottom" highlights the unfortunate damage that's been done. But images of once-pristine rivers can also challenge us to work harder on regaining that lost clarity. And the "thickets of wild roses in full bloom" he found on the Cottonwood's banks still scent the air each June.

Not every river ran clear back then. In one entry, Nicollet describes the water of the Blue Earth as "yellowish, as if yellow clay were in suspension." He noted that the Dakota named the Minnesota River "Mini Sotta" which means "cloudy waters" and that the Maple River was called "Rhdirhditan Wapata," meaning "river of mud." Some rivers are simply turbid by nature.

The Dakota and Ojibwa river names that Nicollet carefully recorded in his journals and on his map also lend historic perspective to river identity. The Rush River isn't just a stream in a hurry. Once bounded by vast wetlands, the Rush was known to the Dakota as "Wanyecha Oju, or "Rush River" for the rushes that grew along its banks then.

In his research on Nicollet's map, Robert Douglas, professor of geography at Gustavus Adolphus College in St. Peter, has visited many of the geographic points for which Nicollet recorded longitude and latitude. Nicollet used only a sextant, a barometer, a compass, and a chronometer. Douglas's modern technology (a global positioning system, or GPS, unit) verified the accuracy of Nicollet's readings, sometimes to within a few hundred feet. Reading his journals helps you find many of the exact spots where he camped.

For the imaginative canoeist, Nicollet's journals and his 1843 map add a fascinating historic dimension to river adventures in southern Minnesota. In his journals, Nicollet either mentions, or describes in detail, 30 of the rivers in this guide. The only four not mentioned are the Long Prairie, Minnehaha Creek, the Root, and the Whitewater.

Nicollet's *Map of the Hydrographical Basin of the Upper Mississippi River* was originally published in 1843 by the U.S. government and reprinted in 1965 from the original copperplates by the Minnesota Historical Society. A 41" by 34" reprint is available online or from the museum shop at the Nicollet County Treaty Site History Center in St. Peter, (507) 934-2160, http://www.nchsmn.org/.

Another voice from rivers past can be heard in a British geologist's writings. *A Canoe Voyage up the Minnay Sotor* by George W. Featherstonhaugh (one pronunciation is "Fanshaw") is an interesting journal-style travelogue written in 1835 about a canoe voyage from Green Bay, Wisconsin, to the source of the Minnesota River. (The book also describes travels to other parts of America.) This intrepid explorer traversed Wisconsin by paddling up the Fox River and down the Wisconsin River. He and his voyageur crew then canoed up the Mississippi River to Fort Snelling. From there, they crossed southern Minnesota by paddling up the Minnesota (Minnay Sotor) River to Big Stone Lake.

Musically inclined paddlers will be interested to read that Featherstonhaugh noted the following: "Amongst their other qualifications, I had required that those who were to accompany me should be well acquainted with the popular Canadian airs, and be able to sing them after the old approved fashion of keeping time with their paddles." Featherstonhaugh's style is chattier than Nicollet's, and his comments on human nature, especially as exhibited by the Canadian voyageurs, are often incisive and witty. Copies of a 1970 printing of both volumes of Featherstonhaugh's work are available from the Minnesota Historical Society Press which has an online store (http://shop.mnhs.org/index.cfm?CFID=1650426&CFTOKEN=95045660).

APPENDIX 4
Paddling Instruction and Paddling Clubs in or Near Minnesota

INSTRUCTION
The best way for novices to learn good basic skills and for beginners and intermediate paddlers to improve their skills is to take paddling classes. Here's a list of places offering formal instruction:

Bear Paw Outdoor Adventure Resort, White Lake, WI 54491, (715) 882-3502; www.bearpawinn.com. Offers a full range of kayak and canoe instruction, with classes on the Wolf River in Nicolet National Forest.

Canoe U (www.rapidsriders.net). The Rapids Riders (see below) host annual camping and instruction weekends in May and June, with formal instruction in paddling and cruising skills, solo and tandem whitewater canoeing, and whitewater kayaking, taught by instructors certified by the American Canoe Association.

Minnesota Canoe Association (www.canoe-kayak.org) is developing a program of formal and informal instruction. Contact Education Director David Shanteau (education@canoe-kayak.org) for more information.

University of Minnesota-Duluth's National Kayak and Canoe Institute, Duluth, MN, (218) 726-7128; www.umdrsop.org. Classes in four ability levels and private instruction are offered in coastal kayaking, whitewater kayaking, whitewater rescue, tandem river tripping, whitewater open canoeing, and instructor training. Guided sea-kayaking trips on Lake Superior are offered. The institute also sponsors the St. Louis River Whitewater Rendezvous and the Two Harbors Kayak Festival.

Nicolet College Outdoor Adventure Series, Rhinelander, WI (www.nicolet.tec.wi.us). The curriculum includes canoeing and sea-kayaking instruction, useful seminars, and fantastic trips.

PADDLING CLUBS
Many paddling clubs sponsor paddling classes. In addition, paddling with experienced canoeists and kayakers is a great way to improve your skills while hanging out with people who love to be on the water. These groups welcome nonmembers on their trips. The list covers the whole state (and a bit of South Dakota).

Minnesota Canoe Association, Inc. (MCA), P.O. Box 13567, Dinkytown Station, Minneapolis, MN 55414 (www.canoe-kayak.org). *An umbrella organization that sponsors summer paddling cruises and certified instruction, publishes a newsletter (Minnesota Paddler), promotes paddling and paddling safety, fosters the environmental health of rivers and lakes, and is an affiliate of the American Canoe Association (ACA). The following are MCA affiliates:*

Headwaters Canoe Club; contact Frannie Tjader, (218) 444-5477.

Inland Sea Kayakers (www.inlandsea kayakers.org, info@inlandseakayakers.org) is an organization of sea-kayaking enthusiasts who promote safe sea-kayaking through education, instruction, and leadership, offer instruction and training, schedule trips throughout the kayaking season, and promote conservation of water resources and adjacent lands for recreational purpose.

Mankato Paddling and Outings Club (www.hickory tech.net/~mrbscr) is an active and enthusiastic club that focuses on canoeing and kayaking as well as biking, cross-country skiing, hiking, and camping. Club members paddle daily when water levels are good. Paddlers of all skill levels are welcome to join. The club schedules regular outings and social events, meets twice a month in North Mankato, and participates in the DNR Adopt-A-River Program. Contact Peggy Kreber, (507) 931-6419; mankato@canoe-kayak.org.

Mississippi Whitewater Park Development Corporation (MWPDC) (www. whitewaterpark.canoe-kayak.org). The MWPDC is a citizen group devoted to advancing the creation of a whitewater park at Lower St. Anthony Falls, at the site of the only waterfall on the entire Mississippi River, via re-creation of rapids adjacent to the two locks and dams now in that area in the heart of Minneapolis. The Mississippi Whitewater Park, still in its planning stages, is projected to put tens of thousands of people each year into these rapids, mainly in inflatable rafts. Contact Bill Tilton, whitewater park@canoe-kayak.org.

Rapids Riders (www. rapidsriders. net, rapidsriders @rapidsriders.net) is a Twin Cities–based whitewater kayak and canoe club that offers paddling instruction by ACA-certified instructors and conducts annual river cleanups to help improve paddling resources.

River Ramblers (www.river-ramblers.org) has a standard schedule of great annual paddling trips of all kinds. Nonmembers are welcome to join the trips.

South Dakota Canoe Association (www.sdcanoe. org) sponsors outings on South Dakota and Minnesota rivers and welcomes nonmembers on trips. Contact David Greenlee, (605) 594-6287 (greenlee@alliancecom.net) for more information.

Superior Kayak and Outdoor Adventure Club (SKOAC) (www.skoac.org). This Twin Cities–based volunteer organization of sea kayakers holds ACA-certified skills workshops and sponsors club trips, both for sea-kayaking and for other outdoor endeavors.

Minnesota Rovers Outings Club (www.mnrovers. org, info@mnrovers.org) is a volunteer group devoted to all kinds of active outings, including paddling. Weekly meetings are held in the Twin Cities Metro area. Members can use the club's paddling equipment free for club outings (limited supply).

Sierra Club, North Star Chapter (www.northstar. sierraclub.org) schedules canoe outings each summer.

APPENDIX 5
Environmental Organizations Focused on Rivers

Water quality is an issue dear to the hearts of all Minnesota paddlers. Joining a group of like-minded folks is a great way to help your favorite river. There's strength in numbers.

Cannon River Watershed Partnership (CRWP), www.crwp.net.

Chippewa River Watershed Project www.chippewa river.com. To get involved in helping the Chippewa, volunteer for the Citizen Monitoring Network (Standard, River Transect, or Biological Monitoring) or make a donation to the project's Endowment Fund. Contact Kylene Olson in Montevideo, (320) 269-2139, ext. 116.

Clean Up the River Environment (CURE) www. curemnriver. org. An active and effective grassroots group with the goals of improving water quality and environmental health and improving economic opportunity in the Upper Minn-esota River watershed, CURE offers lots of ways to get involved, including its annual spring River and History Weekend (featuring great river trips), summer field trips to ecologically important sites in the watershed, fall river cleanups, and, of course, membership. For more information, contact Dixie Tilden in Montevideo, (320) 269-2984 or (877) 269-2873.

Coalition for a Clean Minnesota River (CCMR), www.newulmweb.com/ccmr. This coalition of more than 40 organizations and hundreds of individuals works on river restoration. Using an old school building in New Ulm's Riverside Park, the group is creating a Regional River History Center, with public computer access. Politically active and assertive, CCMR gets river issues into the news. The coalition lobbied successfully for the American Heritage Rivers Program and also for the federal–state Conservation Reserve Enhancement Program (CREP), which protects erosion-prone riparian land in the Minnesota River watershed (more than 100,000 acres enrolled and more in the works). CCMR's political strength is rooted in its membership numbers. To join or to learn more, contact Scott Sparlin in New Ulm, (507) 359-2346.

Crow River Organization of Water (CROW), www.crowriver.org. This joint powers board sponsors four great outreach programs, including Citizen Stream Monitoring (weekly stream assessment), Storm Drain Stenciling, Riverwatch (invertebrate monitoring), and River Cleanup. CROW is a busy group: in 2005, 280 River Cleanup volunteers from 10 cities in the watershed netted 6.1 tons of garbage. To volunteer for any of these programs, contact Watershed Coordinator Diane Sander in Buffalo, (763) 682-1933, ext. 3.

Eagle Bluff Environmental Learning Center, www.eagle-bluff.org. The bluff country rivers' biggest champion, Joe Deden, is the director of Eagle Bluff. The center offers a wide range of outdoor education programs for children and adults and a full calendar of special events, including Dinners on the Bluff, programs accompanied by amazing gourmet meals cooked with locally grown ingredients. Sign up for their electronic newsletter and attend one of the events: you'll definitely want to join. For more information, call Eagle Bluff, (888) 800-9558 or (507) 467-2437.

Friends of the Minnesota Valley (FMV) www.friends ofmnvalley.org. FMV is the main private support group for the Lower Minnesota River watershed.

Friends of the Mississippi River, www.fmr.org. The annual Mississippi Challenge (www.mississippichallenge. org) is a two-day, 44-mile event that takes paddlers from Coon Rapids Dam through downtown Twin Cities and down to Grey Cloud Island. It's not only an exciting and fascinating paddle but also a great way for paddlers to raise money for Mighty Miss. Other ways to get involved in the Friends include volunteer planting, weeding, and restoration projects and Special Places Tours. For membership info, contact the Friends, (651) 222-2193.

Friends of the Sauk River, www.geocities.com/ sauk_friends/. This group is a new citizens organization whose mission is to improve, protect, and enjoy the natural resources of the Sauk River watershed. Future activities include a river celebration, river cleanup days, and monitoring programs. Contact mrbender@stcloudstate.edu.

Friends of the Snake River, www.snakerivermn.org. Founded by Dr. Thomas Waters, professor emeritus at the University of Minnesota, this group works to protect the Snake's wild and beautiful river environment through education and supporting public policy changes. They are currently focusing on the threat posed by ATV use in the watershed. The group also sponsors the annual Snake River Canoe Race. Contact Tom Mortenson at tom@post-secondary.org.

Friends of the Upper Mississippi River Refuges, www.friendsofuppermiss.org. This organization's Web site lists lots of ways you can volunteer, from surveying woodcocks to adopting a landing. Contact Steve Sherwood in Winona, (507) 454-6227.

Joseph R. Brown Minnesota River Center, www. hendersonmn.com. Here's one for history buffs. Housed in the former Sibley County Courthouse (on the Historic Register) in Henderson are displays and exhibits of Minnesota River valley history. Contact Director Larry Granger, (507) 248-3719.

Minnesota River Basin Data Center, http://mrbdc. mnsu.edu/, has an extensive database of current data on the rivers in the Minnesota River basin.

Minnesota River Watershed Alliance, www.friends ofmnvalley.org. The Alliance combines the forces of CURE, CCMR, and FMV: There's strength in numbers. Their current project is adding 15,000 more acres to the Conservation Reserve Enhancement Program (CREP II).

Minnesota Waters, www.minnesotawaters.org is the confluence of two active and effective statewide citizen groups, the Rivers Council of Minnesota (www.rivers mn.org) and the Minnesota Lakes Association (www.mn lakes.org), which happened on January 1, 2006. All three Web sites will be operational for some time. Sign up for their enewsletter, The Confluence.

Mississippi River Basin Alliance http://www. mrba.org/.

Redwood-Cottonwood Rivers Control Area (RCRCA), (www.rcrca.com). This Web site is a good source of river data. RCRCA also sponsors annual canoe trips on both rivers.

Vermillion River Watershed Joint Powers Organization, www.co.dakota.mn.us/vermillionjpo.

The following watershed groups need volunteers for their Citizen Monitoring Projects:

Hawk Creek Watershed Project: Contact Project Coordinator Darrell Schindler in Olivia, (320) 523-3666.

Rush River Watershed: Contact Scott Kudelka in Gaylord, (507) 237-5435, ext. 103.

Lower Minnesota River Watershed Initiative: Contact District Administrator Terry Schwalbe in Chaska, (952) 227-1037, www.watersheddistrict.org.

Long Prairie Watershed District: Contact Kitty Tepley in Long Prairie, (320) 732-2644.

APPENDIX 6
10 Easy Ways to Make a River Happy

If you're not a joiner, there are other ways than joining an environmental group to help your favorite river. This list was adapted from the Cannon River Watershed Partnership Web site:

• **Sweep your street gutters clean.** Think of a gutter as a dry streambed connected via the storm sewers to the nearest river. When it rains, the dry streambed fills and everything in the gutter is washed downstream into the river. Organic debris that you sweep out of the gutter before it rains is phosphorus that doesn't reach the river.

• **Minimize paved surfaces on your property.** Less pavement means less runoff.

• **Plant or mulch bare soil and avoid edging your sidewalks.** Uncovered soil is quick to run off.

• **Catch roof runoff with rain gardens** (www.dnr.state.mn.us/volunteer/mayjun04/raingardens.html) and rain barrels (www.rainbarrelguide.com).

• **Aim your downspouts onto grass and wash your car on the grass.** Grass filters out contaminants that will otherwise head for the river.

• **Keep household chemicals and paints from washing into street gutters.**

• **Use nonphosphorus fertilizer on established lawns.** Unless indicated by a soil test, phosphorus is rarely needed to keep a lawn healthy and thus just runs off. Phosphorus runoff is one of the bad guys in river ecology.

• **Collect your pet's waste.** Enough said.

• **Buy organically grown vegetables and meats from local growers whenever possible.** You reward growers who use less of the fertilizer and chemicals that are washed into your rivers.

• **If you have unpaved drainage ditches on your land, allow wetland plants to grow in them without mowing.** Wetland plants are great natural filtering agents.

APPENDIX 7
Useful Web Sites

WATER LEVELS
USGS http://waterdata.usgs.gov/mn/nwis/rt
NOAA http://www.crh.noaa.gov/ahps2/index.php?wfo=mpx
EIMS http://es.metc.state.mn.us/eims/rivers_streams/index.asp?optn=10
DNR http://www.dnr.state.mn.us/river_levels/index.html
USACE http://www.mvp-wc.usace.army.mil/dcp/
American Whitewater http://www.americanwhitewater.org/region/MW/

WEATHER
NOAA http://www.nws.noaa.gov/forecasts/graphical/sectors/uppermissvly.php

MINNESOTA DNR
Phone (888) 646-6367 (MINNDNR)
Home http://www.dnr.state.mn.us/index.html
State Parks http://www.dnr.state.mn.us/state_parks/index.html
State Park Campsite Reservations http://www.stayatmnparks.com
Canoe Routes http://www.dnr.state.mn.us/canoeing/index.html
Public Water Access Maps http://www.dnr.state.mn.us/water_access/counties.html

TOPOGRAPHICAL MAPS
Google Earth (free) http://earth.google.com
Topofusion (free demo) http://www.topofusion.com/

Topozone (free demo) http://www.topozone.com/
PADDLING CLUBS AND INSTRUCTIONS
(see Appendix 4)

ENVIRONMENTAL
(see Appendix 5 for organization Web sites)
What's in Our Water http://www.mepartnership.org/sites/WHATSINOURWATER/
Minnesota Water: Let's Keep it Clean http://www.cleanwatermn.org/